# America's TEST KITCHEN

# PRAISE FOR OTHER AMERICA'S TEST KITCHEN TITLES

"This tome definitely raises the bar for all-in-one, basic, must-have cookbooks. . . . Kimball and his company have scored another hit."   Portland Oregonian on *The America's Test Kitchen Family Cookbook*

"A foolproof, go-to resource for everyday cooking."
Publishers Weekly on *The America's Test Kitchen Family Cookbook*

"For anyone looking for a lighter way of cooking, this book and its 300 recipes would be a most valuable resource."   Providence Journal on *The Best Light Recipe*

"Further proof that practice makes perfect, if not transcendent. . . . If an intermediate cook follows the directions exactly, the results will be better than takeout or mom's."   The New York Times on *The New Best Recipe*

"Exceptional renditions with thorough instruction…"
Publishers Weekly on *Cooking at Home with America's Test Kitchen*

"Like a mini-cooking school, the detailed instructions and illustrations ensure that even the most inexperienced cook can follow these recipes with success."
Publishers Weekly on *Best American Side Dishes*

"Makes one-dish dinners a reality for average cooks, with honest ingredients and detailed make-ahead instructions."   The New York Times on *Cover & Bake*

"*Steaks, Chops, Roasts & Ribs* conquers every question one could have about all things meat."
The San Francisco Chronicle on *Steaks, Chops, Roasts & Ribs*

"The best instructional book on baking this reviewer has seen."
Library Journal (starred review) on *Baking Illustrated*

"A must-have for anyone into our nation's cooking traditions—and a good reference, too."
Los Angeles Daily News on *American Classics*

"If you've always wanted to make real Italian dishes as close to the Italian way as we can make them in America, here's a cookbook that shows you how."   Pittsburgh Post-Gazette on *Italian Classics*

"*Cook's Illustrated* to the rescue. . . . *Perfect Vegetables* belongs on every cooking reference shelf. Here's to our health."   Pittsburgh Tribune-Review on *Perfect Vegetables*

AMERICA'S TEST KITCHEN
17 Station Street, Brookline, MA 02445

Library of Congress Cataloging-in-Publication Data
The Editors at America's Test Kitchen

THE BEST OF AMERICA'S TEST KITCHEN 2007:
The Year's Best Recipes, Equipment Reviews, and Tastings

1st Edition

ISBN-13: 978-1-933615-09-7  Hardcover: $35.00 US/$41.50 CAN
ISBN-10: 1-933615-09-5
1. Cooking. 1. Title
2006

Manufactured in the United States of America

10 9 8 7 6 5 4 3

Distributed by America's Test Kitchen
17 Station Street, Brookline, MA 02445

EDITOR: Elizabeth Carduff
ASSOCIATE EDITORS: Charles Kelsey, Rachel Toomey
ASSISTANT EDITOR: Elizabeth Wray Emery
ART DIRECTOR, SERIES, AND COVER DESIGNER: Carolynn DeCillo
DESIGNERS: Christian Steinmetz, Matthew Warnick
SENIOR PRODUCTION MANAGER: Jessica Lindheimer Quirk
FRONT COVER PHOTOGRAPH: Carl Tremblay
COVER STYLING: Marie Piraino
INTERIOR & BACK COVER PHOTOGRAPHERS: Keller + Keller, Carl Tremblay, and Daniel J. van Ackere
COPYEDITOR: Evie Righter
PROOFREADER: Debra Hudak
INDEXER: Elizabeth Parson

PICTURED ON THE FRONT COVER: Ultimate Turtle Brownies (page 279)

# THE BEST OF
# America's
# TEST KITCHEN

## THE YEAR'S BEST RECIPES, EQUIPMENT REVIEWS, AND TASTINGS

# 2007

BY THE EDITORS AT
AMERICA'S TEST KITCHEN

# CONTENTS

# INTRODUCTION

**GROWING UP IN A SMALL VERMONT TOWN IN THE**
Green Mountains, I never once heard the word "best."
That would imply that there were other things (or other
people) that were not quite as good. And since the prevail-
ing approach to life was that one ought to be ever grateful
for whatever one receives, the notion of "best" was simply
not part of the vernacular. The molasses cookies, the baking powder biscuits, the anadama bread were all really
good, all the time. But one batch was never the best batch.

That, of course, provided a bit of a philosophical problem
when it came to really bad situations. When the baler broke,
and it couldn't be fixed using baling twine, pliers, a ham-
mer, or a grease gun, that was serious business, especially
if the weather was unsettled. Much the same could be said
of a cow that died giving birth or a tractor that needed a
new clutch. Oddly enough, these were never considered bad
days—they were just part of the give-and-take of living.
And, never forget, there was still noontime dinner at the
yellow farmhouse that was part of the schedule every day,
no matter whether it had started out good or bad.

Not being a true Vermonter (if you were not born in
Vermont, don't even think about passing yourself off as a
local), I tend to differ. I can remember years when the sap
ran for almost a whole month or the day when the molasses cookies were perfect: crisp on the outside and chewy on
the inside. And, it ought to be said, every batch of biscuits
was in fact unique. Some days they rose better than others;
some days they were flakier and just melted in the mouth.
And there were days when we did get all the hay in the
barn before it rained and days that it poured unexpectedly
as the hay sat sodden, cut and raked into wet rows where it
slowly rotted. Even the most die-hard farmer ought to call
that a bad day.

America's Test Kitchen is much like a big farm. There
are dozens of people at work, some testing stews, some
putting handheld mixers through their paces, while others
taste-test semisweet chocolate or white wine vinegar. On a
good day, we find that the cheapest pot is better than the
most expensive one, that the bargain supermarket brand
tops the pricey mail-order product, and that the quick and
easy version of a classic French or Italian dish is actually
fresher tasting and almost as good as the three-hour version. That's how we define "best" here in the test kitchen.
The results are unexpected and favorable. We got more
than we had hoped for.

So *The Best of America's Test Kitchen* is like a whole month
of perfect spring weather. You get the best of a whole year
of *Cook's Illustrated* and *Cook's Country* magazines (along
with the special issues: *Holiday Baking* and *Summer Grilling*).
In addition, we include the best recipes and other content
from all of the books we published this year including *The
America's Test Kitchen Family Cookbook, The Best Light Recipe,*
and *The Best 30-Minute Recipe.* Although a Vermonter might
reject the notion of "best," he or she would certainly appreciate good value and for anyone who is penny-wise (but not
necessarily pound-foolish), this book is a bargain. We cherry-
pick our best material and put it all together in one book and
put it in your hands at a reasonable price. Enough said.

I remember a very hot day in July back in the early
1960s when I spent most of it underneath a 1949 Farmall
replacing the clutch. (I was the only one small enough to
crawl underneath and get the job done.) When I finally
finished, I was awfully proud of my handiwork; it was the
first time I had done a man's job in the presence of men.
I guess I expected a round of applause or a backslap or
two. What I got instead was a modest, "Well, it works," as
Charlie Bentley hopped on, started the motor, and slipped
it into first.

I have come to realize, after all these years, that Charlie
had paid me the highest compliment. So, if you spend
time with this book and like what you see, just send us a
brief note that reads, "Well, it works." We'll understand.

CHRISTOPHER KIMBALL
Founder and Editor
*America's Test Kitchen*

CHEESE STRAWS

# STARTERS & SALADS

# GOUGÈRES

### MAKES FIFTEEN 2-INCH PUFFS

**WHAT MAKES THIS A BEST RECIPE:** A perfect gougère, or cheese choux pastry, has a crisp, caramel-colored exterior that yields to a tender, slightly moist interior. It should taste nutty from the browned cheese and a little eggy. Unfortunately, most are amateurish affairs, either dry and bitter or soft and gooey. In all our testing, we discovered that this classic French appetizer, which has only a few ingredients, isn't hard to make but requires some careful attention to technique and cooking times. The traditional method involves bringing water or milk, salt, and butter to a boil in a saucepan. When the mixture reaches a rolling boil, flour is vigorously beaten in to make a paste that is then stirred over low heat to develop stringy strands of gluten, which will give the dough elasticity and strong oven spring when baked. Cooking this simple dough (called *pâte à choux*) for just three minutes ensures optimum gluten development and using a food processor when adding the eggs eliminates the risk that the eggs will start to cook when they meet the hot paste. Unlike most recipes, we use an egg white in addition to two whole eggs, which contributes to an appealing golden color and delicate flavor.

> 2 large eggs plus 1 large egg white
> 6 tablespoons water
> 5 tablespoons unsalted butter, cut into 10 pieces
> 2 tablespoons whole milk
> ¼ teaspoon salt
> ½ cup (2½ ounces) unbleached all-purpose flour, sifted
> 3 ounces Gruyère, Emmentaler, or Swiss cheese, shredded (about 1 cup)
> Pinch cayenne pepper

**1.** Beat the eggs and egg white in a measuring cup or small bowl; you should have ½ cup (discard the excess). Set aside.
**2.** Bring the water, butter, milk, and salt to a boil in a small saucepan over medium heat, stirring once or twice. When the mixture reaches a full boil (the butter should be fully melted), immediately remove the saucepan from the heat and stir in the flour with a heatproof spatula or wooden

As you pipe mounds of this cheesy batter onto the baking sheet, slowly pull up the pastry bag.

spoon until combined and the mixture clears the sides of the pan. Return the saucepan to low heat and cook, stirring constantly, using a smearing motion, until the mixture is slightly shiny, looks like wet sand, and tiny beads of fat appear on the bottom of the saucepan, about 3 minutes (the paste should register 175 to 180 degrees on an instant-read thermometer).
**3.** Immediately transfer the mixture to a food processor and process with the feed tube open for 10 seconds to cool slightly. With the machine running, gradually add the eggs in a steady stream. When all the eggs have been added, scrape down the sides of the bowl and add the Gruyère and cayenne to the food processor. Process for 30 seconds, until a smooth, thick, sticky paste forms.
**4.** Adjust an oven rack to the middle position and heat the oven to 425 degrees. Spray a large baking sheet with nonstick cooking spray and line it with parchment paper; set the sheet aside.
**5.** Fold down the top 3 or 4 inches of a large pastry bag fitted with a ½-inch plain tip to form a cuff. Hold the bag open with one hand in the cuff and fill the bag with the paste. Unfold the cuff, place the bag on a work surface, and, using your hands, push the paste toward the tip of the pastry bag. Twist the top of the bag and pipe the paste onto the prepared baking sheet into 15 evenly spaced 1½-inch mounds. Use the back of a teaspoon dipped in a bowl of cold water to even out the shape and smooth the surface of the piped mounds.

**6.** Bake for 15 minutes (do not open the oven door), then reduce the oven temperature to 375 degrees and continue to bake until golden brown and fairly firm, 8 to 10 minutes longer. Remove the baking sheet from the oven. With a paring knife, cut a ¾-inch slit into the side of each puff to release steam; return to the oven, turn off the oven, and prop the oven door open with the handle of a wooden spoon. After 10 minutes, transfer the puffs to a wire rack. Serve warm.

**WHERE THINGS CAN GO WRONG:** Small variations in oven temperature will lead to wildly different results in both color and texture so be sure your oven is accurate or use an oven thermometer.

**WHAT YOU CAN DO AHEAD OF TIME:** You can prepare the paste (through step 3) up to 2 hours in advance of baking it; transfer it to a medium bowl and press a sheet of plastic wrap that has been sprayed with nonstick cooking spray directly on the surface and store at room temperature until proceeding with the recipe. You can also fully bake and cool the gougères and store them at room temperature for up to 24 hours or freeze in a zipper-lock bag for up to 1 month. Before serving, crisp room-temperature gougères in a 300-degree oven for 5 to 8 minutes; crisp frozen gougères for 8 to 10 minutes.

## NOTES FROM THE TEST KITCHEN

### A PASTRY BAG IS ESSENTIAL
No matter how careful we tried to be, we found that the choux paste was just too sticky to be successfully worked without a pastry bag. As you pipe mounds of this cheesy batter onto the baking sheet slowly pull up the pastry bag. If you prefer smaller gougères, simply use a smaller tip but pay close attention as they bake because smaller puffs may require a shorter baking time.

### BAD PUFFS, GOOD PUFFS
If removed from the oven too early, the gougères will collapse as they cool (left). Proper baking ensures crisp, well-risen gougères (right).

**FALLEN PUFF**          **FULLY RISEN PUFF**

# CHEESE STRAWS
MAKES 14 STRAWS

**WHAT MAKES THIS A BEST RECIPE:** Cheese straws are an old-fashioned appetizer that never fail to impress. What we like best about this recipe (apart from how easy it is to make) is that it delivers crunchy cheese straws with real cheese flavor. Most recipes, including the one on the back of the Pepperidge Farm Puff Pastry box, call for only ¼ cup cheese but we found it took a full cup of grated Parmesan to produce cheese straws with a good, hearty flavor. We tried a few other cheeses, including Asiago, smoked cheddar, and manchego, but only Parmesan and Asiago retained their full-flavored punch after baking (the other cheeses tasted bland against the rich dough). We also tried adding various herbs and spices, such as fresh thyme, smoked paprika, and chili powder, but tasters preferred the batches seasoned only with a little salt and black pepper. As for our technique, instead of cutting the dough into two pieces and sandwiching the cheese between them, we pressed the grated cheese onto both sides of a single piece of dough using a rolling pin. (We tried pressing the cheese into just one side of a single piece of dough, but there was simply not enough surface area to hold a cup of cheese.) The exposed cheese then melted and toasted as the pastry puffed in the oven. At 425 degrees, the straws took only 10 minutes to bake through. They emerged from the oven with a crisp, airy texture and an undeniable cheese flavor that is a classic.

1  (9 by 9½-inch) sheet frozen puff pastry, thawed on the counter for 10 minutes (see page 8 for more information)
2  ounces Parmesan or Asiago cheese grated (1 cup)
¼  teaspoon salt
¼  teaspoon pepper

**1.** Adjust the oven racks to the upper-middle and lower-middle positions and heat the oven to 425 degrees. Line 2 baking sheets with parchment paper and set them aside. Place the puff pastry on a sheet of parchment and sprinkle with ½ cup of the cheese and ⅛ teaspoon each of salt and pepper. Place a sheet of parchment over the cheese and, using a rolling pin, press the cheese into the dough by gently rolling the pin back and forth. Without removing the parchment, carefully flip the dough over, cheese-side down. Remove the top layer of parchment and sprinkle with the remaining cheese, salt, and pepper. Cover the pastry with the parchment. Measure the piece of dough and continue to roll it out, if necessary, to form a 10 ½-inch square.

**2.** Remove the top sheet of parchment and, using a sharp knife or pizza cutter, cut the dough into fourteen ¾-inch-wide strips. Gently twist each strip of dough and transfer it to a parchment-lined baking sheet, spacing the strips about 1 inch apart.

**3.** Bake immediately until fully puffed and golden brown, about 10 minutes, reversing the positions of the baking sheets from top to bottom halfway through the baking time. Remove the straws to a wire rack to cool for 5 minutes before serving.

**WHERE THINGS CAN GO WRONG:** We found that it's best to work with puff pastry that isn't fully thawed. If it is completely thawed, you will likely have trouble working with it and twisting it into the desired shape before baking.

**WHAT YOU CAN DO AHEAD OF TIME:** The cheese straws, once completely cooled, can be stored in an airtight container at room temperature for up to 3 days.

## NOTES FROM THE TEST KITCHEN

### HOW TO SHAPE CHEESE STRAWS
Holding one strip of dough at each end, gently twist the dough in opposite directions and transfer it to a parchment-lined baking sheet. Repeat with the remaining pieces of dough, spacing the strips about 1 inch apart.

# LIGHT ARTICHOKE DIP
SERVES 10 TO 12

**WHAT MAKES THIS A BEST RECIPE:** When developing *The Best Light Recipe,* we immediately zeroed in on this appetizer as one in dire need of a test kitchen makeover. Sure, there are myriad light versions of this ubiquitous dip, but most of them just swap out lowfat or nonfat dairy for their full-fat counterparts or, worse yet, use yogurt instead of mayonnaise. And the truth is that most full-fat versions needed a makeover too, because they are bland and also don't taste much like artichokes. So our goal was twofold: to both substantially lighten this dip and give the flavors a fresher, less dated spin. The classic recipe is generally just a combination of sour cream, cream cheese, and mayonnaise blended with jarred artichoke hearts and Parmesan and then baked. And yes, it is creamy, but woefully lacking in any distinct flavor. We found that the trick to making a flavorful and light version of this classic, one that was creamy and had real artichoke flavor, came down to both technique and ingredients. After trying both jarred and canned artichokes, we still didn't have the clean artichoke flavor we were after. Frozen artichokes were closer to the real thing and when roasted, their flavor deepened and cut through all the dairy. We also took the extra time to sauté onion and garlic, which further boosted the taste overall. And by using high-quality Parmesan, we found we could cut the amount needed almost by half. With these steps (plus using reduced-fat dairy), we were able to cut the calories found in a traditional recipe by half to just 110 per ¼-cup serving and the fat grams to 7, down from 20. And, we had fashioned a dip with fresh, sophisticated flavors that was anything but a relic.

DIP
- 2 (9-ounce) boxes frozen artichokes (do not thaw)
- 2 teaspoons olive oil
  Salt and pepper
- 1 medium onion, minced (about 1 cup)
- 2 garlic cloves, minced
- 1 cup reduced-fat mayonnaise
- ½ cup light cream cheese, at room temperature (see page 258)

1 ounce Parmesan cheese, grated (½ cup)
1 tablespoon fresh lemon juice
1 tablespoon minced fresh thyme
    Pinch cayenne pepper

TOPPING
1 cup fresh breadcrumbs (see note)
2 tablespoons grated Parmesan cheese
    Nonstick vegetable or olive oil spray

**1. FOR THE DIP:** Adjust an oven rack to the middle position and heat the oven to 450 degrees. Line a rimmed baking sheet with foil. Toss the frozen artichokes with 1 teaspoon of the oil, ½ teaspoon salt, and ¼ teaspoon pepper until evenly coated, and spread over the prepared baking sheet. Roast, rotating the baking sheet from front to back, until the artichokes are browned at the edges, 20 to 25 minutes. Let the artichokes cool and chop coarse. Reduce the oven temperature to 400 degrees.

**2.** Meanwhile, combine the onion, garlic, the remaining 1 teaspoon oil, and ½ teaspoon salt in a 10-inch nonstick skillet. Cover and cook over medium-low heat, stirring occasionally to prevent burning, until softened, 8 to 10 minutes.

**3.** Add the mayonnaise, cream cheese, Parmesan, lemon juice, thyme, and cayenne to the onion mixture and stir to combine, smearing any lumps of cream cheese against the side of the skillet to break them up. Gently fold in the chopped artichokes; season with salt and pepper to taste. Scrape the mixture into an ungreased 8-inch-square baking dish.

**4. FOR THE TOPPING:** Toss the breadcrumbs and Parmesan together in a medium bowl until combined and sprinkle evenly over the top of the dip. Spray the topping lightly with vegetable oil. Bake until browned, 20 to 25 minutes. Serve immediately.

**WHERE THINGS CAN GO WRONG:** It's important that the cream cheese be at room temperature, otherwise it will not mix well and distribute evenly. Also, the consistency of this dip is best when warm, so make sure it comes out of the oven just as your guests are starting to arrive.

**WHAT YOU CAN DO AHEAD OF TIME:** The dip can be prepared (without the crumb topping) and refrigerated, covered tightly with plastic wrap, for up to 3 days. To bake, sprinkle the breadcrumb topping over the dip, spray with vegetable oil, and bake as directed. There is no need to increase the baking time.

## NOTES FROM THE TEST KITCHEN

### SORTING OUT LOWFAT MAYONNAISE CHOICES

Because mayonnaise is fatty by definition (it's mostly oil and egg yolks), lowfat mayonnaise is a popular product among the diet-conscious. Hellmann's has always been the winner of taste tests here–both full-fat and light varieties. But with the arrival of their Reduced Fat "Just 2 Good" mayo with only 2 grams of fat per tablespoon (as compared to their light mayo with 4.5 grams and full fat with 11 grams), we wondered if it mattered which one we used. In short, we found that if you're spreading it on a sandwich or using a small amount (as you might for tuna salad), go with the Hellmann's Light. But if you're using a lot of it in a dip (with other ingredients that will overshadow the taste of the mayo), use Hellmann's Reduced Fat "Just 2 Good" (to reap the benefit of saving all those calories).

**HELLMANN'S LIGHT**
Use this higher fat choice when you only need a small amount.

**HELLMANN'S REDUCED FAT "JUST 2 GOOD":**
Use this lowest fat option when making flavorful dips where you need a large amount.

### MAKE YOUR OWN BREADCRUMBS

It's a snap to make fresh breadcrumbs, and white sandwich bread is our top choice for making them. Just tear pieces of sandwich bread into quarters and pulse in a food processor to coarse crumbs, about 8 pulses. One slice of bread should yield about 1 cup fresh crumbs. Does it matter which brand of sandwich bread you use? After a blind tasting of the eight leading brands of sandwich bread, there were two that came out on top: **Arnold Country Classics White** and **Pepperidge Farm Farmhouse Hearty White.** Both were consistently ranked as having the best texture and flavor. Whether you're making breadcrumbs, croutons, or just a sandwich, it's worth reaching for one of these.

Properly ground breadcrumbs should measure between ⅛ and ¼ inch.

# BAKED BRIE EN CROÛTE

SERVES 8 TO 10

**WHAT MAKES THIS A BEST RECIPE:** Baked Brie en croûte is one of those appetizers that when executed properly takes center stage at any party. That said, most baked Brie recipes end up on appetizer tables as an unappealing and runny mass of cheese and soggy pastry. Our challenge was to find a way to crisp up the pastry while softening the cheese to the point that it was appealingly warm and soft but not oozing out of the pastry onto the plate. The solution was somewhat counterintuitive but it worked beautifully: wrap the cheese in the pastry and give it a brief stay in the freezer before baking (and bake it in a very hot oven so the pastry becomes golden brown quickly). This method maintains the cheese at just the right soft consistency but allows the pastry to become crisp and remain sturdy. What also pleased us about this recipe is that store-bought puff pastry makes it foolproof and easy to prepare. We leave a circle on the top free of pastry so you can add the condiment of your choice, though we like apricot or fig jam or any kind of chutney.

1   (9 by 9 ½-inch) sheet frozen puff pastry, thawed
1   large egg, beaten lightly
1   (8-ounce) wheel firm Brie cheese
¼   cup apricot preserves or hot pepper jelly

**1.** Roll the puff pastry into a 12-inch square on a lightly floured counter. Using a pie plate or other round guide, trim the pastry to a 9-inch circle with a paring knife. Brush the edges lightly with the beaten egg. Place the Brie in the center of the pastry circle and, following the photos, wrap it in the pastry. Brush the exterior of the pastry with beaten egg and transfer to a parchment-lined baking sheet. Freeze for 20 minutes.

**2.** Adjust an oven rack to the middle position and heat the oven to 425 degrees. Bake the cheese until the exterior is a deep golden brown, 20 to 25 minutes.

**3.** Transfer to a wire rack. Spoon the preserves into the exposed center of the Brie. Cool for about 30 minutes. Serve with crackers or bread.

**WHERE THINGS CAN GO WRONG:** If you use a soft and very ripe Brie, you won't get the best results and the cheese will be too runny after it is baked. Also, don't be tempted to skip the freezing step as this keeps the cheese from melting too much during baking.

**WHAT YOU CAN DO AHEAD OF TIME:** The Brie can be prepared through step 1 (but do not freeze) and refrigerated, wrapped tightly in plastic wrap, for up to 24 hours. Freeze for 20 minutes before continuing with step 2.

## NOTES FROM THE TEST KITCHEN

### HOW TO WRAP THE BRIE IN PUFF PASTRY

**1.** Place the round of Brie in the center of the pastry circle. Lift the pastry up over the cheese, pleating it at even intervals.

**2.** Press the pleated edge of pastry up into a rim, which will later be filled with the preserves or jelly.

### WORKING WITH PUFF PASTRY

Puff pastry is too difficult to make for all but the most accomplished baker. Thankfully, Pepperidge Farm Puff Pastry sheets are available in virtually every supermarket and work well. Each 1-pound package contains two 9 by 9 ½-inch sheets. Because the dough is frozen, however, it must be defrosted before it can be worked with, otherwise it can crack and break apart. We have found that thawing the dough in the refrigerator overnight is the best method but it takes some forethought. Countertop defrosting works too, but don't rush it. Depending upon the ambient temperature, it may take between 30 and 60 minutes. The dough should unfold easily, but feel firm. If the seams crack, rejoin them by rolling them smooth with a rolling pin. And if the dough warms and softens, place it in the freezer until once again firm.

# POACHED SHRIMP SALAD
## WITH AVOCADO AND GRAPEFRUIT
### SERVES 4

**WHAT MAKES THIS A BEST RECIPE:** When developing salad recipes for *The Best Light Recipe,* we looked for combinations of fresh, bright flavors, healthful ingredients, and dressings that wouldn't tip the fat scales. Instead of a shrimp salad that relied on mayonnaise or a traditional vinaigrette for flavor, we wanted a lighter salad where the shrimp took center stage. Most recipes call for cooking shrimp in simmering water but shrimp go from undercooked to overcooked in a matter of seconds. By adding the shrimp to boiling water, then turning off the heat and throwing the lid on the pot, we let residual heat gently cook the shrimp—a foolproof process that takes 8 minutes. Because the shrimp are in the poaching liquid (flavored with lemon juice, bay leaf, and peppercorns) for so long, they actually pick up some flavor, too. Once done, the shrimp are shocked in ice water to immediately halt any further cooking. We then made a dressing in the blender using a portion of the avocado as a stand-in for the oil, along with grapefruit juice, lime juice, and honey. Whether you're counting your calories or not, this is a winning dinner salad (with just 280 calories and 9 grams of fat per serving).

SHRIMP

1   lemon, halved
1   bay leaf
½   teaspoon peppercorns
1   pound extra-large shrimp (21 to 25 per pound), peeled and deveined

SALAD AND VINAIGRETTE

2   ruby red grapefruits, segmented and juice reserved
1   avocado, cut into ½-inch dice (see page 17)
2   tablespoons fresh lime juice
½   teaspoon honey
1 ½   teaspoons grated fresh ginger
½   teaspoon salt
¼   teaspoon pepper
1   tablespoon chopped fresh mint

2   ounces snow peas (about 24), strings removed and cut lengthwise into ⅛-inch strips
16   Bibb lettuce leaves, washed and dried

**1. TO POACH THE SHRIMP:** Pour 3 cups water into a medium saucepan. Squeeze the juice of both lemon halves into the water; add the squeezed halves to the water with the bay leaf and peppercorns. Bring to a boil over high heat and boil for 2 minutes. Remove the pan from the heat and add the shrimp. Cover and let stand off the heat for 8 minutes. Have ready a medium bowl filled with ice water.

**2.** Drain the shrimp into a colander, discarding the lemon halves, bay leaf, and peppercorns. Immediately transfer the shrimp to the ice water to stop the cooking and chill, about 3 minutes. Drain the shrimp and transfer them to a large dry bowl; refrigerate until needed.

**3. TO PREPARE THE VINAIGRETTE:** Place the reserved grapefruit juice in a ¼-cup measure. If necessary, add enough water to equal ¼ cup. Puree the juice, one-quarter of the avocado, lime juice, honey, ginger, salt, and pepper together in a blender until smooth.

**4.** To serve, remove the bowl of chilled shrimp from the refrigerator and add the grapefruit segments, mint, snow peas, and remaining avocado. Pour the dressing over the mixture and toss gently to coat. Arrange the lettuce leaves on four plates and top with the shrimp mixture. Drizzle each salad with any dressing left in the bowl.

**WHAT YOU CAN DO AHEAD OF TIME:** The shrimp can be poached up to 2 days in advance and refrigerated, wrapped tightly in plastic wrap.

## NOTES FROM THE TEST KITCHEN
### DEVEINING SHRIMP

**1.** After removing the shell, use a paring knife to make a shallow cut along the back of the shrimp so that the vein is exposed.

**2.** Use the tip of the knife to lift the vein out of the shrimp. Discard the vein by wiping the blade against a paper towel.

GREEN SALAD WITH ROASTED PEARS

# GREEN SALAD
## WITH ROASTED PEARS AND BLUE CHEESE
### SERVES 4 TO 6

**WHAT MAKES THIS A BEST RECIPE:** When you want a winter salad that is a little out of the ordinary (or if you're wondering what to do with the rock-hard pears in the supermarket in January), this one tastes great and is special enough to serve guests, too. The secret to success here is roasting the pears in a really hot oven. In fact, we found it's even essential to heat your baking sheet as you're preheating the oven so that the pears start browning right away. To expedite the caramelization, we coat the pears in maple syrup mixed with grated ginger, which also imparts nice flavor to the salad overall. Our favorite pear variety for roasting is the Bartlett pear; their sweet and flowery flavor intensifies in the oven, making them the perfect choice for this salad.

¼ cup maple syrup
1 tablespoon grated fresh ginger
3 firm pears, preferably Bartlett
Salt and pepper
2 tablespoons cider vinegar
1 small shallot, minced (1 tablespoon)
3 tablespoons extra-virgin olive oil
2 bunches watercress, thick stems removed
1 head Bibb lettuce, torn into bite-sized pieces
4 ounces blue cheese, crumbled (about 1 cup)

**1.** Line a rimmed baking sheet with foil. Adjust an oven rack to the lower-middle position, place the prepared baking sheet on the rack, and heat the oven to 500 degrees. Whisk the maple syrup and ginger together in a bowl. Peel and quarter the pears lengthwise. Core the pears, then halve each quarter lengthwise.

**2.** Toss the pears with 3 tablespoons of the syrup mixture. Spread the pears in a single layer on the preheated baking sheet and season with salt and pepper. Roast until browned on the bottom, about 15 minutes. Flip each slice and roast until tender and deep golden brown, about 5 minutes. Let the pears cool on the baking sheet while preparing the salad.

**3.** Whisk the vinegar, shallot, oil, and salt and pepper to taste into the remaining syrup mixture. Combine the watercress and lettuce in a large serving bowl. Gently toss with the vinaigrette. Scatter the pears and blue cheese on top and serve.

**WHERE THINGS CAN GO WRONG:** If you try to roast the pears in an oven that isn't hot enough, you'll end up with mushy pears, regardless of the type or firmness.

**WHAT YOU CAN DO AHEAD OF TIME:** The pears can be roasted up to 3 hours in advance, but keep them at room temperature until ready to serve.

## NOTES FROM THE TEST KITCHEN

### A QUICK PEAR PRIMER
Although there are dozens of pear varieties, the most common choices in the supermarket are Bosc, Anjou, and Bartlett. We decided to find out which varieties were best for roasting, poaching, and eating out of hand.

Easily recognizable for their dull, brownish skin, Bosc pears are very sweet when ripe and have a hearty (some would say mealy) texture. We found that Boscs were best poached. The moist heat softened their texture and made them more appealing. In contrast, roasting emphasized their mealy qualities.

Anjou pears, with their light yellow-green hue, are creamy, tender, and incredibly juicy when ripe. They can be eaten out of hand and are great for roasting; the hot oven concentrates their mild flavor.

Bartletts are our favorite. Yellow when underripe, these pears turn a beautiful greenish-yellow when ready to eat. Their sweet, flowery flavor becomes more powerful when they are roasted, which is why they are our number-one choice for our Green Salad with Roasted Pears and Blue Cheese.

BOSC

ANJOU

BARTLETT

# COOL AND CREAMY MACARONI SALAD

### SERVES 8 TO 10

**WHAT MAKES THIS A BEST RECIPE:** Macaroni salad has to be one of the easiest and most versatile side dishes. And it goes with everything from a simple sandwich to grilled or roasted fish or meat. But there isn't a member of the test kitchen who hasn't been enticed by a bowl of macaroni salad in all its tangy-sweet glory, only to be disappointed by a mouthful of diluted mush. And we'd also received pleas of help from many readers tired of dumping out soggy macaroni salad at the end of a summer barbecue or picnic on the beach. So what is the solution to perfecting such a seemingly simple dish so that the macaroni was neither drowning in watery mayonnaise nor so soft that it had no bite whatsoever? The answer, it turns out, was not what you might expect. Since cooked macaroni tends to soak up mayonnaise like a sponge, you need to undercook the macaroni and leave it a little wet so that it absorbs the water over time, not the mayo. As for the flavorings, we stayed with the traditional combination of lemon juice, Dijon mustard, cayenne, and garlic powder (fresh garlic is too overpowering). We also found that if the seasonings were tossed with the pasta and allowed to sit briefly before the mayonnaise was added, the salad tasted brighter and fresher.

|   | Salt |
|---|---|
| 1 | pound elbow macaroni |
| ½ | small red onion, minced |
| 1 | celery rib, minced |
| ¼ | cup minced fresh parsley |
| 2 | tablespoons fresh lemon juice |
| 1 | tablespoon Dijon mustard |
| ⅛ | teaspoon garlic powder |
|   | Pinch cayenne pepper |
| 1½ | cups mayonnaise |
|   | Pepper |

**1.** Bring 4 quarts water to a boil in a large pot for the macaroni. Add 1 tablespoon salt and the macaroni to the boiling water and cook, stirring, until nearly tender, about 5 minutes. Drain in a colander and rinse with cold water until cool, then drain briefly so that the macaroni remains moist. Transfer to a large bowl.

**2.** Stir in the onion, celery, parsley, lemon juice, mustard, garlic powder, and cayenne, and let sit until the flavors are absorbed, about 2 minutes. Add the mayonnaise and let sit until the salad texture is no longer watery, 5 to 10 minutes. Season with salt and pepper to taste. Serve.

**WHAT YOU CAN DO AHEAD OF TIME:** The salad can be covered and refrigerated, wrapped tightly in plastic wrap, for up to 2 days. You may need to add a little warm water to adjust the consistency before serving.

---

## GREAT DISCOVERIES

### LEAVE THE MACARONI WET

Over the years, I have become the macaroni salad expert in the test kitchen. Or so I thought. Until I tackled this particular assignment for *Cook's Country,* I had always firmly believed that it was essential to shake the cooked macaroni dry. I even advocated going to the trouble of spreading the cooked macaroni out on paper towels so as to remove any excess water from both the exterior and the crooks of the pasta. Yes, I know that drying pasta on paper towels sounds absurd (and time-consuming), but I was convinced that even a little excess water would make my salad mushy and soggy.

Well, it turns out that I was making work for myself. If you undercook the macaroni, it's far more likely to retain decent texture in the salad. The other key finding from my latest round of macaroni salad tests was even more important. Don't toss the drained pasta with the mayonnaise right away. The pasta is a sponge, especially right after it has been cooked. If it has no alternative, the pasta will soak up the mayonnaise and the noodles will turn mushy. However, if you leave the noodles a bit wet after they are drained, the pasta will soak up this water—not the mayonnaise—and the effect on the noodles is minimal. We concluded that if the macaroni soaks up too much mayonnaise it turns mushy, but if it soaks up a little water the texture remains firm and chewy.

JULIA COLLIN DAVISON | SENIOR FOOD EDITOR, BOOKS

# ALL-AMERICAN POTATO SALAD

SERVES 4 TO 6

**WHAT MAKES THIS A BEST RECIPE:** Traditional American potato salad, containing mayonnaise, mustard, vinegar, pickles, celery, onion, and sometimes hard-cooked eggs, is a deli-case staple. Though simple to make, most versions are sloppy, mushy, and bland. Our first task was to determine the best potato variety for our salad. We tried Red Bliss (firm but bland) and russets (mushy but great-tasting), but ultimately settled on Yukon Golds, which offered the best balance of sturdiness and flavor. With the potatoes chosen, it was time to focus on the dressing. We made a bright and creamy mayonnaise-based dressing, which we cut with tangy sour cream and sweet yellow mustard. To further intensify the dressing, we tried adding various vinegars and lemon juice, but they tended to overwhelm the other flavors. It wasn't until we added some pickle juice—yes, the liquid in the pickle jar—that our dressing really came together. Although the dressing had great flavor, it was merely coating the potatoes, not getting inside. We decided to borrow a technique from French-style potato salads in which a simple vinaigrette is drizzled over the drained potatoes when they are still hot, and is absorbed by them as they cool. Pouring a mayonnaise-based dressing over hot potatoes would result in a runny mess, but singling out a couple of strongly flavored ingredients to pour over the hot potatoes—in this case the mustard and pickle juice—proved just the trick.

2 pounds Yukon Gold potatoes (about 4 medium), peeled and cut into ¾-inch cubes
    Salt
3 tablespoons dill pickle juice
1 tablespoon yellow mustard
½ cup mayonnaise
¼ cup sour cream
¼ cup finely chopped dill pickles
1 celery rib, chopped fine
½ small red onion, chopped fine
½ teaspoon celery seed
    Pepper
2 hard-cooked eggs, peeled and cut into ¼-inch dice (optional)

Yukon Gold potatoes offer the best balance of sturdiness and flavor.

**1.** Cover the potatoes with water by 1 inch in a large saucepan and bring to a boil over high heat. Stir in 1 teaspoon salt, reduce the heat to medium-low, and simmer until the potatoes are tender, 10 to 15 minutes.

**2.** Drain the potatoes thoroughly and spread them in a single layer on a rimmed baking sheet. Mix 2 tablespoons of the pickle juice and the mustard together in a small bowl. Drizzle the pickle juice mixture over the potatoes and gently toss until evenly coated. Refrigerate the potatoes until cooled, about 30 minutes.

**3.** Mix the mayonnaise, sour cream, chopped pickles, celery, red onion, remaining 1 tablespoon pickle juice, ½ teaspoon salt, celery seed, and ¼ teaspoon pepper together in a large bowl. Add the cooled potatoes and gently toss to combine. Cover and refrigerate until thoroughly chilled, about 30 minutes. Gently stir in the eggs, if using, just before serving.

**WHERE THINGS CAN GO WRONG:** Make sure not to overcook the potatoes or the salad will be quite mushy. Keep the water at a gentle simmer and use the tip of a paring knife to judge the doneness of the potatoes. If the knife inserts easily into the potato pieces, they are done.

**WHAT YOU CAN DO AHEAD OF TIME:** The potato salad can be refrigerated in an airtight container for up to 2 days.

# CHICKEN SALAD
## WITH AVOCADO, MANGO, AND CITRUS DRESSING
### SERVES 6

**WHAT MAKES THIS A BEST RECIPE:** For many cooks, mayonnaise is the go-to ingredient for turning last night's leftovers into chicken salad. Fine for a simple sandwich, but mayonnaise is more about luscious texture than interesting flavor, as the creamy fat tends to dull the impact of other ingredients, no matter how aggressively you empty your spice cabinet. Instead, we thought a vinaigrette-dressed chicken—something you might serve on a bed of greens as a light dinner—would have fresher, bolder flavors. Unfortunately, we realized right away that this was easier said than done: Because oil and vinegar separate so easily, they cling poorly to chicken, yielding greasy, watery salads. To solve this problem, we needed to create an emulsion (a suspension of two liquids that don't naturally mix). Looking for an ingredient that would help emulsify the dressing, we turned to avocado, which with all its creamy fat, worked perfectly, blending well with citrus juice and a little oil to make a fine, cohesive dressing. Using a blender was key, though, since its fast-moving blade makes it more effective at emulsifying the ingredients into small droplets that stay suspended (instead of separating) than whisking by hand does. This bright creamy dressing pairs nicely with shredded chicken, mango, and other fresh seasonings to make a lively dinner salad.

1   ripe avocado
½   cup fresh orange juice
1   teaspoon finely grated lime zest
3   tablespoons juice from 2 limes
2   tablespoons canola oil
1   tablespoon plus 1 teaspoon honey
    Salt and pepper
1   mango, ripe but firm, cut into ½-inch dice
½   small red onion, diced small (about ⅓ cup)
1   jalapeño chile, minced
3   tablespoons chopped fresh mint
5   cups shredded roast chicken, at room temperature

**1.** Halve and pit the avocado. In a blender, puree half the avocado, orange juice, lime zest and juice, oil, honey, 1¼ teaspoons salt, and ½ teaspoon pepper until smooth. Transfer to a large bowl.

**2.** Dice the remaining avocado half into ½-inch pieces. Add the avocado, mango, onion, chile, and mint to the vinaigrette; toss gently to combine. Add the chicken and toss gently to combine; let stand at room temperature for 15 minutes. Season with salt and pepper to taste and serve immediately.

## NOTES FROM THE TEST KITCHEN

### FULLY COOKED CHICKEN FOR SALAD
For a quicker, easier chicken salad, we wondered how the fully cooked chicken options at the market would fare. In a word, great. The assertive flavors of our chicken salad minimized any differences among the five chickens we tried, including our freshly made roasted chicken, two supermarket rotisserie chickens, and a garlicky bird from Boston Market (a fast-food chain restaurant). Even the Tyson Heat 'N Eat Whole Chicken—fully cooked, by Tyson, and shrink-wrapped—fared just as well. And since it's sold refrigerated, you don't have to wait for it to cool down before shredding and dressing it. The convenience comes at a small price: These birds, especially the rotisserie specimens, can be pretty salty. You will want to use a light hand when seasoning.

### PREPARING AVOCADOS

**1.** After slicing the avocado in half around the pit, lodge the edge of the knife blade into the pit and twist to remove. Use a large wooden spoon to pry the pit safely off the knife.

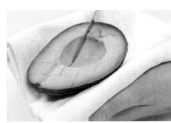

**2.** Use a dish towel to hold the avocado steady. Make ½-inch-crosshatch incisions in the flesh of each avocado half with a knife, cutting down to but not through the skin.

**3.** Separate the diced flesh from the skin with a soup spoon inserted between the skin and the flesh, gently scooping out the avocado cubes.

# SOUPS & STEWS

# HOT AND SOUR SOUP

SERVES 6 TO 8

**WHAT MAKES THIS A BEST RECIPE:** The ideal hot and sour soup is spicy, bracing, rich, and complex. It can also take a good part of the day to prepare, and an extensive list of hard-to-find ingredients makes it even less accessible for the average home cook. We were able to simplify this soup without compromising its singular flavor by substituting ingredients that can be found at most any local supermarket. The main hurdle was to strike a balance between the "hot" and "sour" components of the soup. The "hot" side of the soup was created with two heat sources— penetrating white pepper and fiery chili oil. Creating the "sour" side presented more challenges. The traditional sour component in this soup is Chinese black vinegar, a low-acid vinegar with a distinctive flavor. For a workable substitute, we settled on a tablespoon each of balsamic and red wine vinegar (though we still recommend seeking out Chinese black vinegar—which is available at most Asian markets—as its flavor is unique). Thin strips of pork and cubes of tofu add substance to the soup, while fine wisps of egg lend a pleasing contrast in texture. Cornstarch is a key ingredient as well: not only does it tenderize the pork, it also stabilizes the egg, keeping it from blending into the soup and muddying its appearance. Wood ear mushrooms and lily buds were replaced with fresh, mild shiitake mushrooms and crispy, mildly tangy canned bamboo shoots. A sprinkling of raw, crisp scallions adds the finishing touch, and our soup strikes a perfect balance of flavor, texture, and color.

- 7 ounces extra-firm tofu, drained
- 4 tablespoons soy sauce
- 1 teaspoon toasted sesame oil
- 3 tablespoons plus 1½ teaspoons cornstarch
- 1 boneless center-cut pork chop, ½ inch thick (about 6 ounces), trimmed of fat and cut into 1-inch by ⅛-inch matchsticks
- 3 tablespoons plus 1 teaspoon cool water
- 1 large egg
- 6 cups low-sodium chicken broth
- 1 cup bamboo shoots (from one 5-ounce can), sliced lengthwise into ⅛-inch-thick strips
- 4 ounces shiitake mushrooms, stemmed and sliced ¼ inch thick
- 5 tablespoons Chinese black vinegar (see note at right)
- 2 teaspoons chili oil
- 1 teaspoon ground white pepper
- 3 medium scallions, sliced thin, for serving

**1.** Place the tofu in a pie plate and set a heavy plate on top. Weight with 2 heavy cans and let stand at least 15 minutes (the tofu should release about ½ cup of liquid). Whisk 1 tablespoon of the soy sauce, sesame oil, and 1 teaspoon of the cornstarch in a medium bowl. Toss the pork with the marinade and set aside for at least 10 minutes (but no more than 30 minutes).

**2.** Combine 3 tablespoons cornstarch with 3 tablespoons cool water in a small bowl and set aside. Mix the remaining ½ teaspoon cornstarch with the remaining 1 teaspoon cool water in another small bowl. Add the egg and beat with a fork until combined. Set aside.

**3.** Bring the broth to a boil in a large saucepan over medium-high heat. Reduce the heat to medium-low and add the bamboo shoots and mushrooms. Simmer until the mushrooms are just tender, about 5 minutes. While the broth simmers, dice the tofu into ½-inch cubes. Add the tofu and pork, including the marinade, to the soup, stirring to separate any pieces of pork that stick together. Continue to simmer until the pork is no longer pink, about 2 minutes.

**4.** Stir the cornstarch mixture to recombine. Add to the soup and increase the heat to medium-high. Cook, stirring occasionally, until the soup thickens and turns translucent, about 1 minute. Stir in the vinegar, chili oil, pepper, and remaining 3 tablespoons soy sauce, and turn off the heat.

**5.** Without stirring the soup, use a soup spoon to slowly drizzle very thin streams of the egg mixture into the pan in a circular motion. Let the soup sit for 1 minute, then return the pan to medium-high heat. Bring the soup to a gentle boil, then immediately remove from the heat. Gently stir the soup once to evenly distribute the egg. Ladle the soup into bowls and top with the scallions. Serve immediately.

**WHERE THINGS CAN GO WRONG:** Make sure to turn off the heat before drizzling the egg mixture into the soup. If the soup is simmering during this process, the egg won't form its distinctive light and wispy strands.

**WHAT YOU CAN DO AHEAD OF TIME:** The soup is best eaten as soon as it is made.

## NOTES FROM THE TEST KITCHEN

**USE BLACK VINEGAR**
Hot and Sour Soup will have the most authentic and distinct flavor when made with Chinese black vinegar—its flavor is so unique that we recommend seeking it out. Look for black vinegar in Asian supermarkets. If you can't find it, a combination of red wine vinegar and balsamic vinegar can be substituted: Use only 1 tablespoon each of red wine vinegar and balsamic vinegar for the 5 tablespoons Chinese black vinegar called for in the recipe.

**FREEZE THE PORK**
Cutting pork into thin strips can be a challenge. We've found the easiest way to do so is to freeze the pork chop for 15 minutes before slicing.

**A LESS SPICY SOUP**
A combination of white pepper and chili oil makes this soup very spicy. To make it less spicy, omit the chili oil altogether, or add only 1 teaspoon.

**IT'S ALL ABOUT BALANCE**
Warm and cool, crunchy and soft, sweet and pungent—in Chinese cuisine, striking a delicate balance between contrasting elements is often more crucial than ingredient specifics. The sources of this soup's namesake elements, hot and sour, vary from recipe to authentic recipe, but we achieved the most satisfying balance when we combined white peppercorns with black vinegar.

## GREAT DISCOVERIES

### THE MYSTERIOUS POWERS OF CORNSTARCH

Most cooks keep a box of cornstarch on hand for a single purpose: thickening. So did we—until we noticed that cornstarch was working its magic in other ways as well. Predictably, adding cornstarch (3 tablespoons) to our soup thickened it. What was surprising, however, were the two other uses we found for cornstarch. Adding just 1 teaspoon of cornstarch to the pork marinade of soy sauce and sesame oil caused the marinade to cling to and coat the meat during cooking, creating a protective sheath that slowed the inevitable rise in temperature that separates moist, tender pork from dry, chalky pork jerky. And adding just ½ teaspoon of cornstarch to the egg that's drizzled into the soup at the end of cooking seemed to have a tenderizing effect. Cornstarch stabilizes liquid proteins when they're heated, staving off excessive shrinkage and contraction. So this last bit of cornstarch helped the egg cook up lighter and softer.

REBECCA HAYS | MANAGING EDITOR, COOK'S ILLUSTRATED

# BEEF AND VEGETABLE SOUP
SERVES 6 TO 8

**WHAT MAKES THIS A BEST RECIPE:** A really good beef and vegetable soup usually starts with homemade beef stock, which can take all day to prepare. Using canned beef broth, however, is almost always disappointing. But because canned broth is so convenient, we wanted to see if we could find a way to make it work and create a really flavorful, hearty soup that tasted like beef—not the can it came from. The key turned out to be quite simple: Use meat, and use lots of it, both to enhance the broth and as a soup ingredient. After testing a variety of cuts (most of which were too chewy or too greasy), we settled on using boneless blade steak—it has big beefy flavor, is not terribly fatty, and is inexpensive. The steaks are browned to build flavor, then the broth is added. All beef broth tasted tinny, but combining it with chicken broth, water, and a little tomato paste gave us a rich and balanced base for the soup. Herbs and garlic are then added to the pot (we like a combination of bay leaves and thyme, along with a whole head of garlic), and the whole is simmered until the meat is tender and the broth is flavorful. Once tender, the meat is shredded and added back to the soup with the vegetables. Tasters really liked the sweetness of onions and carrots and acidity of tomatoes, which they thought added a complex edge to the soup. Almost any vegetable will work however—everything from potatoes and parsnips to peas and spinach—so we have provided information on page 23 to enable you to create your own variation.

BROTH

3 pounds blade steaks, 1 inch thick
  Salt and pepper
2 tablespoons vegetable oil
1 tablespoon tomato paste
4 cups low-sodium chicken broth
4 cups low-sodium beef broth
2 cups water
1 garlic head, top third cut off and discarded,
  loose outer skins removed
2 bay leaves
½ teaspoon dried thyme

BEEF AND VEGETABLE SOUP

## SOUP

- 1 tablespoon unsalted butter
- 1 onion, minced (about 1 cup)
- 2 carrots, peeled, halved lengthwise, and sliced ¼ inch thick
- 1 (14.5-ounce) can diced tomatoes, drained
  Salt and pepper
  Chopped fresh parsley, for serving

**1.** FOR THE BROTH: Season the blade steaks with salt and pepper. Heat 1 tablespoon of the oil in a large Dutch oven over medium-high heat until shimmering. Add half of the steaks and cook until well browned on both sides, about 8 minutes. Set the steaks aside on a plate. Repeat with the remaining tablespoon oil and steaks.

**2.** Pour off the fat from the Dutch oven and return to medium-high heat. Add the tomato paste and cook, mashing the paste with a wooden spoon for about 30 seconds. Add the chicken broth, beef broth, and water, and scrape any browned bits from the bottom of the pot with a wooden spoon. Return the steaks and any accumulated juice to the pot. Add the garlic, bay leaves, and thyme and bring to a simmer. Using a wide, shallow spoon skim off any foam or fat that rises to the surface. Reduce the heat to medium-low and simmer gently (do not boil) until the meat is tender, about 2 hours.

**3.** Transfer the steaks and the garlic head to a rimmed plate to cool. Once cool enough to handle, shred the meat into bite-sized pieces, discarding any fat. Using tongs, squeeze the garlic cloves into a small bowl. Mash with a fork until a paste forms. Pour the broth through a fine-mesh strainer. Return the shredded beef and garlic paste to the broth.

**4.** FOR THE SOUP: Melt the butter in a clean large Dutch oven over medium heat. Add the onion and carrots and cook until the onion is softened but not browned, about 5 minutes. Add the tomatoes and the broth. Bring to a simmer, reduce the heat to medium-low, and cook until the carrots are tender, about 20 minutes. Season with salt and pepper to taste and sprinkle with the parsley. Serve.

**WHERE THINGS CAN GO WRONG:** Don't let the broth boil or it will be cloudy. Make sure the broth simmers slowly so that it comes out clear. Also, at the outset, some impurities will rise to the surface—they should be skimmed with a wide spoon.

**WHAT YOU CAN DO AHEAD OF TIME:** The broth can be made and refrigerated in an airtight container for up to 3 days or frozen for up to 2 months. When ready to finish the soup, bring the broth to a simmer before proceeding with step 4.

## NOTES FROM THE TEST KITCHEN

### CUSTOMIZE YOUR SOUP
It may be impossible to please all of the people all of the time, but that doesn't mean you can't try. Beef and Vegetable Soup is easily customized to use vegetables you like and/or have on hand. Feel free to mix and match, but don't add more than 2 cups of long-cooking root vegetables, pasta, or rice. The vegetables can cook right in the soup pot, but the pasta and rice should be precooked so they don't make the broth too thick. Below are some ideas for different vegetables to try, along with some brief instructions on how to prepare them, how much to use, and when to add them to the soup.

#### LONG-COOKING VEGETABLES
**RED POTATOES.** Use up to 2 cups scrubbed and diced red potatoes and add them with the broth in step 4.
**PARSNIPS.** Use up to ½ cup peeled and diced parsnips and add them with the broth in step 4.
**SWEET POTATOES.** Use up to 2 cups peeled and diced sweet potatoes and add them with the broth in step 4.

#### LAST-MINUTE VEGETABLES AND STARCH
These vegetables require no preparation; simply add them to the soup at the designated time.
**FROZEN LIMA BEANS.** Add up to ½ cup 5 minutes before the soup is done.
**FROZEN PEAS.** Add up to 1 cup 2 minutes before the soup is done.
**BABY SPINACH.** Add up to 2 cups just 1 minute before the soup is done.
**PASTA, EGG NOODLES, OR RICE.** Cook and drain and add up to 2 cups just before serving.

### TWO BROTHS ARE BETTER THAN ONE
We found that a beef soup made with all canned beef broth turned out weak and metallic-tasting. On the other hand, using all chicken broth gave the soup an overpowering chicken flavor. We solved the problem by using a mixture of the two broths, creating a rich and balanced base for our soup.

### THE BEEFIEST CUT
We tested a variety of cuts before landing on the right choice—blade steaks.

# CHICKEN NOODLE SOUP

SERVES 8 TO 10

**WHAT MAKES THIS A BEST RECIPE:** Making chicken noodle soup at home can be a satisfying process. But no one wants to spend all that time and effort making it only to have the chicken turn out dry and stringy and the broth watery and tasteless. This recipe is easy to follow, with a streamlined process that promises moist, tender meat and a richly flavored broth. The key is to use chicken parts rather than a whole chicken. Dark meat provides much more flavor than white meat does, but we found that tasters only wanted tender chunks of white meat in the finished soup. To solve this dilemma we decided to make the broth with dark meat, then quickly poach the white meat in the broth to finish the soup. The juicy meat of chicken thighs was the best option for the dark meat. After browning the thighs to intensify their flavor, we simmered them in water with a little salt and some bay leaves. The result was a broth that had the cleanest, most intense chicken flavor that cooked in a fraction of the time it took to cook a whole chicken. Raw, boneless, skinless chicken breasts are then added to the simmering broth and poached. Once cooked through, the meat is removed from the broth, cooled, and shredded. Only the breast meat is added back to the soup (the dark meat can be reserved for another use). For additional flavor components, we liked the classic combination of onion, carrot, and celery. Sautéing the vegetables in a thin film of oil (rather than just poaching them in the broth) intensified their flavors. The vegetables finish cooking in the broth, simmering for about 15 minutes, along with some chopped fresh thyme, to meld all the components together. Better than anything that comes out of a can, and easier than most homemade chicken soups that require whole birds and many hours on the stove, this soup deeply satisfies as only chicken soup can.

### BROTH

- 12 bone-in, skin-on chicken thighs (about 4 pounds)
  Salt and pepper
- 1 tablespoon vegetable oil
- 1 onion, chopped (about 1 cup)
- 3 quarts water

A bowl of homemade soup might not cure the common cold (but it will make you feel better).

- 2 bay leaves
- 2 boneless, skinless chicken breasts (about 1 pound)

### SOUP

- 1 tablespoon vegetable oil
- 1 onion, minced (about 1 cup)
- 1 carrot, peeled and sliced thin
- 1 celery rib, halved lengthwise, then sliced thin
- 2 teaspoons minced fresh thyme
- 6 ounces wide egg noodles
- ¼ cup minced fresh parsley
  Salt and pepper

**1. FOR THE BROTH:** Pat the chicken thighs dry with paper towels and season with salt and pepper. Heat the oil in a large Dutch oven over medium-high heat until smoking. Cook half of the thighs skin side down until deep golden brown, about 6 minutes. Turn the thighs and lightly brown on the second side, about 2 minutes. Transfer the thighs to a strainer-lined large bowl. Repeat with the remaining thighs and transfer to the strainer; discard the fat in the bowl. Pour off the fat from the pot, add the onion, and cook over medium heat until just softened, about 3 minutes. Meanwhile, remove and discard the skin from the thighs. Add the thighs, water, bay leaves, and 1 tablespoon salt to the pot. Cover and simmer for 30 minutes. Add the chicken breasts and continue simmering until the broth is rich and flavorful, about 15 minutes.

**2.** Strain the broth into a large container, let stand at least 10 minutes, then skim the fat off the surface. Meanwhile, transfer the chicken to a cutting board to cool. Once cooled, remove the thigh meat from the bones and shred; refrigerate for up to 2 days or freeze for up to 1 month. Shred the breast meat and reserve for the soup.

**3. FOR THE SOUP:** Heat the oil in the now-empty Dutch oven over medium-high heat until shimmering. Add the onion, carrot, and celery and cook until the onion has softened, 3 to 4 minutes. Stir in the thyme and broth and simmer until the vegetables are tender, about 15 minutes. Add the noodles and shredded breast meat and simmer until the noodles are just tender, about 5 minutes. Off the heat, stir in the parsley and season with salt and pepper to taste. Serve.

**WHAT YOU CAN DO AHEAD OF TIME:** The broth (and shredded breast meat) for the soup can be refrigerated for up to 2 days or frozen for up to 1 month before being used to make soup. To avoid soggy noodles and vegetables, finish the soup (step 3) just before you plan on serving it.

## NOTES FROM THE TEST KITCHEN

### GET THE FAT OUT
Chicken thighs add flavor to the broth, as well as fat. Removing the skin after browning the thighs helps cut down on the greasiness, but some fat will still float to the surface as the broth cools.

To remove the fat, place a single paper towel on the surface of the slightly cooled broth. Gather the corners of the paper towel and lift the towel out of the broth, allowing the excess broth to drip back into the container. Repeat with additional paper towels until all of the surface fat is removed.

### THIGHS IF YOU WANT
Most people prefer chicken noodle soup with chunks of white meat. If you prefer dark meat in your soup, you can omit the chicken breasts entirely and add the shredded thigh meat to the soup instead. The thigh meat can also be reserved for a salad or pot pie.

# HEARTY SLOW-COOKER BEEF STEW
### SERVES 6 TO 8

**WHAT MAKES THIS A BEST RECIPE:** The slow cooker is a convenient kitchen tool for busy cooks. But when it comes to beef stew, most slow-cooker recipes are disappointing. The meat isn't browned and lacks flavor, while the long cooking time makes for mushy vegetables. Worse yet, the meat and vegetables heat up, but the flavors never really marry, producing a dish that is watery and flavorless. Our recipe for slow-cooker beef stew produces chunks of tender meat, a broth with just-the-right thickness, and perfectly cooked vegetables every time. How did we do it? We started with generous pieces of beef chuck (a cut that is ideal for long, slow cooking) and browned them well for maximum flavor. We then browned the onions and added a bit of tomato paste, but the base for our stew was still missing something—the color was washed out and it lacked truly meaty flavor. After several failed attempts at trying to solve these problems, we hit upon an unusual solution. Soy sauce was the surprise ingredient here, giving our stew the rich, brown color and intense savory flavor we sought. To thicken our stew we tried the usual suspects of flour, cornstarch, and even potato flakes, but we had the best results when we tried an unlikely ingredient: Minute Tapioca. Commonly used to thicken fruit pies, we found tapioca ably thickened the stew's broth and withstood the long cooking without leaving a starchy aftertaste. All that was left to do was solve the problem of the mushy vegetables. We tried roasting the vegetables separately before adding them to the pot. They tasted great, but an hour of chopping and roasting made our recipe way more complicated and time-consuming than we wanted. It was then that we had the idea to steal a trick often used in grilling and made a "hobo pack." The vegetables are wrapped in foil and placed on top of the beef in the slow cooker, which protects their sweet, earthy flavor and prevents them from overcooking—a simple technique that worked perfectly. This is a no-hassle beef stew that rivals any stovetop version.

5   pounds boneless beef chuck-eye roast, trimmed and cut into 1½-inch cubes
    Salt and pepper
3   tablespoons vegetable oil
4   onions, minced (about 4 cups)
1   (6-ounce) can tomato paste
2   cups low-sodium chicken or beef broth
3   tablespoons soy sauce
1   pound carrots, peeled and cut into 1-inch pieces
1   pound parsnips, peeled and cut into 1-inch pieces
1   pound red potatoes (about 3), cut into 1-inch pieces
1½  teaspoons minced fresh thyme
2   bay leaves
2   tablespoons Minute Tapioca
2   cups frozen peas, thawed

**1.** Pat the beef dry with paper towels, then season with salt and pepper. Heat 1 tablespoon of the oil in a large nonstick skillet over medium-high heat until just smoking. Add half of the beef and brown on all sides, about 8 minutes. Transfer the beef to the slow-cooker insert and repeat with the remaining beef.

**2.** Add 1 tablespoon of the oil, onions, and ¼ teaspoon salt to the empty skillet and cook until golden brown, about 6 minutes. Add the tomato paste and cook, stirring well, for 2 minutes. Add the broth and soy sauce, bring to a simmer, and transfer to the slow-cooker insert.

**3.** Toss the carrots, parsnips, potatoes, ½ teaspoon of the thyme, and the remaining 1 tablespoon oil in a large bowl and season with salt and pepper. Wrap the vegetables in a foil packet that will fit into the slow cooker. Stir the bay leaves and tapioca into the slow-cooker insert; set the vegetable packet on top of the beef.

**4.** Set the slow cooker to high, cover, and cook for 6 to 7 hours. (Or cook on low for 10 to 11 hours.) Transfer the vegetable packet to a plate. Carefully open the packet (watch for steam) and stir the vegetables and juices into the stew. Add the remaining 1 teaspoon thyme and the peas and let stand until the peas are heated through, about 15 minutes. Discard the bay leaves, season with salt and pepper to taste, and serve.

**WHERE THINGS CAN GO WRONG:** Make sure not to remove the lid from the slow cooker during the cooking process. Doing so will result in a loss of precious heat and will extend the cooking time.

**WHAT YOU CAN DO AHEAD OF TIME:** You can do most of the prep for this recipe the night before the ingredients go into the slow cooker. Prepare the recipe through step 2 and refrigerate the browned beef and onion mixture in separate containers. In the morning, transfer everything to the slow cooker and proceed with step 3. The cooking time will run to the high end of the ranges given in the recipe.

## NOTES FROM THE TEST KITCHEN

### BEEF STEW SECRETS
Beef stew made in a slow cooker tends to have three big problems: it's watery, it's bland, and the vegetables cook to mush. Here's how we solved these problems.
- To thicken the stew without giving it a starchy texture, use Minute Tapioca.
- For big beefy flavor, slip in a few tablespoons of soy sauce.
- For perfectly cooked vegetables, steam them in a "hobo pack" (see below) on top of the stew.

### MAKING A HOBO PACK
To make a hobo pack, place the vegetables on one side of a large piece of heavy-duty aluminum foil. Fold the foil over, shaping it into a packet that will fit into your slow cooker, then crimp to seal the edges. Also, we found that if you are going to leave the stew in the slow cooker for more than 10 hours it was best to cut the vegetables into larger, 1½- to 2-inch pieces.

HEARTY SLOW-COOKER BEEF STEW

# 30-MINUTE PANTRY CLAM CHOWDER

### SERVES 6 TO 8

**WHAT MAKES THIS A BEST RECIPE:** We love homemade clam chowder, with its rich, creamy texture and full clam flavor. But making clam chowder at home has a few big drawbacks. For one, it's time consuming. The clams must first be washed and scrubbed clean, then steamed and chopped before being added to the chowder. Clams can also be expensive, and that price adds up quickly when a typical recipe calls for at least seven pounds. Add to that the fact that clams are not terribly forgiving—you must cook them soon after their purchase—and the idea of a quick clam chowder made with canned clams sounds very appealing. But many recipes using canned clams come out too rich, too creamy, and utterly lacking the sweet, briny flavor of clams. Our quick clam chowder has the smooth, lush texture and distinct clam flavor of a classic clam chowder—without the time, expense, and inconvenience typically involved. After many hours in the kitchen, we learned that the secret to making a good quick clam chowder is to use both chopped clams and clam juice and to use them generously. (We like Doxsee Minced Clams teamed with Doxsee brand clam juice, as well as Snow's Minced Clams and Snow's clam juice. These clams are neither too tough nor too soft, and have a good natural clam flavor.) Making the chowder predominantly out of these two ingredients ensured a full clam flavor that takes center stage. We then added waxy red boiling potatoes, which have a firm but tender texture and don't break down easily when cooked. A generous amount of bacon adds smoky flavor and a welcome complexity, while garlic, onion, and bay leaves further round out the chowder's flavor without overwhelming the star ingredient. We were also careful not to over-thicken the chowder, a common mistake. We found that ¼ cup of flour was all that was needed to provide enough starch to give the chowder body, but not make it pasty or gluey. (In addition, the flour also acts as a stabilizer and prevents the chowder from separating and curdling.) Finishing the chowder with a cup of cream smoothed out the clam flavor and gave the soup a silky texture. With this recipe, you can easily have great clam chowder at home.

4 (6.5-ounce) cans minced clams
3 (8-ounce) bottles clam juice
1½ pounds red potatoes (4 or 5 medium), cut into ½-inch chunks
1 teaspoon fresh thyme or ¼ teaspoon dried
2 bay leaves
4 slices bacon, minced
1 onion, minced (about 1 cup)
 Salt
2 garlic cloves, minced
¼ cup unbleached all-purpose flour
1 cup heavy cream
2 tablespoons minced fresh parsley
 Pepper

**1.** Drain the clams, reserving the juice and set the clams aside. Add the bottled clam juice to the reserved clam juice to measure 5 cups (if necessary, add water). Bring the clam juice, potatoes, thyme, and bay leaves to a boil, covered, in a large saucepan. Reduce to a simmer and continue to cook, covered, until needed in step 3.

**2.** Meanwhile, cook the bacon in a large Dutch oven over medium-high heat until the fat is partially rendered, about 2 minutes. Add the onion and ¼ teaspoon salt and continue to cook, stirring occasionally, until softened and slightly browned, about 8 minutes.

**3.** Stir in the garlic and cook until fragrant, about 30 seconds. Stir in the flour and cook until lightly browned, about 1 minute. Slowly stir in the clam juice and potato mixture, scraping up any browned bits. Bring to a simmer and cook until the potatoes are tender, 7 to 10 minutes.

**4.** Stir in the clams, cream, and parsley. Return to a simmer and cook for 2 minutes. Off the heat, remove the bay leaves, season with salt and pepper to taste, and serve.

**WHERE THINGS CAN GO WRONG:** Both canned clams and bottled clam juice are often salty, so be careful when seasoning the chowder. Be sure to add the clams at the end of the cooking time—canned minced clams can become tough and bland if simmered for an extended period of time. Cooking the clams for just 2 minutes ensures that they remain tender and full of flavor.

**WHAT YOU CAN DO AHEAD OF TIME:** The chowder is best eaten as soon as it is made.

# LIGHT CREAM OF BROCCOLI SOUP

### SERVES 4

**WHAT MAKES THIS A BEST RECIPE:** This soup has all the creaminess and richness of regular cream of broccoli soup, but with less than half the calories and a fraction of the fat—just 120 calories and 5 grams of fat per serving. Plus this soup is bursting with broccoli flavor—unlike other versions where large amounts of cream and butter dilute the vegetal flavor and dull its color. Rather than sauté the vegetables with up to half a stick of butter, we sweat the broccoli stalks and onion in just a teaspoon of oil and some salt (the more tender broccoli florets are added later in the cooking process). Cooked over medium-low heat with the lid on, the vegetables steam in the moisture they release, resulting in deep, concentrated flavor. A combination of chicken and vegetable broths provides a pleasing balance of depth and lightness, while some white wine adds a hint of acidity. The biggest challenge was deciding what type of dairy to use. Taking a cue from other lowfat cream of vegetable soups, we tried substituting lowfat milk for the cream, but the result was a soup that lacked body and flavor. Hoping for a creamier (but still lower-fat) product, we then moved on to evaporated milk but tasters complained it was too sweet, with an off flavor. The winner turned out to be half-and-half. We found that just ½ cup gave us the smooth, rich, creamy texture we sought without eclipsing the flavor of the broccoli.

1½   pounds broccoli (about 1 large bunch), florets cut into 1-inch pieces, enough stalks peeled and chopped fine to make ¾ cup (discard any remaining stalks)
1     onion, minced (about 1 cup)
1     teaspoon vegetable oil
      Salt
3     garlic cloves, minced
1     tablespoon unbleached all-purpose flour
¼     cup dry white wine
1     bay leaf
1½   cups low-sodium chicken broth
1½   cups low-sodium vegetable broth
½     cup half-and-half
      Pepper

**1.** Combine the chopped broccoli stalks, onion, oil, and ½ teaspoon salt in a large saucepan. Cover and cook over medium-low heat, stirring often, until softened, 8 to 10 minutes. Stir in the garlic and cook until fragrant, about 30 seconds.

**2.** Stir in the flour and cook for 1 minute. Whisk in the wine with the bay leaf and cook until the wine is absorbed, about 1 minute. Whisking constantly, gradually add the broths. Bring to a boil over medium-high heat. Cover, reduce the heat to medium-low, and simmer until slightly thickened and the broth no longer tastes of flour, about 5 minutes. Add the florets and continue to simmer, uncovered, until tender, 7 to 10 minutes. Remove the bay leaf.

**3.** Puree the mixture in a blender (or food processor) until smooth, and return to a clean saucepan. Stir in the half-and-half and cook over low heat until just hot (do not boil), about 3 minutes. Season with salt and pepper to taste and serve immediately.

**WHERE THINGS CAN GO WRONG:** To preserve its green color, cook the broccoli until it is just tender. Also, do not boil the soup once the half-and-half has been added. Boiling will cause the half-and-half to curdle.

**WHAT YOU CAN DO AHEAD OF TIME:** The soup is best eaten as soon as it is made.

## NOTES FROM THE TEST KITCHEN

### USE TWO BROTHS
This soup tastes best when made with both chicken broth and vegetable broth; however, for a vegetarian soup, you can use all vegetable broth (the soup will taste sweeter).

### PREPARING BROCCOLI

**1.** Place the head of broccoli upside down on the cutting board and, using a large knife, trim the florets very close to their heads and cut into 1-inch pieces.

**2.** Lay the stalks on the cutting board and square them off with a large knife, to remove the outer ⅛ inch, which is quite tough. Cut the stalks in half lengthwise and chop fine.

# HEARTY VEGETABLE SOUP
## SERVES 6 TO 8

**WHAT MAKES THIS A BEST RECIPE:** Brothy vegetable soups with bits of vegetables are pleasing, but they never seem to be sufficiently filling. Our goal was to create a thick and hearty vegetable soup, one that could be elevated to main-course status. Using long-simmering starchy root vegetables or dried beans is a common way to create a real soup, but we were hoping to find a quicker solution. We started with a soup base of winter vegetables (carrots, parsnips, and onions) along with some starchy potatoes. Once the vegetables were tender, we pureed a portion of them and returned the puree to the broth. This addition did indeed augment the base as well as infuse the broth with more vegetable flavor, but the soup was still not hearty enough. Thinking more starch was in order, we then tried adding pureed canned beans but tasters didn't like the mealy, grainy texture the beans contributed. Cooked rice wasn't any better, giving the soup an overwhelming rice flavor and unappealing viscous texture. The surprise solution was several slices of toasted bread. Pureed along with some of the broth, the bread gave the soup an almost creamy consistency without interfering with the vegetable flavor. For variety in color and texture, we added chopped fresh spinach and frozen lima beans, as well as white beans, only not pureed this time. A light drizzle of sweet-tart balsamic vinegar brought all the flavors together and was the perfect finishing touch.

2   tablespoons vegetable oil
3   carrots, peeled and chopped
2   parsnips, peeled and chopped
2   onions, chopped (about 2 cups)
6   garlic cloves, minced
8   cups low-sodium chicken broth
12  ounces russet potatoes (about 2 medium), peeled and cut into 1-inch pieces
2   teaspoons minced fresh thyme
1   sprig fresh rosemary
1   bay leaf
2   slices hearty white sandwich bread, lightly toasted
2   cups curly spinach, stemmed and chopped
1   (15-ounce) can cannellini beans, drained and rinsed
1   (10-ounce) package frozen baby lima beans or peas
    Balsamic vinegar
    Salt and pepper

**1.** Heat the oil in a large Dutch oven over medium-high heat until shimmering. Add the carrots, parsnips, and onions and cook until lightly browned and softened, 5 to 7 minutes. Add the garlic and cook until fragrant, about 30 seconds. Add the broth, potatoes, thyme, rosemary, and bay leaf and bring to a boil. Reduce the heat to low, cover, and simmer until the vegetables are soft, about 15 minutes.

**2.** Remove and discard the rosemary and bay leaf. Transfer 3 cups of solids, 1 cup of broth, and the bread to a blender and puree until smooth. Stir the puree back into the pot, add the spinach, cannellini beans, and lima beans, and cook over medium heat until the spinach is tender and the beans are heated through, about 8 minutes. Stir in 1 tablespoon of vinegar and season with salt and pepper to taste. Serve, passing extra vinegar at the table.

**WHAT YOU CAN DO AHEAD OF TIME:** The soup can be made and refrigerated in an airtight container for up to 3 days. This soup does not freeze well.

## NOTES FROM THE TEST KITCHEN

### REINING IN ROSEMARY'S FLAVOR
Rosemary has an overpowering pine-like flavor that can dominate other flavors even in small amounts. To keep the flavor of the rosemary in the background, we simmer the sprig in the soup to extract its flavor. After about 15 minutes, once the rosemary has lightly perfumed the broth, we remove it from the pot and discard it.

### PUREEING SOUPS SAFELY
Fill the blender workjar only two-thirds full, hold the lid in place with a folded kitchen towel, and pulse rapidly a couple of times before letting the machine run continuously. These preliminary steps prevent pressure from building up inside the blender jar that can force the lid off the blender and spray soup skyward.

# FAST CURRIED CAULIFLOWER SOUP

SERVES 6

**WHAT MAKES THIS A BEST RECIPE:** Flavorful, inexpensive, and readily available, cauliflower is one of our favorite candidates for a cream of vegetable soup. The challenge in trying to make a rich, creamy cauliflower soup in just 30 minutes is that cauliflower—unlike many other vegetables—does not cook quickly. We solved this problem by simmering the cauliflower with the broth rather than adding it later, to allow more time for the florets to become tender. In another pot, we cooked the aromatics. By the time we had developed the aromatic base, the contents of both pots could be combined and the partially cooked cauliflower only required a few minutes more simmering to finish cooking with the base. When flavoring this soup, we did not want to overshadow the straightforward, earthy taste of the cauliflower, but we thought that we could make a few simple additions for complexity. After some trial and error, we settled on a small amount of curry powder and fresh ginger. In addition to onion, the sweet, pungent flavor of these two ingredients complemented the cauliflower perfectly. Adding a little tangy yogurt at the end helped to further brighten the flavors.

        3   cups low-sodium chicken broth
    1½   pounds cauliflower florets, chopped (5 cups)
        2   tablespoons unsalted butter
        1   onion, minced (about 1 cup)
              Salt
        1   tablespoon grated fresh ginger
        2   teaspoons curry powder
      ½   cup plain yogurt
      ½   cup whole milk
              Pepper
        1   tablespoon minced fresh cilantro

**1.** Bring the broth and cauliflower to a boil, covered, in a large saucepan and set aside.

**2.** Meanwhile, melt the butter in a large saucepan over medium heat. Add the onion and ½ teaspoon salt and cook until softened, 3 to 5 minutes.

**3.** Stir in the ginger and curry powder and cook until

fragrant, about 1 minute. Stir in the broth and cauliflower mixture. Bring to a simmer and cook until the cauliflower is tender, 10 to 13 minutes.

**4.** Puree the soup in batches in a blender (or food processor) until smooth. Return the pureed soup to the pot and stir in the yogurt and milk. Return to a brief simmer, then remove from the heat. Season with salt and pepper to taste and sprinkle with the cilantro before serving.

**WHERE THINGS CAN GO WRONG:** After adding the yogurt make sure not to boil the soup, which can cause the yogurt to become curdled and grainy.

**WHAT YOU CAN DO AHEAD OF TIME:** The soup can be pureed, cooled, and refrigerated for up to 3 days. To serve, bring to a simmer over low heat and finish the soup as directed in step 4.

## NOTES FROM THE TEST KITCHEN

### TIMESAVING TIP

Many supermarkets now sell cauliflower florets already trimmed and ready to cook—a certain time-saver for the busy cook. The prepared florets, available in 12-ounce bags in some markets, can often be found along with the prewashed lettuces. If you buy cauliflower by the head, rather than the prepped florets, you will need a 2 ½-pound head of cauliflower for this recipe.

### EQUIPMENT: BLENDERS

Blenders don't typically see a lot of action in the test kitchen and so in the past we've recommended buying a sturdy but reasonably priced one. Recently, however, we've noticed an increasing number of high-end blenders on the market claiming to excel at a whole host of tasks. Wondering if blenders had finally become an essential kitchen tool (and thus worth a higher price tag), we brought eight high-end blenders (and one under $50) into the kitchen and put them through a battery of tests. What did we find out? That it is jar design, not power, that separates a so-so blender from a superior one. Tapered jars with a narrow base were the strongest performers because they funnel food down into the blades and yield nearly flawless purees—the reason you want a blender in the first place. Our top pick is the **Braun Power Max Blender.** With its highly tapered jar and reasonable price tag ($49), we find it hard to beat.

# 30-MINUTE RED LENTIL SOUP

### SERVES 6

**WHAT MAKES THIS A BEST RECIPE:** For a 30-minute meal, this soup is superbly satisfying, both in terms of complex flavors and intense richness. Lentils are popular for a couple of reasons: One, they don't require soaking before cooking—a big plus; and, two, they cook up in a relatively short amount of time. Red lentils, in particular, are our favorite for this soup because they lack a seed coat, which means they take only about 20 minutes to cook. Moreover, once cooked they form a smooth, thick puree—perfect for a hearty soup. To maximize the efficiency of making this recipe, we started cooking the lentils before preparing anything else, allowing time to build a flavorful base. (We then married the broth and the base together.) As for the seasonings, we kept in mind the lentil's popularity in India and used a flavor combination common to that cuisine. So, in addition to the staples of onion, ginger, and garlic, we also added garam masala, a spice blend consisting of coriander, cardamom, cumin, cinnamon, and cloves. This spice combination gives the soup intriguing undertones with very little effort. Beyond the aromatics, the soup distinguishes itself with the addition of coconut milk. The fragrant, slightly sweet milk adds a lovely depth of flavor as well as a silken, creamy texture.

|     |                                               |
| --- | --------------------------------------------- |
| 4   | cups low-sodium chicken broth                 |
| 2   | cups water                                    |
| 2   | cups split red lentils                        |
|     | Salt                                          |
| 1   | tablespoon vegetable oil                      |
| 1   | onion, minced (about 1 cup)                   |
| 4   | garlic cloves, minced                         |
| 1   | tablespoon grated fresh ginger                |
| 1½  | teaspoons garam masala                        |
| 1   | (14-ounce) can light coconut milk             |
| ½   | cup minced fresh cilantro                     |
|     | Pepper                                        |
| 3   | plum tomatoes, cored, seeded, and chopped coarse |

**1.** Bring the broth, water, lentils, and ½ teaspoon salt to a boil, covered, in a large saucepan. Reduce to a simmer and continue to cook, covered, until needed in step 3.

**2.** Meanwhile, heat the oil in a large saucepan over medium-high heat until shimmering. Add the onion and ¼ teaspoon salt and cook until softened and lightly browned, 3 to 5 minutes.

**3.** Stir in the garlic, ginger, and garam masala and cook until fragrant, about 1 minute. Stir in the broth mixture and coconut milk, scraping up any browned bits. Bring to a simmer and cook until the lentils are tender and the soup is thickened, about 15 minutes.

**4.** Off the heat, stir in the cilantro and season with salt and pepper to taste. Sprinkle the individual bowls of soup with the chopped tomatoes before serving.

**WHAT YOU CAN DO AHEAD OF TIME:** The soup can be prepared through step 3 and refrigerated in an airtight container for up to 3 days or frozen up to 1 month. Reheat the soup over low heat, adding water to adjust the consistency, before proceeding with step 4.

## NOTES FROM THE TEST KITCHEN

### USE YOUR TIME WISELY
When trying to make a soup in less than 30 minutes it pays to multitask. To optimize the preparation, mince the garlic and ginger while the onion is cooking. Also, prepare the garnishes while the soup simmers.

### GARAM MASALA
This soup gets it distinctive flavor from garam masala—a unique spice blend that is used in Indian cooking. This complex-flavored spice mix can be found in most markets, but if you have a hard time locating it we've developed a mix of common spices that will replicate the flavor. For your own spice blend mix together 1 tablespoon each of cinnamon, cardamom, coriander, cumin, and ¼ teaspoon ground cloves.

### COCONUT MILK
Make sure to purchase coconut milk, not cream of coconut—they are vastly different products. Coconut milk is made from shredded coconut meat steeped in water, which is then strained, pressed, and mashed to release as much liquid as possible. Cream of coconut is a sweet, thick concoction used in cocktails, not soups.

# DAUBE PROVENÇAL

SERVES 4 TO 6

**WHAT MAKES THIS A BEST RECIPE:** At its best, daube Proven-çal (also known as daube niçoise) is a memorable beef stew with all the elements of the best French fare: tender pieces of beef, luxurious sauce, and complex flavors, including olive oil, olives, garlic, wine, herbs, oranges, tomatoes, mushrooms, and anchovies. Unfortunately, this stew is often a one-note wonder, with a single flavor dominating the rest—beef stew with olives, or beef stew with oranges. Our version combines these strong, independent flavors in a way that all the elements stand out but none dominates, creating a robust but cohesive stew. We started with the meat and knew we wanted chuck-eye roast for the best flavor and texture (it's tough but softens nicely during long, slow cooking). We then began to methodi-cally test the other ingredients, hoping to strike a perfect bal-ance. Tasters loved the earthiness of porcini mushrooms and the briny character of niçoise olives. Tomatoes added a wel-come brightness, orange peel a subtle floral element, and herbs such as thyme and bay leaves are a natural addition to any dish from Provence. Despite some initial protests that anchovies and salt pork don't belong in a beef stew, they added an unde-niable depth of flavor and complexity that we found to be essential. And rather than use a roux (a butter and flour thick-ener) we found that sprinkling flour right into the pot with the vegetables and tomato paste created a braising liquid that thickened to the consistency of a rich sauce. With so many bold ingredients, the half bottle of red wine in our working recipe had fallen quietly into the background, so we carefully began to add more. To our surprise we found that we could use the entire bottle, so long as we simmered the stew for a little extra time to allow the flavors to meld. Because of this slightly longer cooking time, we decided to cut the meat into larger, 2-inch pieces. This not only prevented the beef from overcooking and drying out, it also added to the rustic qual-ity of this dish. We like to serve this stew with egg noodles or boiled potatoes.

¾ ounce dried porcini mushrooms, rinsed well
3½ pounds boneless beef chuck-eye roast, trimmed and cut into 2-inch chunks

1½ teaspoons salt
1 teaspoon pepper
4 tablespoons olive oil
5 ounces salt pork, rind removed
4 carrots, peeled and cut into 1-inch rounds
2 onions, halved and cut into ⅛-inch-thick slices
4 garlic cloves, sliced thin
2 tablespoons tomato paste
⅓ cup unbleached all-purpose flour
1 bottle bold red wine
1 cup low-sodium chicken broth
1 cup water
4 strips orange zest, removed with a vegetable peeler, each strip about 3 inches long, cleaned of white pith, and cut lengthwise into thin strips
1 cup niçoise olives, pitted and drained well
3 anchovy fillets, minced
5 sprigs fresh thyme, tied together with kitchen twine
2 bay leaves
1 (14.5-ounce) can whole tomatoes, drained and cut into ½-inch dice
2 tablespoons minced fresh parsley

**1.** Cover the mushrooms with 1 cup hot tap water in a small microwave-safe bowl. Cover with plastic wrap, cut several steam vents in the plastic, and microwave on high power for 30 seconds. Let stand until the mushrooms soften, about 5 minutes. Lift the mushrooms from the liq-uid and chop into ½-inch pieces (you should have about 4 tablespoons). Strain the liquid through a fine-mesh strainer lined with one paper towel into a medium bowl. Set the mushrooms and liquid aside.

**2.** Adjust an oven rack to the lower-middle position and heat the oven to 325 degrees. Pat the beef dry with paper towels, then season with the salt and pepper. Heat 2 tablespoons of the oil in a large Dutch oven over medium-high heat until shimmering and add half the beef. Cook without moving the pieces until well browned, about 2 minutes on each side, for a total of 8 to 10 minutes, reducing the heat if the fat begins to smoke. Transfer the meat to a medium bowl. Repeat with the remaining oil and meat.

**3.** Reduce the heat to medium and add the salt pork, car-rots, onions, garlic, and tomato paste to the now-empty pot. Cook, stirring occasionally, until light brown, about 2 min-utes. Stir in the flour and cook, stirring constantly, about 1 minute. Slowly add the wine, gently scraping the pan bottom to loosen the browned bits. Add the broth, water, beef, and

any juice in the bowl. Increase the heat to medium-high and bring to a full simmer. Add the mushrooms and their liquid, orange zest, ½ cup olives, anchovies, thyme, and bay leaves, distributing evenly and arranging the beef so it is completely covered by the liquid. Cover partially and place in the oven. Cook until a fork inserted in the beef meets little resistance (the meat should not be falling apart), 2½ to 3 hours.

**4.** Discard the salt pork, thyme, and bay leaves. Add the tomatoes and remaining ½ cup olives; warm over medium-high heat until heated through, about 1 minute. Cover the pot and allow the stew to settle, about 5 minutes. Using a spoon, skim the excess fat from the surface of the stew. Stir in the parsley and serve.

**WHAT YOU CAN DO AHEAD OF TIME:** Once the salt pork, thyme, and bay leaves are removed in step 4, the daube can be cooled and refrigerated in an airtight container for up to 4 days. Before reheating, skim the hardened fat from the surface, then continue with the recipe.

## NOTES FROM THE TEST KITCHEN

### SUBSTITUTIONS
If niçoise olives are not available, pitted Kalamata olives, though not authentic, can be substituted. Our favorite cut of beef for this recipe is chuck-eye roast, but any boneless roast from the chuck will work.

### "SIMMER" IN THE OVEN
While most stew recipes are cooked on the stovetop, we prefer to simmer our daube in the oven. The evenly distributed heat of the oven results in a stew with a silkier sauce and much more intense flavor.

### SHOPPING FOR KEY INGREDIENTS
Here are some notes on buying the key ingredients in our daube.
**SALT PORK.** Cured (but not smoked) pork belly gives the stew richness and flavor. Buy a piece that's at least 75 percent meat, with a minimum of fat.
**OLIVES.** Use briny niçoise olives and pit them. Cook some of the olives with the stew, then add more just before serving to maximize their impact.
**ANCHOVY FILLETS.** No one will be able to detect their flavor, but anchovies add earthiness to this dish. Meaty Ortiz anchovies (in olive oil) won a test kitchen tasting.
**RED WINE.** Choose something bold, such as Cabernet (Côtes du Rhône or Zinfandel will also work), and simmer for at least 2½ hours to cook off the raw flavor that an entire bottle contributes to the pot.
**TOMATOES.** Progresso whole tomatoes were the winner of a test kitchen tasting. To preserve their lively flavor, add the drained tomatoes just before serving.

# QUICK BLACK BEAN SOUP
#### SERVES 6

**WHAT MAKES THIS A BEST RECIPE:** Traditional black bean soup is typical of a long-simmered soup that delivers big flavor. The soup begins with dried beans that are usually soaked hours ahead of cooking. Then, the beans are simmered with a ham hock and aromatic vegetables like onion, garlic, and bell pepper. Next a sofrito—a combination of finely diced garlic, onion, and pepper—is slowly cooked down in a separate pot until the flavors are concentrated. The sofrito is added to the bean mixture and the soup is cooked further to allow the flavors to meld. Our quick black bean soup has the complexity and depth of flavor characteristic of a long-simmered traditional black bean soup, but it takes only a fraction of the time to make. The first thing we got rid of was the dried beans (and thus the overnight soaking and hours of simmering). Instead, we turned to canned beans. Pureeing a portion of them and adding them to chicken broth gives the soup a more intense black bean flavor than if we left them all whole. Spicy chorizo replaces the ham hock, and sautéing it lends an essential smoky, meaty flavor. The preparation of the vegetables was the main hurdle in trying to keep this soup simple and quick. We tried simmering the drained and rinsed canned beans with sautéed chopped aromatics (skipping the mincing to save time), but the beans simply didn't absorb the vegetables' flavor. Then we had another thought: Since we were bringing out the food processor anyway to puree some of the beans, we realized we could also use it to process the vegetables. This worked perfectly, with the vegetables and their juices giving off a more pronounced flavor in a shorter period of time. Oregano, cumin, cayenne, and Tabasco add the requisite spice and heat, while some cilantro and a squeeze of lime brighten up the whole thing. We're willing to bet no one will guess this black bean soup took only 30 minutes to prepare.

3   cups low-sodium chicken broth
6   ounces chorizo, diced
1   onion, chopped (about 1 cup)
1   red bell pepper, stemmed, seeded, and chopped
6   garlic cloves, chopped

        Salt
4   (15-ounce) cans black beans, drained and rinsed
1   cup water
1   tablespoon minced fresh oregano or 1 teaspoon dried
½   teaspoon ground cumin
½   teaspoon cayenne pepper
½   cup minced fresh cilantro
    Tabasco
2   limes, quartered, for serving

**1.** Bring the broth to a boil, covered, in a large saucepan and set aside.

**2.** Meanwhile, cook the chorizo in a large Dutch oven over medium heat until browned and the fat is rendered, about 5 minutes.

**3.** While the chorizo cooks, pulse the onion, bell pepper, and garlic in a food processor until finely minced, 20 to 30 seconds, scraping down the sides of the bowl as needed. Remove the puree to a bowl.

**4.** Stir the processed vegetables and ½ teaspoon salt into the Dutch oven and cook until the vegetables are dry and beginning to brown, 6 to 8 minutes. While the vegetables cook, puree 4 cups of the beans and the water together in the food processor until smooth.

**5.** Stir the oregano, cumin, and cayenne into the Dutch oven and cook until fragrant, about 1 minute. Stir in the broth, pureed beans, and remaining whole beans. Bring to a simmer and cook until the whole beans have warmed through, about 5 minutes. Off the heat, stir in the cilantro and season with salt and Tabasco to taste. Serve with the lime wedges.

**WHAT YOU CAN DO AHEAD OF TIME:** The soup can be refrigerated in an airtight container for up to 3 days or frozen for up to 1 month.

## NOTES FROM THE TEST KITCHEN

### TIMESAVING TIP
Don't bother washing the food processor bowl or blade after processing the vegetables—you will need to use them again to puree the beans.

### PERFECT PUREE
When it comes to the thickness of black bean soup, opinions vary. Some like it totally smooth, others like a more chunky soup. To satisfy both groups we pureed about three-quarters of the beans and left the remainder whole.

# WHITE CHICKEN CHILI
SERVES 8

**WHAT MAKES THIS A BEST RECIPE:** White chicken chili is a lighter and more brothy counterpart to conventional red meat chili—and with only 320 calories and 4.5 grams of fat per serving, it's a lower-fat alternative too. Versions of this chili vary, but most contain chicken and white beans (or hominy corn) and are vibrantly flavored with a variety of fresh chiles and spices. Two things make this version a standout, particularly among other lowfat chilis, which are usually wimpy and bland. The first is our technique for cooking the chicken. We start with bone-in, skin-on chicken breasts that are lightly browned on both sides before the skin is removed. The breasts are then simmered in broth, shredded, and returned to the chili towards the end of cooking, resulting in extremely moist and flavorful pieces of meat. This works much better than using ground chicken, which lacks substance, or diced chicken breasts that become dry and stringy after a long simmer. The other factor that makes this white chicken chili such a success is the selection of fresh chiles we used and the way in which we combined them. To intensify the chili's flavor we added a trio of earthy poblanos, sweet Anaheims, and piquant jalapeños, which gave the stew a rich, complex flavor. Even so, something was still missing. After some experimentation, we decided to sauté the chiles and remove half of them before continuing on with the process of making the chili. Once the chili had simmered for a spell, we stirred in the reserved chiles along with some raw minced jalapeño. This gave the chili bright flavor and a welcome textural contrast, as these chiles were still slightly firm. A generous amount of cumin and dried oregano, along with some scallions, cilantro, and fresh lime juice, provides the perfect finish.

3   pounds bone-in, skin-on chicken breasts
    (2 whole breasts, split)
    Salt and pepper
1   teaspoon vegetable oil
3   poblano chiles, stemmed, seeded, and chopped medium
3   medium Anaheim chiles, stemmed, seeded, and chopped medium

1 medium jalapeño chile, plus 1 small jalapeño chile, seeds and ribs removed and set aside (see note below), flesh minced

2 onions, minced (about 2 cups)

6 garlic cloves, minced

2 tablespoons ground cumin

2 tablespoons dried oregano

8 cups low-sodium chicken broth

2 (15-ounce) cans cannellini beans, drained and rinsed

¼ cup fresh lime juice (3 limes)

¼ cup minced fresh cilantro

4 scallions, sliced thin

**1.** Season the chicken breasts with salt and pepper. Heat the oil in a large Dutch oven over medium-high heat until just smoking. Sear the chicken, skin side down, until browned, about 4 minutes. Flip the chicken and sear on the second side until browned, about 4 minutes. Transfer the chicken to a plate and remove and discard the skin.

**2.** Add all of the chiles except the small jalapeño, onions, garlic, cumin, oregano, and 1 teaspoon salt to the Dutch oven. Cover and cook over medium-low heat, stirring often, until the vegetables are softened, 12 to 15 minutes. Transfer half of the chile mixture to a clean plate and set aside.

**3.** Stir in the broth, chicken, and beans. Bring to a boil over medium-high heat, reduce the heat to medium-low, and simmer, stirring occasionally, until the chicken is fully cooked, about 20 minutes. Using tongs, transfer the chicken to a large plate. Continue to simmer the chili, uncovered, until it has thickened, 35 to 40 minutes.

**4.** When the chicken is cool enough to handle, shred the chicken into bite-sized pieces, discarding the bones. Stir the shredded chicken, reserved chile mixture, lime juice, cilantro, scallions, and small jalapeño into the chili. If the chili is too thick, stir in water to thin it. Season with salt and pepper to taste and serve.

**WHAT YOU CAN DO AHEAD OF TIME:** The chili can be refrigerated in an airtight container for up to 3 days or frozen for up to 1 month.

## NOTES FROM THE TEST KITCHEN

### TAMING CHILE HEAT
Most of a chile's heat resides in the ribs and the seeds. If you prefer more heat, we suggest mincing the ribs along with the seeds and adding them to the recipe to taste. If you prefer less heat, discard the seeds and ribs.

# LIGHT TURKEY CHILI
SERVES 8

**WHAT MAKES THIS A BEST RECIPE:** This chili is rich, meaty, and thick with just the right amount of spices—a no-fuss turkey chili that rivals its beef counterpart, without all the fat. Rather than sauté the aromatics in a large amount of oil, we learned we could cook the garlic, bell pepper, onion, and spices over low heat in just a tablespoon of oil along with some salt. The salt draws moisture from the vegetables, and covering them as they cook traps the moisture in and allows the vegetables to "sweat" in their own juices. This technique results in a deep concentration of flavor with a minimal amount of fat. Many recipes for lowfat turkey chili add the spices after the turkey has already browned, but we knew that with such a small amount of fat in the recipe, the ground spices needed to have direct contact with the cooking oil, and have plenty of time in the pot to "bloom." Adding the spices at the outset along with the aromatics gave them ample to time to develop their flavors fully. And although we didn't want a chili with killer heat, we did want real warmth and depth of flavor. We used a hefty 4 tablespoons of chili powder, added plenty of coriander, cumin, and oregano, and tossed in some red pepper flakes and cayenne for heat. Choosing the right type of meat was another important element in creating a satisfying lowfat turkey chili: 99 percent lean turkey was dry and stringy, but 93 percent lean was just right, remaining moist and juicy even after a long simmer. We did find however that it was important to add half the meat to the cooked vegetables and the remaining half after the chili had simmered for an hour—this kept some of the meat in larger pieces. When adding the second pound of meat to the chili, it is important to pat the meat into a ball, and then break off pieces to add it to the simmering chili. This prevents the meat from cooking in long strands. A combination of chicken broth and the juice from canned tomatoes gave our chili a rounded and well-balanced flavor. Finally, tasters preferred a combination of both crushed and diced tomatoes, along with kidney beans, for a substantial lowfat turkey chili (with just 340 calories and 10 grams of fat per serving) that will satisfy even the heartiest appetite.

| | |
|---|---|
| 2 | onions, minced (about 2 cups) |
| 1 | red bell pepper, stemmed, seeded, and cut into ½-inch pieces |
| 6 | garlic cloves, minced |
| ¼ | cup chili powder |
| 1 | tablespoon ground cumin |
| 2 | teaspoons ground coriander |
| ½–1 | teaspoon red pepper flakes |
| 1 | teaspoon dried oregano |
| ¼–½ | teaspoon cayenne pepper |
| 1 | tablespoon vegetable oil |
| | Salt |
| 2 | pounds 93 percent lean ground turkey |
| 2 | (15-ounce) cans dark red kidney beans, drained and rinsed |
| 1 | (28-ounce) can diced tomatoes |
| 1 | (28-ounce) can crushed tomatoes |
| 2 | cups low-sodium chicken broth |
| 2 | limes, cut into wedges, for serving |

**1.** Combine the onions, bell pepper, garlic, chili powder, cumin, coriander, pepper flakes, oregano, cayenne, oil, and ½ teaspoon salt in a large Dutch oven. Cover and cook over medium-low heat, stirring often, until the vegetables are softened, 8 to 10 minutes.

**2.** Add half the turkey and increase the heat to medium-high. Cook, breaking up the meat with a wooden spoon, until no longer pink and just beginning to brown, about 4 minutes. Stir in the beans, diced tomatoes with their juice, crushed tomatoes, broth, and 1 teaspoon salt. Bring to a boil over medium-high heat; reduce the heat to medium-low and simmer, uncovered, until the chili has begun to thicken, about 1 hour.

**3.** Pat the remaining 1 pound of turkey together into a ball, then pinch off teaspoon-sized pieces of meat and stir them into the chili. Continue to simmer, stirring occasionally, until the turkey is tender and the chili is rich and slightly thickened, about 40 minutes longer (if the chili begins to stick to the bottom of the pot, stir in ½ cup water). Season with salt to taste. Serve with the lime wedges and garnishes (see note), if desired.

**WHAT YOU CAN DO AHEAD OF TIME:** The chili can be refrigerated in an airtight container for up to 3 days or frozen for up to 1 month.

## NOTES FROM THE TEST KITCHEN

### TURKEY TEXTURE
Substituting ground turkey (or chicken) for ground beef in a chili is a well-known way to reduce fat and calories. But after a few hours of simmering, the texture and flavor of ground poultry don't compare to that of beef. It doesn't brown as well as beef nor does it impart the same meaty flavor—and the texture can be soft and unappetizing. After many tests we discovered a few solutions. First, we sauté just half of the ground poultry at the start, breaking it up into little pieces with a spoon, to really distribute the flavor while it simmers. Then we increase the dish's meatiness by adding chicken broth to the chili. As it simmers, it thickens and lends a meatier flavor to the chili. And for improved texture and moisture, we add the remaining ground poultry toward the end of the simmering time. We pinch the poultry into small pieces before stirring them in to mimic the crumbled appearance of ground beef.

### CHOOSE YOUR GARNISHES
While an ungarnished bowl of chili is good, the right garnishes can make a bowl of chili even tastier. In order to keep the amount of fat and calories under control, we prefer to use garnishes like chopped tomatoes, sliced scallions, and fresh cilantro instead of sour cream and cheese.

### THE SPICE IS RIGHT
If you like a spicy chili use the larger amount of red pepper flakes and cayenne listed.

### SWEAT VEGETABLES AND SLASH FAT
Rather than sauté the vegetables, we sweat them with much less fat. Turn the heat down to medium-low, toss the vegetables with just 1 tablespoon of oil and some salt, and put the lid on. This simple technique allows the vegetables to "sweat" in their own juices, resulting in a deep concentration of flavor.

### INGREDIENTS: CHICKEN BROTH
What chicken broth product should you reach for you when you haven't got time for homemade? We recommend choosing a mass-produced, lower-sodium brand and checking the label for evidence of mirepoix ingredients, such as carrots, celery, and onions. **Swanson Certified Organic Chicken Broth** was our clear favorite, with tasters calling it "very chickeny, with straightforward and honest flavors." But the less expensive, third-place Swanson Natural Goodness was solid as well. And if you don't mind adding water, Better Than Bouillon Chicken Base came in a very close second and was the favorite of several tasters.

# VEGETABLES & SIDE DISHES

# THE ULTIMATE VEGETABLE TORTA

SERVES 6 TO 8

**WHAT MAKES THIS A BEST RECIPE:** Like many authentic regional Italian recipes, this one made its way to American shores a little road weary (and often changed for the worse). A crustless tart made with layers of vegetables bound together by cheese and custard, vegetable torta takes time and attention to execute correctly. But done right, it's a great make-ahead dish that showcases the best of summer's bounty—plus it's a vegetarian main course that never fails to please. We hit upon the main problem with this recipe immediately: The vegetables release lots of water during cooking, creating a soggy, flavorless tart. Salting and carefully pressing the vegetables (except the pepper) was the first step in solving this problem but then we still had to figure out how to cook each one, which proved more difficult (in fact, a logistical nightmare). After multiple time-consuming and frustrating rounds of tests, we learned that we could roast the eggplant, microwave the zucchini (between layers of paper towels), and simply bake the tomatoes in the torta (no precooking required). As for the red bell peppers, they were sturdy enough to just roast along with the eggplant. The major challenge of this torta solved, we turned our attention to the crust and the custard. We decided to add a simple breadcrumb crust by mixing fresh breadcrumbs with melted butter since this gave the torta a more finished and uniform appearance and kept the custard from sticking to the sides of the pan. And for a flavorful custard, we included mashed roasted garlic (we roasted it along with the eggplant), Asiago cheese, herbs, and a hefty does of lemon juice. Served warm or at room temperature, this torta is worth the time it takes to make it. In fact, we'd call it a stunner.

## VEGETABLES

3  eggplants (about 1 pound each), halved crosswise and cut lengthwise into ½-inch-thick slices, outer thin slices of skin from each half discarded
    Kosher salt

3  tablespoons olive oil, plus additional oil for brushing wire racks

1  garlic head, outer papery skins removed and top third of head cut off and discarded

Pepper

2  red bell peppers

2  large ripe tomatoes (about 8 ounces each), cored and cut into ¼-inch-thick slices

4  zucchini (about 8 ounces each), cut on a steep bias into ¼-inch-thick slices

## CRUST

4  slices high-quality sandwich bread, torn into quarters

3  tablespoons unsalted butter, melted, plus more for the pan

1½  ounces Asiago cheese, grated (about ⅔ cup)

## CUSTARD AND GARNISH

3  large eggs

¼  cup heavy cream

2  teaspoons minced fresh thyme

2  tablespoons fresh lemon juice

2  ounces Asiago cheese, grated (about 1 cup)

2  tablespoons thinly sliced fresh basil

**1. FOR THE VEGETABLES:** Sprinkle both sides of the eggplant slices with a generous 1 tablespoon kosher salt; transfer the salted eggplant to a large colander set over a bowl. Let stand until the eggplant releases about 2 tablespoons liquid, about 30 minutes. Arrange the eggplant slices in a single layer on a double layer of paper towels; cover with another double layer of paper towels. Firmly press each slice to flatten and remove as much liquid as possible.

**2.** While the eggplant drains, adjust the oven racks to the upper-middle and lower-middle positions; heat the oven to 450 degrees. Set 2 wire racks on 2 rimmed baking sheets; brush both racks with oil. Place the garlic cut-side up on a sheet of aluminum foil and drizzle with 1½ teaspoons of the oil; wrap the foil tightly around the garlic and set aside.

## NOTES FROM THE TEST KITCHEN

**A WET TORTA IS A BAD TORTA**
Why bother salting and pressing all those vegetables? Because our moisture removal techniques extract more than 4 cups of liquid from the vegetables, which otherwise would make a very soggy torta.

**3.** Arrange the salted and pressed eggplant slices on the oiled racks; brush the slices on both sides with 2 tablespoons of the oil and sprinkle with pepper.

**4.** Brush the bell peppers with the remaining 1½ teaspoons oil and place 1 pepper on each wire rack with the eggplant. Place the baking sheets in the oven; place the foil-wrapped garlic on the lower oven rack alongside the baking sheet. Roast the vegetables until the eggplant slices are soft, well browned, and collapsed, and the peppers are blistered and beginning to brown, 30 to 35 minutes, rotating the baking sheets and turning the peppers over halfway through the baking time. Transfer the peppers to a medium bowl, cover with plastic wrap, and set aside; allow the eggplant to cool on wire racks. Continue to roast the garlic until the cloves are very soft and golden brown, 10 to 15 minutes longer. Set the garlic aside to cool. Reduce the oven temperature to 375 degrees.

**5.** While the vegetables roast, arrange the tomato slices on a double layer of paper towels; sprinkle with 1 teaspoon kosher salt. Let stand 30 minutes, then cover with another double layer of paper towels; gently press the tomatoes to remove moisture.

**6.** While the vegetables roast and the tomatoes stand, sprinkle both sides of the zucchini slices with a generous 1 tablespoon kosher salt; transfer the salted zucchini slices to a large colander set over a bowl. Let the zucchini stand until it releases about ⅓ cup liquid, about 30 minutes. Place a triple layer of paper towels on a large, microwave-safe plate. Arrange a third of the zucchini slices on the paper towels; cover with another triple layer of towels, pressing to remove moisture. Repeat, arranging the remaining zucchini in two additional layers separated by a triple layer of paper towels, and placing a triple layer of paper towels on top of the final zucchini layer. Place another heavy, microwave-safe plate on the zucchini stack; press firmly to compress. Microwave the stack on high power until steaming, about 10 minutes. Using potholders, carefully remove the stack from the microwave and let stand 5 minutes; remove the top plate.

**7.** When the peppers are cool, remove the skins. Slit the peppers pole to pole; discard the stem and seeds. Unfurl the peppers so they lie flat; cut each pepper lengthwise into 3 pieces.

**8.** FOR THE CRUST: Pulse the torn bread in a food processor until coarsely ground, about ten 1-second pulses. With the machine running, pour the melted butter through the feed tube and process until combined, about 4 seconds. Add ⅔ cup Asiago and pulse to combine, about three 1-second pulses. Transfer the mixture to a bowl. Do not wash the food processor.

**9.** Thoroughly grease a 9-inch springform pan with softened butter. Measure out 1 cup of the breadcrumb mixture and sprinkle in the bottom of the springform pan; using the flat bottom of a measuring cup, press the crumbs into an even layer. Holding the pan upright, press an additional 1¼ cups breadcrumb mixture into the sides of the pan, forming a thick, even layer that stops about ¼ inch from the top of the pan. Reserve the leftover breadcrumb mixture.

**10.** FOR THE CUSTARD: Squeeze the garlic head at the root end to remove the cloves from the skins. In a small bowl, mash the cloves with a fork and place in the food processor; add the eggs, cream, thyme, and lemon juice. Process until thoroughly combined, about 30 seconds.

## NOTES FROM THE TEST KITCHEN

### MAXIMIZING THE FLAVOR OF THE VEGETABLES
After slicing, salting, and pressing, each vegetable requires a special technique to remove even more liquid.

**EGGPLANT.** The eggplant should be roasted in a 450-degree oven until browned and dry. (Both the garlic and red peppers don't have as much excess moisture, but their flavors benefit from roasting, too.)

**ZUCCHINI.** Zucchini will fall apart if roasted. We had better luck microwaving it between paper towels weighted with heavy plates.

**TOMATOES.** The tomatoes don't require precooking—they will continue to dry out if baked on top of the torta.

**11. TO ASSEMBLE AND BAKE:** Arrange a single layer of eggplant on top of the breadcrumb crust, tearing the pieces as needed to cover the entire bottom surface. Sprinkle evenly with 2 tablespoons cheese. Arrange a single layer of zucchini and sprinkle with 2 tablespoons cheese. Repeat with another layer of eggplant and cheese. Layer in all the red pepper pieces; sprinkle with 2 tablespoons cheese. Pour half of the custard over the vegetables; tilt the pan and shake gently from side to side to distribute it evenly over the vegetables and down the sides. Repeat the layering of eggplant and zucchini, sprinkling each layer with 2 tablespoons cheese (about 4 more layers). Pour the remaining custard over the vegetables; tilt and gently shake the pan to distribute. Arrange the tomato slices around the perimeter of the pan, overlapping to fit, then fill in the center with the remaining slices. Press the tomatoes gently with your hands. Sprinkle the torta with 3 tablespoons of the reserved breadcrumb mixture and discard any remaining breadcrumbs.

**12.** Set the torta on a baking sheet and bake on the lower-middle rack until the tomatoes are dry, the breadcrumb topping is lightly browned, the center of the torta looks firm and level (not soft or wet), and the torta registers an internal temperature of 175 degrees on an instant-read thermometer, 75 to 90 minutes. Cool the torta for 10 minutes on a wire rack; run a thin-bladed knife around the inside of the pan to loosen, then remove the springform pan ring.

**13. TO SERVE:** Slide a thin metal spatula between the crust and pan bottom to loosen. Let stand 20 minutes longer (to serve warm) or cool to room temperature, sprinkle with the basil, and cut into wedges.

**WHERE THINGS CAN GO WRONG:** If you fail to properly salt and press the vegetables, you will end up with a soggy, unsliceable mess. This recipe is not quick. You must execute each step but the results are worth the time and effort.

**WHAT YOU CAN DO AHEAD OF TIME:** The eggplant, garlic, and peppers can be roasted, cooled, wrapped in plastic, and refrigerated for up to 24 hours before assembly. Or the torta can be assembled, baked, cooled, removed from the springform pan, wrapped in plastic, and refrigerated overnight. Allow the torta to stand at room temperature for about 1 hour before serving.

# ROASTED MAPLE-MUSTARD GREEN BEANS
SERVES 4

**WHAT MAKES THIS A BEST RECIPE:** When green beans are fresh picked at the height of summer, you really can't go wrong regardless of how you prepare them—just a quick steaming, some salt, and a pat of butter and they're ready for the table. But try that with supermarket green beans in January and you'll be sorry. These beans need some special attention (and dressing up) to be palatable. Looking for an alternative to our many recipes for braised green beans and green bean casseroles, we decided to try roasting them to see if it was possible to breathe new life into over-the-hill supermarket beans. Roasted in a hot oven with only oil, salt, and pepper, an entire baking sheet of beans disappeared faster than french fries. Our repeated tests confirmed that roasting consistently transforms geriatric specimens into deeply caramelized, full-flavored beauties. Here's why: As green beans mature, their fibers toughen and their sugars are converted to starch. The hot, dry heat of the oven helps to reverse the aging process. Fibers break down and an enzymatic reaction causes the starch to turn back into sugar, restoring sweetness. Although we loved these beans straight up, we wanted a version that was a little dressier and could hold its own at Sunday dinner alongside a roast pork loin or a simple roast chicken. These sweet-savory beans with two kinds of mustard and maple syrup fit the bill perfectly and the addition of matchstick carrots makes for a beautiful platter.

1 tablespoon maple syrup
1 tablespoon Dijon mustard
1 tablespoon grainy mustard
  Pinch cayenne pepper
1 pound green beans, stem ends snapped off
2 carrots, peeled and cut into matchsticks (see page 227)
1 tablespoon vegetable oil
  Salt
1 tablespoon minced fresh parsley

**1.** Adjust an oven rack to the middle position and heat the oven to 450 degrees. Combine the maple syrup, mustards, and cayenne in a small bowl.

**2.** Line a rimmed baking sheet with aluminum foil and arrange the beans and carrots on the sheet. Drizzle with the oil and, using your hands, toss to coat evenly. Sprinkle with ½ teaspoon salt, toss to coat, and distribute in an even layer. Roast for 10 minutes.

**3.** Remove the baking sheet from the oven. Using tongs, coat the beans and carrots evenly with the maple-mustard mixture and redistribute in an even layer. Continue roasting until the carrots and beans are dark golden brown in spots and the beans are starting to shrivel, 10 to 12 minutes longer.

**4.** Season with salt to taste and toss well to combine. Transfer to a serving dish, sprinkle with the parsley, and serve.

## NOTES FROM THE TEST KITCHEN

### LINE THE BAKING SHEET
An aluminum foil liner prevents burning on dark nonstick baking sheets. When using baking sheets with a light finish, foil is not required, but we recommend it for easy cleanup.

### SHRIVEL ACTION
Wrinkles aren't always a sign of overzealous cooking. For roasted green beans, shriveled exteriors indicate a successful transformation from bland and stringy to tender and flavorful.

# PAN-ROASTED BROCCOLI
## WITH SPICY SOUTHEAST ASIAN FLAVORS
### SERVES 4

**WHAT MAKES THIS A BEST RECIPE:** Like rice, bread, or salad, broccoli is a weeknight staple: a quick, versatile, go-to item you can count on when you want a warm green vegetable on your plate. And while steamed broccoli has its virtues, it loses its appeal when it appears as a side dish more than once a week. So how could we transform the humble broccoli into a side dish that might even find a place on the table when company is coming? The idea of roasting broccoli—especially in a skillet on the stovetop—had long intrigued us, but dried-out, shriveled florets and chewy stems were too often the result when we put broccoli in a dry pan over high heat. On our journey to better pan-roasted broccoli, we first removed the florets and trimmed them each to an even size, and then trimmed the stems and sliced them on the bias into long, coin-like shapes of equal thickness to prevent overcooking and create the greatest amount of surface area for browning. Next we assembled the broccoli in an even layer in a relatively hot, lightly oiled skillet. We had hoped the heat would promote caramelization and that the bit of oil would keep things from drying out, but it soon became clear that some moist heat (in other words, steam) would be necessary if the broccoli was to cook through without burning or drying out. Once the broccoli began to brown, we added a little water seasoned with salt and pepper, covered the skillet, and let it steam. Two minutes later, when the broccoli turned bright green, we removed the lid and allowed the excess moisture to evaporate while the broccoli continued to cook. Because the hardier stems take longer to cook than the more delicate florets, we found that adding the pieces in a two-step process (browning the stems first, then tossing in the florets) prevented the florets from becoming limp and overcooked. After spending less than 10 minutes at the stove, we now had a flavorful broccoli dish with mostly bright green florets and toasty brown stems that could be eaten simply as is, although we decided to make things more interesting by adding a mixture of peanut butter, hoisin sauce, lime juice, brown sugar, and chili sauce—plus a garnish of chopped roasted peanuts.

3    tablespoons water

¼    teaspoon salt

⅛    teaspoon pepper

1    tablespoon creamy peanut butter

1    tablespoon hoisin sauce

2    teaspoons fresh lime juice

2    garlic cloves, minced

1    teaspoon brown sugar

¾    teaspoon Asian chili sauce

2    tablespoons vegetable oil

1¾   pounds broccoli (about 1 large bunch), florets cut
     into 1½-inch pieces, stems trimmed, peeled, and
     cut on the bias into ¼-inch-thick slices about
     1½ inches long (see page 29)

¼    cup fresh basil, chopped

2    tablespoons chopped roasted unsalted peanuts

**1.** Stir the water, salt, and pepper together in a small bowl until the salt dissolves; set aside. In a separate small bowl combine the peanut butter, hoisin sauce, lime juice, garlic, brown sugar, and chili sauce; set aside.

**2.** In a 12-inch nonstick skillet, heat the oil over medium-high heat until just beginning to smoke. Add the broccoli stems in an even layer and cook, without stirring, until browned on the bottoms, about 2 minutes. Add the florets to the skillet and toss to combine; cook, without stirring, until the bottoms of the florets just begin to brown, 1 to 2 minutes longer.

**3.** Add the water mixture and cover the skillet; cook until the broccoli is bright green but still crisp, about 2 minutes. Add the basil and the peanut butter mixture and toss until the broccoli is evenly coated and heated through, about 30 seconds. Transfer to a serving dish, top with the chopped peanuts, and serve immediately.

**WHERE THINGS CAN GO WRONG:** Avoid buying broccoli with stalks that have dry cracks or that bend easily or with florets that are yellow or brown. If your broccoli stalks are especially thick, split them in half lengthwise before slicing so they cook evenly.

# SAUTÉED MUSHROOMS
## WITH BACON AND PEARL ONIONS
### SERVES 4

**WHAT MAKES THIS A BEST RECIPE:** When we have the funds or good fortune to get our hands on a batch of freshly foraged chanterelles, we've learned it's best to keep their preparation very simple. It takes little besides a hot pan with some butter and garlic to appreciate their intense flavor. But this is a rarity for most of us. Besides the oversized portobello, which we generally reserve for grilling, the only affordable mushrooms we can always locate for a quick stovetop sauté are common white buttons. With their mild flavor and rubbery texture when cooked, we had never considered them good for much other than salad bars and takeout pizza. But were we being fair? With the right technique, however, we were able to turn this always available, affordable mushroom into a tasty side dish. Unlike steaks or cutlets, which begin to sear immediately upon hitting a hot pan, button mushrooms don't begin to brown until their water has been driven off. Our trick was to overload the skillet to start, the theory being that once the water has evaporated and the mushrooms have shrunk, the pan would no longer be crowded. We were at first alarmed by the flood of liquid that resulted, but patience (and high heat) prevailed. After about 13 minutes (what most recipes give as a total cooking time for sautéed mushrooms), the skillet was dry, and, more importantly, the mushrooms had shrunk to fit the skillet in a single layer and begun to brown nicely. It seemed a short dash from here to the finish line: keep the heat high, shake the pan occasionally, and cook the contents until well browned. But now the skillet was too dry. Even over more moderate heat, the pan would begin to burn, which made the mushrooms taste bitter. The solution was simple enough. Once the mushrooms had given off their water, we lowered the heat and added a little fat to prevent burning. With the technique in place, we decided to work on incorporating some flavorful seasonings. Bacon, pearl onions, sweet port wine, and blue cheese completed the transformation of these basic mushrooms from salad bar staple to super side dish.

4 slices bacon, cut crosswise into ½-inch strips

½ pound frozen pearl onions (about 1⅓ cups)

1 teaspoon sugar

½ cup ruby port

1½ pounds white mushrooms, quartered if medium or halved if small

1 tablespoon unsalted butter

1 tablespoon minced fresh parsley

Salt and pepper

2 ounces blue cheese, crumbled (about ½ cup) (optional)

**1.** Cook the bacon in a large skillet over medium-high heat until beginning to render fat, about 1 minute. Add the onions and sugar and cook, stirring occasionally, until the bacon is crisp and the onions are light brown, about 8 minutes. Using a slotted spoon, transfer the onions and bacon to a medium bowl. Reserve 1 tablespoon of bacon fat in a small bowl; discard the remaining fat. Add ¼ cup of the port to the skillet and return to medium-high heat; simmer about 30 seconds, scraping up any browned bits with a wooden spoon. Pour the port into the bowl with the bacon and onions; wipe out the skillet with paper towels.

**2.** Heat the reserved bacon fat in the skillet over medium-high heat until shimmering but not smoking. Add the mushrooms and cook, stirring occasionally, until the mushrooms release liquid, about 5 minutes. Increase the heat to high and cook, stirring occasionally, until the liquid has completely evaporated and the mushrooms start to brown, about 8 minutes longer.

**3.** Add the butter, reduce the heat to medium, and continue to cook, stirring once every minute, until the mushrooms are dark brown, about 8 minutes longer. Add the bacon-onion mixture and the remaining ¼ cup port; cook, stirring frequently, until the liquid has evaporated and the mushrooms are glazed, about 2 minutes. Stir in the parsley and season with salt and pepper to taste. Transfer to a serving dish, sprinkle with the blue cheese (if using), and serve.

**WHERE THINGS CAN GO WRONG:** Do not thaw the pearl onions or they will become mushy before they can cook to light brown.

# CREAMY PEAS
## WITH HAM AND ONION
SERVES 4 TO 6

**WHAT MAKES THIS A BEST RECIPE:** Although we think most vegetables are better fresh than frozen, peas are an exception. Because their natural sugars turn to starch within hours after being picked, fresh peas are mealy unless cooked the same day they are harvested. Frozen peas are harvested, cooked, and frozen within hours of being picked, which locks in their sweet flavor. In a head-to-head tasting of major brands of frozen peas and fresh peas from the supermarket, there was no contest—the frozen peas were sweeter and more tender.

For this recipe, we wanted to figure out the best way to bring frozen peas back to life and unlock their flavor. And while we were at it, we wanted to come up with a recipe that would be more interesting than plain peas. This workhorse vegetable is endlessly variable and when prepared correctly, can be a winning (and convenient) side dish. Most cooks dump the peas into a pot of salted water or microwave them. Once tender, the peas are drained and tossed with butter and seasonings. This simple method isn't bad, but it leaves the peas short on flavor. We knew we could do better. Our first thought was to cook the peas in something more flavorful than salted water; we hoped the cooking liquid could also work as a sauce. So we piled ingredients into a saucepan and brought the liquid (heavy cream) to a boil. Unfortunately, by the time the cream had reduced to a saucy consistency, the peas had turned army green. We had better luck when we added the peas (still frozen) to an almost finished sauce. By the time the peas were tender, they had soaked up plenty of flavor and the sauce was the perfect consistency. To jazz up our creamy peas, we added smoky ham, red onion, and fresh tarragon.

2 tablespoons unsalted butter

6 ounces ham steak, cut into ½-inch pieces

1 red onion, halved and sliced thin

⅔ cup heavy cream

1 tablespoon minced fresh tarragon or parsley

Salt and pepper

1 pound frozen peas, not thawed

For a side dish worthy of a holiday table, cook frozen peas in an almost finished and flavorful cream sauce with ham steak and red onion.

**1.** Melt the butter in a large skillet over medium-high heat. Add the ham and cook until browned, about 5 minutes. Add the onion and cook until softened and beginning to brown, about 5 minutes.

**2.** Add the cream, tarragon, and salt and pepper to taste. Bring to a simmer and cook until the cream just begins to thicken, about 3 minutes. Stir in the peas, cover, and cook until tender, about 5 minutes. Season with salt and pepper to taste and serve.

**WHERE THINGS CAN GO WRONG:** Because the cream is reduced to the proper consistency before the peas are added to the pan, the peas should be cooked with the cover on.

## NOTES FROM THE TEST KITCHEN

### GIVE FROZEN PEAS A CHANCE
In the test kitchen, we've come to depend on frozen peas. Not only are they more convenient than their fresh comrades in the pod, but also they taste better. In test after test, we've found that frozen peas are tender and sweet, while fresh peas are starchy and bland. Finding good frozen peas is not hard. After tasting peas from the two major national frozen food purveyors, Birds Eye and Green Giant, along with organically grown peas from Cascadian Farm, our panel found little difference among them. All of the peas were sweet and fresh, with a bright green color.

# SUGAR-GLAZED ROASTED CARROTS
### SERVES 4 TO 6

**WHAT MAKES THIS A BEST RECIPE:** Let's face it, carrots are not the sexiest vegetable in the produce aisle. But at most times of year, they are reliable and when roasted can make an excellent side dish. The perfect roast carrots are tender and sweet, with a caramelized crust. High heat and sugar are the usual means of coaxing this kind of browning out of carrots, but it's a high-wire act. Carrots can go from crunchy and pale to mealy and charred in a matter of minutes. Our first decision took place in the produce aisle. Although baby carrots require no preparation (just open the bag and dump into a pan), the results we got with them were disappointing. After 10 minutes in the oven, they were shriveled and soggy. Maybe the pool of water in most bags of baby carrots was the culprit. In any case, these carrots are often bland and woody. It was worth taking an extra 10 minutes to peel and cut grown-up-sized carrots ourselves. When we tested roasting times and temperatures, we found that shorter and hotter were better. When cooked for a long time in a moderate oven, the carrots ended up soggy and overcooked before any real caramelization could occur. We had the best results in a very hot oven set to 475 degrees. Heating the baking sheet before adding the carrots jump-started the browning process. In less than 20 minutes, the carrots were perfectly cooked. Carrots tossed in butter browned a bit better than those tossed in oil, but the addition of sugar—just 1 tablespoon for 1½ pounds of carrots—made a big difference. Granulated sugar was up to the job, but we got really dramatic results when we tried dark brown sugar. After peeling umpteen pounds of carrots, we had finally developed a reliable recipe. Best of all, it was quick and easy. Carrots were never so appealing.

1½  pounds medium carrots, peeled and cut into 2 by ½-inch pieces (see page 52)
2  tablespoons unsalted butter, melted
1  tablespoon dark brown sugar
½  teaspoon salt
½  teaspoon pepper

**1.** Adjust an oven rack to the middle position and heat the oven to 475 degrees. Heat a rimmed baking sheet in the oven for 10 minutes.

**2.** Toss the carrots, melted butter, brown sugar, salt, and pepper in a medium bowl until thoroughly combined. Remove the hot baking sheet from the oven and place the carrots on it in a single layer. Roast until the carrots are beginning to brown on the bottom, about 15 minutes.

**3.** Remove the pan from the oven, toss the carrots to redistribute, and continue to roast until tender and deep amber in color, about 3 minutes. Serve.

**WHERE THINGS CAN GO WRONG:** If the carrots have very narrow tips, trim the thin ends; they scorch easily.

## NOTES FROM THE TEST KITCHEN

### HOW TO CUT CARROTS

To ensure even cooking, we cut the carrots into 2 inch by ½-inch pieces—not necessarily an easy task given that carrots vary in thickness from end to end. Here's how to produce pieces that are evenly sized.

**1.** Cut a peeled carrot into thirds, with each piece measuring roughly 2 inches long.

**2.** Cut each piece in half or quarters lengthwise to yield pieces that are ½ inch thick.

### OUR FAVORITE VEGETABLE PEELERS

Vegetable peelers fall into two main categories: the traditional peeler (whose blade is in line with the handle) and the Y-shaped peeler, whose blade sits perpendicular to the handle. The traditional peelers were comfortable and slick, especially when used for delicate tasks such as peeling carrots. On the other hand, the Y-shaped peelers proved their mettle by mowing over thick-skinned fruits and vegetables. The **Oxo I-Series Peeler** (right), $10, which comes with replaceable blades and a weighted handle for greater control, was the best overall peeler we tested. The runner-up, the Y-shaped **Kuhn Rikon Peeler** (left), $3.49, takes off very wide, thick strips of peel, making it especially good on winter squash or celery root.

# LIGHT EGGPLANT PARMESAN
### SERVES 6

**WHAT MAKES THIS A BEST RECIPE:** Eggplant Parmesan is classic Italian comfort food, sharing a place in our hearts with meat and cheese lasagna and fettuccine Alfredo. Although eggplant Parmesan tastes awfully good, it needed quite a makeover to be included in *The Best Light Recipe.* Our original recipe not only tipped the scale, it broke the scale altogether, with 760 calories, 59 grams of fat, and 140 milligrams of cholesterol per serving. The reasons were obvious. In most recipes, slices of eggplant are coated with a standard breading of flour, egg, and breadcrumbs, and then shallow fried. Given the porous nature of eggplant, oil gets absorbed into the thirsty flesh and the surrounding crumbs. The fried eggplant is then layered with shredded mozzarella cheese, and topped with tomato sauce that includes more oil and grated Parmesan cheese. We needed a fresh take on this classic Italian dish and we were determined to cut the calories and fat in half at the very least, without sacrificing taste. We decided to try a method that had been successful with our Light Chicken Parmesan (page 184). We dipped the eggplant in beaten egg whites (instead of whole eggs), then in crispy, pretoasted and seasoned panko (Japanese-style breadcrumbs). After a quick mist with vegetable oil spray, we baked the eggplant in a hot oven until it was tender on the inside and crisp on the outside. Hoping we were onto something, we layered the eggplant with a quick tomato sauce (containing just 1 teaspoon of oil), shredded reduced-fat mozzarella, and grated Parmesan cheese. Our hopes were soon dashed when we retrieved the eggplant from the oven. The once-crisp exterior had turned the texture of wet cardboard, and all tasters felt that the breading was overwhelming, especially on the underside of the eggplant that hadn't had the benefit of the heat. This layer had dramatically absorbed moisture from the sauce and fat from the cheese. We solved this problem by breading the eggplant on just one side and then layering it, naked side down, in the casserole. There was less breading to absorb any moisture from the tomato sauce, and less to interfere with the delicate eggplant flavor. In addition to the one-sided breading technique, we used less tomato sauce in the casserole than a traditional recipe, and saved a large portion of it to serve on the side. The eggplant was no longer blanketed in a dull coating of breadcrumbs, and our judicious use of tomato sauce was a success. With a skinny 330 calories and only 9 grams of fat per serving, we had more than met our expectations. This was still comfort food, satisfying and soothing. But with numbers like this, it was comfort without a catch.

| | |
|---|---|
| 2 | eggplants (1 pound each), ends trimmed, cut crosswise into ⅓-inch-thick rounds |
| | Kosher salt |
| 2 | (28-ounce) cans diced tomatoes |
| 4 | garlic cloves, minced |
| 1 | tablespoon tomato paste |
| 4 | teaspoons extra-virgin olive oil |
| ⅛ | teaspoon red pepper flakes |
| ½ | cup plus 2 tablespoons minced fresh basil |
| | Salt and pepper |
| 1½ | cups panko (Japanese-style breadcrumbs) |
| 1 | ounce Parmesan cheese, grated (about ½ cup), plus extra for serving |
| ½ | cup unbleached all-purpose flour |
| 1½ | teaspoons garlic powder |
| 3 | large egg whites |
| 1 | tablespoon water |
| | Vegetable oil spray |
| 8 | ounces reduced-fat mozzarella cheese, shredded (about 2 cups) |

**1.** Toss half of the eggplant with 1 teaspoon kosher salt, then place in a large colander set over a bowl. Repeat with the remaining eggplant and 1 more teaspoon kosher salt, and transfer to the colander with the first batch. Let sit until the eggplant releases about 2 tablespoons liquid, 30 to 40 minutes. Spread the eggplant slices on a triple layer of paper towels and cover with another triple thickness of paper towels. Press firmly on each slice to remove as much liquid as possible, and wipe off the excess salt.

**2.** Meanwhile, process the tomatoes with their juice in a food processor until mostly smooth, fifteen to twenty 1-second pulses; set aside. Cook the garlic, tomato paste, 1 teaspoon of the oil, and pepper flakes in a medium saucepan over medium heat until the tomato paste begins to brown, about 2 minutes. Stir in the pureed tomatoes and cook until the sauce is thickened, about 25 minutes. Off the heat, stir in the ½ cup minced basil and season with salt and pepper to taste. Cover and set aside until needed.

**3.** Adjust the oven racks to the lower-middle and upper-middle positions and heat the oven to 475 degrees. Combine the breadcrumbs and remaining 1 tablespoon oil in a large nonstick skillet and toast over medium heat, stirring often, until golden, about 10 minutes. Spread the breadcrumbs into a shallow dish and let cool slightly; when cool, stir in the ½ cup Parmesan. Combine the flour, garlic powder, and ½ teaspoon pepper in a second shallow dish. In a third shallow dish, whisk the egg whites and water together.

**4.** Line 2 rimmed baking sheets with foil and coat with vegetable oil spray. Season the eggplant with pepper. Lightly dredge one side of each eggplant slice in the seasoned flour, shaking off the excess. Dip the floured side of the eggplant into the egg whites, and then coat the same side with the breadcrumbs. Press on the crumbs to make sure they adhere. Lay the eggplant breaded side up on the prepared baking sheets in a single layer.

**5.** Lightly spray the top of the eggplant slices with vegetable oil spray. Bake until the top of the eggplant slices are crisp and golden, about 30 minutes, rotating and switching the baking sheets halfway through baking.

**6.** Spread 1 cup of the tomato sauce in the bottom of a 13 by 9-inch baking dish. Layer in half of the eggplant slices breaded side up, overlapping the slices to fit. Distribute ½ cup of the sauce over the eggplant; sprinkle with half of the mozzarella. Layer in the remaining eggplant breaded side up and dot with 1 cup of the sauce, leaving the majority of the eggplant exposed so it will remain crisp; sprinkle with the remaining mozzarella. Bake until bubbling and the cheese is browned, about 10 minutes. Cool for 5 minutes, then sprinkle with the 2 tablespoons minced basil and serve, passing the remaining sauce and extra Parmesan separately.

**WHERE THINGS CAN GO WRONG:** Take care not to let the eggplant sit salted for more than the time given or it will be overly salty and limp.

**WHAT YOU CAN DO AHEAD OF TIME:** The sauce can be refrigerated in an airtight container for up to 3 days or frozen for up to 3 months.

## NOTES FROM THE TEST KITCHEN

### WHY WE SALT EGGPLANT
The tradition of salting eggplant serves two functions. The first is that it makes eggplant firmer by removing water, which also prevents it from soaking up excess oil. The second is that salt masks the bitterness inherent in the vegetable.

# OVEN-FRIED ONION RINGS

MAKES 24 RINGS, SERVES 4 TO 6

**WHAT MAKES THIS A BEST RECIPE:** Onion rings are the ubiquitous accompaniment to burgers and fried seafood, and a treat for kids and grown-ups alike. But hardly anyone dares to make them at home and with good reason: they create a mess and are rarely worth all the bother that making them entails. Oven-fried onion ring recipes, however, promised to eliminate the mess associated with deep-frying, but they don't really work—at least none of the recipes we've tried. In these early tests, we achieved dehydrated, tough, or soggy onion rings but we never came close to the deep-fried crunch and flavor of the real thing. Deep-fried onion rings start with sliced onions that are dunked in a thick batter, usually made with flour, egg, and liquid. When fried, the batter forms a crisp shell that helps the onions steam and become tender. When we tried it in the oven, however, the batter slid off the rings and stuck to the baking sheet. Dredging the rings in flour first helped—the batter now had something to cling to. As for what went into the batter, a combination of buttermilk, egg, and flour was perfect, especially when seasoned with cayenne, salt, and pepper. We then tossed the batter-dipped onion rings with breadcrumbs, but tasters wanted more crunch. At our local supermarket, we bought anything that looked like it might make a good crumb coating, including cornmeal, cornflakes, Melba toast, Ritz crackers, saltines, and potato chips. Back in the test kitchen, we found that a combination of saltines and potato chips worked perfectly. The potato chips were super crunchy and baked up to a golden brown crust that almost seemed deep-fried, and the lean crackers absorbed any excess grease. It was almost impossible to tell that these super-crunchy onion rings had come out of the oven. For four to six servings of rings, made from two large onions on two baking sheets, 6 tablespoons of vegetable oil was just right, giving the rings a good sear without making them too oily. Admittedly, these onion rings, like many oven-fried recipes, are not low in fat, but, frankly, that was not our goal. We wanted deep-fried flavor without the mess—and this recipe delivers on both counts.

What could be better with a burger or steak than crispy, crunchy onion rings that you don't have to fry?

½ cup unbleached all-purpose flour
1 large egg, at room temperature
½ cup buttermilk, at room temperature
¼ teaspoon cayenne pepper
½ teaspoon salt
¼ teaspoon black pepper
30 saltines
4 cups kettle-cooked potato chips
2 large yellow onions, cut into 24 large rings, ½ inch thick
6 tablespoons vegetable oil

**1.** Adjust the oven racks to the lower-middle and upper-middle positions and heat the oven to 450 degrees. Place ¼ cup of the flour in a shallow baking dish. Beat the egg and buttermilk together in a medium bowl. Whisk the remaining ¼ cup flour, cayenne, salt, and black pepper into the buttermilk mixture. Pulse the saltines and chips together in a food processor until finely ground and place in a separate shallow baking dish.

**2.** Working one at a time, dredge each onion ring in the flour, shaking off any excess. Dip in the buttermilk mixture, allowing the excess to drip back into the bowl, then drop into the crumb coating, turning the ring to coat evenly. Transfer to a large plate and repeat with the remaining onion rings.

**3.** Pour 3 tablespoons of the oil onto each of 2 rimmed baking sheets. Place in the oven and heat until just smoking, about 8 minutes. Carefully tilt the heated sheets to coat them evenly with the oil, then arrange the onion rings in a single layer on both sheets. Bake, flipping the onion rings over and switching and rotating position of baking sheets halfway through baking, until golden brown on both sides, about 15 minutes. Transfer the onion rings to paper towel–lined plates to drain briefly. Serve immediately.

**WHERE THINGS CAN GO WRONG:** If they are to cook evenly, the onions must be cut evenly, into ½-inch-thick rounds. Pull apart the rings in each round, discarding any that are less than 2 inches in diameter.

**WHAT YOU CAN DO AHEAD OF TIME:** The onion rings can be breaded in advance and refrigerated for up to 1 hour. Let them sit at room temperature for 30 minutes before baking; if baked straight from the fridge, the onions will not soften properly and will remain crunchy.

## NOTES FROM THE TEST KITCHEN

### HOW WE GOT A DEEP-FRIED COATING WITHOUT A DEEP-FRYER
Our oven-fried onion rings are so crisp and crunchy that you'd swear they came straight from the fryer. The secret is a coating made with kettle-cooked potato chips and saltines ground to fine crumbs. When crumbled, the kettle chips produce a golden brown crust that almost seems deep-fried, and the crushed saltines add a nice salty kick and absorb any excess grease from the potato chips.

**SALTINES**
Help absorb excess grease.

**KETTLE CHIPS**
Mimic a fried crust.

# STUFFED CABBAGE ROLLS
## WITH SWEET AND SOUR TOMATO SAUCE
MAKES 18 ROLLS, SERVES 6 TO 8

**WHAT MAKES THIS A BEST RECIPE:** This recipe is from the grandmother of one of our test cooks. None of the other stuffed cabbage recipes we tried in our research for *The America's Test Kitchen Family Cookbook* even came close to the hearty, well-rounded flavor of this one. The filling, a simple mixture of white rice and ground beef seasoned with grated onion, salt, and pepper, is enveloped by the large outer leaves of the cabbage. The remaining cabbage is then shredded and the rolls are placed on top to steam, while the shredded cabbage wilts down to eventually become part of the sauce. Made primarily of diced tomatoes and tomato puree, the sauce gets flavor from the shredded cabbage, as well as most of its sweet and sour taste from brown sugar and lemon juice. However, the real magic happens when the clove-studded onion and the crushed gingersnaps are added to the pan. The gingersnaps and onion (along with the optional raisins) add sweetness, spice, and body to the sauce. In turn, the sauce flavors the modest meat stuffing, making this dish the ultimate in comfort food. There's just no improving on a recipe this good.

Salt
1 head green cabbage (2 pounds), cored
¼ cup long-grain white rice
1 onion, grated on the large holes of a box grater
1½ pounds (80 percent lean) ground beef
Pepper
1 (14.5-ounce) can diced tomatoes
1 (28-ounce) can tomato puree
2 cups water
6 tablespoons light brown sugar
3 tablespoons fresh lemon juice
1 onion, peeled
8 whole cloves
12 small gingersnaps (3 ounces), pounded into coarse crumbs
½ cup raisins (optional)

**1.** Bring 4 quarts water and 1 tablespoon salt to a boil in a large Dutch oven over high heat. Add the cored head of cabbage and cook until the outer leaves just begin to wilt, about 3 minutes. Following the photos, use tongs to remove the outer 20 leaves from the simmering head of cabbage, one at a time, as each wilts and transfer them to a colander to cool. Remove the remaining blanched head of cabbage and let it cool. Do not discard the water.

**2.** Return the water to a boil over high heat. Add the rice and cook until tender, about 13 minutes. Drain the rice through a strainer, rinse it to cool, and let it drain thoroughly. In a medium bowl, combine the cooked rice, grated onion, beef, ½ teaspoon salt, and ¼ teaspoon pepper.

**3.** Trim any tough ribs from the cabbage leaves and tightly roll 2 tablespoons of the meat mixture into each leaf (you will have about 18 rolls). Shred the remaining blanched cabbage (both the head and any remaining leaves).

**4.** Scatter half of the shredded cabbage leaves in the large Dutch oven. Arrange the cabbage rolls, seam-side down, on top of the shredded cabbage, fitting them in snugly to prevent unrolling. (If you are using a smaller pot, arrange the rolls in two layers.) Sprinkle the remaining shredded cabbage over the rolls.

**5.** Combine the diced tomatoes with their juice, tomato puree, water, 3 tablespoons of the brown sugar, the lemon juice, and ½ teaspoon salt, then pour the liquid over the cabbage. Stud the peeled onion with the cloves and submerge it in the liquid. Bring the mixture to a boil, then reduce it to a simmer, cover, and cook for 30 minutes.

**6.** Discard the clove-studded onion. Sprinkle the crushed gingersnaps and raisins (if using) into the pot and shake the pot gently to incorporate them without disturbing the cabbage rolls. Continue to simmer, uncovered, until the sauce begins to thicken, about 1 hour.

**7.** To serve, gently transfer the cabbage rolls to a serving dish (or individual plates) using a slotted spoon. Add the remaining 3 tablespoons brown sugar to the sauce and season with salt and pepper to taste. Spoon some of the sauce over the rolls and pass the extra sauce separately.

**WHERE THINGS CAN GO WRONG:** Be gentle when handling the cabbage rolls as they have a tendency to break apart when cooking.

**WHAT YOU CAN DO AHEAD OF TIME:** The cooked cabbage rolls and sauce can be refrigerated in an airtight container for up to 2 days or frozen for up to 1 month. Transfer the refrigerated cabbage rolls and sauce (if frozen, defrost in the refrigerator overnight) to an ovensafe dish and wrap tightly in foil. Bake in a 350-degree oven until hot, about 50 minutes. Remove the foil and continue to bake until the rolls are heated through, about 10 minutes longer.

## NOTES FROM THE TEST KITCHEN

### HOW TO ASSEMBLE CABBAGE ROLLS

**1.** Cut out and discard the cabbage core, using a paring knife.

**2.** Using tongs, gently transfer the outer leaves of the cabbage to a colander as they blanch and wilt. Grasp the leaves from the cored end.

**3.** Remove the thick rib from the base of the cabbage leaves by cutting along both sides of the rib to form a narrow triangle.

**4.** With the core end of the cabbage leaf facing you, arrange 2 tablespoons of the filling just above the area where the thick rib has been removed.

**5.** Fold the sides of the cabbage leaf over the filling.

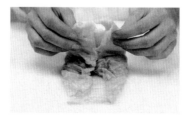

**6.** Roll the bottom edge of the leaf up over the filling into a tight and tidy roll.

# BUTTERMILK MASHED POTATOES
## WITH LEEKS AND CHIVES
### SERVES 4

**WHAT MAKES THIS A BEST RECIPE:** Creamy yet tangy, these mashed potatoes are easy enough to end up on your dinner table on a busy weeknight. So what's different about buttermilk mashed potatoes as opposed to those made with milk or cream? It turns out that you can't just substitute buttermilk for other dairy—that is unless you like curdled potatoes. Buttermilk curdles at 160 degrees, a temperature reached almost instantly when the cold liquid hits steaming-hot potatoes. And while you can wait for the potatoes to cool off before adding the buttermilk, the best solution is to add melted butter to the buttermilk—the fat keeps the buttermilk from curdling. When mixed with room-temperature buttermilk, melted butter acts as an insulating agent, with the fat coating the proteins in the buttermilk and protecting them from heat shock. The only other important factor here is the potatoes themselves and how we cooked them. The test kitchen has found that simmering whole russets in their jackets yields the best potato flavor and silkiest texture but we wanted to simplify things. After much testing we found that we could peel and cut Yukon Golds before simmering and still have creamy, smooth potatoes since they have less starch than russets or red potatoes and do not absorb as much water during cooking. So all it takes for great buttermilk mashed potatoes is the right potato and the right technique. And a little butter. Sautéed leeks and some chives jazz this recipe up a notch but they're great without them too.

---

2  pounds Yukon Gold potatoes (4 medium), peeled and cut into 1-inch chunks

1  bay leaf
   Salt

7  tablespoons unsalted butter (6 tablespoons, melted and cooled)

1  medium leek, white and light green parts, rinsed well, quartered, and cut into ¼-inch slices

⅔  cup buttermilk, at room temperature

3  tablespoons minced fresh chives
   Pepper

---

**1.** Place the potatoes and bay leaf in a large saucepan and add cold water to cover by 1 inch and 1 tablespoon salt. Bring to a boil over high heat, then reduce the heat to medium and simmer until the potatoes break apart when a paring knife is inserted, about 18 minutes. Drain the potatoes, discard the bay leaf, and return the potatoes to the saucepan set on the still-hot burner.

**2.** While the potatoes are cooking, melt 1 tablespoon of the butter in a small nonstick skillet over medium heat. Add the leek and cook, stirring occasionally, until lightly browned and wilted, about 8 minutes.

**3.** Using a potato masher, mash the potatoes until a few small lumps remain. Gently add 6 tablespoons melted butter and the buttermilk to a small bowl and mix until combined. Add the butter-buttermilk mixture, leeks, and chives to the potatoes; using a rubber spatula, fold gently until just incorporated. Season with salt and pepper to taste. Serve immediately.

**WHERE THINGS CAN GO WRONG:** Be sure to bring the buttermilk to room temperature and mix with the cooled melted butter before adding it to the potatoes or it will curdle.

## NOTES FROM THE TEST KITCHEN

**THE SECRET TO BUTTERMILK MASHED POTATOES**
When mashed potatoes turn out dry, it's partly because the starch granules haven't ruptured and broken down. Thorough cooking makes the granules dissolve, yielding mashed potatoes that are smooth rather than grainy.

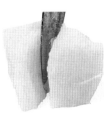

**NOT QUITE DONE**
Potatoes that remain intact when pierced with a paring knife need more cooking.

**OVERDONE**
Potatoes that have begun to disintegrate will result in soupy mashed potatoes.

**JUST RIGHT**
Potatoes that break apart when pierced with a paring knife are ready to be mashed.

# CRISPY POTATO PANCAKES
## SERVES 4

**WHAT MAKES THIS A BEST RECIPE:** With its lacy, golden brown exterior and creamy interior, a good potato pancake is hard to beat. Traditional potato pancakes are made with grated potatoes (squeezed dry to remove excess moisture), eggs, onions, and a dry binder (usually flour or matzo meal). Formed into flat disks, they are fried in a pan of hot oil until golden brown. You can fry only a few pancakes at a time, so keeping the first batches hot while making more is always a challenge. No wonder most cooks save potato pancakes for special occasions. For this recipe, we made potato pancakes suitable for a weeknight dinner by using frozen hash-brown potatoes. (They've been shredded and squeezed dry, which is half the work.) We microwaved the frozen potatoes with butter for flavor as well as moisture and were pleasantly surprised by the results. Because we were not grating potatoes, the idea of grating onions (the usual procedure in most recipes) seemed silly. Minced onions were too crunchy, but scallions provided the same flavor without any textural distraction. A single egg helped bind the potatoes and scallions, but we needed a dry binder, too. Flour gave the pancakes a pasty texture. Matzo meal worked fine, but not everyone has this ingredient on hand. Cornstarch worked just as well and is a staple in most kitchens. Now that we had simplified our ingredient list, we needed a method to match. Instead of pan-frying, we oven-fried our pancakes in a single batch on an oiled baking sheet. Preheating the baking sheet turned out to be essential—without this step the pancakes were not sufficiently crisp. Going one step further, we coated each potato ball with vegetable oil spray before pressing it into a ½-inch-thick disk on the hot oiled baking sheet. This method evenly (and lightly) coated the entire surface of each pancake with fat, helping to reproduce the texture and color characteristic of skillet-frying. Tasters marveled at the creamy interior and extra-crispy exterior of the pancakes—and no one guessed we had started with frozen hash browns. Serve these crisp pancakes with sour cream and/or applesauce.

Do you love potato pancakes but hate shredding potatoes and frying them? We have a solution.

2   tablespoons vegetable oil
5   cups frozen shredded hash-brown potatoes
4   tablespoons (½ stick) unsalted butter
1   large egg
2   scallions, chopped fine
1   tablespoon cornstarch
½   teaspoon salt
½   teaspoon pepper
    Vegetable oil spray

**1.** Adjust an oven rack to the upper-middle position and heat the oven to 475 degrees. Coat a rimmed baking sheet with the vegetable oil.

**2.** Place the hash browns and butter in a large microwave-safe bowl. Cover tightly with plastic wrap and microwave on high power until the butter is melted and the hash browns are defrosted, about 5 minutes. Remove the plastic wrap, stir well, and let cool.

**3.** Whisk the egg, scallions, cornstarch, salt, and pepper together in a medium bowl until thoroughly combined.

Add to the hash-brown mixture and stir until incorporated. Divide the mixture into 10 equal-sized balls and set aside on a large plate.

**4.** Place the oiled baking sheet in the oven and heat until the oil is just beginning to smoke, about 6 minutes. Remove the baking sheet from the oven and, working quickly, place the potato balls on the hot baking sheet. Spray each ball with vegetable oil spray, then press each one into a ½-inch-thick disk using a metal spatula (spray the back of the spatula with vegetable oil spray if the potato balls start to stick). Bake until the potato pancakes are golden brown on the bottom, about 10 minutes. Flip the pancakes over, press down using a metal spatula, and bake until crisp and golden brown on the second side, about 8 minutes more. Place the pancakes on a large paper towel–lined plate and let drain briefly. Serve.

**WHERE THINGS CAN GO WRONG:** Allow the microwaved potatoes to cool before stirring in the remaining ingredients, otherwise the heat from the potatoes will cook the egg.

## NOTES FROM THE TEST KITCHEN

### HOW TO MAKE POTATO PANCAKES
Shape the potato mixture into 10 equal-sized balls, then gently place onto a hot oiled baking sheet. Use a greased metal spatula to press each ball into a pancake.

### EASIER THAN YOU THINK
Frozen hash browns are a great way to make quick potato pancakes—no peeling or grating potatoes required.

# ROASTED GARLIC POTATOES
SERVES 4

**WHAT MAKES THIS A BEST RECIPE:** To us, the ultimate roasted garlic potato has a crispy golden shell containing a delicate creamy interior. And every bite should provide a hit of garlic flavor, but without a trace of harshness or bitterness. It all starts with choosing the right kind of potato, and we favored waxy red potatoes, whose high moisture content ensures a creamy interior. A rimmed baking sheet allowed the potatoes to brown better than a high-sided roasting pan (which inhibits evaporation), and preheating the baking sheet helped jump-start the browning process and improved crispness. Using a preheated pan also reduced sticking, letting us use just 3 tablespoons of oil. But to get our potatoes really crisp, we tossed the cut potatoes with a tablespoon of cornstarch, which absorbed the moisture released during cooking before it could turn the potatoes soggy. And to get a potent hit of garlic, we found that mixing the already roasted potatoes with garlic butter was the best approach since the garlic was evenly dispersed and the residual heat from the potatoes mellowed out any harsh garlic overtones.

2 pounds red potatoes (6 medium), cut into 1-inch wedges
1 tablespoon cornstarch
½ teaspoon garlic powder
Salt and pepper
3 tablespoons vegetable oil
1 tablespoon unsalted butter, softened
1 garlic clove, minced
1 teaspoon minced fresh parsley
⅛ teaspoon grated lemon zest

**1.** Adjust an oven rack to the highest position, place a rimmed baking sheet on the rack, and heat the oven to 450 degrees.

**2.** Toss the potatoes, cornstarch, garlic powder, ¾ teaspoon salt, and ¼ teaspoon pepper together in a large bowl. Carefully remove the preheated baking sheet from the oven, add

A hot baking sheet and a dusting of cornstarch create roasted potatoes that are seriously crisp.

the oil, and tilt to evenly coat with the oil. Place the potatoes cut-side down in a single layer on the baking sheet. Roast until browned around the edges, about 30 minutes.

**3.** Meanwhile, mix the butter, garlic, parsley, and zest together in a medium bowl. Remove the baking sheet from the oven and, using a metal spatula, turn the potatoes skin-side down. Roast until the potatoes are crisp and deep golden brown, 10 to 15 minutes.

**4.** Transfer the potatoes to the bowl with the butter mixture and toss until evenly coated. Season with salt and pepper to taste. Serve.

**WHERE THINGS CAN GO WRONG:** Do not be tempted to turn the potatoes more than the recipe indicates—they will not become crispy or brown properly.

## NOTES FROM THE TEST KITCHEN

### ON THE MILD SIDE

For a rich garlic flavor without any harshness or bitterness, we tossed the potatoes with garlic powder before roasting them. Unlike fresh garlic, the powder will not burn in the oven and has a gentle flavor besides. For a hit of fresh garlic, we tossed the roasted potatoes with garlic butter—made with a single minced clove—just before serving.

# SHORT-ORDER HOME FRIES
SERVES 4

**WHAT MAKES THIS A BEST RECIPE:** Any decent grill cook can turn a pile of cubed potatoes into perfectly crisp, impeccably seasoned home-fried potatoes—or so it would seem. While the well-seasoned, flat griddle at the diner certainly helps, the real secret is precooking the potatoes. Most restaurants use leftover roasted or boiled potatoes (preferably medium-starch potatoes that hold their shape well) to make their home fries. But who has precooked potatoes at home? Skip this step and you'll end up with a greasy mound of crunchy potatoes. So why on earth are they called home fries when they are so impractical to make at home? Because we don't want to get up at the crack of dawn to boil or roast potatoes, we turned to the quickest cooker in the kitchen: the microwave. We microwaved diced potatoes with a bit of butter, and after just five minutes the potatoes were parcooked and ready for the skillet. We decided to use a nonstick skillet so that we could "home-fry" the potatoes without using an excess of butter. To develop a crust we packed the potatoes down with a spatula (to approximate the effect of the heavy cast-iron tool used in many diners to press the potatoes flat against the griddle) and let them cook undisturbed. After five minutes, the potatoes were beginning to develop a nice, hearty crunch, so we tossed them around, packed them down again, and waited some more. After repeating this process a few more times, the potatoes were evenly browned and extra-crusty. The last step was flavoring. Sautéed onion was a must. Taking a clue from a local diner, we tried sprinkling the home fries with a bit of garlic salt just before serving. Its deep, savory flavor nicely balanced the sweetness of the onion and potatoes. Finally, we had hassle-free home fries worthy of their name.

1½   pounds Yukon Gold potatoes (3 medium), cut into ¾-inch chunks
4   tablespoons (½ stick) unsalted butter
1   onion, minced (about 1 cup)
½   teaspoon garlic salt
½   teaspoon salt
   Pepper

SHORT-ORDER HOME FRIES

**1.** Arrange the potatoes in a large microwave-safe bowl, top with 1 tablespoon of the butter, and cover tightly with plastic wrap. Microwave on high until the edges of the potatoes begin to soften, 5 to 7 minutes, shaking the bowl (without removing the plastic) to redistribute the potatoes halfway through cooking.

**2.** Meanwhile, melt 1 tablespoon of the butter in a large nonstick skillet over medium heat. Add the onion and cook until softened and golden brown, about 8 minutes. Transfer to a small bowl.

**3.** Melt the remaining 2 tablespoons butter in the skillet over medium heat. Add the potatoes and pack them down with a spatula. Cook, without moving, until one side of the potato pieces is brown, 5 to 7 minutes. Turn the potatoes, pack down again, and continue to cook until well browned and crisp, 5 to 7 minutes. Reduce the heat to medium-low and continue cooking, stirring the potatoes every few minutes until crusty, 9 to 12 minutes. Stir in the onion, garlic salt, salt, and pepper to taste. Serve.

**WHERE THINGS CAN GO WRONG:** Remember to reduce the heat to medium-low in step 3 for the last 9 to 12 minutes of cooking, or else the home fries will burn.

## NOTES FROM THE TEST KITCHEN

### THE BEST POTATO FOR HOME FRIES
High-starch/low-moisture potatoes, such as russets, may be great for baking and mashing, but when it comes to home fries they are not the best choice. The fluffy flesh of these potatoes breaks down in the skillet, leaving nothing but a greasy pool of stodgy spuds. For tender tubers that retain their texture, we prefer medium-starch or waxy varieties such as Yukon Gold, all-purpose, and red potatoes. They hold their shape in the skillet, develop a great crust, and fry up to a beautiful golden brown.

**RUSSET POTATOES**
A falling-apart mess

**YUKON GOLD POTATOES**
Intact, crisp, and browned

# POTATOES LYONNAISE
SERVES 3 TO 4

**WHAT MAKES THIS A BEST RECIPE:** One of the hallmark dishes of France's premier gastronomic city, pommes de terre Lyonnaise (aka potatoes Lyonnaise) is a study in simple elegance. Although originally conceived as a dish of economy (that is, an easy way to use up leftover boiled potatoes), it has eventually come to represent the best of classic French bistro cuisine: buttery, browned potato slices interwoven with strands of sweet, caramelized onion and lightly sprinkled with fresh, grassy parsley. The modern reality, however, is often far removed from that buttery, earthy ideal. Most versions we tested were greasy and heavy rather than rich and complex. Having no leftover cooked potatoes on hand (as is the case for most home cooks), we borrowed a technique from our home fries (see page 60) and began by microwaving the ¼-inch-thick slices of potato until barely tender in a tablespoon of melted butter. Then, using just one more tablespoon of butter (most classic recipes call for 4 to 6 tablespoons), a simple brown-and-flip approach, and medium-high heat, we cooked the potatoes until golden brown in less than 15 minutes. Potatoes Lyonnaise would just be sautéed potatoes if not for the addition of onion, the definitive ingredient of dishes prepared à la Lyonnaise. To achieve sweet, concentrated flavor, we covered the skillet and cooked the onion slices on medium once they had released some moisture. Deglazing the pan with just a small amount of water prevented the onion slices from scorching and gave them the opportunity to cook further in their own flavorful juice. Putting the steps together in an efficient manner was easy. While the onion cooked, the potatoes began their warm-up in the microwave. Once the onion finished cooking and was removed to a nearby bowl, the potatoes took their place in the pan. To meld the flavors, we tossed the onion back into the pan along with the potatoes and briefly sautéed the two together. The finishing touches: adding a little salt and pepper along the way and a sprinkling of fresh parsley at the end. Now we had an updated version of a French classic that was good enough (and quick enough) to make even without leftover potatoes.

Medium-starch Yukon Golds are best for Potatoes Lyonnaise, and after a jump start in the microwave, they are ready for the pan.

  3  tablespoons unsalted butter
  1  large onion (about 14 ounces), halved and sliced ¼ inch thick (about 3 cups)
     Salt
  2  tablespoons water
1 ½  pounds Yukon Gold potatoes (3 medium), peeled and sliced crosswise into ¼-inch rounds
     Pepper
  1  tablespoon minced fresh parsley

**1.** Melt 1 tablespoon of the butter in a large, heavy nonstick skillet over medium-high heat. When the foaming subsides, add the onion and ¼ teaspoon salt and stir to coat; cook, stirring occasionally, until the onion begins to soften, about 3 minutes. Reduce the heat to medium and cook, covered, stirring occasionally, until the onion is lightly browned and softened, about 12 minutes longer, deglazing with water when the pan gets dry, about halfway through cooking time. Transfer to a bowl and cover. Do not wash the skillet.

**2.** While the onion cooks, microwave 1 tablespoon of the butter on high power in a large microwave-safe bowl until melted, about 45 seconds. Add the potatoes to the bowl and toss to coat with the melted butter. Microwave on high power until the potatoes just start to turn tender (see the photos) about 6 minutes, tossing halfway through the cooking time. Toss the potatoes again and set aside.

**3.** Melt the remaining tablespoon butter in the skillet over medium-high heat. When the foaming subsides, add the potatoes and shake the skillet to distribute evenly. Cook, without stirring, until browned on the bottom, about 3 minutes. Using a spatula, stir the potatoes carefully and continue to cook, stirring every 2 to 3 minutes, until the potatoes are well browned and tender when pierced with the tip of a paring knife, 8 to 10 minutes more. Sprinkle with ¼ teaspoon salt and ¼ teaspoon pepper.

**4.** Add the onion back to the skillet and stir to combine; cook until the onion is heated through and the flavors have melded, 1 to 2 minutes. Season with salt and pepper to taste. Transfer to a large plate and sprinkle with the parsley. Serve.

**WHERE THINGS CAN GO WRONG:** Toss the potatoes at the halfway point during their brief spell in the microwave to prevent uneven cooking. If using a lightweight skillet, you will need to stir the potatoes in step 3 more frequently to prevent burning.

## NOTES FROM THE TEST KITCHEN

### HOW TO TELL IF THEY'RE DONE
A few crucial seconds separate perfectly tender potatoes Lyonnaise from mealy (overdone) and "al dente" (underdone) misfires. Because microwave ovens vary widely in terms of power, visual clues are especially useful in this recipe.

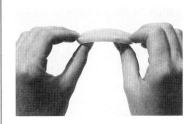

**UNDERCOOKED.** Potatoes look translucent and rubbery.

**JUST RIGHT.** Mostly opaque, potatoes resist slightly when bent.

**OVERCOOKED.** Potatoes yield easily, flaking apart when bent.

# DOWN 'N' DIRTY RICE

### SERVES 4 TO 6

**WHAT MAKES THIS A BEST RECIPE:** The culinary traditions of Cajun country run deep and are fiercely held, and dirty rice is just one of the many specialties you'll find there. For generations, Cajun cooks, like frugal cooks everywhere, were determined to use every part of the animals they raised. And dirty rice allowed them to make use of chicken giblets—the gizzard, heart, kidneys, and liver—for flavoring. At the same time it turned the rice brown, hence the name. But dirty rice isn't just about appearances—it's about turning a bland white grain into a rich, meaty side dish. Because modern home cooks don't have a ready supply of giblets (and may not be much interested in having such a supply in any case), we wanted to find a way to make dirty rice with nothing more than familiar supermarket staples. After trying everything from bacon and sausage to hamburger meat, we found that ground pork came closest to producing the flavor we'd gotten when we made a batch of dirty rice with the real thing—giblets. But this dish was a still a long way from that real thing. Because chicken livers are still widely available, we wondered if this one member of the original foursome would do the trick. Sure enough, tasters agreed that rice made with both chicken livers and ground pork lived up to the name "dirty." Add to the pot the classic Cajun trinity of onion, celery, and bell pepper, and pass a bottle of hot pepper sauce at the table, and there you have a real taste of Louisiana.

| | |
|---|---|
| 1 | tablespoon vegetable oil |
| 8 | ounces ground pork |
| 1 | onion, minced (about 1 cup) |
| 1 | celery rib, chopped fine |
| 1 | red bell pepper, stemmed, seeded, and chopped fine |
| 3 | garlic cloves, minced |
| 4 | ounces chicken livers, rinsed, trimmed of fat, and chopped fine |
| ¼ | teaspoon dried thyme |
| ¼ | teaspoon cayenne pepper |
| | Salt |
| 2¼ | cups low-sodium chicken broth |
| 2 | bay leaves |
| 1½ | cups long-grain white rice, rinsed |
| 3 | scallions, sliced thin |

**1.** Heat the oil in a large Dutch oven over medium heat until shimmering. Add the pork and cook until browned, about 5 minutes. Stir in the onion, celery, and bell pepper and cook until softened, about 10 minutes. Add the garlic, chicken livers, thyme, cayenne, and 1 teaspoon salt and cook until browned, 3 to 5 minutes. Transfer to a fine-mesh strainer set over a bowl and cover with foil.

**2.** Increase the heat to high and add the chicken broth, bay leaves, and rice to the empty pot. Scrape the pot bottom with a wooden spoon to remove the browned bits. Bring to a boil, reduce the heat to low, cover, and cook until the rice is tender, 15 to 17 minutes. Remove from the heat, discard the bay leaves, and fluff the rice with a fork. Gently stir in the drained meat and vegetable mixture (discarding the accumulated juices) and sprinkle with the scallions. Serve immediately, with a bottle of hot sauce at the table if desired.

## NOTES FROM THE TEST KITCHEN

### LIGHT AND FLUFFY DIRTY RICE

In our initial testings, the ground pork had a tendency to make the rice clumpy and greasy. By cooking the "dirty" ingredients separately from the rice and draining off the fat from the mixture, we were able to keep the rice light and fluffy.

### THE BEST WAYS TO RINSE RICE

We may like our rice dirty, but gummy is another story. Rinsing the rice removes much of the exterior starch, thereby preventing the grains from sticking together. The resulting rice cooks up light and fluffy, making it perfect for dirty rice, rice pilafs, or even rice salads. To rinse the rice, place it in a bowl, cover with cold water, and swish around to release the starch. Change the water as necessary until the water is nearly clear. Alternatively, you can place the rice in a fine-mesh strainer set over a large bowl. Run water over the rice and use your hands to swish the rice around to release excess starch. Pour off the water and repeat until the water is no longer cloudy.

# SWEET POTATO CASSEROLE

SERVES 10 TO 12

**WHAT MAKES THIS A BEST RECIPE:** Every Thanksgiving, without fail, millions of households across the country prepare the butter-laden, overspiced, marshmallow-topped side dish we all know and love as Sweet Potato Casserole, but with all of that fat, sugar, and spice, the flavor of the sweet potatoes gets lost. Thinking that the supporting ingredients ought to play second fiddle to the potatoes while still giving a fond nod to the familiar notion of a sweet potato casserole, we set out to update this home-style classic. Most of the recipes we researched added a great deal of sugar, cream, butter, and eggs to mashed sweet potato. Toppings, we were pleased to find, ranged far beyond marshmallows to include everything from a simple scattering of nuts to such glorifications as canned pineapple rings, maraschino cherries, cornflakes, Rice Krispies, breadcrumbs, and our favorite, streusel. The streusel's crisp texture and bittersweet flavor—dark brown sugar balanced by slightly bitter pecans—held the filling's richness at bay. And we liked the fact that the pecans added a nice texture to the dish and also became crunchy in the oven.

We were surprised to find that three-quarters of the recipes we found called for canned sweet potatoes. They have all the spunk (and flavor) of wet cardboard, so we ruled them out from the start. In terms of precooking the potatoes, we found that roasting, as opposed to boiling, produced a rich, earthy, intensely sweet flavor. Once the potatoes cooled briefly, we simply scraped the soft flesh free of the papery skins. We pureed half of the potatoes in the food processor until creamy, and folded the other half into the puree just before baking; bites of dense potato were thus suspended throughout the puree. Roasting had so intensified the flavor of the sweet potatoes that the excessive amounts of sugar traditionally added to the filling became superfluous. Any more than a few tablespoons made the filling saccharine. Half-and-half contributed richness without being cloying, and just 5 tablespoons of butter (most recipes included a full stick, or more) further smoothed things out. Recipes typically add whole eggs to the filling, but we thought they made the casserole too stiff. Without any eggs, however, the filling

was too loose and lacked depth of flavor. Yolks alone proved to be the solution, giving the casserole just enough body to be scooped neatly with a serving spoon. To keep the casserole from tasting like a pie and to offset the rich sweetness of the potatoes, we added a little nutmeg in conjunction with a generous grind of black pepper. Vanilla—a stiff shot of it—added surprising dimension by picking up floral undertones. Between the roasted potatoes, a prudent use of sugar and seasonings, and a less sticky-sweet topping, the intense flavor of sweet potatoes was now the focus of this classic casserole. And we'll even bet that no one will miss the marshmallows.

## SWEET POTATOES

7 pounds (6 to 8 medium) sweet potatoes, of equal size

## STREUSEL

5 tablespoons unsalted butter, cut into 5 pieces and softened, plus more for the pan
½ cup (2½ ounces) unbleached all-purpose flour
½ cup (3½ ounces) packed dark brown sugar
¼ teaspoon salt
1 cup pecans

## FILLING

5 tablespoons unsalted butter, melted
2 teaspoons salt
½ teaspoon ground nutmeg
½ teaspoon pepper
1 tablespoon vanilla extract
4 teaspoons fresh lemon juice
Granulated sugar
4 large egg yolks
1½ cups half-and-half

**1. FOR THE SWEET POTATOES:** Adjust an oven rack to the lower-middle position and heat the oven to 400 degrees. Poke the sweet potatoes several times with a paring knife and space evenly on a rimmed baking sheet lined with aluminum foil. Bake the potatoes, turning them once, until they are very tender and can be squeezed easily with tongs, 1 to 1½ hours (or 45 minutes for small sweet potatoes). Remove the potatoes from the oven and cut in half lengthwise to let the steam escape; cool at least 10 minutes. Reduce the oven temperature to 375 degrees.

**2. FOR THE STREUSEL:** While the potatoes are baking, butter a 13 by 9-inch baking dish. Pulse the flour, brown sugar, and salt in a food processor until blended, about four

1-second pulses. Sprinkle the butter pieces over the flour mixture and pulse until a crumbly mass forms, six to eight 1-second pulses. Sprinkle the nuts over the mixture and pulse until combined but some large nut pieces remain, four to six 1-second pulses. Transfer the streusel to a medium bowl and return the now-empty bowl to the processor.

**3.** Once the potatoes have cooled slightly, use the spoon to scoop the flesh into a large bowl; you should have about 8 cups. Transfer half of the potato flesh to the food processor. Using a rubber spatula, break the remaining potato flesh in the bowl into coarse 1-inch chunks.

**4. FOR THE FILLING:** Add the melted butter, salt, nutmeg, pepper, vanilla, and lemon juice to the potatoes in the food processor and process until smooth, about 20 seconds. Taste for sweetness, then add up to 4 tablespoons granulated sugar, if necessary; add the yolks. With the processor running, pour the half-and-half through the feed tube and process until blended, about 20 seconds; transfer to the bowl with the potato pieces and stir gently until combined.

**5. TO ASSEMBLE AND BAKE:** Pour the filling into the prepared baking dish and spread into an even layer with the spatula. Sprinkle with the streusel, breaking up any large pieces with your fingers. Bake until the topping is well browned and the filling is slightly puffy around the edges, 40 to 45 minutes. Cool at least 10 minutes before serving.

**WHERE THINGS CAN GO WRONG:** For even cooking, buy potatoes that are uniform in size. Avoid potatoes larger than 1½ pounds; they require a longer roasting time and tend to cook unevenly. Because natural sugar levels in sweet potatoes vary greatly depending on variety, size, and season, it's important to taste the filling before adding sugar. If the filling is bland, add up to 4 tablespoons sugar; if the potatoes are naturally sweet, you may opt to omit the sugar altogether. When sweetening the filling, keep in mind that the streusel topping is quite sweet.

**WHAT YOU CAN DO AHEAD OF TIME:** The potatoes can be baked up to 2 days ahead. Scrape the flesh from the skins and refrigerate in an airtight container.

## NOTES FROM THE TEST KITCHEN

### HOW TO TELL IF THEY'RE DONE
Sweet potatoes take longer than you might think—up to 1½ hours in a 400-degree oven. Here are two ways to determine whether they are properly cooked.

**SQUEEZE.** Although the outside might be tender the center can still be firm. Before removing the sweet potatoes from the oven, squeeze them with a pair of tongs—they should give all the way to the center without resistance.

**PEEK.** If you have doubts, cut the sweet potatoes in half lengthwise. If you see whitish marbling (uncooked starches that are firm to the touch), press the halves back together, wrap the potatoes individually in foil, and continue roasting until the marbling disappears.

### BYE BYE MOISTURE
Instead of boiling sweet potatoes (as most recipes direct), we baked ours for a lighter, fluffier casserole. As soon as the sweet potatoes were finished cooking, we cut them in half lengthwise so the steam could escape.

### SWEET POTATOES AND STARCH
After making gluey mashed potatoes in the food processor, we were reluctant to take the same tack with sweet potatoes. But the processor-pureed sweet potatoes—creamy and smooth—were everything the white potatoes hadn't been. First off, the sweet and white potatoes, which are from completely different plant families, have starches that are also very different. Sweet potato starch is similar to cornstarch. The starch granules are about half the size of those in white potatoes, and they are more stable during cooking. Second, sweet potatoes contain an enzyme that when heated converts some starches to sugars. With less starch that is more resistant to breakdown, cooked sweet potatoes are thus rendered creamy—not gluey—by the processor's whirling blade.

### CUT THE RECIPE IN HALF
To serve 4 to 6, halve all the ingredients and bake the casserole in an 8-inch-square prepared baking dish for 35 to 40 minutes.

# CHEESY POTATO CASSEROLE
### SERVES 8 TO 10

**WHAT MAKES THIS A BEST RECIPE:** Every country cook knows the basic recipe for scalloped potatoes: Layer thinly sliced potatoes and cheese in a shallow casserole dish, cover with liquid, and bake. In the best of all worlds, the potatoes form dense layers, the liquid reduces to a creamy, flavorful sauce, and the cheesy crust is golden and crisp. But scalloped potatoes are heavy and bland. Most recipes use only cream and then overload the casserole with cheese. To avoid this sort of gloppy mess, we created a simple sauce with both cream and broth, which allowed the flavor of the potatoes to stand out. Simmering fresh thyme and garlic with the cream and broth made the sauce taste even better. As for the cheese, we decided to pair Gruyère or Swiss (for both their meltability and their flavor) with Parmesan (for its browning ability and its flavor). Russets, all-purpose, and Yukon Gold potatoes all worked well, although russets, with their tender bite and earthy flavor, were our favorite. More important than the potato type, however, was the way they were sliced—very thin, if they were to cook evenly. To finish things off, a top layer of golden, bubbly cheese was nice, but we wanted a really crisp crust. Unconventional as it might seem, we added torn-up bread pieces to the top of the casserole, gently pressing them into the cream, and topping them with cheese. The golden topping looked great and its tasty crunch was a perfect complement to the tender, creamy, potatoes below.

4 garlic cloves, 1 clove cut in half lengthwise, remaining cloves minced

1 tablespoon unsalted butter, softened

4 ounces Gruyère or Swiss cheese, shredded (about 1 cup)

2 ounces Parmesan cheese, grated (about 1 cup)

1½ cups heavy cream

1½ cups low-sodium chicken broth

2 teaspoons minced fresh thyme

⅛ teaspoon nutmeg

¾ teaspoon salt

⅛ teaspoon pepper

2½ pounds russet potatoes (5 medium), peeled and sliced ⅛ inch thick

4–5 slices high-quality white bread, crusts removed and torn into pieces (about 4 cups)

**1.** Adjust an oven rack to the middle position and heat the oven to 350 degrees. Use the cut side of the halved garlic to rub the sides and bottom of a 2-quart shallow baking or gratin dish. Allow the garlic in the dish to dry briefly, about 2 minutes, then coat the dish with the softened butter. Combine the cheeses in a small bowl.

**2.** Bring the minced garlic, cream, broth, thyme, nutmeg, salt, and pepper to a boil in a large saucepan over medium-high heat. Reduce the heat to medium-low and simmer until the liquid is reduced to 2½ cups, about 5 minutes. Remove from the heat and gently stir in the potatoes.

**3.** Spoon half of the potato mixture into the prepared dish. Sprinkle with half of the cheese, add the remaining potato mixture, and press with a spatula to compact. Press the bread pieces into the casserole and bake 40 minutes. Sprinkle the remaining cheese on top and continue baking until golden and bubbling, 25 to 30 minutes. Remove from the oven and let rest 20 minutes before serving.

**WHERE THINGS CAN GO WRONG:** The potatoes must be sliced very thinly (⅛ inch thick), or else they won't cook evenly and you'll end up with an underdone casserole (and crunchy potatoes). It's nearly impossible to slice potatoes this thinly with a knife, making a food processor fitted with a slicing disk or a mandoline a must.

**WHAT YOU CAN DO AHEAD OF TIME:** This casserole can be assembled (do not add the bread to the topping) and refrigerated up to 24 hours ahead. When ready to bake, add the bread and bake according to the recipe.

## NOTES FROM THE TEST KITCHEN

### THE BEST INEXPENSIVE MANDOLINE
We highly recommend using a mandoline to ensure that the potatoes are cut thinly and evenly. We found that you don't have to spend a fortune on this handy slicer; in fact, after testing five models we found several that fit the bill though the best buy was the **Pyrex Slicer** at just $5.99.

# RICE AND GRAINS 101

## LONG GRAIN

Includes most generic rice, as well as basmati (an aged extra-long-grain rice from India), Texmati (a domestic alternative), and fragrant Thai jasmine
**HOW IT LOOKS:** Slender, elongated, four to five times longer than wide
**HOW IT COOKS:** High amylose means a light, fluffy texture with firm, distinct grains, making it especially good for pilafs and salads. Some cooks use the "absorption method" (see page 71), but to our minds, just adding water is a missed flavor opportunity. We prefer the "pilaf method," a sauté-based method that brings out toasted, nutty flavors.

## SHORT GRAIN

Includes sushi rice
**HOW IT LOOKS:** Opaque, almost round grains
**HOW IT COOKS:** The softest, stickiest grain of the bunch (cooked), thanks to low amylose and high amylopectin. These qualities make it ideal for tossing with a light vinegar dressing and wrapping up in sushi rolls. Often steamed, but the basic "absorption method" works so long as the simmer is gentle.

## MEDIUM GRAIN

Includes generic medium-grain rice and specialty rices for dishes like risotto (Arborio) and paella (Valencia)
**HOW IT LOOKS:** Fat, chalky grain, two to three times longer than wide
**HOW IT COOKS:** Higher in amylopectin, medium-grain rice is tender and a bit sticky, and resists turning hard and crunchy as it cools (unlike long grain). It's versatile stuff. When simmered, the grains clump together, making it a good choice to accompany a stir-fry. But it also takes well to the pilaf method, especially in risottos and paellas.

## BROWN RICE

**HOW IT LOOKS:** Light brown bran layer intact (a few greenish grains are normal)
**HOW IT COOKS:** The bran layer, valued for its fiber content, is also something of a nuisance: It slows absorption (brown rice takes nearly twice as long to cook as white) and cooks unevenly on the stovetop (we prefer the oven method). Whether short, medium, or long grain, brown rice has a pronounced chew, nutty flavor, and distinct grains.

## PEARL BARLEY

Hulled whole grains of barley with the bran polished off. Chewy, with a mildly sweet, nutty flavor. Great in soups.

## WHEAT BERRIES

Not berries at all, but whole, husked wheat kernels with bran layer and germ intact. Cooked wheat berries are firm and chewy. Great for cold salads.

## BULGUR

Wheat berries that have been precooked, dried, stripped of their bran, and crushed into pieces. This quick-cooking grain is not the same as cracked wheat, which has not been parcooked.

## QUINOA

This spinach relative is sometimes called a "supergrain" because it contains eight essential amino acids. The tiny seeds expand to four times their size during cooking and turn out light and fluffy.

## WILD RICE

"Real" wild rice is hand-harvested from lakes and rivers and costs as much as $9 per pound. We prefer not-so-wild wild rice—cultivated in man-made paddies—which has a more resilient texture and a much lower price. Cook wild rice at a bare simmer and check it often: It can go from chewy and underdone to mushy and "blown out" in a matter of minutes.

## COOKING RICE AND OTHER GRAINS (FOR 1 CUP RAW)

| GRAIN | RINSE? | BEST METHOD | WATER | COOKING TIME | YIELD |
|---|---|---|---|---|---|
| long-grain rice | yes | pilaf | 1½ cups | 18–20 min | 3 cups |
| medium-grain rice | no | pilaf, absorption | 1⅓ cups | 16–18 min | 3 cups |
| short-grain rice | no | absorption | 1¼ cups | 16–18 min | 2¾ cups |
| brown rice | no | oven | 1½ cups | 1 hr | 2½–3 cups |
| pearl barley | no | pasta | 4 quarts | 25–30 min | 3½–4 cups |
| wheat berries | no | pasta | 4 quarts | 1 hr | 2–2½ cups |
| bulgur | no | absorption* | 1½ cups | 15 min | 2–2½ cups |
| quinoa | yes | absorption | 2 cups | 15–20 min | 3 cups |
| wild rice | no | absorption** | 2 cups | 35–45 min | 3 cups |

**A NOTE ON RINSING:** For the fluffiest long-grain rice, rinse grains to remove some of the surface starches. Don't bother rinsing medium- or short-grain rices, they are meant to be a bit sticky; also, don't rinse brown rice—there is no exterior starch. Always rinse quinoa to remove its bitter coating.
* Modified: Add bulgur to boiling water, then let steep, covered and off heat, for 15 minutes.
** Drain wild rice of excess liquid before serving.

# FOUR METHODS FOR COOKING RICE AND OTHER GRAINS

## ABSORPTION METHOD

Grains are simmered slowly in a measured quantity of liquid until tender. Combine grains, liquid, and salt (½ teaspoon per cup of raw grains) in a heavy-bottomed saucepan. Bring to a boil over medium-high heat. Reduce the heat to low and simmer, covered, until the grains are tender (see the chart on page 70 for times). Let stand off the heat, covered, 10 to 15 minutes. Fluff with a fork and serve.

## OVEN METHOD

Best for situations requiring prolonged, even heating, such as cooking brown rice or larger quantities of white rice.

**1.** Heat the oven to 375 degrees with the oven rack in the middle position. Bring the liquid to a boil, covered, in a saucepan over high heat. Combine the grains, boiling liquid, and salt (½ teaspoon per cup of raw grains) in a baking dish.

**2.** Cover tightly with a double layer of foil. Bake until the grains are tender (see the chart on page 70 for times). Let stand 5 minutes, uncover, fluff with a fork, and serve.

## PILAF METHOD

Grains are cooked in hot butter or oil briefly before adding liquid to impart a toasted, nutty flavor. To make a true pilaf, sauté aromatics like onion and garlic and spices until fragrant before adding the grains.

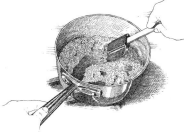

**1.** Heat the butter or oil (2 teaspoons per cup of raw grains) in a saucepan over medium heat. Add the grains and cook, stirring, until the grains become chalky and opaque and stop sticking to the pan, about 3 minutes.

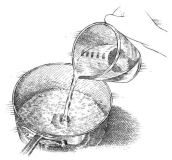

**2.** Add the liquid and salt (½ teaspoon per cup of raw grains), increase the heat, and bring just to a boil. Reduce the heat to low, cover, and simmer until the liquid is absorbed and the grains are tender (see the chart on page 70 for times). Let stand off the heat, covered, 10 to 15 minutes. Fluff with a fork and serve.

## PASTA METHOD

Grains are cooked like pasta—in an abundant quantity of salted, boiling water. Best for very firm, chewy grains or for recipes in which a softer texture is desired, such as cold salads.

**1.** Bring 4 quarts water to a rapid boil over high heat. Add the grains and 2½ teaspoons salt, reduce the heat, and simmer until the grains are tender (see the chart on page 70 for times).

**2.** Drain the grains in a strainer set in a sink. Let stand in the strainer 5 minutes before using or spread out on a parchment-lined baking sheet to cool.

## FOR STOVETOP SUCCESS

**1. PICK THE RIGHT POT:** To avoid scorching, use a sturdy, heavy-bottomed pot with a tight-fitting lid, preferably nonstick. To ensure the pot is big enough for even cooking, dump the raw grains into the pot: If the grains are more than 1½ inches deep, use a larger pot.

**2. GO LOW:** Bring the water to a boil, cover, then turn it down to a bare simmer. If more than a wisp of steam escapes, the flame is too high.

**3. DON'T STIR:** Rice will release extra starch, and other grains may break.

**4. KEEP A LID ON IT:** Don't start checking for doneness until near the end; lifting the lid releases moisture and can result in crunchy grains.

**5. GIVE IT A REST:** Let rice and grains stand for 10 to 15 minutes covered, off the heat, to allow the starch granules to firm up so they won't break.

# EGGS & BREADS

# HUEVOS RANCHEROS

SERVES 2 TO 4

**WHAT MAKES THIS A BEST RECIPE:** While there are many variations on huevos rancheros or "rancher-style eggs," most often the eggs are quickly fried, slipped onto a corn tortilla base, then napped with a fiery, roasted tomato-chile salsa. The star of this dish is most definitely the salsa—traditionally a cooked tomato-based sauce. Given the lackluster quality of most fresh supermarket tomatoes, we started our testing with canned tomatoes but ultimately turned to fresh plum tomatoes—their texture and bright, tart flavor were qualities that canned tomatoes lacked. To tease out more flavor, we roasted the tomatoes along with jalapeño chiles, onion, garlic, and a bit of tomato paste (which added a crucial backbone of flavor). The roasting gently caramelized the vegetables, giving the salsa great depth. After a quick whirl in the food processor, fresh lime juice, cilantro, and some finely chopped jalapeño were added for a zesty, piquant counterpoint.

Moving on to the eggs, after many failed attempts to transfer fried eggs neatly (and still intact) from the pan to the tortillas we stumbled upon a fairly untraditional method of cooking them: poaching the eggs in the salsa. Poaching (rather than frying) made the eggs easier to cook all at once and easy to scoop out of the pan. The eggs also picked up flavor from the salsa and there was now one less pan to wash. Finally, we found it best to bake our tortillas, since frying produced messy, greasy results. But when brushed lightly with oil, sprinkled with salt, and toasted in a hot oven until golden brown, our tortillas turned out crisp and dry—the perfect foil for the soft, creamy poached eggs and fiery salsa.

3    jalapeño chiles, halved, seeds and ribs removed
1½   pounds ripe plum tomatoes (about 8 medium), cored and halved
½    onion, cut into ½-inch wedges
2    garlic cloves, peeled
1    tablespoon tomato paste
     Salt
3    tablespoons vegetable oil
½    teaspoon ground cumin
⅛    teaspoon cayenne pepper
3    tablespoons minced fresh cilantro
     Pepper
1–2  tablespoons fresh lime juice, plus lime wedges for serving
4    corn tortillas
4    large eggs

**1. FOR THE SALSA:** Adjust an oven rack to the middle position and heat the oven to 375 degrees. Mince 1 of the jalapeños and set it aside. In a medium bowl, combine the tomatoes, the remaining jalapeños, onion, garlic, tomato paste, 1 teaspoon salt, 2 tablespoons oil, cumin, and cayenne. Toss to mix thoroughly. Place the vegetables cut side down on a rimmed baking sheet. Roast them until the tomatoes are tender and skins begin to shrivel and brown, 35 to 45 minutes. Cool on the baking sheet for 10 minutes. Increase the oven heat to 450 degrees. Using tongs, transfer the roasted onions, garlic, and jalapeños to a food processor. Process the mixture until almost completely broken down, about 10 seconds, pausing halfway through to scrape down the sides of the bowl with a rubber spatula. Add the tomatoes and process until the salsa is slightly chunky, about 10 seconds more. Add 2 tablespoons cilantro, the reserved minced jalapeño, salt, pepper, and lime juice to taste.

**2. FOR THE TORTILLAS:** Brush both sides of each tortilla lightly with the remaining tablespoon oil, sprinkle both sides with salt, and place them on a clean baking sheet. Bake the tortillas until the tops just begin to color, 5 to 7 minutes. Flip them and continue to bake until they are golden brown, 2 to 3 minutes more.

**3. FOR THE EGGS:** Meanwhile, bring the salsa to a gentle simmer in a 12-inch nonstick skillet over medium heat. Remove the skillet from the heat and make four shallow wells in the salsa with the back of a large spoon. Break 1 egg into a cup, then carefully pour the egg into the well in the salsa. Repeat this process with the remaining eggs. Season each egg with salt and pepper to taste, then cover the skillet and place it over medium-low heat. Cook the eggs until desired doneness: 4 to 5 minutes for runny yolks, 6 to 7 minutes for set yolks.

**4. TO SERVE:** Place the tortillas on serving plates and gently scoop one egg onto each tortilla. Spoon the salsa around each egg, covering the tortillas, but leaving a portion of egg exposed. Sprinkle with the remaining cilantro and serve with lime wedges.

**WHAT YOU CAN DO AHEAD OF TIME:** To save time in the morning, make the salsa the day before and store it overnight in the refrigerator.

## NOTES FROM THE TEST KITCHEN

### HOLDING THE TORTILLAS
If you need to hold the tortillas for a short time, cover the baking sheet with foil.

### WHEN BAD THINGS HAPPEN TO GOOD FOOD
Beans, beef, cheese, guacamole, lettuce, olives, sour cream: To compensate for so-so ingredients, many recipes opt for overkill, turning this simple Mexican breakfast into an egg-adorned plate of "Extreme Nachos." Our version takes a simpler approach, fine-tuning flavor and texture for a few key ingredients. Huevos rancheros should be appetizing—not an appetizer.

### THREE STEPS TO BETTER HUEVOS RANCHEROS

**ROAST.** Slow-roasting improved the flavor of supermarket tomatoes while intensifying the other salsa ingredients.

**TOAST.** Crisping store-bought tortillas in the oven yielded the best texture—light and crispy, not tough or greasy.

**POACH.** Poaching the eggs in small wells made in the salsa improved their flavor and left us with just one pan to wash.

# MAPLE SAUSAGE AND WAFFLE BREAKFAST CASSEROLE
SERVES 6

**WHAT MAKES THIS A BEST RECIPE:** In its simplest form, a breakfast casserole is day-old bread soaked in custard (eggs and cream), then baked until golden and fluffy. Most recipes—including ours—also add sausage and cheese. It's easy to grasp their appeal: you can make them with just a handful of ingredients and assemble everything the night before, so all you have to do in the morning is turn on your oven. A hearty dish by nature, breakfast casserole is by no means light fare, but that doesn't mean it should be so rich you have to let out your belt after breakfast. We like this recipe because it's easy but also tasty (and not so heavy that you feel guilty the rest of the day). After much testing, we realized that heavy cream was one of the culprits in most recipes giving these casseroles their über-richness while also deadening their flavors. Whole milk (and also lowfat milk) works just fine and allows you to actually taste the sausage and cheese. But our most surprising and original finding was about the base of the casserole: the bread. Most recipes use white sandwich bread or even sourdough or French bread. We tried all these—and more—and none delivered the light texture we were after. After scouring the bread aisle for something sweet but not too heavy, we wandered into the frozen food section. Just on a whim, we toasted some frozen waffles and layered them with the other ingredients. The result? A light and airy casserole that couldn't be beat. The waffles were a huge hit with our tasters and as an added bonus paired nicely with crumbled maple sausage. As a finishing touch, we replaced some of the milk with maple syrup.

6–8   frozen waffles (½ inch thick)
12   ounces maple breakfast sausage, crumbled
     Unsalted butter (for the dish)
6   ounces cheddar cheese, shredded (about 1½ cups)
6   large eggs
1¼   cups whole or lowfat milk
¼   cup maple syrup
¼   teaspoon salt
⅛   teaspoon pepper

Company coming? Wake up to this make-ahead casserole that calls for frozen waffles instead of the typical white bread.

**1.** Adjust an oven rack to the middle position and heat the oven to 375 degrees. Arrange the waffles in a single layer on a baking sheet and bake until crisp, about 10 minutes per side.

**2.** Brown the sausage in a nonstick skillet over medium heat, breaking it apart with a spoon, 8 to 10 minutes. Drain on a plate lined with paper towels.

**3.** Butter an 8-inch-square baking dish and add half the waffles in a single layer. Add half of the sausage and ½ cup of the cheese. Repeat the layering of the waffles, sausage, and ½ cup cheese. Whisk the eggs, milk, maple syrup, salt, and pepper together in a medium bowl until combined. Pour the egg mixture evenly over the casserole. Following one of the photos, cover the baking dish with plastic wrap and place the weights on top. Refrigerate the casserole for at least 1 hour or overnight.

**4.** Adjust an oven rack to the middle position and heat the oven to 325 degrees. Let the casserole stand at room temperature for 20 minutes. Uncover the casserole and sprinkle the remaining ½ cup cheese over the top. Bake the casserole until the edges and center are puffed, 45 to 50 minutes. Cool for 5 minutes before serving.

**WHERE THINGS CAN GO WRONG:** Belgian-style frozen waffles are too thick for this recipe. They throw off the waffle/custard ratio, producing a casserole that bakes up dry.

## NOTES FROM THE TEST KITCHEN

### DOUBLING THIS CASSEROLE
To double the recipe, simply double all the ingredients, use a 13 by 9-inch baking dish, and increase the baking time by 30 to 40 minutes.

### THE WEIGHTING GAME
When developing our breakfast casserole recipe, we found that a corner or two of waffle often wouldn't fully absorb the custard, and some unlucky test cook would end up with a mouthful of dry waffle. To remedy the situation, we weighted the casserole and then waited some more (refrigerating the casserole for at least one hour). We found two easy ways to weight the assembled casserole before baking.

**1.** Press plastic wrap directly onto the surface of the casserole, top with another 8-inch-square baking dish, then weight with heavy canned goods.

**2.** Press plastic wrap directly onto the surface of the casserole, then place two 1-pound boxes of brown sugar on the plastic wrap and top with a cast-iron pan.

### TASTE TEST: FROZEN WAFFLES
Although we typically make our waffles from scratch, the use of store-bought waffles in our Maple Sausage and Waffle Breakfast Casserole had us wondering which was best. We corralled eight brands of frozen waffles, ranging from ordinary (Pillsbury Homestyle) to organic (Lifestream Hemp Plus) and tasted them topped with maple syrup. **Eggo Homestyle Waffles** was the undisputed winner. These waffles were praised for their buttery, eggy flavor and crisp exterior.

# STUFFED FRENCH TOAST

SERVES 4

**WHAT MAKES THIS A BEST RECIPE:** Stuffed French toast is the sort of dish most of us only encounter when we're out for brunch, but when a reader wrote in wondering if we could tell her how to make it at home, we decided to take on the challenge. In our opinion, good stuffed French toast marries a creamy filling with a really crisp exterior. And it's this contrast in texture (plus the filling, of course) that distinguishes the stuffed version from ordinary French toast. To "stuff" the French toast, a filling is spread between two slices of regular sandwich bread, with the moist filling acting as a sort of seal. The sandwiches are then dipped in an egg-based batter and cooked in butter, much like regular French toast.

We scoured many cookbooks looking for ideas for the stuffing and we found two different options: jam or sweetened cream cheese. Our tasters overwhelmingly preferred the cream cheese filling, both for its richness and for the fact that it worked better than jam alone at holding the bread slices together. Simply mixed with a little sugar and cinnamon, cream cheese made the perfect filling. We did find, however, that it was easy to vary this simple formula by adding jam, apple butter, or chocolate chips though in our opinion, this simple version just can't be beat.

Satisfied with the stuffing, it was time to focus on the "toast." The typical egg and milk batter used with regular French toast wasn't producing the kind of crisp exterior we envisioned. We found recipes that called for everything from a thick pancake batter to a heavy, cream-based dip, but none gave us a really crisp exterior to contrast with the soft filling. After many failed tests, we tried tempura batter. A thick mixture made with flour, egg, and either sparkling water or beer, this batter traditionally provides a thin, super-crisp coating for seafood and vegetables. Since beer didn't feel appropriate for breakfast, we combined a mixture of sparkling water, flour, and egg. This was perfect; the bread fried up to a crisp golden brown and provided the perfect contrast with the creamy stuffing. Wondering if sparkling water was really essential, we gave tap water a try and it served to create the same great crisp texture.

The crisp exterior on this French toast contrasts perfectly with the sweet cream cheese filling.

6   ounces cream cheese, at room temperature
3   tablespoons sugar
¼   teaspoon ground cinnamon
8   slices high-quality sandwich bread
1   large egg
1   cup cold water
½   cup unbleached all-purpose flour
1   teaspoon vanilla extract
4   tablespoons (½ stick) unsalted butter
    Maple syrup, for serving

**1.** Combine the cream cheese, sugar, and cinnamon in a medium bowl. Spread the mixture on 4 bread slices. Top with the remaining bread slices, pressing down gently to form 4 sandwiches.

**2.** Combine the egg, water, flour, and vanilla in a shallow pie plate. Melt 2 tablespoons of the butter in a large nonstick skillet over medium heat. Dip both sides of 2 of the sandwiches in the batter and place in the skillet. Cook until deep golden brown on both sides, about 3 minutes per side. Repeat this process with the remaining butter and sandwiches.

**3.** Cut the French toast into triangles and serve immediately with maple syrup, if desired.

## NOTES FROM THE TEST KITCHEN

**THE RIGHT BREAD**
We like large sandwich bread for this recipe, with slices about 5 by 4 inches. If you use the smaller, standard-sized sandwich bread, you won't need all of the filling.

# SKILLET STRATA
## WITH SPINACH AND SMOKED GOUDA
SERVES 6 TO 8

**WHAT MAKES THIS A BEST RECIPE:** A strata, in its most basic form, is a layered egg casserole comprising day-old bread, eggs, cheese, and milk. The result is a hearty, savory bread pudding that tastes great, but requires some advance planning since it needs to sit overnight to allow the bread to soak up the milk and eggs. Plus, after an overnight stay in the fridge, it still has to bake for an hour or so. This skillet version, however, delivers the same souffléed richness but requires no advance planning whatsoever, as long as you have an ovenproof skillet and a few simple ingredients on hand. We like the combination of smoked Gouda and spinach in our strata, and we find that frozen chopped spinach (a convenient freezer staple) works great here. To make our strata, we start by sautéing onion in butter until lightly browned, and then we add the bread pieces to the skillet to toast them and dry them out a bit. This is a crucial step because it gives the bread a sturdy structure that keeps it from turning to mush when soaked with the custard. Next, we fold in the spinach and the custard off the heat to avoid scorching the eggs, and to ensure quick, even cooking. (We discovered that the residual heat from the skillet and its contents—the onion-bread mixture—gently thicken the custard, giving the strata a jump start in the oven.) Just before finishing our strata in the oven, we gently press down on the top of it to help the bread soak up the egg mixture. And after just 12 minutes in a hot oven, this strata is ready to eat, golden and puffed high above the rim of the skillet—perfect for a last-minute dinner or a leisurely weekend breakfast.

- 1 (10-ounce) package frozen chopped spinach
- 4 tablespoons (½ stick) unsalted butter
- 1 onion, minced (about 1 cup)
  Salt
- 6 large eggs
- 1½ cups whole milk
  Pepper
- 4 ounces smoked Gouda cheese, shredded (about 1 cup)
- 5 slices high-quality sandwich bread, cut into 1-inch squares
- 2 garlic cloves, minced

**1.** Adjust an oven rack to the middle position and heat the oven to 425 degrees. Meanwhile, place the frozen spinach in a medium microwave-safe bowl and cover tightly with plastic wrap. Microwave the spinach on high until it is thawed, about 4 minutes. When the spinach is cool enough to handle, squeeze it until dry and set it aside.

**2.** Melt the butter in a 10-inch ovensafe nonstick skillet over medium-high heat, swirling to coat the skillet, until the foaming subsides. Add the onion and ½ teaspoon salt and cook until the onion is softened and lightly browned, about 6 minutes.

**3.** Meanwhile, whisk the eggs, milk, and ¼ teaspoon pepper together in a large bowl, then stir in the cheese. Set the mixture aside.

**4.** Add the bread to the skillet and, using a rubber spatula, carefully fold the bread into the onion mixture until it is evenly coated. Cook the bread, folding occasionally, until it is lightly toasted, about 3 minutes. Stir in the garlic and cook until fragrant, about 30 seconds.

**5.** Off the heat, fold in the spinach and the egg mixture until it is slightly thickened and well combined with the bread. Gently press down on the top of the strata to help the bread soak up the egg mixture.

**6.** Bake the strata until the edges and center are puffed and the edges have pulled away slightly from the sides of pan, about 12 minutes, and serve.

**WHERE THINGS CAN GO WRONG:** We strongly recommend that you don't trim the crusts from the bread for this recipe. The crusts add flavor and, more importantly, a lot of structure to the strata. We found that trimming the crusts results in a strata that is dense and eggy. Also using a 10-inch ovensafe nonstick skillet is crucial: If you use a larger skillet, the thickness and texture of the strata will be all wrong; and if you use a conventional skillet, the eggs will stick to the pan.

## NOTES FROM THE TEST KITCHEN

### SQUEEZING SPINACH DRY
Removing the excess moisture from the spinach is key here. After thawing the spinach in the microwave, wrap it in paper towels (or a clean kitchen towel) and squeeze out as much liquid as possible.

SKILLET STRATA

# 30-MINUTE CORNED BEEF HASH

SERVES 4

**WHAT MAKES THIS A BEST RECIPE:** Great corned beef hash requires time (and patience), something that was in short supply as we developed recipes for *The Best 30-Minute Recipe*. How, we wondered, could we peel raw potatoes, cube them, then fry them until golden in rendered bacon fat, layer in the corned beef, and poach eggs in 30 minutes or less? We knew right away that we needed to conquer the longest-cooking element in the recipe—the potatoes—to get this dish on the table quickly. It was clear that partially cooking the potatoes first—before adding them to the pan—would be necessary. But when neither parboiling the potatoes nor microwaving them proved efficient, we turned to the pre-pared potato products available in the supermarket. Frozen (precooked) diced hash browns proved to be the solution to the potato quandary. When microwaved and then added to the skillet, they cooked up golden brown and crusty. As for the eggs, to speed up the process, we poached them in the same pan as the hash by nestling them into shallow indenta-tions in the hash, covering the pan, and cooking over low heat. The results were perfect: eggs with runny yolks conve-niently set in the hash and ready to be served.

| | |
|---|---|
| 4 | slices bacon, chopped |
| 1 | onion, minced (about 1 cup) |
| 4 | cups (20 ounces) frozen diced hash browns |
| 1 | tablespoon vegetable oil |
| | Salt and pepper |
| 2 | garlic cloves, minced |
| ½ | teaspoon minced fresh thyme |
| ⅓ | cup heavy cream |
| ¼ | teaspoon Tabasco |
| 12 | ounces thinly sliced corned beef, cut into ½-inch pieces |
| 4 | large eggs |

**1.** Fry the bacon in a large nonstick skillet over medium-high heat until the fat begins to render, about 2 minutes. Add the onion and cook until softened and lightly browned, about 8 minutes.

**2.** Meanwhile, toss the potatoes with the oil, ½ teaspoon salt, and ¼ teaspoon pepper in a medium microwave-safe bowl. Tightly cover the bowl with plastic wrap and microwave on high until the potatoes are hot, about 5 minutes.

**3.** Stir the garlic and thyme into the onion mixture and cook until fragrant, about 30 seconds. Stir in the hot potatoes, cream, and Tabasco. Using the back of a spatula, gently pack the potatoes into the pan, and cook the hash undisturbed for 2 minutes. Flip the hash, one portion at a time, and lightly repack it into the pan. Repeat the flipping process every few minutes until the potatoes are nicely browned, 6 to 8 minutes.

**4.** Stir in the corned beef and lightly repack the hash. Make four shallow indentations (about 2 inches wide) in the sur-face of the hash.

**5.** Crack 1 egg into each indentation and sprinkle the eggs with salt and pepper. Reduce the heat to medium-low, cover the pan with a tight-fitting lid, and continue to cook until the eggs are just set, about 5 minutes. Serve immediately.

**WHERE THINGS CAN GO WRONG:** Make sure that the inden-tations for the eggs are not too deep, otherwise the eggs will not cook evenly and in time. We had a number of tests yield eggs with hard yolks and uncooked whites (not really the poached egg ideal). Shallow indentations however allowed the eggs to lay more evenly, which ensured perfectly set eggs every time.

## NOTES FROM THE TEST KITCHEN

**MAKING SENSE OF FROZEN POTATOES**
In the vast world of frozen potatoes the term "hash browns" can be used to describe several different varieties. We found the best results with diced hash browns, which are sometimes labeled "Southern" style. They are often sold in 2-pound bags.

**GOT EXTRA TIME?**
If you want to use fresh potatoes (which will add a few extra minutes to the recipe), substitute 1½ pounds russet potatoes (3 or 4 medium), scrubbed and cut into ½-inch pieces, for the frozen potatoes. Increase the microwave cooking time to 8 minutes, or until the potatoes are tender around the edges, shaking the bowl halfway through. Proceed with the recipe as directed.

# FAMILY-SIZE TOMATO, BACON, AND GARLIC OMELET

### SERVES 4

**WHAT MAKES THIS A BEST RECIPE:** Here we set out to see if we could make one big omelet that would serve a family of four. Our initial tests were disastrous, with runny eggs on top and burnt eggs underneath. Obviously, flipping a behemoth, eight-egg omelet was out of the question but then we risked scorched eggs on the bottom. So to coordinate all the cooking, we added the sautéed filling ingredients along with the eggs and cooked them over medium heat until just beginning to set. Then we lowered the heat, sprinkled the cheese on top, and covered the skillet; in just five minutes the omelet was ready to serve. Shaping this supersized omelet was as simple as sliding it halfway out of the pan and then folding it over onto itself—the residual heat was also enough to finish melting the cheese perfectly.

|   |   |
|---|---|
| 8 | large eggs |
|   | Salt and pepper |
| 8 | slices bacon, minced |
| 1 | large tomato, cored, seeded, and chopped fine |
| ½ | green bell pepper, cored, seeded, and chopped fine |
| 4 | garlic cloves, minced |
| 2 | tablespoons unsalted butter |
| 3 | ounces pepper Jack cheese, shredded (about ¾ cup) |

**1.** Whisk the eggs, ½ teaspoon salt, and ⅛ teaspoon pepper together in a large bowl. Set aside.

**2.** Fry the bacon in a 12-inch nonstick skillet over medium-high heat until crisp, about 8 minutes. Stir in the tomato and bell pepper and cook until the vegetables are softened, about 6 minutes. Stir in the garlic and cook until fragrant, about 30 seconds. Transfer the mixture to a paper towel–lined plate and wipe the skillet clean with paper towels. Return the skillet to medium heat.

**3.** Melt the butter in the skillet, swirling to coat the skillet, until the foaming subsides. Add the eggs and bacon mixture to the pan and cook, stirring gently in a circular motion, until the mixture is slightly thickened, about 1 minute. Following the photo, use a rubber spatula to pull the cooked edges of the egg toward the center of the pan, tilting the pan so the uncooked egg runs to the cleared edge of the pan. Repeat until the bottom of the omelet is just set but the top is still runny, about 1 minute. Cover the skillet, reduce the heat to low, and cook until the top of the omelet begins to set but is still moist, about 5 minutes.

**4.** Remove the pan from the heat. Sprinkle the cheese evenly over the omelet, cover, and let it sit until the cheese partially melts, about 1 minute. Following the photo, slide half of the omelet onto a serving platter using a rubber spatula, then tilt the skillet so the remaining omelet flips over onto itself, forming a half-moon shape. Cut the omelet into wedges and serve immediately.

**WHERE THINGS CAN GO WRONG:** Chop the filling ingredients finely to keep your omelet intact when it comes time to flipping it out onto a platter.

## NOTES FROM THE TEST KITCHEN

### HOW TO MAKE AN OVERSIZED OMELET

**1.** To cook the omelet evenly, pull the cooked edges of egg toward the center of the pan and allow raw egg to run to the edges.

**2.** When the omelet is set on the bottom but still very runny on the top, cover the skillet and reduce the heat to low.

**3.** After the top of the omelet begins to set, sprinkle with the cheese, replace the cover, and let the omelet rest off the heat until the cheese has partially melted.

**4.** After using a rubber spatula to slide half of the omelet out onto a platter, tilt the skillet so that the omelet folds over onto itself to make a half-moon shape.

# FLAKY BUTTERMILK BISCUITS

MAKES 12 BISCUITS

**WHAT MAKES THIS A BEST RECIPE:** Closer to pastry than dinner roll, these flaky, rich, golden biscuits have striated layers of tender, buttery dough. Perhaps because they require more work than the typical fluffy biscuit, truly flaky biscuits have become scarce, while their down-market imitators (supermarket "tube" biscuits) are alarmingly common. So, how does one make a biscuit flaky? Our investigation was initially sidetracked by regional squabbling over the relative merits of butter versus lard, buttermilk versus milk, and brands of flour. Testing showed that while these choices affect flavor and texture, they are not at the heart of what makes a biscuit flaky. Instead, it is how those ingredients are handled. Enter, the puff-pastry technique: a method of rolling and folding dough multiple times to creates layers. Like folding then refolding a business letter (called a "turn" each time you roll and fold the dough), this action flattens the cold butter in the dough into thin sheets, which get sandwiched between equally thin layers of flour. In the oven, the butter melts and steam fills the spaces left behind, creating a biscuit with flaky, buttery layers. This technique (found in most of the flaky biscuit recipes we researched) worked well for us. However, in the process we learned a few tricks that make it work even better. For example, to ensure that the butter does not soften and mix with the flour (which makes short and crumbly biscuits) during the folding and rolling, we chill the mixing bowl and all of the wet and dry ingredients (instead of just the butter) before mixing. This trick buys enough time to complete two sets of turns—the number of turns that we determined gives us the optimum number of layers—with the cold butter still intact. Also, we discovered that changing the way we cut the butter into the flour helps create biscuits with better rise and more discrete flaky layers. Cutting the butter into the flour until pebble-sized pieces appear—the common method—just wasn't giving us the lift we needed. We also found that pieces in the shape of pebbles were the wrong shape. Flaky pieces—which roll out into bigger, longer thin sheets—produce biscuits that turned heads. As our biscuits rise in the oven, they form beautiful flaky layers with browned edges.

2½ cups (12½ ounces) unbleached all-purpose flour, plus extra for dusting
1 tablespoon baking powder
½ teaspoon baking soda
1 teaspoon salt
2 tablespoons vegetable shortening, cut into ½-inch chunks
8 tablespoons (1 stick) cold unsalted butter, lightly floured and cut into ⅛-inch slices (see the photo on page 84), plus 2 tablespoons butter, melted
Vegetable oil spray
1¼ cups cold buttermilk, preferably lowfat

**1.** Adjust an oven rack to the lower-middle position and heat the oven to 450 degrees. Whisk the flour, baking powder, baking soda, and salt together in a large bowl.

**2.** Add the shortening to the flour mixture, breaking up the chunks using your fingertips until only small, pea-sized pieces remain. Working in batches, drop the butter slices into the flour mixture and toss to coat. Following the photo on page 84, pick up each slice of the butter and press it between floured fingertips into flat, nickel-sized pieces. Repeat this process until all the butter is incorporated, and toss to combine. Freeze the mixture (in the bowl) until chilled, about 15 minutes.

**3.** Spray a 24-inch-square area of work surface with vegetable oil spray. Spread the spray evenly across the surface with a kitchen towel or paper towel. Sprinkle ⅓ cup of the extra flour across the sprayed area, and gently spread the flour across the work surface with your palm to form a thin, even coating. Add all but 2 tablespoons of the buttermilk to the chilled flour mixture. Stir briskly with a fork until a ball forms and no dry bits of flour are visible, adding the remaining buttermilk as needed (the dough will be sticky and shaggy but should clear the sides of the bowl). With a rubber spatula, transfer the dough onto the center of the prepared work surface, dust the surface lightly with flour, and, with floured hands, bring the dough together into a cohesive ball.

**4.** Pat the dough into an approximate 10-inch square. Then roll it into an 18 by 14-inch rectangle about ¼ inch thick, dusting the dough and rolling pin with flour as needed. Following the photos on page 84, use a bench scraper or thin metal spatula to fold the dough into thirds, brushing any excess flour from the surface. Lift a short end of the dough and fold it in thirds again to form an approximate 6 by 4-inch rectangle. Rotate the dough 90 degrees, dust the work surface underneath with flour, and roll and fold the dough again. Dust with flour as needed.

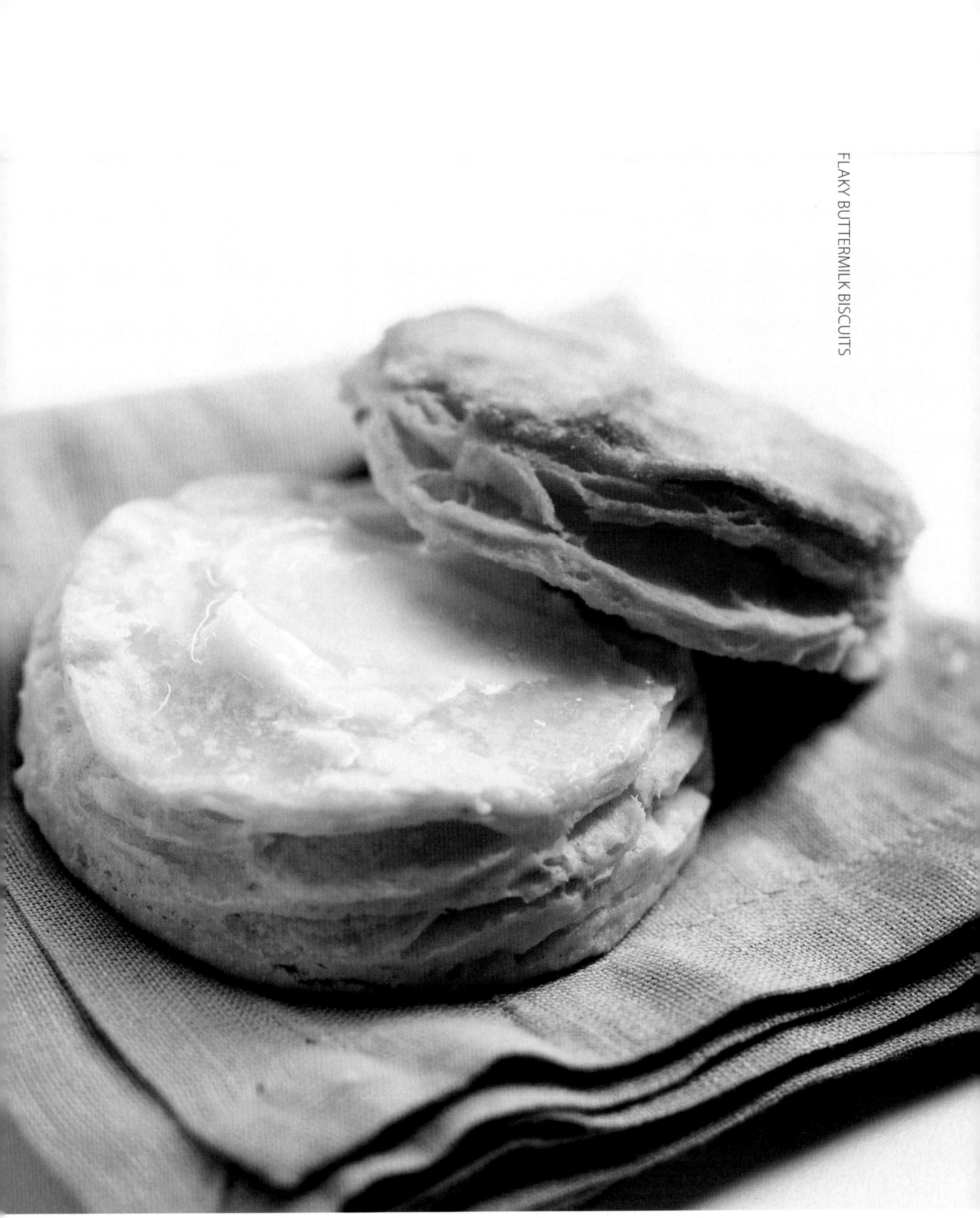

FLAKY BUTTERMILK BISCUITS

**5.** Roll the dough into a 10-inch square about ½ inch thick. Flip the dough and cut 9 rounds with a floured 3-inch biscuit cutter, dipping the cutter back into the flour after each cut. Carefully invert and transfer the rounds to an ungreased baking sheet, spaced 1 inch apart. Gather the dough scraps into a ball and roll and fold once or twice until the scraps form a smooth dough. Roll the dough into a ½-inch-thick round, cut 3 more 3-inch rounds, and transfer them to the baking sheet. Discard the excess dough.

**6.** Brush the biscuit tops with melted butter. Bake, without opening the oven door, until the tops are golden brown and crisp, 15 to 17 minutes. Let the biscuits cool on the baking sheet for 5 to 10 minutes before serving.

**WHERE THINGS CAN GO WRONG:** The dough is a bit sticky both when it comes together and during the first set of turns. Set aside about 1 cup of extra flour for dusting the work surface, dough, and rolling pin to prevent sticking. (Be careful not to incorporate large pockets of flour into the dough when folding it over.) Also, when cutting the biscuits, press down with firm, even pressure—do not twist the cutter, as this will pinch the edges of the biscuit, causing uneven rising.

**WHAT YOU CAN DO AHEAD OF TIME:** The recipe may be prepared though step 2, transferred to a zipper-lock freezer bag, and frozen for several weeks. Let the mixture sit at room temperature for 15 minutes before proceeding with the recipe.

## GREAT DISCOVERIES

### CREATING A NONSTICK WORK SURFACE

It was a catch-22. Our flaky biscuit dough had to be wet—a dry dough makes a dry biscuit—but it also had to be rollable. The only way I could successfully roll it was to scatter heaps of flour across the work surface, most of which ended up in the dough (which meant it was no longer wet). I needed to create a very thin, uniform layer of flour to keep the dough from sticking to the work surface during the crucial rolling process. The solution was a simple one. One morning, I gave the work surface a quick blast from a can of vegetable oil spray. (My hope was that the spray coating would help the flour adhere more evenly to the work surface.) I rolled out the next batch of dough and, to my delight, it released easily—and without much flour sticking to it.

SEAN LAWLER | ASSOCIATE EDITOR, COOK'S ILLUSTRATED

## NOTES FROM THE TEST KITCHEN

### MAKING THE "LAYERED LOOK" WORK FOR YOU

A strategic process of pinching, folding, and refolding creates stratified layers of air, fat, and flour—yielding ultra-flaky layers.

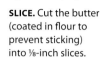

**SLICE.** Cut the butter (coated in flour to prevent sticking) into ⅛-inch slices.

**PRESS.** Pinch the butter slices between well-floured fingertips into flat, nickel-sized pieces.

**FOLD.** With a bench scraper or metal spatula, fold the dough into thirds (like a business letter).

**REFOLD.** Starting at one of the short ends, fold the dough into thirds again, rotate it 90 degrees, roll it out, and repeat the process.

**FLAKY BUTTER = FLAKY BISCUITS**

FLAKY SHEETS COMBINED BY HAND ➔ FLAKY BISCUITS

PEBBLY PIECES COMBINED IN A FOOD PROCESSOR ➔ REGULAR BISCUITS

# MULTIGRAIN BREAD

MAKES TWO 9 BY 5-INCH LOAVES

1¼ cups (6¼ ounces) 7-grain hot cereal mix
2½ cups (20 ounces) boiling water
3 cups (15 ounces) unbleached all-purpose flour, plus extra for dusting
1½ cups (7½ ounces) whole wheat flour
4 tablespoons honey
4 tablespoons (½ stick) unsalted butter, melted and cooled slightly
2½ teaspoons instant or rapid-rise yeast
1 tablespoon salt
¾ cup unsalted pumpkin or sunflower seeds
½ cup old-fashioned rolled oats or quick oats

**WHAT MAKES THIS A BEST RECIPE:** We were determined to make a sandwich-style multigrain bread that didn't require lots of time and special equipment. That meant no overnight sponges, and no need for either a super-hot oven or baking stone as there would be for a rustic free-form loaf. We were after a loaf with substance (no fluff like the store-bought version) and hearty, multigrain flavor: a bread recipe that only required a modest amount of effort. Most of the recipes we researched had lengthy ingredient lists, which included obscure grains (read: lots of trips to different stores), but the techniques were straightforward enough. Unfortunately, these recipes produced poorly risen loaves, dense and heavy as bricks. So what's our secret for a complexly flavored multigrain bread with a light texture? First, we used a 7-grain hot cereal mix, a handy blend of ground whole grains, including hard-to-find varieties (no running around town looking for specific whole grains). We discovered that steeping the grain mixture in boiling water and cooling it before adding it to the dough works best (our bread had distracting crunchy bits when we added the dry grain cereal directly to the dough). This cereal mix gives our bread its great flavor and an interesting textural contrast—something that was missing when we tried other grain combinations. We also learned that the right mix of flours (3 cups of all-purpose and 1½ cups whole wheat) and kneading the dough in a standing mixer on a moderately low speed for about 10 minutes are crucial for giving our bread the lightness we were after. Too much whole wheat flour in the mix made dense loaves, and kneading the dough for a short amount of time produced loaves with a poor rise. And employing a traditional bread-mixing technique called an autolyse—a resting period just after the initial mixing of water and flour that gives the flour time to hydrate—kept this bread from being crumbly and dry (this step also makes the dough less tacky and thus easier to work). Our multigrain bread baked up with a nice chew, without being tough, and pumpkin or sunflower seeds added a welcome (gentle) crunch. As a final touch, we rolled the shaped loaves in oats, giving them a finished, professional look.

**1.** Place the cereal mix in the bowl of a standing mixer and pour the boiling water over it. Let it stand, stirring occasionally, until the mixture cools to 100 degrees and resembles thick porridge, about 1 hour. Whisk the flours together in a medium bowl.

**2.** Once the grain mixture has cooled, add the honey, melted butter, and yeast and stir to combine. Attach the bowl to a standing mixer fitted with a dough hook. With the mixer running on low speed, add the flours, ½ cup at a time, and knead until the dough forms a ball, 1½ to 2 minutes. Cover the bowl with plastic wrap and let the dough rest 20 minutes. Add the salt and knead on medium-low speed until the dough clears the sides of the bowl, 3 to 4 minutes (if it does not clear the sides, add 2 to 3 tablespoons of additional all-purpose flour and continue mixing). Continue to knead the dough for 5 more minutes. Add the seeds and knead for another 15 seconds. Transfer the dough to a floured work surface and knead it by hand until the seeds are dispersed evenly and the dough forms a smooth, taut ball. Place the dough into a greased container with a 4-quart capacity. Cover the container with plastic wrap and let the dough rise until doubled in size, 45 to 60 minutes.

**3.** Adjust an oven rack to the middle position and heat the oven to 375 degrees. Spray two 9 by 5-inch loaf pans with nonstick cooking spray. Transfer the dough to a lightly floured work surface and pat it into a 12 by 9-inch rectangle. Cut the dough in half crosswise with a knife or bench scraper.

**4.** Working with one piece of dough at a time, with the short side facing you, roll the dough piece into a log, keeping the roll taut by tucking it under itself as you go. To seal the loaf, pinch the seam gently with your thumb and forefinger. Spray the loaf lightly with water or vegetable oil spray and then roll it in an even coating of oats. Place the loaf seam-side down in one of the prepared loaf pans, pressing the dough gently into the corners. Cover the loaf lightly with plastic wrap and repeat this process with the remaining piece of dough and oats.

**5.** Let the loaves rise until almost doubled in size, 30 to 40 minutes. (The dough should barely spring back when poked with your knuckle.) Bake the loaves until the internal temperature on an instant-read thermometer registers 200 degrees, 35 to 40 minutes. Remove the loaves from the pans and cool them on a wire rack before slicing, about 3 hours.

**WHERE THINGS CAN GO WRONG:** Don't confuse 7-grain hot cereal mix with boxed, cold breakfast cereals that may also be labeled "7-grain." These cold cereals will turn to complete mush when covered with hot water—ruining the bread dough.

## NOTES FROM THE TEST KITCHEN

### SAFE STORAGE
Leftover bread can be wrapped in a double layer of plastic wrap and stored at room temperature for 3 days; wrapped in an additional layer of aluminum foil the bread can be frozen for up to 1 month.

### PACKAGE DEAL
Scavenging for different grains (left) can be an invigorating challenge, but it also eats up precious time. We prefer the ease of one-stop shopping: One bag of hot cereal mix (right) has seven grains. Our favorite brands: **Arrowhead Mills** and **Bob's Red Mill**.

### LOAVES' LABOR LOST
Few of the recipes we found delivered a multigrain bread with a great flavor and a light texture. Here are two of the offenders.

**LIKE A BRICK**
Great flavor, but a laundry list of ingredients weighs the loaf down into a dense, brick-like solid.

**LIKE WHITE BREAD**
Fluffy sandwich-style texture, but so few grains it's almost like plain old white bread.

# PARKER HOUSE ROLLS
MAKES 24 ROLLS

**WHAT MAKES THIS A BEST RECIPE:** Few dinner rolls are as traditionally American as the Parker House roll, a uniquely folded, slightly sweet roll created at the Parker House Hotel in Boston in the mid-19th century. But could they be streamlined? In our opinion, there's no reason for these rolls to be complicated because truth be told, they are prepared from a pretty simple bread dough. All of the recipes we researched use all-purpose flour for a light texture, and most are fairly rich, loaded with milk, eggs, butter, and sugar. Some veered close to breakfast goods, something we wanted to avoid. Our basic working recipe came about fairly easily. After fiddling with some proportions we attained a balanced flavor—not too rich or too sweet—and a tender crumb. So, how did we speed up the slow natural rising process of a bread dough? We made our own "proofing box," a warm box that professional bakers use to incubate dough. We mimicked this technique by heating our oven to 200 degrees for a few minutes then shutting it down. The dough flourished in this warm environment, doubling in just 45 minutes, half of what it took at room temperature. Even with another 45 minutes for the second rise, we still were able to get the rolls in the oven in just about two hours. With our speedy rising under control, we took a good look at shaping our rolls, perhaps the trickiest part of the recipe. Rolls are conventionally "rounded" before shaping, or rolled tight between your palm and the work surface. This technique uses the tension of the tacky dough to tighten it into a perfect sphere. When we tried making rolls skipping the rounding step the results were dismal: misshapen rolls with a poor crumb. Suffice it to say we learned our lesson, rounding was one corner we couldn't cut. Moving on to creating the classic Parker House roll shape, we found it best to lightly flatten the dough with your palm, then roll it into an oval with a small rolling pin (or wooden spoon handle). After brushing the disk with butter, one side of the dough is folded over the other. A quick brush with more butter ensured a crispy browned top.

| 1¼ | cups whole milk |
|---|---|
| 2 | tablespoons sugar |
| 1 | envelope (about 2¼ teaspoons) instant or rapid-rise yeast |
| 1 | large egg, lightly beaten |
| 4–4¼ | cups (20 to 21½ ounces) unbleached all-purpose flour, plus extra for dusting |
| 1½ | teaspoons salt |
| 14 | tablespoons (1¾ sticks) unsalted butter, 8 tablespoons cut into 8 pieces and softened |

**1.** Adjust an oven rack to the lowest position and heat the oven to 200 degrees. Once the oven reaches 200 degrees, maintain the oven temperature for 10 minutes, then turn off the heat.

**2.** Heat the milk and sugar together in a small saucepan or in the microwave until the mixture is lukewarm (about 110 degrees). Whisk in the yeast and egg and set aside. Combine 4 cups of the flour and salt in the bowl of a standing mixer fitted with a paddle and mix at the lowest speed to blend, about 15 seconds. With the mixer running at low speed, add the liquid mixture in a steady stream. Mix until the flour is moistened, about 1 minute. With the mixer still running, slowly begin to add 8 tablespoons of the softened butter, 1 piece at a time, until it is incorporated into the dough. Increase the speed to medium and beat until the dough is thoroughly combined and scrappy, about 2 minutes longer.

**3.** Replace the paddle with a dough hook and knead the dough at medium speed until it is smooth but still sticky, about 6 minutes (adding more flour in 1-tablespoon increments, if necessary for the dough to clear the sides of the bowl). Scrape the dough out of the mixing bowl and onto a lightly floured work surface. Knead the dough by hand until it is very smooth and soft, but no longer sticky, about 1 minute. Transfer the dough to a very lightly oiled large bowl. Cover the bowl with plastic wrap and place it in the warmed oven until the dough doubles in size, about 45 minutes.

**4.** Once the dough has doubled, press it down, replace the plastic wrap, and allow the dough to rest for 5 minutes. Meanwhile, melt the remaining 6 tablespoons of butter and liberally brush 3 tablespoons of it on the bottom and sides of a large rimmed baking sheet.

**5.** Divide the relaxed dough into 2 equal pieces and, with your hands, pull and shape each piece until it is 18 inches long and about 1 ½ inches across. With a bench scraper, cut each length of dough into twelve 1½-inch pieces (each piece will weigh about 1½ ounces). Loosely cover all 24 pieces with plastic wrap. Following the photos, round and shape the rolls, then place them on the prepared baking sheet in three evenly spaced rows. Lightly brush the tops of the rolls with the remaining 3 tablespoons of melted butter and loosely cover them with plastic wrap. Set the rolls in a warm place and let them rise until almost doubled in size and touching each other, about 45 minutes.

**6.** When the rolls are almost fully risen, adjust the oven rack to the middle position and heat the oven to 375 degrees. Bake the rolls until the tops are dark golden brown, 20 to 22 minutes. Transfer the rolls to a wire rack and cool them for 10 minutes. Serve warm.

**WHERE THINGS CAN GO WRONG:** When rounding the dough and shaping the rolls, it is important to keep the remaining dough covered, otherwise it will quickly dry out and develop a skin. Also, here's a tip when rolling the dough out: It is important to keep the edges thicker than the center so that they will adhere to each other when the dough is folded and not puff open during baking. We learned the hard way, as batch after batch of poorly rolled dough unfolded in the oven to look like open clams.

**WHAT YOU CAN DO AHEAD OF TIME:** After transferring the dough to an oiled bowl in step 3, cover the bowl tightly with plastic wrap and refrigerate the dough for up to 16 hours. Before continuing with step 4, remove the dough from the refrigerator and let stand at room temperature for 30 minutes. Alternatively, after laying the shaped rolls on the prepared baking sheet in step 5, cover the baking sheet tightly with plastic wrap and refrigerate the rolls for up to 16 hours. Before baking in step 6, let the rolls sit at room temperature until they have nearly doubled in size and spring back slowly when indented with a finger, 30 to 60 minutes.

# NOTES FROM THE TEST KITCHEN

### FLOUR THE ROLLING PIN, NOT THE WORK SURFACE

Rolling the dough into symmetrical rounds takes a little practice, but you will quickly get the hang of it. A dry, unfloured work surface helps because the dough will stick a little. Also, use a thin dowel or the handle of a wooden spoon to flatten the rolls. Whatever your choice, lightly flour it or the dough will stick to it.

### PARKER HOUSE DOUGH IN A FOOD PROCESSOR

We prefer to knead this dough in a standing mixer, but a food processor can do the job. If using a food processor, heat the milk and sugar together in a small saucepan or in the microwave until the mixture is lukewarm (about 110 degrees). Whisk in the yeast and egg and set aside. Pulse 4 cups of the flour and salt in a food processor fitted with a steel blade to combine. With the processor running, add the liquid mixture in a steady stream and mix until the flour is moistened, about 30 seconds. Stop the processor and add 8 tablespoons softened butter and pulse until incorporated into the dough, about ten 1-second pulses. Let the dough rest for 2 minutes then process until a rough ball forms, about 8 seconds. Turn the dough out onto a clean counter and knead by hand to form a smooth, round ball, about 5 minutes, adding the remaining ¼ cup flour as needed to prevent the dough from sticking to the counter. Transfer to a lightly oiled bowl, cover with plastic wrap, and let rise as directed in step 3.

### SHAPING PARKER HOUSE ROLLS

**1.** With a cupped palm, roll each piece of dough into a smooth, tight ball.

**2.** After rolling each piece of dough into a smooth, tight ball, press the balls into ½-inch-thick rounds.

**3.** Roll the flattened dough into an oval using the lightly floured handle of a wooden spoon or a thin dowel, leaving the edges thicker than the middle.

**4.** Lightly brush the dough with melted butter, then fold the dough in half and gently seal the edges.

# DATE-NUT BREAD

MAKES ONE 9 BY 5-INCH LOAF

**WHAT MAKES THIS A BEST RECIPE:** Date-nut bread gets a bad rap for being overly dense with a heavy sweetness that overpowers the chewy dates and crunchy nuts. We believe that our recipe rids date-nut bread of its poor reputation (and makes it a bread you'll want to eat year-round, not just at the holidays). Rich in date and nut flavor with a moist, tender texture, this bread is a far cry from the nearly inedible brick-like loaves out there. So, how do we do it? One important key to our success was the mixing method. To achieve a compact-but-not-dense texture in our loaves, we use the quick bread mixing method: wet and dry ingredients are combined separately then quickly blended by hand before baking. We had poor luck using other techniques such as the "creaming" method (softened butter and sugar are whipped together with an electric mixer before adding the other ingredients), which produced breads that were too airy and cake-like. All-purpose flour gave the bread just the right crumb (whole wheat flour made it much too dense) while melted butter makes our recipe both easy and rich (oil created a bland, greasy crumb). To soften the dates and give them a more supple texture in the finished bread we soaked them in hot water and baking soda (which helped break down their fibers). To counteract the sweetness of the dates we used buttermilk which lent the bread a nice tanginess and we also used some of the liquid leftover from softening the dates which helped boost the overall date flavor. Finally, toasting the nuts before adding them to the batter intensifies their flavor and gives them a crisp texture that contrasts well with the soft bites of date and bread.

2 cups (10 ounces) unbleached all-purpose flour, plus extra for dusting

1 cup boiling water

1 teaspoon baking soda

2 cups pitted whole dates, chopped coarse

1 cup pecans or walnuts, chopped coarse

⅔ cup buttermilk

¾ cup packed (5¼ ounces) dark brown sugar

6 tablespoons (¾ stick) unsalted butter, melted and cooled

1 large egg

1 teaspoon baking powder

¼ teaspoon salt

**1.** Adjust an oven rack to the middle position and heat the oven to 350 degrees. Grease a 9 by 5-inch loaf pan, and dust it with flour, tapping out any excess.

**2.** Stir together the water, baking soda, and dates in a medium bowl. Cover and set aside until the dates have softened and the water is lukewarm, about 30 minutes.

**3.** Meanwhile, spread the nuts on a rimmed baking sheet and toast them in the oven until fragrant, 5 to 10 minutes. Set them aside.

**4.** Stir the buttermilk and sugar together in a medium bowl. Add the melted butter and egg, and stir until combined. Stir in the date mixture until combined. In another medium bowl, whisk together the flour, baking powder, salt, and nuts. Stir the buttermilk mixture into the flour mixture with a rubber spatula until just moistened. Scrape the batter into the prepared pan and smooth the surface with a rubber spatula.

**5.** Bake until the loaf is dark brown and a skewer inserted in the center comes out clean, 55 to 60 minutes, rotating the pan halfway through baking. Cool the loaf in the pan for 10 minutes, then transfer it to a wire rack and cool at least 1 hour before serving.

**WHAT YOU CAN DO AHEAD OF TIME:** The loaf can be wrapped in plastic wrap and stored at room temperature for up to 3 days.

## NOTES FROM THE TEST KITCHEN

### CHOPPING DRIED FRUIT
Dried fruit, especially dates, very often sticks to the knife when you try to chop it. To avoid this problem, coat the blade with a thin film of nonstick cooking spray just before you begin chopping. The fruit slides right off the slick blade. Also, as you chop the dates, watch for and remove the pits and stems, which seem to adhere persistently even to pitted dates.

# COFFEECAKE MUFFINS
MAKES 12 MUFFINS

**WHAT MAKES THIS A BEST RECIPE:** This recipe was inspired by coffeecake muffins one of our test cooks came across at a local bake sale. But while these muffins looked the part, veined with cinnamon and topped with streusel, the flavor and texture didn't come close to that of real coffeecake. We wondered what it would take to make great coffeecake in miniature. After testing many coffeecake muffin recipes in our test kitchen, all of which were chewy and disappointing, we simply made our favorite coffeecake recipe and divided the batter among muffin cups, topping each with a portion of streusel. This didn't work as well as we thought it would: The batter didn't rise properly, and the muffins were very crumbly. Our observation? Because of their shape, muffins require a stiffer batter than cakes. Switching to a basic muffin recipe, we made batch after batch in which we altered various ingredients to reach a richer, cakier consistency. Butter was the answer; the more we added, the richer the flavor and the more cake-like the consistency. A full stick of butter yielded the texture we were after, and a judicious amount of sour cream (¾ cup)—an ingredient that typically gives coffeecake its full flavor—provided optimal taste and texture. With the basics of our muffins in the basket, we focused on other aspects of the recipe like streamlining the mixing method and incorporating the streusel. Because we were working with muffin batter (a quick bread essentially) we used the quick bread mixing method of combining the wet and dry ingredients separately before blending them together. This is typically done by hand, but as we were chopping the nuts for the streusel in the food processor, we thought we could save dirtying at least one bowl by finishing the batter in the food processor. This worked like a charm, and all we had left to do was decide how to finish our batter with the streusel. We settled on topping our muffins with streusel in addition to stirring a portion of the streusel mixture into the prepared batter.

Topped with streusel and rich but sturdy, these muffins share the best of both coffeecake and muffin.

½ cup pecans

¼ cup packed (1¾ ounces) dark brown sugar

1 teaspoon ground cinnamon

2 cups (10 ounces) unbleached all-purpose flour

1 cup (7 ounces) granulated sugar

1 teaspoon salt

8 tablespoons (1 stick) unsalted butter, cut into ½-inch pieces and softened

1½ teaspoons baking powder

½ teaspoon baking soda

¾ cup sour cream

1 large egg

1 teaspoon vanilla extract

**1.** Adjust an oven rack to the middle position and heat the oven to 350 degrees. Generously coat a 12-cup muffin tin with vegetable oil spray.

**2.** Process the nuts, brown sugar, and cinnamon in a food processor until the nuts are the size of sesame seeds, about ten 1-second pulses. Transfer the mixture to a medium bowl.

**3.** Return the bowl and metal blade to the food processor, add the flour, granulated sugar, and salt and process until combined, about five 1-second pulses. Sprinkle the butter evenly over the flour mixture and process until the butter is oat-sized, about eight 1-second pulses. Remove 1 cup of the flour-butter mixture and, using a fork, stir it into the reserved brown sugar mixture until combined to make streusel. Set aside ¾ cup of the streusel for the muffin batter and the remaining portion for topping the muffins.

**4.** Add the baking powder and baking soda to the flour mixture in the food processor bowl and process until combined, about five 1-second pulses. Whisk together the sour cream, egg, and vanilla. Add it to the flour mixture. Process until the batter is just moistened, about five 1-second pulses. Add the reserved ¾ cup streusel to the flour mixture and process until the streusel is just distributed throughout the batter, about five 1-second pulses.

**5.** Use a large ice-cream scoop or measuring cup to divide the batter evenly among the prepared muffins cups. Sprinkle with the remaining streusel, pressing lightly so that it sinks slightly into the batter. Bake until a toothpick inserted into the center of a muffin comes out with a few crumbs attached, about 18 minutes. Let the muffins cool in the pan on a wire rack for 2 minutes, then run a knife around each one to loosen. Gently transfer the muffins to a wire rack, let cool for 5 minutes, and serve warm.

**WHERE THINGS CAN GO WRONG:** Be careful not to overprocess the batter in step 4, or you run the risk of muffins with a tough, chewy texture.

## NOTES FROM THE TEST KITCHEN

### THE ICING ON THE COFFEECAKE
These muffins are great eaten as is, warm from the oven. But when you crave a little extra sweetness, here's a quick way to make an easy icing to drizzle over them. Follow the recipe through step 5, placing a sheet of parchment paper beneath the wire rack as the muffins cool. Whisk 1 cup confectioners' sugar and 2 tablespoons water in a medium bowl until smooth. Spoon 2 teaspoons of the icing over each muffin, letting it run down the sides.

### NO FOOD PROCESSOR, NO PROBLEM
If you don't have a food processor, first chop the nuts with a knife. Proceed with the recipe, mixing the ingredients in a large bowl with a wooden spoon or spatula, but use a wire whisk to work the butter into the dry ingredients in step 3.

# MORNING GLORY MUFFINS

## MAKES 12 MUFFINS

**WHAT MAKES THIS A BEST RECIPE:** Morning Glory Muffins are meant to be loaded with the healthy, energy-inducing ingredients that, like a bowl of cereal and fruit, will get your day off to a great start. The problem is that most of these "healthy" muffins are dark, overly moist, and not worth eating. These sweet, moist muffins, however, are chock full of fruit (coconut, raisins, and pineapple), nuts, and shredded carrot but still taste great and have a true muffin-like texture. Generally, a muffin recipe "loaded" with add-ins means it's loaded with problems. Adding other ingredients to a basic muffin batter can easily throw off the whole balance—especially if the add-ins contain a lot of moisture. For example, we found that if we didn't remove the excess moisture from canned pineapple, we wound up with gummy muffins. And grated carrot is tricky too. Anything beyond 2 cups destroyed the lift and made the muffins too dense. And while these muffins baked up beautifully tender and moist without the addition of nuts, a handful was certainly a welcome addition for textural contrast. But we found that just throwing them in raw didn't do much. A quick spell in the oven gave the nuts the crunch they needed, as well as making their flavor more pronounced in the chorus of other ingredients.

½ cup walnuts or pecans

2¼ cups (11¼ ounces) unbleached all-purpose flour

2 teaspoons baking soda

1 teaspoon ground cinnamon

½ teaspoon salt

1¼ cups (8¾ ounces) sugar

3 large eggs

8 tablespoons (1 stick) unsalted butter, melted and cooled

1 teaspoon vanilla extract

4 carrots, peeled and grated (2 cups)

1 (8-ounce) can crushed pineapple, drained and pressed dry with paper towels

½ cup sweetened shredded coconut

½ cup raisins

**1.** Adjust an oven rack to the middle position and heat the oven to 375 degrees. Generously coat a 12-cup muffin tin with vegetable oil spray.

**2.** Meanwhile, spread the nuts on a rimmed baking sheet and toast them in the oven until fragrant, about 5 minutes. When they're cool enough to handle, coarsely chop them and set aside.

**3.** Whisk the flour, baking soda, cinnamon, and salt together in a large bowl. In a separate bowl, whisk the sugar, eggs, melted butter, and vanilla until smooth. Gently fold the egg mixture into the flour mixture with a rubber spatula until just combined. Fold the carrots, pineapple, coconut, raisins, and toasted nuts into the batter.

**4.** Use a large ice-cream scoop or measuring cup to divide the batter evenly among the prepared muffin cups. Bake until golden and a toothpick inserted into the center of a muffin comes out with just a few crumbs attached, 25 to 30 minutes.

**5.** Let the muffins cool in the pan on a wire rack for 5 minutes, then run a knife around each one to loosen. Flip the muffins out onto the wire rack. Let them cool for 10 minutes before serving.

## NOTES FROM THE TEST KITCHEN

### ARE HIGH-PRICED TINS WORTH THE MONEY?

With price tags ranging from $5 to a whopping $26, we wondered if there was a good reason for shelling out the big bucks for a simple muffin tin. It turns out that there are differences in the way the tins performed. The best tins browned the muffins evenly; the worst tins browned the muffins on top, but left them pale and underbaked on the bottom. Darker coated metals, which absorb heat, do the best job of browning baked goods. Heavy-duty (and higher-priced) models did not produce muffins that were any better than those baked in the least expensive model. The supermarket staple Baker's Secret ($5.69) performed well and finished in a respectable second place. But **Wilton Ultra-Bake** ($9.99) was the clear winner, in part because of its generous 2-inch lip.

# LIGHT CINNAMON ROLLS
## WITH BUTTERMILK ICING
MAKES 9 ROLLS

**WHAT MAKES THIS A BEST RECIPE:** Truthfully, we find it nearly impossible to pass up good cinnamon rolls. Their hypnotic scent and creamy-sweet glaze make them much too hard to resist. But with 11 grams of fat and 380 calories per roll, these were certainly not an everyday breakfast treat. From the beginning we decided against a yeast-raised cinnamon roll recipe: We didn't want to spend our time waiting for dough to rise. Instead we wanted the ease and convenience of a roll that relied on baking powder and baking soda for lift. Throwing this dough together was a snap and it was ready to shape and cut right away (no proofing necessary). After a quick knead (just 30 seconds), the dough is patted out into a rectangle, topped with the sugar filling, rolled up, sliced, and baked. Sure it was easy enough make these rolls, but they were still loaded with fat and calories. So how did we transform them? For starters, we cut nearly a stick of butter from the recipe. Close analysis of traditional quick bread cinnamon roll recipes revealed that the dough itself didn't really require that much butter—only 2 tablespoons were necessary. But, we observed that a glut of butter is typically used to grease the pan, bind the sugary filling, and brush the dough. We figured that some of this butter might be unnecessary and our hunch was right. For instance, a thin coating of vegetable oil spray was a good low-calorie substitute for the butter used to grease the pan. And tasters didn't miss the butter when we omitted it from the traditional brown sugar filling. In the end though, we did wind up using 1 extra tablespoon (in addition to the 2 tablespoons already in the dough) to brush the dough before adding the sugar filling. This small amount of butter flavored the interior of the rolls, and kept them moist as well. Finally, brushing the tops of the rolls with butter before baking was a waste of fat and calories—the butter's richness was undetectable when we topped the rolls with our light and creamy icing. (Light cream cheese mixed with a little confectioners' sugar and buttermilk is our secret for the icing.) Heavy cream—typically found in most traditional

doughs—was another sinful ingredient to get the boot. Surprisingly, we found that a hefty dose of buttermilk made a great substitute for the cream, and it gave our rolls a tender, moist crumb without adding a ton of fat and calories. Tasters also liked the tanginess that it added to the dough—a nice counterpoint to the sweetness of the filling and icing. Our lowfat cinnamon rolls have all of the appeal of their seductive full-fat cousins, and because they have only 4.5 grams of fat and 280 calories per roll, we have no qualms reaching for them. One final note: These rolls are best eaten as soon as they are iced, but they hold up well at room temperature for up to 2 hours.

### FILLING
- ⅓ cup packed (2⅓ ounces) dark brown sugar
- ⅓ cup (2⅓ ounces) granulated sugar
- 2 teaspoons ground cinnamon
- ⅛ teaspoon ground cloves
- ⅛ teaspoon salt

### DOUGH
- 2½ cups (12½ ounces) unbleached all-purpose flour, plus extra for dusting
- 2 tablespoons granulated sugar
- 1¼ teaspoons baking powder
- ½ teaspoon baking soda
- ½ teaspoon salt
- 1¼ cups buttermilk
- 3 tablespoons unsalted butter, melted and cooled

### ICING
- 2 tablespoons light cream cheese, at room temperature
- 2 tablespoons buttermilk
- ¾ cup (3 ounces) confectioners' sugar

**1.** Adjust an oven rack to the upper-middle position and heat the oven to 425 degrees. Spray an 8-inch-square baking pan and a wire rack with vegetable oil spray, and set aside.

**2. FOR THE FILLING:** Mix all the ingredients together and set aside.

**3. FOR THE DOUGH:** Whisk the flour, granulated sugar, baking powder, baking soda, and salt together in a large bowl. In a separate bowl, whisk the buttermilk and 2 tablespoons of the melted butter together. Stir the buttermilk mixture into the flour mixture with a wooden spoon until the liquid is absorbed (the dough will look very shaggy),

There is no butter in the filling for our Light Cinnamon Rolls, yet they still taste rich (and are irresistible).

about 30 seconds. Transfer the dough to a floured work surface and knead until just smooth and no longer shaggy, about 30 seconds.

**4.** Following the photos, pat the dough with your hands into a 12 by 9-inch rectangle. Brush the dough with the remaining tablespoon of melted butter. Sprinkle evenly with the filling, leaving a ½-inch border of plain dough around the edges. Press the filling firmly into the dough. Using a bench scraper or metal spatula, loosen the dough from the work surface. Starting at the long side, roll the dough, pressing lightly, to form a tight log. Pinch the seam to seal. Roll the log seam-side down and cut it evenly into 9 pieces with dental floss. With your hand, slightly flatten each piece of dough to seal the open edges and keep the filling in place.

**5.** Arrange the rolls in the prepared baking pan (3 rows of 3 rolls). Cover the pan with foil and bake for about 12 minutes. Remove the foil and bake until the edges of the rolls are golden brown, 12 to 14 minutes longer.

**6.** Use an offset metal spatula to loosen the rolls from the pan. Wearing oven mitts, place a large plate over the pan and invert the rolls onto the plate. Place the greased wire rack over the plate and flip the rolls onto the rack. Let the rolls cool for 5 minutes before icing.

**7.** TO ICE THE ROLLS: While the rolls are cooling, line a rimmed baking sheet with parchment paper (for easy cleanup). Set the rack of cooling rolls over the baking sheet. Whisk the cream cheese and buttermilk together in a large nonreactive bowl until thick and smooth (the mixture will look like cottage cheese at first). Sift the confectioners'

sugar over the mixture, and then whisk until a smooth icing forms, about 30 seconds. Spoon the icing evenly over the rolls and serve.

**WHERE THINGS CAN GO WRONG:** Make sure that you knead the dough just 30 seconds or the rolls will be tough. Also, when shaping the rolls, don't be afraid to use a little extra flour on the work surface if the dough seems a little sticky.

## NOTES FROM THE TEST KITCHEN

### WHY DENTAL FLOSS?
When it comes to slicing our rolls before baking them, we don't reach for a knife, we reach for dental floss. Eccentric as it seems, using dental floss (make sure it's unflavored) lets you smoothly cut through soft dough without squeezing the filling out of place (which happens when using a knife).

### MAKING CINNAMON ROLLS

**1.** Pat the dough into a 12 by 9-inch rectangle and brush it with melted butter. Sprinkle the filling evenly over the dough, leaving a ½-inch border. Press the filling firmly into the dough.

**2.** Loosen the dough from the work surface with a bench scraper, and starting at a long side, roll the dough, pressing lightly, to form a tight log. Pinch the seam to seal.

**3.** Roll the log seam-side down and, using dental floss, cut the formed roll into 3 even segments. Then cut each segment into 3 rolls, for a total of 9.

**4.** With your hand, slightly flatten each piece of dough to seal the open edges and keep the filling in place.

# CHALLAH

MAKES 1 LARGE LOAF

**WHAT MAKES THIS A BEST RECIPE:** Challah, the saffron-hued, braided bread traditionally made for most Jewish holidays, is one of those breads that is best baked at home. The mass-produced challah available at local grocery stores and bakeries is typically dry and disappointingly bland. Good challah is rich with eggs and lightly sweetened, with a dark, shiny crust and a firm but light and tender texture. The ingredients for challah are pretty standard bread-making fare: flour, yeast, water or milk, eggs, sugar, salt, and butter or oil. As far as what flour to use, we found that standard all-purpose flour works fine (protein-rich bread flour made our loaves too tough). And concerning the debate over whether to use milk or water in the dough, our tasting panel preferred loaves made with water. Milk-based loaves baked up too dense and heavy, as did loaves made with too many eggs. And while eggs are the heart and soul of good challah (contributing flavor, tenderness, and its trademark yellow tinge), that does not mean it should be super eggy (like a rich brioche). After some experimentation we found that 2 whole eggs with an additional yolk was optimal. (What do we do with the extra egg white? We'll get to that later.) For fat we liked the flavor and texture that butter added (oil didn't do much for us), and found that 4 tablespoons lent the perfect amount of richness.

Our biggest challenge turned out to be the braiding. The recipes that we researched all had different braiding instructions. A real mess of confusion, these recipes came with complicated diagrams of multiple strands of interwoven dough (much like a macramé project). After numerous misshapen challahs, we came up with a simple solution. We divided the dough into two pieces, one half the size of the other, and made two simple three-stranded braids. Then we glued the smaller braid to the top of the large one using an egg wash made with the leftover egg white. After brushing the entire loaf with more egg wash (for a glossy and dark finished exterior) and baking it, the bread emerged from the oven looking like authentic challah with the illusion of complicated knotwork.

3–3¼  cups (15 to 16¼ ounces) unbleached all-purpose flour, plus extra for dusting

¼  cup (1¾ ounces) sugar

1  envelope (about 2¼ teaspoons) instant or rapid-rise yeast

1¼  teaspoons salt

2  large eggs plus 1 large egg yolk

4  tablespoons (½ stick) unsalted butter, melted

½  cup plus 1 tablespoon warm water (about 110 degrees)

1  large egg white (for the egg wash)

1  teaspoon poppy or sesame seeds (optional)

**1.** Whisk together 3 cups of the flour, sugar, yeast, and salt in a medium bowl. Set it aside. Mix together the 2 eggs, yolk, melted butter, and ½ cup warm water in the bowl of a standing mixer fitted with a dough hook. Add the flour mixture to the wet mixture and knead at low speed until a dough ball forms, about 5 minutes, adding the remaining ¼ cup flour, 1 tablespoon at a time, as needed to prevent the dough from sticking. Whisk the egg white with the remaining 1 tablespoon warm water in a small bowl, cover with plastic wrap, and refrigerate.

**2.** Transfer the dough to a lightly oiled large bowl, turning the dough over to coat it with oil. Cover the bowl with plastic wrap and let the dough rise in a warm place until doubled in size, 1½ to 2 hours. Gently press the dough to deflate it, cover it with plastic wrap, and let it rise until doubled in size again, 40 to 60 minutes.

**3.** Lightly grease (or line with parchment) a large baking sheet and set it aside. Transfer the dough to a lightly floured work surface. Divide the dough into 2 pieces, one roughly half the size of the other. (The small piece will weigh about 9 ounces, the larger piece about 18 ounces.) Divide the large piece into 3 equal pieces. Roll each piece of dough into a 16-inch-long rope, about 1 inch in diameter. Following the photos, line up the ropes of dough side by side and pinch the top ends together. Take the dough rope on the left and lay it over the center rope. Take the dough rope on the right and lay it over the center rope. Repeat this process until the ropes of dough are entirely braided, then pinch the bottom ends together. Place the braid on the prepared baking sheet. Divide the smaller piece of the dough into 3 equal pieces. Roll each piece into a 16-inch-long rope, about ½ inch in diameter. Braid them together, pinching the bottom ends to seal. Brush some of the egg wash on top of the large loaf and following the photo, place the small braid on top of the larger braid. Then tuck both ends under the braid. Loosely

drape the loaf with plastic wrap and let it rise in a warm place until the loaf becomes puffy and increases in size by one-third, 30 to 45 minutes.

**4.** Adjust an oven rack to the lower-middle position and heat the oven to 375 degrees. Brush the loaf with the remaining egg wash and sprinkle it with poppy or sesame seeds, if using. Bake until the loaf is golden brown and an instant-read thermometer inserted into the side of the loaf reads 190 degrees, 30 to 40 minutes. Place the baking sheet on a wire rack. Cool the loaf completely before slicing.

**WHAT YOU CAN DO AHEAD OF TIME:** After the dough has been braided and the loaf formed in step 3, it can be covered with plastic wrap and refrigerated for up to 16 hours. Before baking in step 4, let the loaf sit at room temperature until it has nearly doubled in size and springs back slowly when indented with a finger, 30 to 60 minutes. Bake and cool as directed in step 4.

## NOTES FROM THE TEST KITCHEN

### BRAIDING CHALLAH

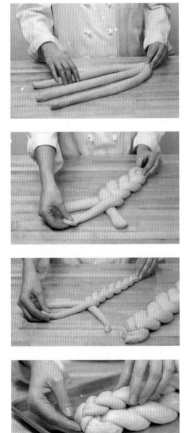

**1.** Divide the large piece of dough into 3 ropes, each about 16 inches long and 1 inch thick. Line the three ropes up side by side and pinch the top ends together to seal.

**2.** Take the dough rope on the left and lay it over the center rope. Take the dough rope on the right and lay it over the center rope. Repeat until the dough is entirely braided.

**3.** Divide the smaller piece of dough into 3 ropes, each about 16 inches long and ½ inch thick. Braid as directed above.

**4.** Brush the larger braid with some of the egg wash, and secure the smaller braid on top. Tuck both ends under the braid.

# ORANGE DROP DOUGHNUTS
MAKES 24 TO 30 DOUGHNUTS

**WHAT MAKES THIS A BEST RECIPE:** We think that everyone loves hot, homemade doughnuts, but in this day and age, most people are daunted by the effort it takes to make them. And we seem to have lost sight of the drop doughnuts popular a generation ago. These old-fashioned "drop and fry" doughnuts couldn't be easier, but making them lighter and rich with orange flavor was clearly our challenge. This classic recipe was popularized by Betty Crocker in the late 1940s and 1950s. Dropping spoonfuls of cake-style doughnut batter—leavened with quick-acting baking powder—into hot oil yields fresh doughnuts in minutes. There's no waiting for the doughnuts to proof, as there is with yeast-raised doughnuts (which also require fussy rolling or stamping). We started our initial testing by trying some of the classic recipes we researched—which, in truth, were pretty good, but a bit dense and light on orange flavor. Looking to the flour quantity first, we found that some recipes use nearly 3 cups of flour for 24 doughnuts. These heavy (yet tasty) lead balloons fell straight to the bottom of tasters' bellies. Two cups of flour—paired with 2 teaspoons of baking powder—worked much better. And two eggs and a little melted butter made our doughnuts properly rich. As for liquid ingredients, some recipes call for milk as well as orange juice. But diluting the orange flavor just seemed wrong, so we added only juice. For even more orange flavor though, we stirred a whopping tablespoon of grated orange zest into the batter—far more than the teaspoon or so found in older recipes. Finally, we took a cue from a few recipes and rolled the hot doughnuts in a batch of homemade orange-flavored sugar. With three applications of orange flavor (and the zest and juice from three oranges), there was no doubt that our simple recipe had great orange presence. Plus you'll love the powerful citrus aroma that drifts through your kitchen as you fry them.

#### ORANGE-SUGAR COATING
½ cup (3½ ounces) sugar

1 teaspoon grated orange zest

DOUGHNUTS

About 2 quarts vegetable oil

2 cups (10 ounces) unbleached all-purpose flour

2 teaspoons baking powder

¼ teaspoon salt

2 large eggs

½ cup (3½ ounces) sugar

1 tablespoon grated orange zest

½ cup orange juice

2 tablespoons unsalted butter, melted

**1.** FOR THE COATING: Pulse the sugar and zest in a food processor until blended, about 5 pulses. Transfer the mixture to a medium bowl. (If making by hand, toss the zest and sugar in a medium bowl using a fork until evenly blended.)

**2.** FOR THE DOUGHNUTS: Heat 3 inches of vegetable oil in a 4-quart saucepan until the temperature reaches 350 degrees. Whisk the flour, baking powder, and salt together in a medium bowl. Whisk the eggs, sugar, and zest together in a large bowl. Whisk in the orange juice, then the melted butter, until well combined. Stir in the flour mixture until evenly moistened.

**3.** Using two dinner teaspoons, carefully drop heaping spoonfuls of the batter into the hot oil. (You should be able to fit about 6 spoonfuls in the pan at one time. Do not overcrowd.) Fry, maintaining the oil temperature between 325 and 350 degrees, until the doughnuts are crisp and deeply browned on all sides, 3 to 6 minutes. Using a slotted spoon, transfer the doughnuts to a plate lined with paper towels. Drain for 5 minutes. Add the doughnuts to the bowl of orange sugar, toss until well coated, and then transfer them to a serving plate. Repeat this process with the remaining batter, regulating the oil temperature as necessary. The doughnuts are best served warm.

**WHERE THINGS CAN GO WRONG:** Frying your doughnuts in oil heated to the exact temperature is key here. If the oil is too cool, the doughnuts turn out greasy and pale. And if it is too hot, the doughnut exterior burns before the interior even has a chance to cook through. For perfectly cooked doughnuts, we recommend using a candy thermometer (or instant-read thermometer that registers high temperatures) to monitor and maintain the correct temperature of the oil.

## NOTES FROM THE TEST KITCHEN

### HOW TO MAKE ORANGE DROP DOUGHNUTS

**1.** To avoid splashes of oil, use two dinner teaspoons to "drop" the doughnut batter carefully into the oil.

**2.** When the doughnuts are deep brown and float to the top of the oil, use a slotted spoon to transfer them to a plate lined with paper towels.

**3.** Let the doughnuts drain for 5 minutes, then transfer them to the orange sugar and toss until coated.

### NO THERMOMETER, NO PROBLEM

Properly heated oil (usually between 325 and 375 degrees) ensures that deep-fried food will become crisp and browned. Oil that's too cool will yield pale, greasy food. A good candy thermometer or instant-read thermometer that registers high temperatures is a great tool, but with a little testing you can tell if the oil is ready for frying.

When you think the oil might be ready, drop a small piece of bread (with the crust removed) or a small spoonful of batter into the hot oil. If the bread or batter sizzles and fine bubbles appear, the oil is just right and you can add your first batch of food. If there's no action in the pan and your bread or batter just sits there, the oil isn't hot enough. Wait a minute or two, and try again with more bread or more batter.

If the oil bubbles furiously or the bread or batter colors almost instantly, the oil is much too hot. Take the pan off the heat and wait a few minutes before adding the first batch of food.

**TOO COOL**
No bubbles

**JUST RIGHT**
Some bubbles

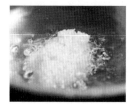

**TOO HOT**
Lots of bubbles

For a double dose of flavor, the cheese is baked into the muffins and sprinkled on top.

# SAVORY CHEESE MUFFINS

### MAKES 12 MUFFINS

**WHAT MAKES THIS A BEST RECIPE:** Muffins aren't just for breakfast. In fact, we think there is nothing better than a savory muffin to accompany stew, chili, or a salad for lunch. Here we found an easy way to turn sweet breakfast muffins into a quick and savory alternative to dinner rolls or biscuits. We simply replace the sugar with cheese, spices, and scallions—no rising time or shaping required. And these muffins are simple to throw together in a hurry, just combine the flour, other dry ingredients, cheese, and scallions in one bowl, whisk the milk, melted butter, sour cream, and egg together in a second bowl, and then gently stir the wet and dry ingredients together. The batter is ready in the time it takes to preheat the oven. And, although you can add almost any kind of cheese, our tasting panel liked the combination of pungent blue cheese tempered with nutty Parmesan. Sprinkling the grated Parmesan over the batter after it's portioned into the muffin tin ensures that the muffin tops will be especially cheesy, browned, and crisp. For a big cheese presence, shred the Parmesan on the large holes of a box grater. (Or, if you prefer, use an equal amount of shredded cheddar in place of the blue cheese.) One caution: These muffins taste best when served warm.

|       |                                                |
|-------|------------------------------------------------|
| 3     | cups (15 ounces) unbleached all-purpose flour  |
| 1     | tablespoon baking powder                       |
| 1     | teaspoon salt                                  |
| ¼     | teaspoon cayenne pepper                         |
| ⅛     | teaspoon pepper                                |
| 4     | ounces blue cheese, crumbled (about 1 cup)     |
| 2     | scallions, chopped                             |
| 1¼    | cups whole milk                                |
| 3     | tablespoons unsalted butter, melted            |
| 1     | large egg, beaten                              |
| ¾     | cup sour cream                                 |
| 1     | ounce Parmesan cheese, shredded (about ½ cup)  |

**1.** Adjust an oven rack to the middle position and heat the oven to 350 degrees. Generously coat a 12-cup muffin tin with vegetable oil spray.

**2.** Whisk the flour, baking powder, salt, cayenne, and pepper together in a large bowl. Mix in the blue cheese and scallions, breaking up any clumps, until the cheese is coated with flour. Whisk the milk, butter, egg, and sour cream together in a medium bowl. Gently fold the wet ingredients into the dry ingredients with a rubber spatula until just combined. Use a large ice-cream scoop or measuring cup to divide the batter evenly among the prepared muffin cups. Sprinkle the Parmesan over the batter in each cup.

**3.** Bake until light golden brown and a toothpick inserted into the center of a muffin comes out with a few crumbs attached, 25 to 30 minutes.

**4.** Let the muffins cool in the pan on a wire rack for 5 minutes, then run a knife around each one to loosen. Flip the muffins out onto a wire rack and let them cool for 10 minutes. Serve warm.

## NOTES FROM THE TEST KITCHEN

### TESTING BAKING POWDER FOR FRESHNESS

Baking powder will lose its leavening ability with time. We suggest writing the date the can was opened on a piece of tape affixed to the can. After 6 months, the baking powder should be tested to see if it's still good. Mix 2 teaspoons of baking powder with 1 cup of hot tap water. If there's an immediate reaction of fizzing and foaming, the baking powder is fine. If the reaction is delayed or weak, throw the baking powder away and buy a fresh can. A can of baking powder that has been opened for a year or more should be replaced.

# PEPPERONI PAN PIZZA

MAKES TWO 9-INCH PIZZAS, SERVING 4 TO 6

**WHAT MAKES THIS A BEST RECIPE:** This recipe was created in response to a reader's request for a pan pizza recipe that rivaled Pizza Hut's. It was an unusual request, but we were up for the challenge. Great pan pizza—named for the pan in which the dough is risen and cooked—has an irresistible crust that's crispy on the bottom and soft and chewy in the middle. The generous amount of oil first poured into the pan creates the crisp bottom; the soft interior is harder to figure out.

Pan pizza isn't something you find in most cookbooks, so we turned to the Internet. After a few clicks, we found a Web site that claimed to reveal the secret Pizza Hut formula. We doubted the recipe was authentic, but we decided to try it because it included a novel ingredient: powdered milk.

Classic pizza dough contains flour, yeast, water, and olive oil, but never milk. We knew, though, that many tender yeast breads are made with milk. Could powdered milk be the key to soft pizza dough?

This dough was tender, with just the right chew. Because most cooks don't have powdered milk on hand, we wondered if fresh milk would work. It did. In fact, the texture of the crust was even better. Whole milk was fine, but dough made with skim milk rose better and baked up especially soft and light.

All-purpose flour, which yields softer baked goods than bread flour, was the right choice, as was a healthy dose of olive oil (2 tablespoons). Although sugar is not traditional in pizza, tasters thought a little (just 2 teaspoons) made the dough taste better, and we knew that sugar gives yeast a nice jump start. To deliver pan pizzas to the table in record time, we used a warm, turned-off oven to help the dough rise faster. Thirty minutes later, we had dough that was ready to shape.

After producing some less-than-stellar crusts, we discovered it was important not to overwork the dough. Beating the dough into submission with a rolling pin caused it to

tear or snap back like a rubber band. In the end, we used the following hybrid method: We used a rolling pin for the first (and easy) part of the process and then stretched the dough over the tops of our knuckles to finish the job—gently.

With the dough nice and tender, it was time to fine-tune the crispness factor. Three tablespoons of oil in each pan delivered maximum crispness without greasiness. After trying various oven temperatures, we settled on 400 degrees as the best compromise between a crisp bottom and scorched toppings. Everything was now perfect—except for the grease on top of the pies. When just plopped onto the pizza and baked, the pepperoni floated in pools of orange grease. Our first thought was to fry it, as with bacon. But this made the pepperoni too crisp and turned it an ugly shade of brown. So we tried the microwave. Layered between paper towels, the pepperoni slices emerged pliable and brightly colored, while the paper towels were soaked with orange fat—the microwave had done its job. From beginning to end, this pizza can be made in 90 minutes. Not as quick as delivery, but less greasy and with the same great crust.

## DOUGH
- ½ cup olive oil
- ¾ cup plus 2 tablespoons skim milk, warmed to 110 degrees
- 2 teaspoons sugar
- 2⅓ cups (11⅔ ounces) unbleached all-purpose flour, plus extra for dusting
- 1 envelope (about 2¼ teaspoons) instant or rapid-rise yeast
- ½ teaspoon salt

## SAUCE
- 1½ teaspoons olive oil
- 1 garlic clove, minced
- 1 (14.5-ounce) can crushed tomatoes
  Salt and pepper

## TOPPING
- 1 (3.5-ounce) package sliced pepperoni
- 12 ounces part-skim mozzarella cheese, shredded (about 3 cups)

**1. FOR THE DOUGH:** Adjust an oven rack to the lowest position and heat the oven to 200 degrees. When the oven

reaches 200 degrees, turn it off. Lightly grease a large bowl with cooking spray. Coat two 9-inch cake pans with 3 tablespoons oil each.

**2.** Mix the milk, sugar, and the remaining 2 tablespoons oil together in a liquid measuring cup. Mix the flour, yeast, and salt in a standing mixer fitted with a dough hook. Turn the machine to low and slowly add the milk mixture. After the dough comes together, increase the speed to medium-low and mix until the dough is shiny and smooth, about 5 minutes. Turn the dough onto a lightly floured work surface, gently shape it into a ball, and place it in the greased bowl. Cover the dough with plastic wrap and place it in the warm oven until doubled in size, about 30 minutes.

**3. FOR THE SAUCE:** Meanwhile, cook the oil and garlic in a medium saucepan over low heat until fragrant, about 2 minutes. Add the tomatoes, increase the heat to medium, and cook until slightly thickened, 10 to 15 minutes. Season with salt and pepper. Set aside.

**4. TO SHAPE AND TOP THE DOUGH:** Transfer the dough to a lightly floured work surface, divide the dough in half, and lightly roll each half into a ball. Following the photos and working with 1 dough ball at a time, roll and shape the dough into a 9 ½-inch round and press it into an oiled pan. Cover with plastic wrap and set in a warm spot (not in the oven) until puffy and slightly risen, about 20 minutes. Meanwhile, heat the oven to 400 degrees.

**5.** While the dough is rising, place half of the pepperoni slices in a single layer on a large, microwave-safe plate lined with 2 paper towels. Cover with 2 more paper towels and microwave on high for 30 seconds. Discard the paper towels and set the pepperoni aside. Repeat this process with the remaining pepperoni.

**6.** Remove the plastic wrap from the dough. Ladle ⅔ cup sauce on each dough round, leaving a ½ inch border around the edges. Sprinkle each round with 1½ cups cheese and top with the pepperoni. Bake the pizzas until the cheese is melted and the pepperoni is browning around the edges, about 20 minutes. Remove the pizzas from the oven and let them rest in the pans for 1 minute. Using a spatula, transfer the pizzas to a cutting board, cut each into 8 wedges, and serve.

## NOTES FROM THE TEST KITCHEN

### THE AMAZING SHRINKING PEPPERONI
Microwaving pepperoni eliminates the possibility that it will turn your pizza into a grease trap. You can see just how much fat is rendered in only 30 seconds by comparing the size of the slices before and after microwaving.

**BEFORE**          **AFTER**

### HOW TO MAKE PAN PIZZA

**1.** Roll the dough outward from the center in all directions to form a 7-inch circle.

**2.** With the dough draped over your knuckles, gently stretch it, using the weight of the dough to make a 9½-inch circle that is slightly thinner at the center.

**3.** Place the dough in the oiled cake pan and gently push it to the edge, taking care not to let too much oil spill over the top.

### PIZZA DOUGH WITHOUT A STANDING MIXER
In step 2, mix the flour, yeast, and salt together in a large bowl. Make a well in the flour, then pour the milk mixture into the well. Using a wooden spoon, stir until the dough becomes shaggy and difficult to stir. Turn out onto a heavily floured work surface and knead, incorporating any shaggy scraps back into the dough. Knead until the dough forms a cohesive ball and is smooth, about 10 minutes. Shape into a ball and proceed as directed.

# HOW TO SUBSTITUTE INGREDIENTS

We know that our carefully tested recipes are often subjected to abuse by our readers (and even by members of our staff), and we know the kinds of disasters that can result. For the record, we forgive you. No one wants to run out to the market for just one ingredient. Perhaps something you've got on hand will do the trick. With that in mind, we tested scores of widely published ingredient substitutions to figure out which ones work under what circumstances and which ones simply don't work. If you are going to substitute ingredients, you may as well do it better and smarter. Here's how.

## FLOURS

The texture of baked goods depends on, among many other things, the protein content of the particular flour used to prepare them.

### ALL-PURPOSE FLOUR
The kitchen workhorse and pantry staple, all-purpose flour has a protein content ranging between 10 and 12 percent. This staple has no substitute.

### CAKE FLOUR
With just 6 to 8 percent protein, cake flour will impart a more tender, delicate, fine-crumbed texture to baked goods.
TO REPLACE: **1 cup cake flour**
• ⅞ cup all-purpose flour + 2 tablespoons cornstarch

### BREAD FLOUR
Bread flour has close to 14 percent protein. This ensures strong gluten development and thereby a sturdy dough.
TO REPLACE: **1 cup bread flour**
• 1 cup all-purpose flour
**CAUTION:** Breads and pizza crusts may bake up with slightly less chew, but the results will be acceptable.

## DAIRY PRODUCTS

### WHOLE MILK AND HALF-AND-HALF
Use the formulas below to substitute one dairy product for another.
TO REPLACE: **1 cup whole milk**
• ⅝ cup skim milk + ⅜ cup half-and-half
• ⅔ cup 1% milk + ⅓ cup half-and-half
• ¾ cup 2% milk + ¼ cup half-and-half
• ⅞ cup skim milk + ⅛ cup heavy cream
TO REPLACE: **1 cup half-and-half**
• ¾ cup whole milk + ¼ cup heavy cream
• ⅔ cup skim or low-fat milk + ⅓ cup heavy cream

### HEAVY CREAM
Evaporated milk can be used in place of heavy cream to enrich soups and sauces.
TO REPLACE: **1 cup heavy cream**
• 1 cup evaporated milk
**NOT SUITABLE FOR:** Whipping, or baking recipes.

### EGGS
All our recipes are tested with large eggs, but substitutions are possible. For half of an egg, whisk the yolk and white together and use half of the liquid.

| LARGE | JUMBO | EXTRA-LARGE | MEDIUM |
|-------|-------|-------------|--------|
| 1 = | 1 | 1 | 1 |
| 2 = | 1½ | 2 | 2 |
| 3 = | 2½ | 2½ | 3½ |
| 4 = | 3 | 3½ | 4½ |
| 5 = | 4 | 4 | 6 |
| 6 = | 5 | 5 | 7 |

## CULTURED DAIRY PRODUCTS

### BUTTERMILK
Regular milk can be "clabbered" with an acidic ingredient such as lemon juice, vinegar, or cream of tartar; the acid will react with baking soda to produce leavening and will approximate the tang of buttermilk in most pancake batters and baked goods.
**NOTE:** Lemon juice is our first choice.
TO REPLACE: **1 cup buttermilk**
• 1 cup milk + 1 tablespoon lemon juice
• 1 cup milk + 1 tablespoon white vinegar
• 1 cup milk + 1 teaspoon cream of tartar
Let stand to thicken, about 10 minutes.
**NOT SUITABLE FOR:** Raw applications, such as a buttermilk dressing.

### SOUR CREAM AND PLAIN, WHOLE MILK YOGURT
These can be swapped for each other in equal measure in most baking recipes with good results, but since sour cream has more than four times the fat, expect cakes and muffins baked with yogurt to have a slightly drier texture. Flavored yogurts such as lemon and vanilla can be substituted for plain in recipes where the flavors won't clash.
TO REPLACE: **1 cup sour cream**
• 1 cup plain whole milk yogurt
TO REPLACE: **1 cup plain yogurt**
• 1 cup sour cream
**CAUTION:** Nonfat and lowfat yogurts are too lean to use in place of sour cream.

## LEAVENERS

### YEAST
Our favorite is instant yeast (also sold as rapid-rise yeast and bread-machine yeast) because it is fast acting and can be stirred directly into the other dry ingredients. Active dry yeast, on the other hand, must be dissolved in warm water (around 110 degrees) before being added to the rest of the ingredients. Other than the method of incorporation, instant and active dry yeast are interchangeable.

### BAKING POWDER
All chemical leavening is based on the reaction of an acid and a base, or alkali (almost always baking soda), to produce the carbon dioxide gas that makes the baked good rise. Baking powder contains an acid along with baking soda and a small amount of cornstarch to absorb moisture and keep the mixture shelf-stable.
TO REPLACE: **1 teaspoon baking powder**
• ¼ teaspoon baking soda + ½ teaspoon cream of tartar. Use right away.

**NOTE:** ¼ teaspoon of baking soda is the leavening equivalent of 1 teaspoon of baking powder.

## SUGARS AND OTHER SWEETENERS

### GRANULATED SUGAR
This staple has no substitute.

### BROWN SUGAR
Granulated sugar and molasses make a close approximation.
TO REPLACE: **1 cup light brown sugar**
• 1 cup granulated sugar + 1 tablespoon molasses
TO REPLACE: **1 cup dark brown sugar**
• 1 cup granulated sugar + 2 tablespoons molasses
Pulse the molasses in a food processor along with the sugar, if desired, or simply add it along with the other wet ingredients.

### POWDERED SUGAR
Because it contains cornstarch, powdered sugar should not be substituted for either brown or granulated sugar in most recipes.
TO REPLACE: **1 cup powdered sugar**
• 1 cup granulated sugar + 1 teaspoon cornstarch ground together in a blender (not a food processor)
**CAUTION:** This works very well for dusting over desserts, less so in icings and glazes.

### SUPERFINE SUGAR
This is handy for cold drinks, as it dissolves more readily than granulated sugar.
TO REPLACE: **1 cup superfine sugar**
• 1 cup granulated sugar ground in a food processor for 15 seconds

### LIQUID SWEETENERS
Replacing some of the sugar in a recipe with honey, molasses, or maple syrup to add an extra dimension of flavor is a simple matter, provided you account for the extra moisture.
TO REPLACE: **sugar with liquid sweetener**
• Reduce the liquid in a recipe by ¼ cup for each cup of liquid sweetener added
**CAUTION:** As liquid sweeteners vary in moisture content, acidity, and even sweetness, it is usually not a good idea to replace more than half of the sugar in a recipe with a liquid sweetener.

## WINE

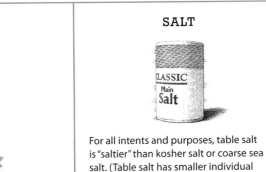

Vermouth makes an acceptable substitute for white wine in recipes that don't call for very much. Nonalcoholic substitutes are more difficult to come by. For soups and pan sauces, the best course of action is to use extra broth, adding wine vinegar (red or white, depending on the recipe) or lemon juice just before serving.
TO REPLACE: **½ cup wine**
• ½ cup broth + 1 teaspoon wine vinegar
• ½ cup broth + 1 teaspoon lemon juice

## SALT

For all intents and purposes, table salt is "saltier" than kosher salt or coarse sea salt. (Table salt has smaller individual crystals, so more crystals of table salt than kosher or coarse sea salt will fit into a measuring spoon.)
TO REPLACE: **1 tablespoon table salt**
• 1½ tablespoons Morton Kosher Salt or fleur de sel
• 2 tablespoons Diamond Crystal Kosher Salt or Maldon Sea Salt
**CAUTION:** Kosher salt and coarse sea salt do not dissolve as readily as table salt; for this reason, we do not recommend using them in baking recipes.

## HERBS

Dried herbs are more potent than fresh. They are best used in longer-cooking recipes like soups and stews, while fresh herbs are best added near the end of cooking.

TO REPLACE: **1 tablespoon fresh herbs**
• 1 teaspoon dried herbs
**CAUTION:** Many dried herbs, such as basil, chives, dill, parsley, and tarragon, are tasteless and should be avoided.

# PASTA

# CREAMY CARBONARA

SERVES 4 TO 6

**WHAT MAKES THIS A BEST RECIPE:** Carbonara is fast (it takes just 20 minutes to prepare) and convenient (it relies on staples most cooks always have on hand), but, unfortunately, most recipes offer nothing more than a dry, stodgy tangle of noodles strewn with chunks of cheese. Not this version. We love this recipe because it marries steaming hot pasta with fresh eggs and cheese to create a rich and creamy sauce. Add some salty, chewy bacon, minced garlic, and a good hit of black pepper and you can't possibly go wrong. The secret to our recipe was that we added heavy cream, dry white wine, and some pasta cooking water with the eggs to loosen the sauce to just the right consistency when we tossed it with the hot pasta. Although we call for spaghetti in this recipe, you can substitute any long thin pasta, such as linguine or fettuccine.

    3   large eggs
    2   ounces Pecorino Romano cheese, grated (about 1 cup)
    2   tablespoons heavy cream
    ½   pound thick-cut bacon, cut into ½-inch pieces
    3   garlic cloves, minced
    1   teaspoon pepper
    ½   cup dry white wine
    1   tablespoon salt
    1   pound spaghetti

**1.** Bring 4 quarts water to a boil in a large pot for the pasta. Whisk the eggs, Pecorino Romano, and cream together in a medium bowl; set aside.

**2.** Meanwhile, cook the bacon in a large skillet over medium heat until crisp, about 8 minutes. Transfer to a small bowl with a slotted spoon. Pour off all but 2 tablespoons of the bacon fat. Add the garlic and pepper to the skillet and cook over medium heat until fragrant, about 30 seconds. Slowly whisk the garlic mixture into the egg mixture.

**3.** Add the wine to the skillet and simmer over medium heat, scraping the bottom of the pan to remove browned bits, until reduced by half, about 5 minutes. Slowly whisk the wine mixture into the egg mixture.

**4.** Meanwhile, add the salt and the pasta to the boiling water. Cook, stirring often, until the pasta is al dente. Reserve 1 cup of the pasta cooking water, then drain the pasta and return it to the pot. Immediately pour the egg mixture over the pasta and toss to combine with ½ cup of the reserved cooking water. Add the bacon and thin the sauce with the remaining cooking water as necessary. Serve immediately.

**WHERE THINGS CAN GO WRONG:** Curdled eggs will ruin your carbonara. To prevent this from happening, be sure to whisk constantly when adding the hot ingredients to the egg mixture.

## NOTES FROM THE TEST KITCHEN

### THE BEST SPAGHETTI
In the not-so-distant past, American pasta had a poor reputation, and rightly so. It cooked up gummy and starchy, and experts usually touted the superiority of Italian brands. To find out if this was still the case, we tasted eight leading brands of spaghetti—four American and four Italian. Ultimately, American-made **Ronzoni Spaghetti** was the top finisher, with tasters praising its nutty, buttery flavor and superb texture. The two most expensive brands came in last, so save your money and don't bother with the expensive imported pastas—American-made is just fine.

### FRESHLY GROUND PEPPER IS A MUST
Pre-ground pepper gave our carbonara a timid, dusty flavor. We switched to freshly ground, but it still wasn't assertive enough. Instead of increasing the heat with untraditional ingredients such as cayenne pepper or red pepper flakes, we opted to "bloom" the heat out of the black pepper by toasting it in rendered bacon fat before adding it to the pasta. This technique brought out the pepper's earthy complexity as well as more than enough heat.

### WE PREFER PECORINO ROMANO
In our carbonara we favored Pecorino Romano, a sharply flavored sheep's milk cheese, to the milder-tasting Parmesan (you can use Parmesan in a pinch); the Pecorino melted more smoothly, making for a creamier texture.

# FOOLPROOF FETTUCCINE ALFREDO

SERVES 4

Fettuccine Alfredo is all about perfect timing, so prepare the cream sauce while the pasta water is heating.

**WHAT MAKES THIS A BEST RECIPE:** This quintessential Roman dish seems simple enough yet it is deceptively difficult to execute perfectly. All too often, whether made at home or in a restaurant, what you end up with is over-cooked pasta and a nondescript sauce that quickly congeals in the bowl into a solid, sticky mass. The basic ingredients—fresh egg noodles, butter, cheese, and cream—are always the same, but we found that their amounts and how they are combined make all the difference. In developing this recipe, we discovered that we could make a fresher sauce if we reduced only 1 cup of cream and then added an additional half cup to the mixture (many other recipes suggest simmering all the cream until it thickens). A modest 2 tablespoons of butter (many recipes use a full stick) and just ¾ cup Parmesan give the sauce its richness without overwhelming either the texture or the balance. We also like the fact that we were able to avoid using flour to stabilize this delicate sauce since a bit of pasta water was all it took to give it the right body and staying power.

| | |
|---|---|
| 1½ | cups heavy cream |
| 2 | tablespoons unsalted butter |
| | Salt |
| ½ | teaspoon pepper |
| 9 | ounces fresh fettuccine |
| 1½ | ounces Parmesan cheese, grated (about ¾ cup) |
| ⅛ | teaspoon freshly grated nutmeg |

## NOTES FROM THE TEST KITCHEN

### PARMIGIANO-REGGIANO MAKES THE DIFFERENCE

Authentic Parmigiano-Reggiano ($13.99 a pound) is aged for at least 24 months, as opposed to 10 months for most domestic varieties—and this allows more rounded complex flavors and aromas to develop. Want to know if the Parmesan you're buying is authentic? Look for the name stamped on the rind to be sure it's the real deal. On a budget? A good alternative is **DiGiorno Parmesan**, made in Wisconsin ($7.99 a pound), which tasters described as a "bit tangy but still sweet and nutty."

**1.** Bring 4½ quarts water to a boil in a large pot for the pasta. Using a ladle or a heatproof measuring cup, fill each individual serving bowl with about ½ cup boiling water; set the bowls aside to warm.

**2.** Meanwhile, simmer 1 cup of the cream and the butter in a medium saucepan over low heat until the mixture reduces to ⅔ cup, 12 to 15 minutes. Off the heat, stir in the remaining ½ cup cream, ½ teaspoon salt, and pepper.

**3.** Add 1 tablespoon salt and the pasta to the boiling water. Cook, stirring often, until the pasta is just shy of al dente. Reserve ¼ cup of the pasta cooking water, then drain the pasta.

**4.** Meanwhile, return the cream mixture to a simmer over medium-high heat. Add the pasta, Parmesan, and nutmeg to the cream mixture. Cook over low heat, tossing to combine, until the pasta is just al dente and the cheese is melted, 1 to 2 minutes. Stir in the reserved pasta cooking water; the sauce may look rather thin but will gradually thicken as the pasta is served and eaten. Working quickly, empty the serving bowls of the water. Divide the pasta among the bowls and serve immediately.

**WHERE THINGS CAN GO WRONG:** This is a delicate dish where timing and ingredients are everything. Make sure you use fresh fettuccine since the sauce won't cling to the noodles as well with dried (and you're apt to end up with gloppy noodles and sauce that pools in the serving bowls). Also, because the pasta will cook in the sauce for a couple of minutes, it is best to undercook it slightly.

## NOTES FROM THE TEST KITCHEN

### WARM YOUR SERVING BOWLS

The texture of the sauce changes dramatically as the dish stands and cools. Serving the Alfredo in warmed bowls helps it retain its creamy texture.

**WARM BOWL**
Still creamy after 5 minutes

**COLD BOWL**
Congeals in just 60 seconds

### OUR FAVORITE CHEESE GRATER

When we need to grate a hefty amount of hard cheese, like Parmesan, our first choice is not the ubiquitous box grater, but rather a rasp grater, a long flat grater. Shaped like a ruler but with lots and lots of tiny, sharp raised teeth, it makes grating large amounts of hard cheese nearly effortless. Our favorite is the **Microplane Grater**, which has a solid handle that provides great leverage for grating. It also makes quick work of ginger and citrus zest.

### THE BEST FETTUCCINE

While developing our Fettuccine Alfredo recipe, we wondered how "fresh" fettuccine from the supermarket would compare with both fresh pasta from a local Italian market and fresh homemade pasta. All three fresh pastas, including Buitoni (from the supermarket refrigerator section), received high marks from tasters, with an eggy flavor and firm but yielding texture. The pasta we purchased from a local Italian market had the wheatiest flavor and chewiest texture. It was made with a mixture of durum flour and semolina. Durum-only Buitoni and our home-made pasta (made with all-purpose flour) were more bland and soft but still very good. Our advice? If you have access to locally made fresh pasta (especially one made with semolina), give it a try. But **Buitoni Fettuccine** is by far the most convenient option, and it can ably compete with homemade.

# WHOLE WHEAT PASTA
## WITH GREENS, BEANS, AND PANCETTA
### SERVES 4 TO 6

**WHAT MAKES THIS A BEST RECIPE:** Italians have a knack for transforming simple, humble ingredients into remarkable meals, and this rustic trio of pasta, hearty greens, and beans is no exception. Ordinarily, making something out of almost nothing takes time (dried cannellini beans are simmered until tender, then garden-fresh greens are cleaned, cooked, and sea-soned). For this recipe we streamlined the Italian classic with-out forfeiting flavor. Right off the bat, we knew we would have to use canned beans, and to compensate for their flavor defi-ciency, we worked in some heavy-hitting ingredients: hearty pancetta, red pepper flakes, and earthy fontina cheese. For the greens, we chose kale or collard greens for their substantial texture, and appealing vegetal and mineral qualities (no bitter-ness like other greens). Whole wheat pasta unified the beans and greens with its nutty flavor and pleasantly chewy texture, and garlicky breadcrumbs finished everything off, contributing headiness and welcome crunch.

| | |
|---|---|
| 2 | slices high-quality sandwich bread, torn into quarters |
| 3 | tablespoons olive oil |
| 6 | garlic cloves, minced |
| | Salt |
| 3 | ounces pancetta, cut into ½-inch pieces |
| 1 | onion, minced (about 1 cup) |
| ¼ | teaspoon red pepper flakes |
| 1–1½ | pounds kale or collard greens (about 14 cups), thick stems trimmed, leaves chopped into 1-inch pieces and rinsed, water still clinging to leaves |
| 1½ | cups low-sodium chicken broth |
| 1 | (15-ounce) can cannellini beans, drained and rinsed |
| 13¼ | ounces whole wheat spaghetti |
| 4 | ounces fontina cheese, coarsely grated (about 1 cup) |
| | Pepper |

**1.** Pulse the bread in a food processor until coarsely ground. Heat 2 tablespoons of the oil in a 12-inch skillet over medium-high heat. Add the breadcrumbs and cook, stirring frequently, until beginning to brown, about 3 minutes. Stir in 1 tablespoon of the garlic; cook, stirring constantly, until the garlic is fragrant and the breadcrumbs are dark golden brown, about 1 minute. Season the breadcrumbs with salt, transfer to a small serving bowl, and set aside. Wipe out the pan with paper towels.

**2.** Heat the remaining tablespoon oil in the now-empty skillet over medium-high heat. Add the pancetta and cook until crisp, about 8 minutes. Transfer to a small bowl with a slotted spoon.

**3.** Add the onion to the pan and cook until starting to brown, about 5 minutes. Add the remaining tablespoon garlic and pepper flakes. Cook, stirring constantly, until the garlic is fragrant, about 30 seconds.

**4.** Add half of the greens to the pan and toss occasionally until starting to wilt, about 2 minutes. Add the remaining greens, broth, and ¾ teaspoon salt. Cover (the pan will be very full), increase the heat to high, and bring to a strong simmer. Reduce the heat to medium and cook, covered, tossing occasionally, until the greens are tender, about 15 minutes (the mixture will be somewhat soupy). Stir in the beans and pancetta and cook until heated through; remove from the heat and cover.

**5.** Meanwhile, bring 4 quarts water to a boil in a large pot for the pasta. Add 1 tablespoon salt and the pasta to the boiling water. Cook, stirring often, until the pasta is just shy of al dente. Drain the pasta and return it to the pot.

**6.** Add the greens mixture to the pasta and toss to combine. Cook over medium-high heat until the pasta absorbs most of the liquid, about 2 minutes. Add the fontina and season with salt and pepper to taste. Serve immediately, passing the garlic breadcrumbs separately.

## NOTES FROM THE TEST KITCHEN

### THE BEST WHOLE WHEAT SPAGHETTI
For this recipe the nutty flavor of whole wheat pasta added complexity and brought the beans and greens into a pleasing harmony. Of all the brands we tried, our favorite was **Ronzoni Healthy Harvest Whole Wheat Blend Pasta** ($1.79 for 13.25 ounces). Unlike many other brands, it is made from a blend of whole durum wheat and regular semolina—so it's not 100 percent "whole" wheat. Its pleasantly chewy texture and deep, wheaty flavor is worth the nutritional trade-off of just 1 gram less fiber per serving than the most fiber-laden whole wheat brands.

# FETTUCCINE
## WITH SHRIMP, TARRAGON, AND CREAM
SERVES 4 TO 6

**WHAT MAKES THIS A BEST RECIPE:** Shrimp with cream sauce over fresh pasta has become a staple on restaurant menus; even chain restaurants have added it to their repertoires. Most of the time, though, their renditions produce rubbery shrimp in a bland, gluey sauce. This version yields plump, juicy shrimp in a velvety cream sauce. And as an added bonus, it is a recipe that requires little prep time and comes together easily at the last minute. For perfectly tender shrimp, we briefly sautéed them in butter and garlic, and then transferred them to a bowl where the residual heat gently finished cooking them. (By keeping the shrimp out of the cream sauce, they were far less likely to overcook.) And as with our Fettuccine Alfredo (page 110), we made a fresh-tasting sauce with just the right consistency for clinging to the pasta and shrimp by reducing only a portion of the cream and then adding an additional half cup, uncooked, to the mixture. As with many pasta dishes, the last minute of cooking was crucial here. We found it most effective to cook the pasta until not quite al dente, drain it, and then cook it with the reserved shrimp, reduced cream, and bit of fresh tarragon. The shrimp warmed through, the tarragon lightly infused the cream, and the pasta had a chance to finish cooking and absorb the sauce.

1   pound large shrimp (31 to 40 per pound), peeled and deveined (see page 10)
    Salt
2   tablespoons unsalted butter
2   garlic cloves, minced
2   cups heavy cream
1   pound fresh or dried fettuccine
2   tablespoons minced fresh tarragon
    Pepper

**1.** Bring 4 quarts water to a boil in a large pot for the pasta.

**2.** Meanwhile, toss the shrimp with ½ teaspoon salt. Melt the butter in a 12-inch skillet over medium-high heat until foaming. Add the shrimp to the skillet in a single layer and cook until pink on both sides, about 2 minutes. Stir in the garlic and cook until fragrant, about 30 seconds. Transfer the shrimp to a bowl; set aside.

**3.** Add 1½ cups of the cream to the skillet and simmer until the mixture reduces to 1 cup, about 8 minutes. Off the heat, stir in the remaining ½ cup cream and set aside.

**4.** Meanwhile, add 1 tablespoon salt and the pasta to the boiling water. Cook, stirring often, until the pasta is just shy of al dente. Drain the pasta and return it to the pot.

**5.** Stir in the cream, shrimp with any accumulated juice, and tarragon and toss to combine. Continue to cook over low heat until the sauce coats the pasta and the pasta is just al dente. Season with salt and pepper to taste. Serve immediately.

**WHERE THINGS CAN GO WRONG:** Do not cook the sauce over too high a flame or for too long, or it will be gluey instead of creamy. Make sure to cook your pasta until not quite al dente, as it will cook further (and absorb some of the butter and cream) when it is cooked with the sauce.

## NOTES FROM THE TEST KITCHEN

### HOW TO COOK PASTA

If you ask ten cooks how they cook pasta, you're likely to get ten answers. In an effort to standardize pasta cookery, we got the water boiling here in the test kitchen. These test kitchen tricks will guarantee perfect pasta every time.

**USE 4 QUARTS OF WATER.** You'll need a large pot, but this amount of water will ensure that the pasta cooks evenly and won't clump.

**USE PLENTY OF SALT.** Many people dump oil into boiling pasta water thinking that it will keep pasta from sticking together, but this is a myth. Adding oil to the boiling water does not prevent sticking. Frequent stirring does. Skip the oil but make sure to add salt—roughly 1 tablespoon for 4 quarts of water—or the pasta will taste bland.

**TASTE PASTA OFTEN FOR DONENESS.** Reading the instructions on the box is a good place to start, but for al dente pasta, you may need to shave a few minutes off the recommended time. When you start to get close to the recommended cooking time, begin tasting for doneness.

**SAVE SOME COOKING WATER.** Wait! Before you drain that pasta . . . Take a liquid measuring cup and retrieve about ½ cup of the cooking water from the pasta pot. Then go ahead and drain the pasta for just a few moments before you toss it with the sauce. (Don't let the pasta sit in the colander too long; it will get very dry very quickly.) When you toss your sauce with the pasta, add some (or all) of the reserved pasta cooking water to thin the sauce as needed.

# MARINARA SAUCE

MAKES 4 CUPS, ENOUGH TO SAUCE 1 POUND OF PASTA

**WHAT MAKES THIS A BEST RECIPE:** Generally, quick tomato sauces, though convenient, are thin and lack depth of flavor—tasting like unremarkable homemade versions of the jarred spaghetti sauce you buy at the supermarket. We developed this recipe with the goal of producing a sauce from scratch, with complex but fresh flavors, in less than an hour. For rich tomato flavor, we hand-crushed canned whole tomatoes (chopping them by hand makes a mess), and cooked them until they glazed the bottom of the pan. By cooking the tomatoes, without their juice, we were able to intensify their flavor. Then we deglazed the pan with red wine, which added robustness, and tomato juice (reserved from the cans of tomatoes), which fortified the tomato flavor. For fresh, bright flavor to complement the deeper, full-bodied essence of the cooked sauce, we kept ¾ cup of the canned tomatoes out of the pot, then chopped them, uncooked, into the sauce. Last, sugar added at the end of cooking (as in most recipes) balanced out the flavors: too much and the sauce began to taste as if it had come from a jar; too little and the acidity overwhelmed the other flavors.

2 (28-ounce) cans whole tomatoes packed in juice
2 tablespoons olive oil
1 onion, minced (about 1 cup)
2 garlic cloves, minced
½ teaspoon dried oregano
⅓ cup dry red wine, such as Chianti or Merlot
3 tablespoons chopped fresh basil
1 tablespoon extra-virgin olive oil
  Salt and pepper
1–2 teaspoons sugar, as needed

**1.** Pour the tomatoes and juice into a strainer set over a large bowl. Using your hands, open up the tomatoes and remove and discard any fibrous cores. Let the tomatoes drain any excess liquid, about 5 minutes. Remove ¾ cup of the tomatoes from the strainer and set aside. Reserve 2½ cups of the tomato juice and discard the remainder.

Slow, gentle simmering produces great marinara, but we're much too impatient. Using unorthodox cooking methods, we cheated the clock.

**2.** Heat the olive oil in a 12-inch skillet over medium heat until shimmering. Add the onion and cook, stirring occasionally, until softened and golden around edges, 6 to 8 minutes. Add the garlic and oregano and cook, stirring constantly, until the garlic is fragrant, about 30 seconds.

**3.** Add the tomatoes from the strainer and cook over medium-high heat, stirring frequently, until the liquid has evaporated and the tomatoes begin to stick to the bottom of the pan and brown fond forms around the pan edges, 10 to 12 minutes. Add the wine and cook until thick and syrupy, about 1 minute. Add the reserved tomato juice and simmer over medium heat, stirring occasionally and loosening any browned bits, until the sauce is thick, 8 to 10 minutes.

**4.** Pulse the sauce and the reserved tomatoes in a food processor until slightly chunky, about eight 2-second pulses. Return the sauce to the skillet and add the basil and extra-virgin olive oil. Season with salt, pepper, and sugar to taste.

**WHERE THINGS CAN GO WRONG:** Because canned tomatoes vary in acidity and saltiness, it's best to add sugar, salt, and pepper carefully to taste just before serving.

**WHAT YOU CAN DO AHEAD OF TIME:** The sauce can be refrigerated in an airtight container for 4 days, or frozen for up to 2 months.

## NOTES FROM THE TEST KITCHEN

### HOW WE GOT SLOW-SIMMERED FLAVOR FAST
The best marinara has lots of complexity—and demand lots of cooking time. Here's how we sped up the process.

**DRAIN THE JUICE.**
A can of tomatoes has more juice than solids. We jump-start flavor concentration by draining off almost a cup beforehand.

**CARAMELIZE THE SOLIDS.**
Caramelizing the tomato solids briskly in a large skillet before deglazing with ingredients further deepens the flavor profile.

**ADD RAW TOMATOES.**
Reserving a few uncooked tomatoes to add near the end of cooking contributes an extra note of freshness to the cooked sauce.

### OUR FAVORITE HAND BLENDER
A hand, or immersion, blender can save time and effort: no need to blend in batches, no need to wash a food processor. But which brand is best? To find out, we gathered nine models, priced between $13 and $90, and put them to the test. So what makes a better hand blender? The differences aren't obvious. As we've found in past tests, wattage means nothing when it comes to most appliances: The 200- and 400-watt Braun models performed equally well. We did, however, end up with a few design preferences: Stainless steel shafts (rather than plastic) were not better performers, but they do resist staining and can be used in pots sitting over a flame. And come cleanup time, a removable blade end is best. In the end, **KitchenAid's Immersion Blender** ($49.99) was our favorite. Aside from a blending beaker, it offers no extras (some models come with fancy attachments), but it did as good a job at blending as most traditional blenders.

# LIGHT MACARONI AND CHEESE

### SERVES 4

**WHAT MAKES THIS A BEST RECIPE:** Weighing in at about 800 calories and 50 grams of fat per serving, a bowl of homemade mac and cheese should really only be a treat every once in a while, like a slice of cheesecake. The truth, however, is that it winds up on the dinner table much more often because it's easy to prepare and most kids will eat it. For *The Best Light Recipe,* we developed a macaroni and cheese that truly can be used as a weekly workhorse dinner, a version with a reasonable amount of calories (450) as well as far fewer grams of fat (12 grams). Our version is velvety smooth and rich, nothing like other light mac and cheese recipes, which we found to be flavorless (due to the use of large amounts of nonfat cheese) or grainy (because they included ricotta or cottage cheese) when we tested them. Our secret? We fashioned our sauce using 8 ounces of lowfat cheddar cheese and 2 percent milk, and for creamy richness without the fat, we added a can of reduced-fat evaporated milk which rounded out the texture of the sauce and even fooled some of the tasters into thinking they were eating the real deal—full-fat mac and cheese. To thicken the sauce without using a traditional roux, we tried a flour slurry (flour dissolved in a liquid) and a cornstarch slurry (cornstarch dissolved in a liquid). The cornstarch-thickened sauce was the best—smooth and silky—and saved us another 10 or so grams of fat per serving.

Salt
½ pound elbow macaroni (about 2 cups)
1 (12-ounce) can reduced-fat evaporated milk
¾ cup 2 percent milk
¼ teaspoon dry mustard
⅛ teaspoon garlic powder or celery salt (optional)
Pinch cayenne pepper
2 teaspoons cornstarch
8 ounces 50 percent light cheddar cheese, grated (about 2 cups)

**1.** Bring 2½ quarts water to a boil in a large saucepan for the pasta. Add 2 teaspoons salt and the pasta to the boiling water. Cook, stirring often, until the pasta is completely cooked and tender. Drain the pasta and leave it in the colander; set aside.

**2.** Add the evaporated milk, ½ cup of the 2 percent milk, mustard, garlic powder (if using), cayenne, and ½ teaspoon salt to the now-empty saucepan. Bring the mixture to a boil, then reduce to a simmer. Whisk the cornstarch and remaining ¼ cup milk together, then whisk it into the simmering mixture. Continue to simmer, whisking constantly, until the sauce has thickened and is smooth, about 2 minutes.

**3.** Off the heat, gradually whisk in the cheddar until melted and smooth. Stir in the macaroni, and let the macaroni and cheese sit off the heat until the sauce has thickened slightly, 2 to 5 minutes, before serving.

**WHERE THINGS CAN GO WRONG:** Don't be tempted to use either preshredded or nonfat cheddar cheese in this dish—the texture and flavor of the mac and cheese will suffer substantially.

## NOTES FROM THE TEST KITCHEN

### ALL ABOUT LIGHT CHEDDAR CHEESE

High in fat and calories, cheese is an ingredient we usually use with a very light hand when developing lower-fat recipes. But cutting back on or omitting cheese entirely is simply not an option in recipes where cheese takes center stage so we decided to take a look at the variety of light cheddars out there. There are many options ranging from cheeses made with 2 percent milk to those labeled fat-free, 75 percent light (which has only one-quarter the fat of regular cheddar), and 50 percent light (half the fat of regular cheddar).

We tasted all of these options on their own with crackers and in batches of our Light Macaroni and Cheese. The fat-free cheese was immediately out of the running for being rubbery and overly sweet. The 2 percent reduced-fat cheese gained high marks, but it was still a little high in fat for our purposes. The 75 percent light cheddar produced mac and cheese that was grainy with a bitter aftertaste. The 50 percent light cheddar, on the other hand, worked well, and **Cabot 50% Light Cheddar** was the favorite of the tasters for its sharp tanginess. Though it doesn't quite stack up against fine aged cheddar when eaten on a cracker, tasters liked the creaminess and cheesy flavor that it lent to our mac and cheese.

# PASTA PRIMAVERA

SERVES 4

**WHAT MAKES THIS A BEST RECIPE:** There's a reason why pasta primavera—a mixture of vegetables, cream sauce, tomato sauce, and pasta—is a restaurant classic. The average recipe requires two hours, six pots, eight vegetables, and some fancy knife work best left to the pros. What's more, the vegetables have to be cooked twice, first blanched in water to set their color and then sautéed in butter. We streamlined the classic recipe and created a version that requires just two pots, 30 minutes, and a staff of one. For the vegetables we chose asparagus, zucchini, and frozen peas, all of which require minimal prep work. Once the pasta was nearly done, we added the vegetables to the pot to cook. All we had to do was drain the whole pot and marry the pasta and vegetables to the sauce. While most primavera recipes call for two separate sauces—a garlicky mushroom and tomato sauce and a creamy cheese sauce, each made in a separate pan—we collapsed these two into one sauce made in one pan by browning mushrooms and onions in butter, then adding garlic, tomatoes, and cream.

- 2 tablespoons unsalted butter
- 1 onion, minced (about 1 cup)
- 8 ounces white mushrooms, quartered
  Salt and pepper
- 2 garlic cloves, minced
- 1 (14.5-ounce) can diced tomatoes, drained
- 1 cup heavy cream
- 12 ounces egg-enriched dried fettuccine
- 1 pound asparagus, trimmed, spears cut diagonally into 1-inch pieces
- 1 zucchini, cut into ½-inch pieces
- 1 cup frozen peas
- 1 ounce Parmesan cheese, grated (about ½ cup), plus extra for serving
- 1½ tablespoons fresh lemon juice
- ¼ cup chopped fresh basil

**1.** Bring 4 quarts water to a boil in a large pot for the pasta. Meanwhile, melt the butter in a large skillet over medium heat until foaming. Add the onion, mushrooms, ¾ teaspoon salt, and ½ teaspoon pepper and cook until browned, about 8 minutes. Add the garlic and cook until fragrant, about 30 seconds. Stir in the tomatoes and cream and bring to a boil. Remove the pan from the heat; set aside.

**2.** Meanwhile, add 2 tablespoons salt and the pasta to the boiling water. Cook, stirring often, until the pasta is just beginning to soften, about 6 minutes. Add the asparagus and cook for 1 minute, then add the zucchini and cook for 2 minutes, and then add the peas and cook until the pasta is al dente, about 1 minute.

**3.** Drain the pasta and vegetables and return them to the pot. Add the cream sauce, Parmesan, lemon juice, and basil, and toss to combine. Season with salt and pepper to taste. Serve immediately, passing the extra Parmesan separately.

## NOTES FROM THE TEST KITCHEN

### PRIMO PASTA FOR PRIMAVERA

As a rule, we think fresh pasta does a better job of absorbing creamy sauces than dried pasta. But for our Pasta Primavera we found fresh fettuccine was too soft and wilted under the weight of all those vegetables. Regular dried pasta wasn't much better—the noodles were too chewy, and the sauce slid right off. We had the best results with dried egg-enriched fettuccine. These noodles were substantial enough to stand up to the vegetables yet also possess the eggy richness and cream-absorbing ability of fresh pasta. Dried egg-enriched fettuccine (we particularly like **Ronzoni**) is sold in 12-ounce packages, perfect for four people.

### THE BEST SUPERMARKET EXTRA-VIRGIN OLIVE OIL

The first batch of oil that comes from the olives is labeled extra-virgin. It is the most intensely flavored, and it can also be the most expensive—it's easy to pay upwards of $30 dollars for a bottle at specialty food stores. We wondered if we could find a tasty, far less expensive bottle at the supermarket. We waded through the myriad choices available, wondering which one was the best all-purpose oil. **DaVinci Extra-Virgin Olive Oil** is the test kitchen favorite among leading supermarket brands for its ripe, buttery, and complex flavor. Best of all, it costs just $8 per liter.

# SKILLET BAKED ZITI

### SERVES 4

**WHAT MAKES THIS A BEST RECIPE:** Even in its simplest form, good baked ziti is the ultimate comfort food. But the downside is that baked ziti, like lasagna, usually requires many pots and pans, and lots of time. You must sauté aromatics and build a sauce in one pan, boil water and cook pasta in another pot, and then combine everything and bake it for up to an hour. And this can all be for naught, since it often comes out dry, bland, and downright unappealing. For *The Best 30-Minute Recipe,* we were determined to figure out how to get a great baked ziti on the table in just half an hour. The solution? After much experimentation, we found that all that this Italian-American dish needed was a skillet and some restraint—just a few really fresh ingredients are what make it great. And we cooked the ziti from start to finish in an ovenproof nonstick skillet. To make this work, we built a simple, watery tomato sauce—a combination of crushed tomatoes, water, garlic, and red pepper flakes made a loose sauce, which was tasty and coated the pasta evenly and thoroughly. (The nonstick skillet helped the sauce stick to the pasta, not the pan, a minor though important detail.) Once the ziti was nearly tender, we added the cream, basil, and cheese and transferred the skillet to a hot oven. In just 10 minutes the cheese was melted and it was ready to serve.

1 tablespoon olive oil

6 garlic cloves, minced

¼ teaspoon red pepper flakes

   Salt

1 (28-ounce) can crushed tomatoes

3 cups water

12 ounces ziti (3¾ cups)

½ cup heavy cream

1 ounce Parmesan cheese, grated (about ½ cup)

¼ cup minced fresh basil

   Pepper

4 ounces whole milk mozzarella cheese, shredded (about 1 cup)

**1.** Adjust an oven rack to the middle position and heat the oven to 475 degrees.

**2.** Combine the oil, garlic, pepper flakes, and ½ teaspoon salt in a large ovensafe nonstick skillet and sauté over medium-high heat until fragrant, about 1 minute. Add the crushed tomatoes, water, ziti, and ½ teaspoon salt. Cover and cook, stirring often and adjusting the heat as needed to maintain a vigorous simmer, until the ziti is almost tender, 15 to 18 minutes.

**3.** Stir in the cream, Parmesan, and basil. Season with salt and pepper to taste. Sprinkle the mozzarella evenly over the ziti. Transfer the skillet to the oven and bake until the cheese has melted and browned, about 10 minutes. Serve.

**WHERE THINGS CAN GO WRONG:** If your skillet is not ovensafe, be sure to transfer the pasta mixture to a shallow, 2-quart casserole dish before sprinkling it with cheese and baking.

## GREAT DISCOVERIES
### COOKING PASTA WITHOUT WATER

As I worked my way through a multitude of pasta dishes for our 30-minute cookbook, I was desperate for tricks that would allow me to bypass all the usual steps for cooking pasta. I knew one thing: If I could figure out how to maximize the skillet, I'd be off to a running start in terms of beating the clock. After some experimenting, I found that small amounts of pasta, 12 ounces or less, cook beautifully in a large (i.e., 12-inch) skillet in a brothy, creamy, or watered-down sauce. As the pasta cooks, it picks up flavor from the liquid, which reduces to become the sauce. And as an added plus, because I was using a skillet, I could easily incorporate other ingredients if I wanted to—either at the beginning, before I added the pasta and the liquid (like sausage or mushrooms), or at the end, if I had an ingredient that just needed the warmth of the dish to cook through (like thawed frozen peas or fresh asparagus.) So whether you want to make baked pasta or a simple stovetop pasta dish with a tasty sauce, you can do it all in a large skillet—from start to finish.

RACHEL TOOMEY | TEST COOK, BOOKS

# CREAMY SKILLET PENNE
## WITH MUSHROOMS AND ASPARAGUS
SERVES 4

**WHAT MAKES THIS A BEST RECIPE:** Having perfected our technique for creating a simple baked pasta dish in a skillet, we wanted to see how far we could push it. Could we create a more sophisticated skillet pasta dish with multiple ingredients? This proved simple enough since we had already figured out the hard part—the correct ratio of pasta to liquid. For this recipe, we wanted pasta bathed in a creamy sauce along with mushrooms and asparagus. First we sautéed the mushrooms in the skillet and then added the liquids and the penne. We found it necessary to crank the heat up high and really let the mixture simmer so that the pasta absorbed the liquid and became tender—otherwise the finished dish was much too watery. At this point, the dish was rich and satisfying, but wasn't as flavorful as we would have liked, so we added dried porcini mushrooms to perk things up—they did the trick. And incorporating the asparagus was simple—we just stirred it into the skillet in the last few minutes so it could cook through. For a finishing touch, we simply added grated Parmesan, which when mixed with what was left of the pasta cooking liquid created a creamy sauce that coated the pasta perfectly.

1 tablespoon olive oil
10 ounces white mushrooms, sliced
Salt
1 shallot, minced (3 tablespoons)
½ ounce dried porcini mushrooms, rinsed and minced
1 teaspoon minced fresh thyme or ¼ teaspoon dried
6 garlic cloves, minced
½ cup dry white wine
3½ cups water
1 cup heavy cream
8 ounces penne (2½ cups)
1 pound asparagus, trimmed and cut into 1-inch lengths
1 ounce Parmesan cheese, grated (about ½ cup)
Pepper

**1.** Heat the oil in a 12-inch nonstick skillet over medium-high heat until shimmering. Add the white mushrooms and ½ teaspoon salt and cook until the mushrooms are browned, about 8 minutes.

**2.** Stir in the shallot, porcini, and thyme and cook until the shallot has softened, about 1 minute. Stir in the garlic and cook until fragrant, about 30 seconds. Stir in the wine and simmer until almost dry, about 1 minute.

**3.** Stir in the water, cream, and penne. Increase the heat to high and cook, stirring often, until the penne is almost tender and the liquid has thickened, 12 to 15 minutes. Add the asparagus and cook until tender, about 3 minutes more.

**4.** Off the heat, stir in the Parmesan and season with salt and pepper to taste. Serve.

**WHERE THINGS CAN GO WRONG:** Be sure to use the designated 8 ounces (2½ cups) of penne called for in the recipe. Because you cook the pasta in a skillet (instead of a large pot of water), the correct ratio of liquid to pasta is critical to the success of this recipe. If more pasta is added to the skillet, there will not be enough liquid to cook it through. Conversely, if less pasta is added to the skillet, the resulting dish will be quite brothy.

## NOTES FROM THE TEST KITCHEN

**WHAT TO LOOK FOR WHEN BUYING DRIED MUSHROOMS**
While developing this recipe, we noticed disturbing differences in quality from one package of dried porcini mushrooms to another. Also known by their French name, cèpes, dried porcinis should be large, thick, and either tan or brown, not black (bottom). Avoid packages with lots of dust and crumbled bits mixed in (left), and keep an eye out for small pinholes, telltale signs that worms got to the mushrooms (right). Eyeballing is good, but smelling the mushrooms (especially if they are sold loose) is also a helpful way to judge quality. Purchase dried porcinis that boast an earthy (not musty or stale) aroma; mushrooms with no aroma at all are likely to have little or no flavor. Packages of "wild mushroom mix," found in some stores, should not be substituted for porcinis. Although these mixes sometimes include porcinis, they also often include lesser-quality mushrooms whose flavor profiles may not be well suited to the dish.

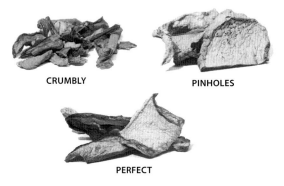

CRUMBLY          PINHOLES

PERFECT

# LIGHT MEAT AND CHEESE LASAGNA

### SERVES 10

**WHAT MAKES THIS A BEST RECIPE:** Few can deny the decadent appeal of meat and cheese lasagna—tender noodles layered with gooey cheese and a rich tomato meat sauce—but at 540 calories and 30 grams of fat per serving, it needed a makeover so it could be more than a special-occasion dish. Unwilling to make sacrifices in flavor and texture (or resort to unrealistically small portion sizes), we made batch after batch until we got it just right. Using ground turkey instead of ground beef or pork, chicken broth, and lots of garlic, red pepper flakes, and basil, we created a lean sauce with great meaty flavor. While a standard lasagna recipe can contain close to a pound of whole milk ricotta cheese, a pound of whole milk mozzarella, and 1¼ cups of grated Parmesan cheese, we swapped in fat-free ricotta and reduced-fat mozzarella, and reduced the amount of Parmesan to ½ cup—just enough to add flavor without tons of fat. This lasagna has all the appeal of the full-fat original, and we cut the calories to 340 and the fat to just 10 grams.

### SAUCE

- 2 (28-ounce) cans diced tomatoes
- 1 onion, minced (about 1 cup)
- 1 teaspoon olive oil
   Salt
- 6 garlic cloves, minced
- 2 tablespoons tomato paste
- ¼ teaspoon red pepper flakes
- 1 pound 93 percent lean ground turkey
- 1 cup low-sodium chicken broth
- 2 bay leaves
- ½ cup minced fresh basil
   Pepper

### FILLING AND PASTA LAYERS

- 1 (15-ounce) container fat-free ricotta cheese
- 12 ounces reduced-fat mozzarella cheese, shredded (about 3 cups)

- 1 ounce Parmesan cheese, grated (about ½ cup)
- ½ cup minced fresh basil
- 1 large egg, beaten lightly
- ½ teaspoon salt
- ½ teaspoon pepper
- 12 no-boil lasagna noodles from one 8-ounce package

**1.** FOR THE SAUCE: Process 1 can of tomatoes with their juice in a food processor until almost smooth, about 5 seconds. Combine the onion, oil, and ½ teaspoon salt in a large nonstick skillet. Cover and cook over medium-low heat until the onion is softened, 8 to 10 minutes.

**2.** Stir in the garlic, tomato paste, and pepper flakes and cook until the garlic is fragrant, about 30 seconds. Stir in half of the ground turkey and cook, breaking the meat into small pieces with a wooden spoon, until the meat loses its raw color but has not browned, about 4 minutes. Add the pureed tomatoes, remaining can of diced tomatoes with their juice, broth, and bay leaves. Bring to a simmer and cook, stirring occasionally, until the flavors are blended and the sauce is thickened, about 45 minutes.

**3.** Stir the remaining turkey into the sauce and continue to simmer, stirring occasionally, until the sauce measures about 6 cups, 20 to 30 minutes. Remove the bay leaves and stir in the basil. Season with salt and pepper to taste.

**4.** FOR THE FILLING: Mix the ricotta, 2 cups of the mozzarella, Parmesan, basil, egg, salt, and pepper together in a large bowl until thoroughly combined (you should have about 3 cups of filling).

**5.** TO ASSEMBLE AND BAKE: Adjust an oven rack to the middle position and heat the oven to 375 degrees. Spray a 13 by 9-inch baking dish with vegetable oil spray. Spread 1½ cups of the sauce evenly over the bottom of the prepared baking dish.

**6.** Lay 3 lasagna noodles on top of the sauce, spaced evenly apart. Place ⅓ cup of the filling on top of each noodle and spread it out evenly over the entire noodle using a rubber spatula. Spread 1 cup of the sauce evenly over the filling. Repeat this layering twice more.

**7.** Lay the remaining 3 noodles over the top. Spread the remaining 1½ cups sauce evenly over the noodles, making sure to cover the edges. Spray a large piece of foil with vegetable oil spray and cover the lasagna tightly.

**8.** Place the lasagna on a rimmed baking sheet and bake for 45 minutes. Remove the foil and sprinkle the lasagna evenly with the remaining 1 cup mozzarella. Continue to bake, uncovered, until the cheese is bubbling and slightly brown,

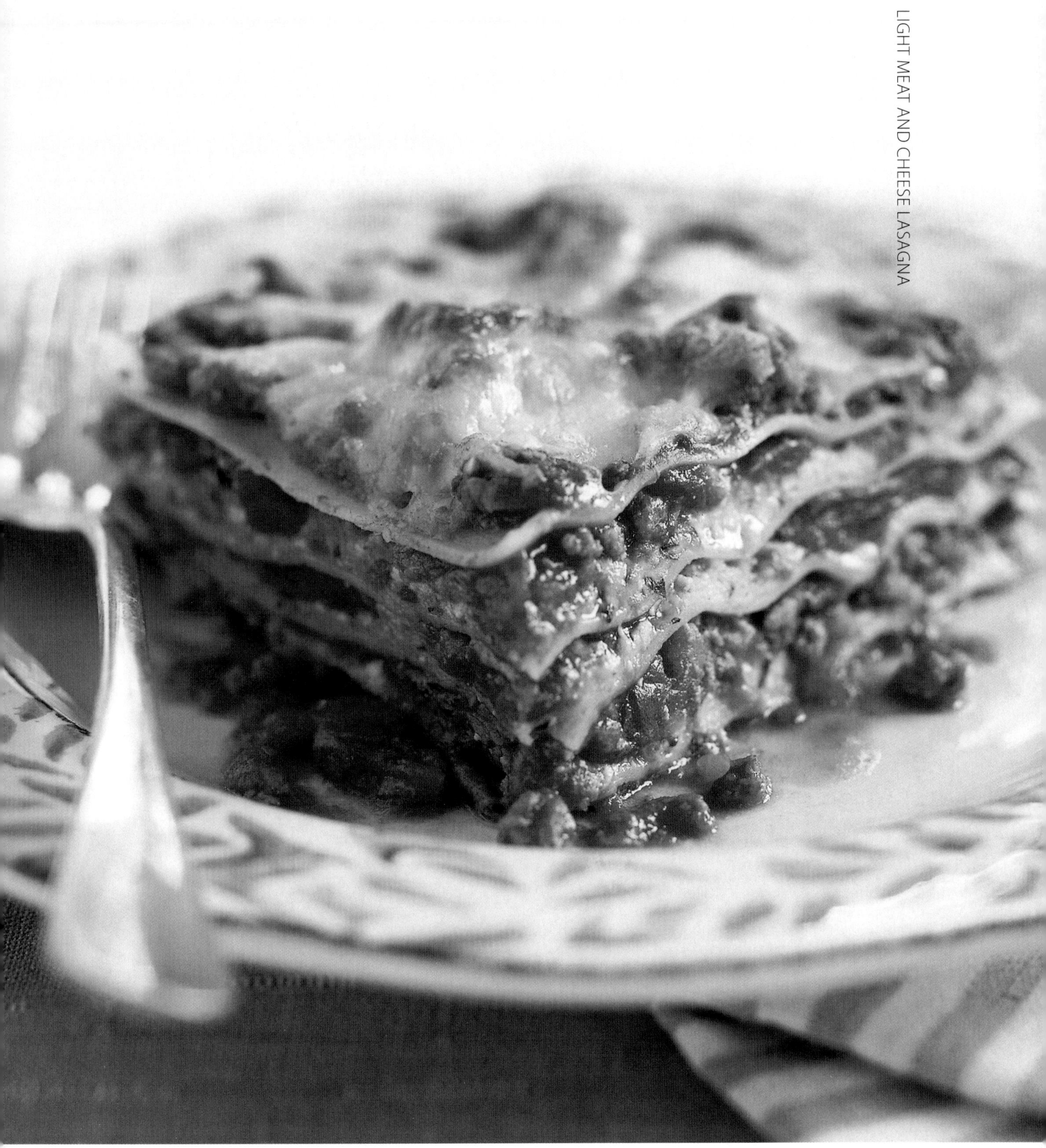

LIGHT MEAT AND CHEESE LASAGNA

10 to 15 minutes longer. Remove from the oven and cool on a wire rack for at least 15 minutes before serving.

**WHERE THINGS CAN GO WRONG:** Do not use ground turkey breast meat (sometimes labeled as 99 percent fat free) for this recipe, or the sauce will be dry and grainy. And fat-free mozzarella will make the filling rubbery.

**WHAT YOU CAN DO AHEAD OF TIME:** The assembled, unbaked lasagna can be held in the refrigerator, wrapped tightly in plastic wrap, for up to 24 hours. Allow the lasagna to sit at room temperature for 1 hour before baking. It can also be frozen, wrapped in an additional layer of foil, for up to 2 months. To bake, defrost the lasagna in the refrigerator for 24 hours, then allow it to sit at room temperature for 1 hour before baking.

## NOTES FROM THE TEST KITCHEN

### CHOOSING A CREAMY RICOTTA
Fat-free ricotta (with 0 grams of fat per cup compared to whole milk ricotta with 32 fat grams per cup) gave us the flavor and moisture we needed for a rich and creamy lasagna filling without any added fat.

### CHOOSING THE RIGHT MOZZARELLA
Reduced-fat mozzarella cheese (with just 18 fat grams per cup of shredded cheese compared to whole milk mozzarella with 28 fat grams per cup) had great melting qualities, good flavor, and even less fat than part-skim mozzarella (with 24 fat grams per cup).

### THE BEST NO-BOIL NOODLES
Much like instant rice, no-boil noodles are precooked at the factory. The extruded noodles are run through a water bath and are then dehydrated mechanically. During baking, the moisture from the sauce softens, or rehydrates, the noodles, especially when the pan is covered as the lasagna bakes. Our favorite no-boil noodles are **Ronzoni Oven Ready Lasagne Noodles,** with their "lightly eggy" and "wheaty" flavor and "tender," "perfectly al dente" texture.

# MEXICAN-STYLE SKILLET VERMICELLI
SERVES 4

**WHAT MAKES THIS A BEST RECIPE:** This skillet supper is based on the traditional Mexican dish *sopa seca*, which translates literally as "dry soup." It begins with an aromatic broth built in a skillet (the soup part), which is poured over thin strands of pasta in a baking dish and baked until the liquid is absorbed and the pasta is tender (the dry part). Authentic versions of the dish, though quick, often require specialty ingredients and several pots and pans. For our version in *The Best 30–Minute Recipe*, we wanted a dish that relied upon easily accessible ingredients and could be made using just one pan—a skillet (see page 118 for more about skillet suppers). Traditionally, this dish is prepared with fideos, thin strands of coiled, toasted noodles, which lend a distinctive background flavor. These noodles are great, but could not be found at our local market. We found that the closest match in texture and depth of flavor was vermicelli, toasted in the skillet until golden brown. We simmered the noodles in a richly flavored broth laced with smoky chipotle chiles in adobo sauce. To round this dish out into a hearty meal, we added chorizo sausage along with canned black beans. A sprinkling of shredded Monterey Jack cheese, melted to form a gooey layer over the noodles, and a little chopped cilantro for freshness, color, and authenticity put the finishing touches on the dish. We like to serve this with sour cream.

8 ounces vermicelli, broken in half
2 tablespoons vegetable oil
8 ounces chorizo sausage, halved and sliced ¼ inch thick
1 onion, minced (about 1 cup)
2 garlic cloves, minced
2 teaspoons minced chipotle chiles in adobo sauce
  Salt
1 (15.5-ounce) can black beans, drained and rinsed
1 (14.5-ounce) can diced tomatoes
1½ cups low-sodium chicken broth
  Pepper
2 ounces Monterey Jack cheese, shredded (about ½ cup)
¼ cup minced fresh cilantro

**1.** Cook the vermicelli with 1 tablespoon of the oil in a 12-inch skillet over medium-high heat, stirring frequently, until toasted and golden, about 4 minutes. Transfer to a paper towel–lined plate and set aside.

**2.** Add the remaining 1 tablespoon oil to the skillet and return to medium heat until shimmering. Add the chorizo, onion, garlic, chipotle, and ½ teaspoon salt and cook until the onion is softened, 3 to 5 minutes.

**3.** Stir in the beans, tomatoes with their juice, broth, and toasted vermicelli. Cover and cook, stirring often and adjusting the heat as needed to maintain a vigorous simmer, until all the liquid is absorbed and the vermicelli is tender, about 10 minutes.

**4.** Season with salt and pepper to taste. Off the heat, sprinkle the Monterey Jack over the top. Cover and let sit off the heat until the cheese melts, about 1 minute. Sprinkle with the cilantro before serving.

**WHERE THINGS CAN GO WRONG:** Remember to break the vermicelli in half, otherwise it will not fit into the skillet and cook evenly.

## NOTES FROM THE TEST KITCHEN

### AN EASY WAY TO BREAK LONG-STRAND PASTA
Though we don't normally recommend breaking pasta strands in half, this step makes it easier to toast vermicelli in a skillet.

**1.** To keep the pasta from flying every which way in the kitchen, roll up the bundle of pasta in a kitchen towel that overlaps the pasta by 3 or 4 inches at both ends.

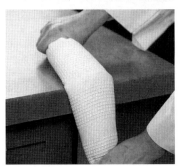

**2.** Holding both ends firmly, center the rolled bundle over the edge of a table or counter. Push down with both hands to break the pasta in the middle of the bundle.

# PASTA
## WITH GARLIC, OLIVE OIL, AND ARTICHOKES
SERVES 4 TO 6

**WHAT MAKES THIS A BEST RECIPE:** Pasta with garlic and oil, or *aglio e olio* in Italian, is among the most satisfying (and simple) pasta dishes. Comprised of kitchen staples, it is certainly quick to throw together, making it the perfect candidate for *The Best 30-Minute Recipe*. However, its simplicity is deceiving; most versions are rife with the flavor of burnt garlic or worse, no garlic presence at all. The key to this recipe (which we dressed up with the addition of artichokes) was the technique used for imbuing the olive oil with garlic. We found that slowly sautéing a large amount of minced garlic (a whopping 4 tablespoons) over a low flame until it turned golden and mellow produced the deep, complex garlic flavor we were after. Accompanied by a fistful of minced parsley, a hit of red pepper flakes, and a splash of fresh lemon juice, our sauce had enough oomph to stand up to a pound of pasta. We finessed our dish even more by holding back some of the raw garlic to season the pasta with before serving, and adding artichoke hearts, which we cooked until lightly browned and tender before adding them to the mix.

7 tablespoons extra-virgin olive oil
12 garlic cloves, minced (about 4 tablespoons)
 Salt
2 (9-ounce) packages frozen artichoke hearts, thawed and drained
1 pound spaghetti
3 tablespoons minced fresh parsley
2 teaspoons fresh lemon juice
¼ teaspoon red pepper flakes
 Pepper
 Grated Parmesan cheese, for serving

**1.** Bring 4 quarts water to a boil in a large pot for the pasta.

**2.** Meanwhile, cook 3 tablespoons of the oil, 3 tablespoons of the garlic, and ½ teaspoon salt in a large nonstick skillet over low heat, stirring often, until the garlic is sticky, foamy, and straw-colored, about 10 minutes. Transfer the garlic to a small bowl.

**3.** Add 1 more tablespoon of oil to the skillet and return to high heat until shimmering. Add the artichoke hearts and ¼ teaspoon salt and cook until lightly browned and tender, about 6 minutes.

**4.** Add 1 tablespoon salt and the pasta to the boiling water. Cook, stirring often, until the pasta is al dente. Reserve ½ cup of the pasta cooking water, then drain the pasta and return it to the pot.

**5.** Stir the artichokes, parsley, lemon juice, pepper flakes, remaining 3 tablespoons oil, toasted garlic mixture, and 2 tablespoons reserved pasta cooking water into the pasta. Season with the remaining raw garlic and salt and pepper to taste. Thin the sauce with the remaining cooking water as needed. Serve, passing the Parmesan separately.

**WHERE THINGS CAN GO WRONG:** When making pasta with garlic and oil, patience is a must. The key to success for this recipe is a slow sauté of the garlic, so don't be tempted to turn up the heat; over high heat garlic can burn in a flash and the taste of burnt garlic will ruin this dish. So keep the heat on low and keep a close eye on the garlic. When it foams and becomes sticky and straw-colored, after about 10 minutes, remove it from the heat.

## NOTES FROM THE TEST KITCHEN

### GARLIC PRESSES SAVE TIME
A defiantly sticky and undeniably stinky job, hand-mincing garlic is a chore most cooks avoid by pressing the cloves through a garlic press. The question for us was not whether garlic presses work, but which of the many available models works best. After squeezing our way through 10 different models, the overall winner was the **Zyliss Nonstick Susi Garlic Press** ($13.95); it was comfortable to use and produced very finely pressed garlic. Its metal frame made short work of two garlic cloves at a time, while its nonstick coating and cleaning attachment (which cleverly stores in the handle of the press) helped to secure its rank.

# CREAMY LOWFAT PESTO
MAKES ABOUT 1 CUP,
ENOUGH TO SAUCE 1 POUND OF PASTA

**WHAT MAKES THIS A BEST RECIPE:** Traditional pesto is made with pureed basil, garlic, nuts, cheese, and a generous amount of olive oil—and with an average of 270 calories and 28 grams of fat per serving, it's definitely not lowfat fare. While most pestos rely on at least ½ cup of oil to emulsify and blend the sauce, for this recipe we used a combination of ¼ cup part-skim ricotta and 2 tablespoons extra-virgin olive oil to give ours its velvety texture. Without all the fat, we found we needed to toast the garlic to tame its bite, and we added a shallot for further allium flavor. To really maximize the basil's flavor, we bruised the leaves before processing them to release their herbaceous oils. Because a little Parmesan packs a lot of flavor, we were able to limit the amount to just ½ cup. And with the cheese's nutty flavor, we found that we didn't miss the nuts that are traditionally part of the recipe. This pesto, with just 6 grams of fat and 80 calories per 2½ tablespoon serving, is a lighter but equally tasty choice for tossing with pasta, as well as using as an all-around condiment.

    4   garlic cloves, unpeeled
    3   cups fresh basil leaves, stems and buds discarded (2 to 3 bunches)
    1   ounce Parmesan cheese, grated (about ½ cup)
    ¼   cup part-skim ricotta cheese
    1   shallot, minced (3 tablespoons)
    2   tablespoons extra-virgin olive oil
        Salt and pepper

**1.** Toast the garlic in a small skillet over medium-heat, shaking the pan occasionally, until the color of the cloves deepens slightly, about 7 minutes. Transfer the garlic to a plate to cool, then peel the cloves and chop or press through a garlic press.
**2.** Place the basil in a heavy-duty gallon-sized zipper-lock bag. Pound the bag with the flat side of a meat pounder or rolling pin until all the leaves are lightly bruised.

Our lowfat pesto relies on part-skim ricotta cheese (rather than lots of oil) for its velvety texture.

**3.** Process the garlic, basil, Parmesan, ricotta, shallot, oil, and ½ teaspoon salt in a food processor until smooth, about 30 seconds, stopping to scrape down the sides of the bowl as needed. Transfer the mixture to a small bowl, and season with salt and pepper to taste.

**WHERE THINGS CAN GO WRONG:** Do not substitute nonfat ricotta for the part-skim ricotta or the pesto will be dry and a bit gummy. Do not include the stems or buds of the basil because they taste bitter.

**WHAT YOU CAN DO AHEAD OF TIME:** The pesto can be covered with a sheet of plastic wrap pressed flush against its surface and refrigerated for up to 3 days.

## NOTES FROM THE TEST KITCHEN

### RELEASING BASIL'S FLAVORFUL OILS
Bruising the basil leaves before processing them in the food processor or blender helps to bring out their sweet flavor. Place the basil leaves in a zipper-lock bag and bruise with a meat pounder or rolling pin.

### TOASTING GARLIC IS ESSENTIAL
Most pesto aficionados spend their time debating over how to puree the basil, but what often gets overlooked is the garlic. We found that raw garlic overwhelmed the herbal flavor of the basil. To mellow that garlic flavor, we decided to toast the unpeeled cloves in a dry pan. This gave the garlic a decidedly nutty flavor, completely devoid of the characteristic raw garlic heat. When processed with the other ingredients, the toasted garlic receded into the background, allowing the full flavor of the basil to shine.

# SLOW-COOKER BOLOGNESE SAUCE
MAKES 12 CUPS, ENOUGH
TO SAUCE 4 POUNDS OF PASTA

**WHAT MAKES THIS A BEST RECIPE:** If you're at all like us, you're finicky about classic pasta sauce recipes, especially one like Bolognese, which when done right is a far cry from a basic meat sauce. Unlike meat sauces in which tomatoes dominate (think jars of spaghetti sauce with flecks of meat in a sea of tomato puree), Bolognese sauce is about the meat, with the tomatoes in a supporting role. Bolognese also differs from many tomato-based meat sauces in that it contains dairy—butter, milk, and/or cream. The dairy gives the meat an especially sweet, appealing flavor. Tradition dictates that when making Bolognese, the cook must exert patience and a watchful eye, hovering over the pot as the aromatics sauté, the meat browns, and small increments of milk and then wine are added and cooked down until they disappear into the meat. All this usually takes about three hours. Bypass these labors, and the result is just not Bolognese—or so we thought. Enter the slow cooker, which we had put to good use developing many a stew and pot roast (though we had not even considered a sauce as complex as Bolognese). We were skeptical at even the thought of it. Yes, the slow cooker is designed for unhurried, unattended simmering (with the top firmly in place so the food is virtually steam cooked), but how would we thicken the sauce and replicate the richness that hours of stovetop cooking delivers? All the recipes we researched more closely resembled waterlogged, flavorless hamburger soup than a rich and deeply flavored Bolognese. That said, with a few tricks we sorted out how to make the sauce. First, since it takes forever for cold ingredients to heat up in a slow cooker, we gave the sauce a running start on the stovetop by softening the vegetables, browning the ground meat, adding the milk, wine, and tomatoes, and then bringing everything to a boil. We then transferred this hot mixture to the slow cooker and cooked it on high with the top off for 7 to 8 hours, which allowed the mixture to reduce down slowly and evenly so that the flavors were concentrated, the sauce silky, and the meat incredibly tender. We think this slow-cooker recipe rivals any prepared by the traditional method. And we intentionally developed a big batch recipe since Bolognese freezes so well.

3 tablespoons unsalted butter

½ onion, minced (about ½ cup)

1 carrot, chopped fine

½ celery rib, chopped fine

3 garlic cloves, minced

3 tablespoons tomato paste

3 pounds meatloaf mix or 1½ pounds ground chuck and 1½ pounds ground pork

Salt and pepper

3 cups whole milk

3 cups dry white wine

2 (28-ounce) cans whole tomatoes, ground in a blender until smooth

1 teaspoon minced fresh thyme

**1.** Melt the butter in a large Dutch oven over medium-high heat. Add the onion, carrot, and celery and cook until softened but not browned, about 6 minutes. Stir in the garlic and tomato paste and cook until fragrant, about 30 seconds. Add the meat, 1 teaspoon salt, and ½ teaspoon pepper and cook, breaking up the meat, until crumbled into tiny pieces and lightly browned, about 5 minutes.

**2.** Add the milk, bring to a vigorous simmer, and cook until the milk evaporates and only clear fat remains, 10 to 15 minutes. Add the wine, tomatoes, and thyme; cover and bring to a boil. Transfer the mixture to a slow cooker, cover, set the temperature to high, and bring to a boil.

**3.** Remove the lid and simmer until the sauce is very thick, 7 to 8 hours. Season with salt and pepper to taste. Serve.

**WHERE THINGS CAN GO WRONG:** Because a lot of steam will rise from the sauce as it cooks, place the slow cooker on a countertop with no cabinetry overhead.

**WHAT YOU CAN DO AHEAD OF TIME:** The sauce can be refrigerated in an airtight container for 4 days, or frozen for up to 2 months. This recipe can be partially made the night before so that it's ready to place in the slow cooker first thing in the morning. Complete step 1 and do step 2 up to the point of transferring the mixture to the slow cooker. Refrigerate the mixture in the Dutch oven overnight. The next morning, bring the mixture back to a boil, transfer it to the slow cooker, and proceed as directed.

## NOTES FROM THE TEST KITCHEN

### FOR EVEN SLOWER COOKING
If you need more than the 7 or 8 hours cooking time called for in the recipe, in step 3 set the lid halfway off the cooker rather than removing it entirely, then simmer the sauce for 10 to 11 hours.

### A SLOW COOKER FOR FAST TIMES
The slow cooker may be the only modern kitchen appliance that saves the cook time by using more of it rather than less. But gone are the days of merely picking out what size you need. We found 40 different models online, which begs the question, is one slow cooker better than another? To find out, we rounded up eight leading models and put them through some very slow tests in the kitchen. We prepared our Bolognese Sauce on high temperature for seven hours in each model and, frankly, each sauce was pretty good. When we prepared a pot roast in our slow cookers, however, we found out that size and shape really matter. We recommend buying an oval slow cooker with a minimum capacity of 6 quarts. Anything smaller and a five-pound chuck roast, pork loin, or brisket will not fit. We also liked models with power lights—without one, it's hard to tell if the slow cooker is on. Our favorite is the **Farberware Millennium 6-Quart Oval Cooker** ($29.99), which won for its shape, performance, and modest price.

### OUR FAVORITE CANNED TOMATOES
Ten months out of the year, the quality of canned tomatoes easily surpasses that of any fresh tomatoes you may be able to find. Picked at the peak of ripeness and canned immediately, they are sweet, flavorful, and convenient. We tasted several brands of both canned diced tomatoes and canned whole tomatoes and discovered that not every brand was up to snuff. Whether you are buying whole or diced tomatoes, look for those that are packed in juice rather than puree, which has an unpleasant cooked flavor. The winning brand of diced tomatoes, **Muir Glen** ($1.79 for 14.5 ounces), uses organic tomatoes and won accolades for its vibrant, fresh-from-the-garden flavor. For whole tomatoes, **Progresso Italian-Style Whole Peeled Tomatoes with Basil** ($1.59 for 28 ounces) was tasters' clear favorite, praised for "the perfect balance of acidic and fruity notes."

# MEAT

# PEPPER-CRUSTED FILET MIGNON
## WITH BLUE CHEESE–CHIVE BUTTER
### SERVES 4

**WHAT MAKE THIS A BEST RECIPE:** The revered elite superstar of steaks, filet mignon usually needs serious help in the kitchen to live up to its reputation on the plate. A relatively mild cut of meat, filet can be crusted with peppercorns, which offer a welcome crunch and flavor boost. We found that using relatively thick-cut (1½-inch to 2-inch) filets were a must for the right ratio of pepper to steak in each bite. And, a copious amount of freshly cracked pepper was key for getting a good crust—however, keeping the crust intact and taming the spicy heat of the peppercorns were our biggest challenges. To keep the crust in place, we had success with a thick paste of cracked peppercorns, oil, and salt rubbed and pressed onto the raw steaks an hour before cooking. Letting the steaks sit before cooking allowed the salt enough time to penetrate and season our thick-cut filets. The resulting finish was crusty and dark brown, and it held tight. To quell the spiciness of the peppercorns we took to heating the peppercorn-oil mixture before rubbing it on the steaks. Cooking the mixture changed the flavor dramatically, toning down the spiciness of the peppercorns, allowing for the more complex, subtle flavors to take center stage.

- 5 tablespoons black peppercorns, cracked (see note)
- 5 tablespoons plus 2 teaspoons olive oil
- 1 tablespoon kosher salt
- 4 center-cut filets mignons, 1½ to 2 inches thick, 7 to 8 ounces each, trimmed of fat and silver skin
- 3 tablespoons unsalted butter, softened
- 1½ ounces mild blue cheese, at room temperature
- ⅛ teaspoon table salt
- 2 tablespoons minced fresh chives

**1.** Heat the peppercorns and 5 tablespoons of the oil in a small saucepan over low heat until faint bubbles appear. Continue to cook at a bare simmer, swirling the pan occasionally, until the pepper is fragrant, 7 to 10 minutes. Remove the pan from the heat and set it aside to cool.

When the mixture cools to room temperature, add the kosher salt and stir to combine. Rub the steaks with the pepper mixture, thoroughly coating the top and bottom of each steak with peppercorns. Cover the steaks with plastic wrap and press gently to make sure the peppercorns adhere. Let stand at room temperature for 1 hour.

**2.** Meanwhile, combine the butter, cheese, and table salt in a medium bowl and mix with a stiff rubber spatula until smooth. Fold in the chives and set aside.

**3.** Adjust an oven rack to the middle position, place a rimmed baking sheet on the oven rack, and heat the oven to 450 degrees. Heat the remaining 2 teaspoons oil in a large skillet over medium-high heat until just smoking. Place the steaks in the skillet and cook, without moving them, until a dark brown crust has formed, 3 to 4 minutes. Flip the steaks and cook until well browned on the second side, about 3 minutes. Remove the pan from the heat and transfer the steaks to the hot baking sheet. Roast 3 to 5 minutes for rare, 5 to 7 minutes for medium-rare to medium. Transfer the steaks to a wire cooling rack, top each one with 1 to 2 tablespoons of the reserved butter, tent loosely with foil, and let them rest for 5 minutes before serving.

## GREAT DISCOVERIES
### TAMING BLACK PEPPERCORNS

Test kitchen staffers with more sensitive palates were relieved to learn that the pungent heat of black peppercorns can be mellowed by a brief simmer in oil. I was pleased with the effect but curious as to the cause. Research revealed that the natural irritant in peppercorns is called piperine. As peppercorns age, the piperine is converted into closely related molecules (called isomers) that have different flavor characteristics and that are less irritating to the nose and throat. Left sitting at room temperature in your cupboard, the peppercorns may take years to undergo this reaction, but the hot oil serves as a catalyst, driving the conversion at hundreds of times its natural speed, quickly tempering the pepper's pungency. As a bonus, piperine and its isomers are oil-soluble, so that during the simmer some of the remaining pepper heat and flavor leaches out of the peppercorns into the surrounding oil. This oil can then be discarded to further reduce the heat of the dish.

SEAN LAWLER | ASSOCIATE EDITOR, COOK'S ILLUSTRATED

# NOTES FROM THE TEST KITCHEN

### WANT IT LESS SPICY?
While heating the peppercorns in oil tempers their pungent heat, this recipe is still fairly spicy. If you prefer a very mild pepper flavor, drain the cooled peppercorns in a fine-mesh strainer in step 1, toss them with 5 tablespoons of fresh oil, add the salt, and proceed.

### CRACKING PEPPERCORNS
Spread half of the peppercorns across a large cutting board. Place a skillet on top, and, pressing down firmly with both hands, use a rocking motion to crush the peppercorns beneath the "heel" of the skillet. Move the skillet back and forth across the cutting board, redistributing the peppercorns as needed. Repeat with the remaining peppercorns.

### TROUBLESHOOTING PEPPER-CRUSTED FILET MIGNON
Choking heat, gray exteriors, peppercorns that fall off with the slightest provocation—we encountered all these problems and more while developing our recipe. To avoid them, take these steps.

**SIMMER.** Gently simmer the peppercorns in olive oil to mellow the heat.

**COAT.** Coat the filets with the pepper-oil mixture, pressing the peppercorns gently into the tops and bottoms of the steaks.

**REST.** Cover with plastic wrap, pressing to make sure the peppercorns adhere. Let rest one hour.

**BROWN.** Sear the steaks in a well-oiled skillet until browned beneath the peppercorn layer.

**ROAST.** Finish cooking in a hot oven to ensure browning on the sides.

# PAN-SEARED INEXPENSIVE STEAK
## WITH MUSTARD-CREAM SAUCE
### SERVES 4

**WHAT MAKES THIS A BEST RECIPE:** We were tired of paying high prices for premium steaks, and wanted to find the best "cheap" steaks—priced under $6.99 per pound—that would deliver solid beefy flavor and tender texture. Our biggest challenge turned out to be identifying the cheap cuts we found. It's hard to know what you're buying when you pick up a "steak" in the grocery store. Names differ from region to region, some cuts are wonderfully tender while others are hopelessly tough, and some recipes recommend cuts that are almost impossible to find. After numerous phone calls and trips to grocery store meat departments and butcher shops, we narrowed our list of cheap steaks down to 12 candidates. We cooked them as we would any steak, creating a nice sear on both sides without overcooking or allowing the fond to burn. Tasters judged most to be too tough and/or lacking beefy flavor, while others were livery or gamey. We tried a variety of preparation methods—salting, aging, tenderizing, marinating—but none really improved flavor and texture. In the end, only two cuts earned favored status: boneless shell sirloin steak (aka top butt) and flap meat steak (aka sirloin tips). If you want to make a pan sauce, you can do so while the steaks rest after cooking but make sure to prepare all the sauce ingredients before cooking the steaks.

- 2 tablespoons vegetable oil
- 2 whole boneless shell sirloin steaks (top butt) or whole flap meat steaks, each about 1 pound and 1¼ inches thick
  Salt and pepper
- 1 shallot, minced (about 3 tablespoons)
- 2 tablespoons dry white wine
- ½ cup low-sodium chicken broth
- 6 tablespoons heavy cream
- 3 tablespoons grainy Dijon mustard

**1.** Heat the oil in a large skillet over medium-high heat until just smoking. Meanwhile, season the steaks with salt and pepper. Place the steaks in the skillet and cook, without moving them, until well browned, about 2 minutes. Flip

To ensure that the meat is tender, slice it against the grain and on the bias.

the steaks and reduce the heat to medium. Cook until well browned on the second side and the internal temperature registers 125 degrees on an instant-read thermometer for medium-rare (about 5 minutes) or 130 degrees for medium (about 6 minutes).

**2.** Transfer the steaks to a large plate and tent them loosely with foil. Let the steaks rest until the internal temperature registers 130 degrees for medium-rare or 135 degrees for medium, 12 to 15 minutes.

**3.** To make the sauce, pour off all but 1 tablespoon of the fat from the now-empty skillet. Return the skillet to low heat and add the shallot. Cook, stirring frequently, until beginning to brown, 2 to 3 minutes. Add the wine and increase the heat to medium-high. Simmer rapidly, scraping up the browned bits on the pan bottom, until the liquid is reduced to a glaze, about 30 seconds. Add the broth and simmer until it has reduced to ¼ cup, about 3 minutes. Add the cream and any meat juice. Cook until heated through, about 1 minute. Stir in the mustard and season with salt and pepper to taste. Set aside.

**4.** Using a sharp knife, slice the steak about ¼ inch thick against the grain on the bias, arrange on a platter or on individual plates, and spoon the sauce over the steak.

**WHERE THINGS CAN GO WRONG:** Bear in mind that even those tasters who usually prefer rare beef preferred these steaks cooked medium-rare or medium because the texture is firmer and not quite so chewy.

## NOTES FROM THE TEST KITCHEN

### CUTTING THE RECIPE DOWN TO SIZE
To serve two instead of four, use a medium skillet to cook a 1-pound steak and halve the sauce ingredients.

### WHEN IS IT DONE?
A great steak starts at the supermarket and ends with proper timing in the kitchen. Chefs who cook hundreds of steaks a week seem to know when a steak is done almost by intuition. Here are some of the more intriguing methods of determining doneness and our assessment of their practicality for home cooks.

**PRESS THE MEAT.** Rare meat feels like the flesh between your thumb and forefinger. For medium meat, make a fist and touch the same part of your hand. Well-done meat feels like the tip of you nose.
**OUR ASSESSMENT.** This method is too vague for most cooks.

**NICK AND PEEK.** Slice into the steak with a paring knife and check the color.
**OUR ASSESSMENT.** The steak has already been butchered once—why do it a second time in the pan and risk losing juices? Fine in an emergency, but not our first choice.

**TAKE THE TEMPERATURE.** Hold the steak up with a pair of tongs and slide an instant-read thermometer through the side, making sure to avoid bone.
**OUR ASSESSMENT.** The most reliable method. Works the first time you try it—and every time thereafter.

# A GUIDE TO INEXPENSIVE STEAKS

We taste-tested 12 inexpensive steaks (all priced at $6.99 per pound or less). We've listed the steaks by the name used in the Uniform Retail Meat Identity Standards (a national system for standardizing terminology for retail cuts of meat), but because supermarkets still often use regional or other names, we've listed the likely alternatives you'll find, too. The "hard-to-find cuts" in the chart are usually sold only at butchers' shops; all other cuts can be found in most supermarkets.

## BEST CUTS FOR PAN-SEARING

### BONELESS SHELL SIRLOIN STEAK
**ALTERNATE NAMES:** Top butt, butt steak, top sirloin butt, top sirloin steak, center-cut roast
**SHOPPING TIPS:** One of the two main muscles from the hip. Can be quite large. Look for a 1-pound piece of uniform, 1¼-inch thickness.
**TASTERS' COMMENTS:** "Tremendous beef flavor" coupled with "very tender" texture make this steak a winner. "Just like butter."

### FLAP MEAT STEAK
**ALTERNATE NAMES:** Top sirloin tips, beef sirloin tips, sirloin tip steak, sirloin flap meat for tips
**SHOPPING TIPS:** Varies widely in size. Ask for a 1-pound steak of even thickness. Avoid small strips of meat or large steaks that taper drastically at one end.
**TASTERS' COMMENTS:** "Great beefy flavor" is the main selling point. Praised as "tender and fun to chew" and "never mushy."

## CUTS BETTER FOR GRILLING

### FLANK STEAK
**ALTERNATE NAMES:** Jiffy steak, London broil
**SHOPPING TIPS:** This wide, thin steak doesn't fit easily in a pan but works great on the grill.
**TASTERS' COMMENTS:** "Pleasant," "mild" flavor, with "just enough chew."

### SKIRT STEAK
**ALTERNATE NAMES:** Philadelphia steak, fajitas meat
**SHOPPING TIPS:** This thin steak can measure more than a foot long, making it better suited for grilling than pan-searing.
**TASTERS' COMMENTS:** Tasters gushed with praise such as "wonderful" and "beefy heaven." The meat is "rich and fatty."

## HARD-TO-FIND CUTS/ BUTCHERS' SPECIALS

### HANGER STEAK
**ALTERNATE NAMES:** Hanging tenderloin, butcher's steak
**SHOPPING TIPS:** Usually a restaurant cut, this thick steak "hangs" between the last rib and the loin.
**TASTERS' COMMENTS:** "Bold, brash beef flavor" and "moderately tender."

### FLAT IRON STEAK
**ALTERNATE NAME:** Blade steak
**SHOPPING TIPS:** Comes from the same muscle as the top blade steak, but the muscle is cut in such a way that the vein is removed at the same time.
**TASTERS' COMMENTS:** "Great beef flavor" and "awesome combination of tender and chewy." Can be livery.

## DISAPPOINTING CUTS

### TOP BLADE STEAK, BONELESS
**ALTERNATE NAMES:** Blade steak, book steak, butler steak, lifter steak, petit steak, flat iron steak, boneless top chuck steak
**TASTERS' COMMENTS:** "Tender and juicy" but undependable. Often tastes "like liver." Watch out for vein that runs through center of steak.

### SHOULDER STEAK, BONELESS
**ALTERNATE NAMES:** Chuck for swissing, boneless clod steak, London broil, boneless shoulder cutlet
**TASTERS' COMMENTS:** "Strong taste veers toward liver," but texture has "decent bite."

### TOP ROUND STEAK
**ALTERNATE NAME:** Inside round cut
**TASTERS' COMMENTS:** "Nice basic beef flavor," but texture is "like bubblegum."

### BOTTOM ROUND STEAK
**TASTERS' COMMENTS:** Overall assessment: "gummy, with flat flavor."

### EYE ROUND STEAK
**TASTERS' COMMENTS:** "Not much meat flavor"; also described as "tough."

### TIP STEAK
**ALTERNATE NAMES:** Sirloin tip steak, round tip steak, knuckle steak
**TASTERS' COMMENTS:** "Spongy," "shallow" beef flavor. Very tough.

# STUFFED FLANK STEAK

### SERVES 8 TO 10

**WHAT MAKES THIS A BEST RECIPE:** Rolled and stuffed flank steak has many advantages: it's a great way to feed a crowd, it's easy to make (and you can do all the work in advance), it's economical, and when properly prepared, it's very flavorful. Even supermarkets offer up packages of stuffed flank steaks, touting them as "great for grilling." However, a big part of success with stuffed flank steak is getting the timing just right. Often, the exterior chars and the inside is still raw.

We set out to build a recipe for stuffed flank steak from the ground up—rolling and stuffing our own—with intentions of demystifying the grilling technique. First, to prepare the flank steak for stuffing, we discovered that freezing it before attempting to butterfly it made for a clean cut ready for stuffing. For the filling, pungent ingredients (such as garlic, capers, and roasted red peppers) were a must, and breadcrumbs helped keep everything nice and tight. Combined with a layer of sliced ham and provolone from the deli, this stuffing was tasty, cheesy, and made a beautiful presentation.

As for grilling technique, a banked fire, with all of the hot coals on one side of the grill worked best when it came to grilling our stuffed steak. We were able to sear the meat over the hot side to achieve a nice brown exterior, and then we moved it over to the cool side (without coals) and covered the grill to finish cooking.

- 1 cup plain dried breadcrumbs
- ¾ cup jarred roasted red peppers, patted dry and coarsely chopped
- ½ cup extra-virgin olive oil
- 2 tablespoons capers, drained
- ¼ cup minced fresh parsley
- 2 garlic cloves, minced
- ¼ teaspoon red pepper flakes
  Salt and pepper
- 1 flank steak (about 2 pounds), frozen for 20 minutes

- 8 ounces Black Forest deli ham, sliced thin
- 8 ounces provolone cheese, sliced thin

**1.** Mix the breadcrumbs, roasted peppers, 2 tablespoons of the oil, capers, parsley, garlic, pepper flakes, and ½ teaspoon salt together in a medium bowl.

**2.** Season the steak with salt and pepper and position it so that the long side faces you. Following the photos, butterfly the steak, and layer the ham, cheese, and seasoned crumbs over the meat. Starting with the short side, roll and tie the steak. Season it with salt and pepper, brush with 2 tablespoons oil, and refrigerate it while the grill is heating.

## NOTES FROM THE TEST KITCHEN

### THE BEST WAY TO STUFF FLANK STEAK

**1.** Slice the chilled steak horizontally, opening the steak as if it were a book. Split the steak to within ½ inch of the edge.

**2.** Layer ham and cheese over the steak, then cover with the crumb mixture, leaving a 1-inch border around the edges of the steak. Pat the crumbs to adhere.

**3.** Starting with a short side, roll up the steak tightly.

**4.** Use kitchen twine to tie the steak at 1-inch intervals. Loop a piece of twine around both ends of the steak to keep the filling from falling out.

**3.** Light a large chimney starter filled with charcoal briquettes (about 100 pieces) and allow it to burn until all the charcoal is covered with a layer of fine gray ash, about 20 minutes. Spread the coals out over half of the grill bottom, leaving the other half with no coals. Set the cooking grate in place, cover, and let the grill heat up for 5 minutes. Use a grill brush to scrape the cooking grate clean.

**4.** Grill the steak over the fire until it is browned on all four sides, about 12 minutes. Move the steak to the cool side of the grill and brush it with 2 tablespoons oil. Cover the grill and cook until an instant-read thermometer inserted into the center of the steak registers 120 degrees, 20 to 30 minutes, rotating and brushing the steak every 10 minutes with 1 tablespoon oil.

**5.** Transfer the steak to a cutting board, tent loosely with foil, and let it rest for 10 minutes. Remove the twine and slice the steak crosswise into ½-inch-thick slices.

**WHERE THINGS CAN GO WRONG:** Checking the internal temperature of stuffed flank steak is a bit tricky. Doing the old "nick and peek" with a knife doesn't really work and causes the stuffing to fall out. An instant-read thermometer is a must for this recipe, and takes all the guesswork out of wondering if the steak is cooked all the way through.

**WHAT YOU CAN DO AHEAD OF TIME:** The stuffed steak, wrapped tightly in plastic wrap, can be refrigerated, for up to 1 day.

## NOTES FROM THE TEST KITCHEN

### STUFFED FLANK STEAK ON A GAS GRILL
Follow the recipe for Stuffed Flank Steak through step 2. Light all the burners on a gas grill and turn the heat to high for 15 minutes. Scrape the cooking grate clean with a grill brush. Grill the steak until browned on all four sides, about 12 minutes. Leave the primary burner on high and turn off all the other burners. Move the steak to the cool side of the grill and proceed as directed in step 4, cooking the steak with the lid down.

# CHARCOAL-GRILLED LONDON BROIL
SERVES 4 TO 6

**WHAT MAKES THIS A BEST RECIPE:** Throwing a big slab of inexpensive meat on the grill sounds easy, but often the result is more like chewing on a rubber tire than a nicely charred, tender steak. Starting with the right cut of London broil (the name given to various cheap cuts of beef) was key to our success. We found the best results with top and bottom round steaks, which seared up well (especially the more uniform bottom round cut). Unfortunately, the steaks had a livery flavor and a good bit of toughness. But we found that salting the meat, wrapping it tightly in plastic wrap, and letting it sit (refrigerated) for at least 3 hours improved the flavor dramatically. The salt drew juice out of the steak and mixed with the salt on the exterior, creating a shallow "brine" that was reabsorbed by the meat as it sat. And it improved the taste by accentuating the steaks' naturally beefy flavors while masking some of the livery ones. That said, we still had problems: the tough, chewy texture and some lingering livery flavor. After trying multiple marinades and tenderizers (all of which failed), we experimented with cooking techniques (searing the meat on the hot side of a grill and then letting it cook through over the cool side). But we were still left with gray bands of overcooked meat surrounding a rosy center. This cut needed less time on the grill—but how could we raise the temperature safely and quickly? When we simply left the meat out at room temperature, after an hour, the internal temperature increased by only 3 degrees; it would take nearly 6 hours to reach 70 degrees—enough time for bacteria to multiply. Taking a cue from Harold McGee's book *On Food and Cooking*, we increased the temperature of the steak from 40 to 70 degrees in just an hour by soaking it (in a zipper-lock bag) in 100-degree water. This allowed us to decrease the grilling time from 22 minutes to just 13, ensuring a steak with a gorgeous rosy interior as well as a decent char. It was the combination of salting (which

Carving grilled London broil into ultra-thin slices is just one of several tricks we used to transform a cheap steak into a terrific meal.

increased beefy flavor) and reduced cooking time (which reduced livery flavor) that was key. So in the end, in addition to choosing the best cut and finessing our technique (including lots of flipping on the grill to counteract buckling), we created a tender, flavorful, and nicely charred steak out of a London broil with the same small arsenal of ingredients used on high-priced, well-marbled cuts of beef.

2  teaspoons kosher salt
1  bottom round steak, 1½ inches thick (2 to 2½ pounds)
1  tablespoon vegetable oil
½  teaspoon pepper

**1.** Sprinkle both sides of the steak evenly with the salt, and wrap it tightly in plastic wrap. Refrigerate the steak for at least 3 hours.

**2.** Fill a large pot or bucket with 1 gallon of warm water (about 100 degrees). Place the wrapped steak into a zipper-lock bag, squeeze out the excess air, and tightly seal the bag. Place the steak in the water, covering with a plate or bowl to keep the bag submerged. Set it aside for 1 hour.

**3.** About 20 minutes before grilling, light a large chimney starter filled with charcoal briquettes (about 100 pieces) and allow it to burn until all the charcoal is covered with a layer of fine gray ash, about 20 minutes. Spread the coals out over half of the grill bottom, leaving the other half with no coals. Set the cooking grate in place, cover, and let the grill heat up for 5 minutes. Use a grill brush to scrape the cooking grate clean.

**4.** Remove the steak from the water and unwrap it. Brush both sides of the steak with the oil (the salt will have dissolved at this point) and sprinkle it evenly with the pepper. Grill the steak directly over the coals, flipping it once every minute, until a dark brown crust forms on both sides, about 8 minutes. Move the steak to the cool side of the grill and cover it. Continue cooking until an instant-read thermometer inserted into the center registers 120 degrees for medium-rare, about 5 minutes, flipping the steak halfway through the cooking time.

**5.** Transfer the steak to a cutting board, tent loosely with foil, and let it rest about 10 minutes. Following the photo on page 138, hold a thin slicing knife at a 45-degree angle to the meat and slice the meat very thinly. Serve.

## NOTES FROM THE TEST KITCHEN

### GAS-GRILLED LONDON BROIL
Because gas grills generally produce less heat than charcoal grills, the steak requires a longer cooking time (and less frequent flipping) to develop a nice char. We have therefore omitted the step of warming the wrapped steak in a water bath and employed metal skewers to keep the steaks from buckling.

**1.** Sprinkle both sides of the steak evenly with the salt, and wrap it tightly in plastic wrap. Refrigerate the steak for at least 3 hours.

**2.** About 20 minutes before grilling, light all the burners on a gas grill and turn the heat to high, close the cover, and heat until very hot, about 15 minutes. Scrape the cooking grate clean with a grill brush.

**3.** Unwrap the steak. Insert 3 metal skewers lengthwise through the center of the steak from one side, spaced about 1 inch apart. Brush both sides of the steak with oil, and sprinkle it evenly with the pepper. Place the steak on the hottest part of the grill. Grill, flipping the steak every 4 minutes, until an instant-read thermometer inserted into the center of the meat registers 120 degrees, 16 to 20 minutes.

**4.** Transfer the steak to a cutting board, tent loosely with foil, and let it rest about 10 minutes. Following the photo on page 138, hold a thin slicing knife at a 45-degree angle to the meat and slice the meat very thinly. Serve.

**WHERE THINGS CAN GO WRONG:** We do not recommend cooking London broil beyond medium-rare as it gets tougher the longer it is cooked. And to get the best sear, and keep the steak from buckling, we found that flipping the meat every minute during the searing process kept the meat flat, allowing for a nicely cooked exterior with great color and flavor.

**WHAT YOU CAN DO AHEAD OF TIME:** The steak can be salted and refrigerated, wrapped tightly in plastic wrap, for up to 24 hours.

## GREAT DISCOVERIES
### WHY DOES SOME MEAT TASTE LIVERY?

While developing the recipe for Charcoal-Grilled London Broil, one of my biggest hurdles was the pervasive presence of "iron-y" and "liver-y" flavors in the bottom round I was using. Through research, I learned that the more active a muscle is the more oxygen it requires to function—and the more oxygen it stores in a protein called myoglobin. So far, so good. The problem comes up when steaks cut from particularly active muscles (the bottom round, for instance, is from the leg) are heated. The heat releases the oxygen from the myoglobin, leaving it free to react with the fatty acids present in all meat to produce liver-y, iron-y flavors in the form of aldehydes. In short, what's causing the off flavors is oxidation. And the longer the cooking time and the higher the temperature, the more oxidation occurs.

Back in the test kitchen, I considered the options. While we usually don't give our steaks a bath before cooking, in the case of London broil, a warm soak really did the trick—by shortening the cooking time considerably. When I grilled a 1½-inch-thick bottom round steak straight from the refrigerator, it took about 22 minutes to achieve a medium-rare center; by that time, the steak had developed an overcooked, gray band around the perimeter. But when I soaked the wrapped steak in 100-degree water for an hour, it reached the same temperature in just 13 minutes—almost half the time! (That's because the refrigerated steak started out at 40 degrees, the bathed steak at 70 degrees, giving it a big jump toward the endpoint of 120 degrees.) Instead of a tough gray band, our soaked steak had subtle gradations of rosy-pink. And most important: The bottom round that cooked for about half the time tasted much less livery.

DAVID PAZMIÑO | TEST COOK, COOK'S ILLUSTRATED

## NOTES FROM THE TEST KITCHEN
### COAXING THE BEST OUT OF LONDON BROIL
A tough, livery, unevenly browned slab of meat that buckles up when grilled? Not a very appealing combination. Instead of admitting defeat—and opting for pricey porterhouse—we stepped up to the challenge. Turns out a tough, cheap steak just needs a bit of old-fashioned pampering to smooth out its rough edges.

**SALT RUBDOWN.** Coating with salt draws juice to the surface, where it eventually dissolves the salt; the juice is then reabsorbed into the steak in the form of a flavorful, concentrated "brine," bringing out beefy flavors and masking livery ones.

**WARM BATH.** Submerging the (wrapped) beef in warm water for the last hour of salting cuts the cooking time by almost 10 minutes—providing less opportunity for fatty acids to break down into off-tasting compounds.

**MUSCLE RELAXATION.** Flipping the meat once per minute keeps the long muscle fibers from contracting and buckling up, making it easier to achieve a good sear.

**STYLISH CUT.** Cutting ultra-thin slices—at a 45-degree angle—shortens the meat's long, tough muscle fibers, dramatically diminishing its chewiness.

# SUNDAY-BEST GARLIC ROAST BEEF

### SERVES 6 TO 8

**WHAT MAKES THIS A BEST RECIPE:** Almost any good home cook can take an expensive prime rib and roast it to perfection, but hand that cook a cheap roast, and disaster likely awaits. Cheap roasts have more gristle, more connective tissue, and flavors that are often sour or livery. With this recipe, however, anyone can turn a cheap cut of meat into the garlicky centerpiece of a special meal for company or a simple Sunday dinner. First, we found that among the cheap roasts available, there is one champ—top sirloin roast. With this cut, you're off to a great start. Our secret for cooking the roast? Start the oven on a high temperature and brown the roast, then lower the temperature to 300 degrees for the remainder of the roasting time. This simple trick gives the exterior a nice browning and the lower heat allows the roast to cook more evenly so you can avoid overcooking the exterior portion in order to cook it through entirely. To dress up our roast, we use garlic in a three-stage process. Slivered garlic (which we toasted in a dry pan to mellow the bite) is inserted into the raw roast, which is then rubbed with a raw garlic-salt paste. The roast sits, covered with the paste for a spell (overnight is best), then the paste is wiped off (it burned and turned bitter during the browning process) before the meat goes in the oven. Once the roast is brown and it's time to lower the oven temperature, we add a third application of garlic in the form of a cooked paste. Hands down, the combination of the roast choice, oven technique, and garlic triple whammy is what makes this a best recipe.

### BEEF

- 8 large garlic cloves, unpeeled
- 1 top sirloin roast with some top fat intact (4 pounds)

### GARLIC-SALT RUB

- 3 large garlic cloves, minced
- 1 teaspoon dried thyme
- ½ teaspoon salt

### GARLIC PASTE

- 12 large garlic cloves, peeled, cut in half lengthwise
- 2 sprigs fresh thyme
- 2 bay leaves
- ½ teaspoon salt
- ½ cup olive oil
  Pepper

### JUS

- 1½ cups low-sodium beef broth
- 1½ cups low-sodium chicken broth

**1. FOR THE BEEF:** Toast the unpeeled garlic cloves in a small skillet over medium-high heat, tossing frequently, until the cloves are spotty brown, about 8 minutes. Set the garlic aside. When cool enough to handle, peel the cloves and cut them into ¼-inch slivers.

**2.** Using a paring knife, make 1-inch-deep slits all over the roast. Insert the toasted garlic into the slits.

**3. FOR THE GARLIC-SALT RUB:** Mix the minced garlic, thyme, and salt together in a small bowl. Rub the mixture all over the roast. Place the roast on a large plate and refrigerate, uncovered, for at least 4 hours or preferably overnight.

## NOTES FROM THE TEST KITCHEN

### THREE CHEAP CUTS

We tested three popular inexpensive roasts and found one champ, one solid pinch hitter, and one roast that you definitely do not want in your lineup.

**BEST BET**

**TOP SIRLOIN ROAST.** This cut from the hip area tasted incredibly meaty and had plenty of marbling, which made for a succulent roast. It can also be labeled as top butt, top sirloin butt, center-cut roast, or spoon roast.

**SECOND CHOICE**

**BLADE ROAST.** This roast from the shoulder was beefy and juicy, and its shape made it very easy to slice. A thin line of sinew was the only unpleasant distraction.

**STEER CLEAR**

**BOTTOM ROUND ROAST.** This roast from the rump area was tough and lacking in flavor. Even worse was the absence of fat and marbling, which made the meat very dry.

**4. FOR THE GARLIC PASTE:** Heat the halved garlic cloves, thyme, bay leaves, salt, and oil in a small saucepan over medium-high heat until the bubbles start to rise to the surface. Reduce the heat to low and cook until the garlic is soft, about 30 minutes. Cool completely, and then strain the mixture, reserving the oil. Discard the herbs and transfer the garlic to a small bowl. Mash the garlic with 1 tablespoon of the garlic oil until a paste forms. Cover and refrigerate the paste until ready to use it. Cover and reserve the garlic oil.

**5.** Adjust an oven rack to the middle position, place a nonstick roasting pan or broiler pan bottom on the oven rack, and heat the oven to 450 degrees. Using paper towels, wipe the garlic-salt rub off the beef. Then, rub the beef with 2 tablespoons of the reserved garlic oil and season it with pepper. Transfer the meat, fat side down, to the preheated pan and roast, turning as needed until the meat is browned on all sides, 10 to 15 minutes.

**6.** Reduce the oven temperature to 300 degrees. Remove the roasting pan from the oven. Turn the roast fat side up and, using a spatula, coat the top of the roast with the garlic paste. Return the meat to the oven and roast until it reaches an internal temperature of 125 degrees on an instant-read thermometer, 50 to 70 minutes. Transfer the roast to a cutting board, tent loosely with foil, and let it rest for 2 minutes.

**7. FOR THE JUS:** Drain the excess fat from the roasting pan and place the pan over high heat. Add the broths and bring them to a boil, scraping the browned bits from the pan bottom. Simmer, stirring occasionally, until the liquid has reduced to 2 cups, about 5 minutes. Add any accumulated juice from the roast and cook for 1 minute. Pour the mixture through a fine-mesh strainer. Slice the roast crosswise against the grain into ¼-inch slices and serve with the jus.

**WHERE THINGS CAN GO WRONG:** When making the jus, taste the reduced broth before adding any of the accumulated meat juice from the roast. The meat juice is well seasoned and may make the jus too salty. Also, a heavy-duty roasting pan with a dark or nonstick finish or a broiler pan is a must for this recipe.

## NOTES FROM THE TEST KITCHEN

### A GARLIC TRIPLE WHAMMY

Not one, not two, but three garlic preparations are used to give our roast beef full garlic flavor without any of that harsh garlic burn. Here's how we do it.

**1.** Toast unpeeled garlic cloves.

**2.** Peel and sliver the cloves and insert the slivers into slits cut into the roast.

**3.** Combine minced garlic with herbs and salt.

**4.** Rub the garlic salt over the roast and refrigerate at least 4 hours.

**5.** Poach halved garlic cloves and herbs in oil. Strain and mash the garlic into a paste.

**6.** Rub the garlic paste over the browned roast.

# FRENCH DIP SANDWICHES
## WITH QUICK JUS
SERVES 4

**WHAT MAKES THIS A BEST RECIPE:** In the test kitchen, we often tire of dishes during the testing process. Chocolate cake, again? Our recipe for Sunday-Best Garlic Roast Beef (page 139) did not suffer this fate, in part because we found that the leftover roast makes incredible French dip sandwiches. The problem, however, was that we had plenty of leftover roast, but rarely any leftover jus. The "dip" in a French dip sandwich, the jus is the most important element—it's used to moisten the beef before assembling the sandwich, and it is served alongside the sandwich for dipping. Here we came up with an easy solution for making a full-flavored jus in no time, without pan drippings. (If you have leftover jus from the roast, that's great: use it.) How did we do it? First, we browned 1 cup of leftover roast beef trimmings in olive oil, then added some onion, a bit of flour (used to give the jus some body), and low-sodium beef broth. The mixture simmers until reduced by half (which gives the jus more body as well as intensifies its flavors) and then it is strained and the solids are discarded. In less than 20 minutes you're left with a bold, beefy jus—perfect for dipping. As far as preparing the roast beef for this sandwich, here's a tip. When you serve your Sunday roast beef, slice as much as you plan to serve that day, and leave the leftover portion of the roast unsliced. It is much easier to carve nice thin slices when the meat is cold and intact. Thin slices of beef are more tender than thick, and make reheating the beef simple and quick. When building the sandwiches, the beef slices are quickly dipped into the hot jus before being layered with sautéed onions and cheese (we like provolone, but Swiss cheese works, too) on buttered and toasted sub rolls. The sandwiches are then broiled until the cheese melts, and served with the extra jus for dipping. These French dip sandwiches are so tasty that you might even find yourself making our recipe for Garlic Roast Beef just for the leftovers!

### JUS
- 1 teaspoon olive oil
- 1 cup leftover roast beef trimmings
- ½ small onion, minced (about ¼ cup)
- 1 teaspoon unbleached all-purpose flour
- 2 cups low-sodium beef broth

### SANDWICHES
- 1 teaspoon olive oil
- 1 onion, halved and sliced thin (about 1 cup)
- 4 (6-inch) sub rolls
- 2 tablespoons unsalted butter, softened
- 4 cups thinly sliced leftover roast beef
- 4 slices provolone (or Swiss) cheese, cut in half

**1. FOR THE JUS:** Heat the oil in a medium skillet over medium-high heat until just smoking. Add the beef and cook until dark brown, about 1 minute. Reduce the heat to medium, add the onion, and cook until slightly softened, about 1 minute. Add the flour and cook, stirring constantly, until fragrant and toasty, about 1 minute. Whisk in the broth, scraping up the browned bits from the pan bottom. Simmer until the liquid is reduced by half, about 10 minutes. Pour the mixture through a fine-mesh strainer and set aside until needed.

**2. FOR THE SANDWICHES:** Position an oven rack 6 inches below the heating element and turn on the broiler. Heat the oil in a small nonstick skillet over medium-high heat until shimmering. Add the onion and cook, stirring frequently, until browned, about 7 minutes.

**3.** Meanwhile, slice the rolls in half lengthwise and spread the interior of both sides with the butter. Place the rolls on a baking sheet, buttered side up, and broil until golden, 1 to 3 minutes. Remove and reserve the top half of each roll.

**4. TO SERVE:** Heat the jus in a small saucepan. Dip the beef slices into the hot jus and place about 4 slices of beef on the bottom half of each roll. Spoon the onions over the beef and arrange the provolone on top. Broil until the cheese has melted. Set the top half of each roll in place and serve with extra jus for dipping.

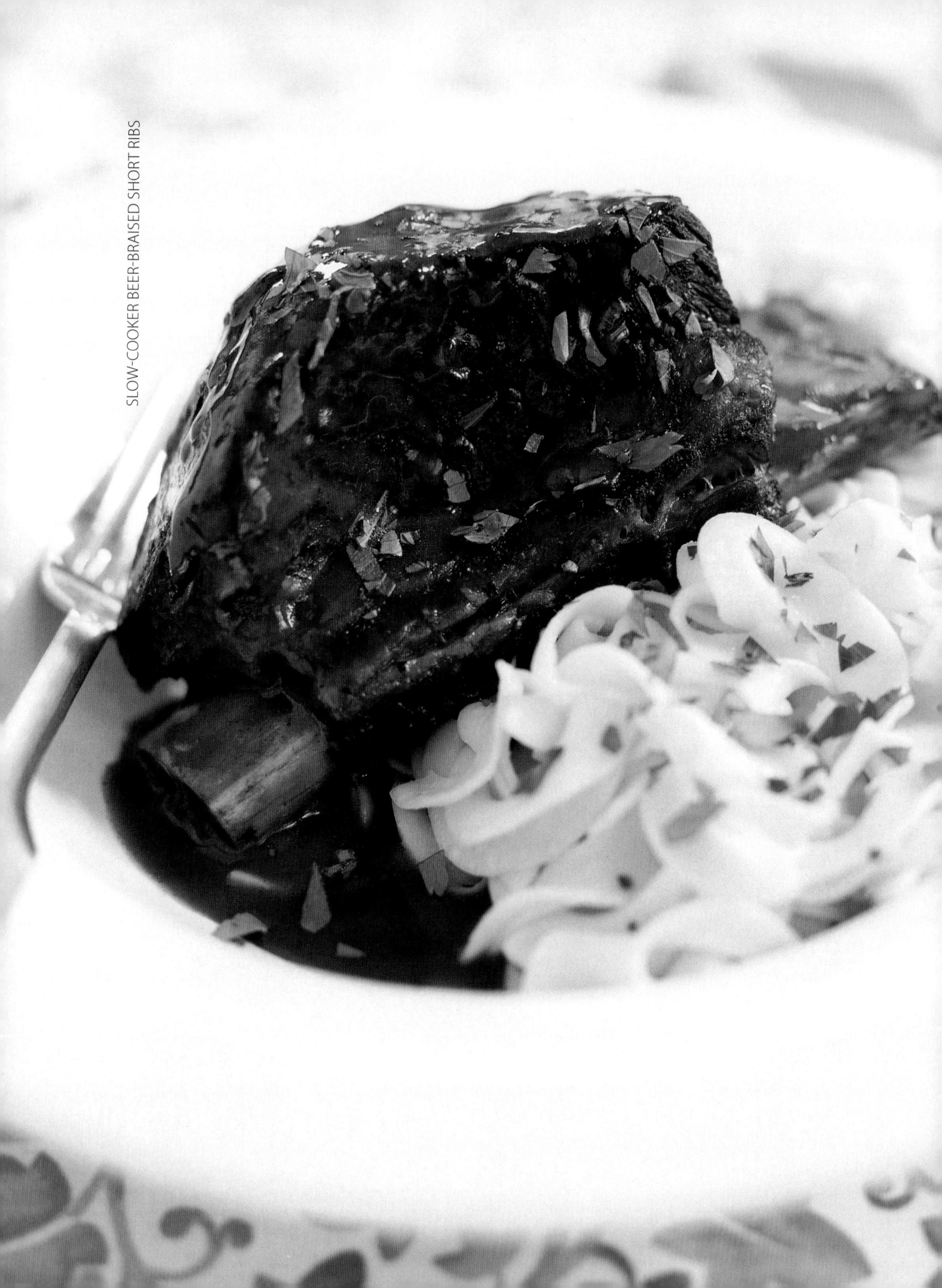

SLOW-COOKER BEER-BRAISED SHORT RIBS

# SLOW-COOKER BEER-BRAISED SHORT RIBS

SERVES 4 TO 6

**WHAT MAKES THIS A BEST RECIPE:** Meaty short ribs are slow food; time and gentle heat turn this tough cut into a blue-ribbon dinner. But we didn't have all day to babysit a simmering pot, so we thought why not use a slow cooker? Our first slew of tests were a disaster, resulting in dull, gray meat swimming in a bland and watery sauce that was capped with nearly an inch of fat. After more testing though, we discovered some key points for extracting as much beefy flavor from this naturally succulent braising cut. Browning the ribs in a skillet before adding them to the slow cooker adds a strong backbone of flavor, as well as renders out a good bit of unwanted fat. And using dark beer as our braising liquid was an epiphany: The beer creates a sauce with a lot of personality (much more than beer cut with chicken and/or beef broth). Tapioca and prunes proved to be the two secret ingredients here. The prunes melt away over the long simmering time, adding color and deep, complex flavor to the sauce, meanwhile, the tapioca worked like a charm to thicken the liquid as it cooked. Finally, to rid our sauce of remaining excess fat, we made our ribs the night before. In the morning, we refrigerated the ribs and sauce separately, then, just before dinner we removed the fat that had solidified on top of the sauce. To serve, we simply reheated the meat and the defatted sauce.

    5   pounds English-style beef short ribs (6 to 8 ribs),
        trimmed of excess fat (see page 146)
        Salt and pepper
    2   tablespoons vegetable oil
    2   tablespoons unsalted butter
    3   pounds onions, halved and sliced thin
    2   tablespoons tomato paste
    2   (12-ounce) bottles dark beer
    2   tablespoons Minute Tapioca
    2   bay leaves
    2   teaspoons minced fresh thyme
    2   tablespoons soy sauce
   12   pitted prunes

    3   tablespoons Dijon mustard
    2   tablespoons minced fresh parsley

**1.** Season the ribs with salt and pepper. Heat the oil in a large skillet over medium-high heat until just smoking. Add half of the ribs, meaty side down, and cook until they are well browned, about 5 minutes. Following the photos, turn each rib on one side and cook until well browned, about 1 minute. Repeat with the remaining sides. Transfer the ribs to a slow-cooker insert, arranging them meaty side down. Repeat with the remaining ribs.

**2.** Pour off all but 1 teaspoon of fat from the skillet. Add the butter and reduce the heat to medium. When the butter has melted, add the onions and cook, stirring occasionally, until well browned, 25 to 30 minutes. Stir in the tomato paste and cook, coating the onions with the tomato paste, until

## NOTES FROM THE TEST KITCHEN

### RIB RULES

**1.** The ribs taste best if fully browned before going into the slow cooker. Brown the meaty side of the ribs, then turn them on each side to finish browning (you can lean the ribs against each other if they won't stand on their own).

**2.** Place the browned ribs in the slow cooker with the meaty side facing down and the bones facing up. This placement will ensure that the meat stays submerged throughout the long cooking time.

### NOT TOO BITTER

Many of the beers we tested in our short ribs recipe turned bitter after 10 hours in the slow cooker. **Newcastle Brown Ale** had a good balance of sweet and bitter flavors and was the test kitchen's top choice. O'Doul's Amber Nonalcoholic Beer was surprisingly good, too—a bit sweet, but still with plenty of personality.

the paste begins to brown, about 5 minutes. Stir in the beer, bring it to a simmer, and cook, scraping the browned bits from the pan, until the foaming subsides, about 5 minutes. Remove the skillet from the heat and stir in the tapioca, bay leaves, 1 teaspoon thyme, soy sauce, and prunes. Transfer the mixture to the slow-cooker insert with the ribs.

**3.** Set the slow cooker on low, cover, and cook until the ribs are fork-tender, 10 to 11 hours. (Alternately, cook on high for 4 to 5 hours.) Transfer the ribs to a baking dish and strain the liquid into a bowl. Cover and refrigerate for at least 8 hours or up to 2 days.

**4.** When ready to serve, use a spoon to skim off the hardened fat from the liquid. Place the short ribs, meaty side down, and liquid in a Dutch oven and reheat over medium heat until warmed through, about 20 minutes. Transfer the ribs to a serving platter. Whisk the mustard and the remaining teaspoon of thyme into the sauce and season with salt and pepper. Pour 1 cup of sauce over the ribs. Sprinkle with parsley and serve, passing the remaining sauce separately.

**WHERE THINGS CAN GO WRONG:** The only way to remove fat from the braising liquid is to prepare this recipe a day or two before you want to serve it. Luckily, the short ribs actually taste better if cooked in advance and then reheated in the defatted braising liquid.

## NOTES FROM THE TEST KITCHEN

### SHORT RIBS
When it comes to choosing a cut of meat for our Slow-Cooker Beer-Braised Short Ribs, you have two options, both of which will deliver good results. English-style short ribs are cut from a single rib bone and feature a long flat bone with a rectangle of meat attached. Flanken-style ribs are cut across several bones and contain two or three small pieces of bone surrounded by pieces of meat. Because flanken-style ribs are more expensive and less widely available, we prefer English-style short ribs.

**ENGLISH-STYLE RIB**

**FLANKEN-STYLE RIB**

# OVEN-BARBECUED BEEF BRISKET
## WITH SMOKY BACON BBQ SAUCE
### SERVES 8 TO 10

**WHAT MAKES THIS A BEST RECIPE:** Down in Texas, the secret to great barbecued brisket is hours and hours of slow, smoky heat. We wanted to know if it were possible to get similar results using our oven. Getting low, even heat was no problem (just turn the oven dial to the desired low temperature), but capturing the smoky flavor of the pit was another story. We recommend pushing aside sauces and marinades featuring liquid smoke. They did little for us. For our technique we poked the brisket with a fork before wrapping it in a pound (yes, 1 pound) of bacon. During its time in the oven, the bacon fat renders and drips into the holes in the meat, giving it noticeably sweet-smoky flavor throughout. Sticking with classic Texas barbecue technique, we massaged our brisket with a spice rub before wrapping it in the bacon. Finally, to get a good crust on our brisket—the hallmark of truly great barbecue—we removed the bacon from the meat toward the end of cooking, used the bacon and meat juice to make a quick barbecue sauce, which we then brushed over the top of the roast before running it under the broiler. The sauce glazed the top of the brisket, turning it almost crisp with a rich mahogany color that will fool even the most ardent barbecue fan.

BBQ RUB

- 4 teaspoons brown sugar
- 4 teaspoons paprika
- 2 teaspoons dry mustard
- 2 teaspoons pepper
- 2 teaspoons salt
- 1 teaspoon onion powder
- 1 teaspoon garlic powder
- 1 teaspoon ground cumin
- ¼ teaspoon cayenne pepper

BRISKET

- 1 brisket roast (4 to 5 pounds), fat trimmed to ¼ inch thick
- 1 pound bacon

## SMOKY BACON BBQ SAUCE

    Bacon from cooked brisket

1  onion, chopped fine (about 1 cup)

½  cup cider vinegar

⅓  cup packed dark brown sugar

1–2 cups low-sodium chicken broth

½  cup ketchup

1  canned chipotle chile in adobo sauce, minced

**1.** FOR THE BBQ RUB: Combine all the dry rub ingredients in a bowl, breaking up any lumps of sugar.

**2.** FOR THE BRISKET: Adjust an oven rack to the upper-middle position and heat the oven to 275 degrees. Massage the dry rub into the meat and following the photo poke the brisket all over with a fork. Arrange half of the bacon strips, overlapping slightly, crosswise on the bottom of a broiler-safe 13 by 9-inch baking dish. Place the brisket, fat-side down, in the bacon-lined pan and place the remaining bacon strips on top, tucking the ends of the strips underneath the brisket following the photo. Cover the pan with foil and roast until a fork inserted into the brisket can be removed with no resistance, about 4 hours.

**3.** Remove the pan from the oven and carefully flip the brisket fat-side up. Replace the foil and return the brisket to the oven. Turn off the oven and allow the brisket to rest in the warm oven for 1 hour.

**4.** FOR THE SAUCE: Pour any accumulated juice into a 1-quart measuring cup and set aside. Remove the bacon from the brisket, chop it into small pieces, and heat it in a medium saucepan over medium heat until the fat has rendered, about 5 minutes. Add the onion and cook until softened, about 5 minutes. Off the heat, add the vinegar and sugar and stir to combine. Return the saucepan to medium heat and reduce the mixture to a syrupy consistency, about 5 minutes.

**5.** Meanwhile, skim the fat from the reserved juice and discard the fat. Add enough broth to the juices to make 3 cups. Add the mixture to the saucepan and reduce it until it measures 3 cups, about 8 minutes. Off the heat, stir in the ketchup and chipotle. Strain the mixture through a fine-mesh strainer, if desired.

**6.** Turn the oven to broil, brush the brisket with 1 cup of the sauce, and broil the brisket until the top is lightly charred and the fat is crisped, 5 to 7 minutes. Transfer the brisket to a cutting board and slice it across the grain into ¼-inch slices. Serve with the remaining sauce.

**WHAT YOU CAN DO AHEAD OF TIME:** Follow the recipe through step 2. In step 3, place the brisket fat-side up on aluminum foil and wrap tightly; reserve the juice in an airtight container. Refrigerate for up to 3 days. When ready to proceed, remove the bacon from the brisket, rewrap the brisket in foil, and cook for 1 hour in a 350-degree oven. Proceed with the recipe from step 4. In step 6, remove the foil from the brisket and proceed as directed.

## NOTES FROM THE TEST KITCHEN

### WHICH BRISKET IS BEST?

Because whole beef briskets can weigh well over 10 pounds, they are typically butchered and sold as two separate cuts—"point" and "flat." The flat cut, the most common in grocery stores, is leaner and thinner, with a rectangular shape and an exterior fat cap. The point cut has an irregular shape and contains large interior fat pockets. Many pitmasters prefer the point cut, believing that its higher fat content keeps the brisket moist over long periods of cooking. For our Oven-Barbecued Beef Brisket, we prefer the flat cut, finding that its external fat cap helps to keep the meat plenty moist. Whichever cut you choose, be sure to purchase a brisket of roughly 4 to 5 pounds that still has a good amount of fat attached. Some butchers cut brisket into small 2- to 3-pound roasts. If this is all that you can find, you can substitute two of the smaller cuts; the cooking time may vary slightly.

**FLAT CUT**
The fat cap on this cut keeps the heat plenty moist.

**POINT CUT**
Although this cut is very moist, most supermarkets don't carry it.

### COAXING BBQ FLAVOR FROM YOUR OVEN

**1.** Massage the dry rub into the meat and poke all over with a fork.

**2.** Arrange half of the bacon strips, overlapping slightly, crosswise on the bottom of a broiler-safe 13 by 9-inch baking dish. Place the brisket, fat-side down, in the bacon-lined pan, and place the remaining strips of bacon on top.

# OVEN-BARBECUED SPARERIBS

SERVES 4

Some recipes muster only the crisp-charred exterior and fall-apart tenderness of outdoor ribs. Ours replicates the smoke flavor, too.

**WHAT MAKES THIS A BEST RECIPE:** The barbecue season for much of the country is cruelly short. When the temperature plunges as fall drifts into winter, it's virtually impossible to maintain the modest grill temperatures required to turn tough cuts of meat tender. So when the craving strikes for smoky spareribs in midwinter, many of us head to the local BBQ shack. This oven method for making barbecued spareribs will allow you to make them yourself anytime—even in the dead of winter. But we only arrived at this method after many missteps. We knew that we could "barbecue" the meat in a low oven until they were fall-apart tender. The problem was infusing them with that trademark (and addictive) smoky flavor.

The indoor barbecued-rib recipes we found were a dubious lot. Most smothered racks in smoke-flavored sauce and baked them slowly. Sure, the ribs tasted OK—slather an old shoe in smoky sauce and it will taste good—but none possessed the deep, rich flavor of true barbecue. Others slicked the ribs with liquid smoke, smearing on a dry rub just before baking—not much better: There's a fundamental difference between ribs that *taste* of smoke and ribs that *are* smoked. After setting off the test kitchen's fire alarms more times than we care to remember, we gave up on wood chips and took inspiration from the Chinese method of using tea to smoke food. Using our own home-rigged smoker—a baking stone, a sturdy baking sheet, a wire rack, and heavy-duty aluminum foil—we found that roasting Lapsang Souchong tea at high heat along with our rack of ribs delivered the authentic smoky flavor we were after. (Popping the ribs in the freezer before subjecting them to this high-heat smoking process allows the meat to withstand both this high-heat smoking and a longer low-heat cooking time.) Adding apple juice to the baking sheet during the cooking time is our real secret, though. The liquid mix turns to steam and the flavor of the apple juice imbues the meat with a subtle sweetness. Some important things to remember: To make this recipe, you will need a baking stone, a sturdy baking sheet with a 1-inch rim, and a wire cooling rack that fits inside it. It's fine if the ribs overlap slightly on the rack.

## RUB

 6 tablespoons yellow mustard
 2 tablespoons ketchup
 3 garlic cloves, minced
 2 teaspoons pepper
 1 tablespoon sweet paprika
 1 tablespoon chili powder
 ½ teaspoon cayenne pepper
 1½ tablespoons kosher salt
 3 tablespoons brown sugar

## RIBS

 2 racks St. Louis–style spareribs, 2½ to 3 pounds each, trimmed of surface fat, membrane removed (see page 150), each rack cut in half
 ½ cup Lapsang Souchong tea leaves (loose or from about 10 teabags), ground to a powder in a spice grinder (about ¼ cup powder)
 ½ cup apple juice

**1.** FOR THE RUB: Combine the mustard, ketchup, and garlic in a small bowl. Meanwhile, combine the pepper, paprika, chili powder, cayenne, salt, and sugar in a separate small bowl.

**2.** FOR THE RIBS: Spread the mustard mixture in a thin, even layer over both sides of the ribs. Coat both sides with the spice mixture, then wrap the ribs in plastic wrap and refrigerate them for at least 8 hours and up to 24 hours.

**3.** Transfer the ribs from the refrigerator to the freezer for 45 minutes. Adjust one oven rack to the lowest position and the second rack to the upper-middle position (at least 5 inches below the broiler). Place a baking stone on the lower rack and heat the oven to 500 degrees. Sprinkle the ground tea evenly over the bottom of a rimmed baking sheet and set a wire rack on the sheet. Place the ribs meat-side up on the rack and cover with heavy-duty foil, crimping the edges tightly to seal. Roast the ribs directly on the stone for 30 minutes, then reduce the oven temperature to 250 degrees, leaving the oven door open for 1 minute to cool. While the oven is open, carefully open one corner of the foil and pour the apple juice into the bottom of the baking sheet. Reseal the foil and continue to roast the ribs until the meat is very tender and begins to pull away from bones, about 1½ hours. (Begin to check the ribs after 1 hour. Leave them loosely covered with the foil for the remaining cooking time.)

**4.** Remove the foil and carefully flip the racks bone-side up. Place the baking sheet on the upper-middle oven rack. Turn on the broiler and cook the ribs until well browned and crispy in spots, 5 to 10 minutes. Flip the ribs meat-side up and cook until well browned and crispy, 5 to 7 minutes more. Cool for at least 10 minutes before cutting into the individual ribs. Serve with barbecue sauce, if desired.

**WHERE THINGS CAN GO WRONG:** A baking stone and a really hot oven are crucial for the smoking process in this recipe. A moderately hot oven and inadequately heated baking stone aren't enough to unlock the tea's smokiness—meaning your ribs will have little to no smoke flavor. We recommend firing up your oven (with the stone in it) right after the ribs go into the freezer for their 45-minute chill. This is plenty of time for the oven and stone to heat up to the right temperature for roasting the tea.

## NOTES FROM THE TEST KITCHEN

### PORK RIBS 101

**SPARERIBS**
Ribs from near the pig's fatty belly. An acceptable choice, but these need a fair amount of home trimming.

**ST. LOUIS–STYLE**
Spareribs that have been trimmed of skirt meat and excess cartilage. Minimal fuss—our top choice.

**BABY BACK**
Smaller, leaner ribs from the (adult) pig's back. Tender, but the meat dries out too quickly for our recipe.

### REMOVING THE MEMBRANE

For this recipe, we recommend removing the thin membrane that lines the concave side of the rib rack. The ribs are easier to manipulate (and eat), and the smoke penetrates both sides of the rack directly.

Before cooking, loosen this membrane with the tip of a paring knife and, with the aid of a paper towel, pull it off slowly, all in one piece.

### WHERE THERE'S SMOKE

Cured over smoldering pine or cypress, Lapsang Souchong tea brews up so smoky that, as a beverage, it's an acquired taste. But as a flavoring agent, it provides the smokiness missing in most indoor rib recipes. Loose tea leaves and tea bags work equally well. (Twining's Lapsang Souchong tea bags are widely available at most supermarkets.)

# GLAZED ALL-BEEF MEAT LOAF

SERVES 6 TO 8

**WHAT MAKES THIS A BEST RECIPE:** It's no secret that "meat loaf" mix—a mixture of ground beef, pork, and veal—makes a stellar loaf. Over the years though we've received a lot of questions about substituting all-beef for meat loaf mix, which is not always available in the market. Wondering if a great all-beef meat loaf were possible, we headed into the test kitchen where our initial test produced an all-beef meat loaf that was chewy with a boring hamburger flavor. We went through 260 pounds of beef to perfect this recipe, a journey that began at the supermarket where we found a dizzying selection of ground beef. After dozens and dozens of tests, we now know that equal parts sirloin and chuck (1 pound of each) provides the perfect balance of juicy, tender meat and assertive beefy flavor. (We also found that 85 percent lean ground beef works in a pinch.) For moisture, flavor, and to help bind our meat loaf, we added Monterey Jack cheese (praised by tasters for its moderate moisture content and neutral flavor). Grating the cheese (on the small holes of a box grater), then freezing it, is a trick that makes the cheese crumbly and easier to evenly incorporate when mixing the loaf ingredients together. It also prevents "hot pockets" of oozing cheese which occurs when the cheese is diced or grated. To give our meat loaf a luxuriously smooth texture we used an unlikely ingredient: gelatin. We got the idea to use gelatin when we were testing different liquids in our meat loaf (the liquid adds moisture and tones down the beef's naturally livery flavor). Reduced veal stock, beef broth, chicken broth, buttermilk, yogurt, and milk (the traditional choice)—we tried them all. The veal stock—a gelatinous ingredient chefs rely on to give savory recipes an unctuous texture—was a big hit. But who has veal stock around except a restaurant? Luckily, powdered gelatin perfectly replicates the gelatinous qualities of the veal stock. Regarding the crowning glory for our meat loaf—its glaze—it's hard to improve on the classic ketchup-based topping, which when run under the broiler intensifies in flavor.

## MEAT LOAF

- 3 ounces Monterey Jack cheese, grated on the small holes of a box grater (about 1 cup)
- 1 tablespoon unsalted butter
- 1 onion, minced (about 1 cup)
- 1 celery rib, minced (about ½ cup)
- 1 garlic clove, minced
- 2 teaspoons minced fresh thyme
- 1 teaspoon paprika
- ¼ cup tomato juice
- ½ cup low-sodium chicken broth
- 2 large eggs
- ½ teaspoon unflavored powdered gelatin
- 1 tablespoon soy sauce
- 1 teaspoon Dijon mustard
- 21 saltine crackers, crushed to fine crumbs (about ⅔ cup)
- 2 tablespoons minced fresh parsley
- ¾ teaspoon salt
- ½ teaspoon pepper
- 1 pound ground sirloin
- 1 pound ground chuck

## GLAZE

- ½ cup ketchup
- 1 teaspoon Tabasco
- ½ teaspoon ground coriander
- ¼ cup cider vinegar
- 3 tablespoons packed light brown sugar

**1. FOR THE MEATLOAF:** Adjust an oven rack to the middle position and heat the oven to 375 degrees. Spread the cheese on a plate and place in the freezer until it is ready to use. Prepare a baking sheet by folding heavy-duty aluminum foil to form a 10 by 6-inch rectangle. Center the foil on a wire cooling rack and place the rack over a rimmed baking sheet. Poke holes in the foil with a skewer (about half an inch apart). Spray the foil with vegetable oil spray.

## NOTES FROM THE TEST KITCHEN

### A GROUND BEEF SUBSTITUTION

If you can't find chuck and/or sirloin, substitute any 85 percent lean ground beef. Handle the meat gently; it should be thoroughly combined but not paste-like. To avoid using the broiler, glaze the loaf in a 500-degree oven; increase the cooking time for each interval by 2 to 3 minutes.

**2.** Heat the butter in a medium skillet over medium-high heat until foaming. Add the onion and celery and cook, stirring occasionally, until beginning to brown, 6 to 8 minutes. Add the garlic, thyme, and paprika and cook, stirring, until fragrant, about 1 minute. Reduce the heat to low and add the tomato juice. Cook, stirring to scrape up the browned bits from the pan bottom, until thickened, about 1 minute. Transfer the mixture to a small bowl and set it aside to cool.

**3.** Whisk the broth and eggs in a large bowl until combined. Sprinkle the gelatin over the liquid and let it stand for 5 minutes. Stir in the soy sauce, mustard, saltines, parsley, salt, pepper, and onion mixture. Crumble the frozen cheese into a coarse powder and sprinkle it over the mixture. Add the ground beef and mix it gently with your hands until it is thoroughly combined, about 1 minute. Transfer the meat to the foil rectangle and shape it into a 10 by 6-inch oval about 2 inches high. Smooth the top and edges of the meat loaf with a moistened spatula. Bake until an instant-read thermometer inserted into the center of the loaf reads 135 to 140 degrees, 55 to 65 minutes. Remove the meat loaf from the oven and turn on the broiler.

**4.** FOR THE GLAZE: While the meat loaf cooks, combine the ingredients for the glaze in a small saucepan. Bring the mixture to a simmer over medium heat and cook, stirring, until it is thick and syrupy, about 5 minutes. Spread half of the glaze evenly over the cooked meat loaf with a rubber spatula. Place the meat loaf under the broiler and cook until the glaze bubbles and begins to brown at the edges, about 5 minutes. Remove the meat loaf from the oven and spread it evenly with the remaining glaze. Place the meat loaf back under the broiler and cook it until the glaze is again bubbling and beginning to brown, about 5 minutes more. Let the meat loaf cool about 20 minutes before slicing it.

**WHERE THINGS CAN GO WRONG:** For the best and most consistent texture, try to buy your beef in packages labeled by primal cut not by fat percentages. This is a more reliable way of assuring the fat content of your meat, a critical factor in turning out a great meat loaf. As a fallback, look for packages that come from an offsite distributor (this will be on the label) as opposed to meat that is ground by the supermarket as most stores don't have the equipment needed to accurately measure fat content.

## GREAT DISCOVERIES
### HOW GELATIN MIMICS VEAL

Many meat loaf recipes call for three different meats (beef, pork, and veal), and each one has a core function. Beef contributes assertive beefiness, while pork adds dimension with flavor and extra fattiness. With veal, it's mostly about the gelatin—a viscous substance with natural water-retaining qualities that help keep a meat loaf moist and unctuous. Gelatin is formed when collagen, the protein in a cow's connective tissue, breaks down during cooking. Collagen is naturally present in cows of all ages, but the collagen in calves (the source of veal) is more loosely structured—and therefore converts to gelatin more easily—than the collagen in an adult cow. In our all-beef meat loaf, we successfully replicated the gelatinous qualities of veal by adding powdered gelatin. So how does it work? Gelatin is a pure protein that suspends water in a mesh-like, semisolid matrix. By slowing down the movement of liquids, gelatin has a stabilizing effect, making it harder for water and other liquids to be forced out, essentially fencing them in. In meat loaf, then, gelatin helps by (1) decreasing the amount of liquid leaking from the meat as the other proteins coagulate and (2) improving the textural feel by making the liquids more viscous even when very hot—sort of a transitional state between liquid and solid. That viscosity translates to a luxuriant texture in the mouth—much like reduced stock, or demi-glace—and the perception of greater richness, as if we had added more fat.

DAVID PAZMIÑO | TEST COOK, COOK'S ILLUSTRATED

## NOTES FROM THE TEST KITCHEN
### TROUBLESHOOTING MEAT LOAF

**GRAY PROBLEM:** The sides of the meat loaf remain crustless.
**SOLUTION:** By opting for a free-form loaf, we achieved an all-over browned crust.

**GREASY PROBLEM:** The meat loaf sits in an unappealing pool of grease.
**SOLUTION:** A foil base, poked with holes and set on a cooling rack, lets juices drain as the loaf cooks.

# SLOPPY JOES
### SERVES 4

**WHAT MAKES THIS A BEST RECIPE:** Sloppy Joes are an ideal weeknight meal—they're quick, easy to prepare, and sure to please kids and grown-ups alike. But all too often they are little more than a sweet, greasy dumping ground for third-rate burger meat. Although the base for Sloppy Joes is pretty constant among most published recipes—ground beef, onion, garlic, spices, something sweet, something sour, something tomato—the end result varies, and usually with disappointing results. They turn out greasy, dry, crumbly, bland, too sweet, too sour, or even too saucy. We knew we could do better, and the key proved to be finding the right balance. We started with the sauce, which is often excessively sweet. Ketchup is a must, but too much made the sauce saccharine. Most recipes also call for copious amounts of sugar, which just made things worse. In search of an alternative, we tested just about every tomato product we could get our hands on. Heinz chili sauce was the right consistency, but it contained flecks of horseradish that turned the sauce bitter. Canned crushed tomatoes needed lengthy cooking, while tomato paste made the sauce dry and stiff. Tomato puree, however, added the strong tomato flavor we wanted. When mixed with ketchup and just a teaspoon of brown sugar, it produced a sauce that was first and foremost about tomatoes, with a gentle sweetness that everyone (even the naysayers in the test kitchen) liked. This combination also strikes a perfect balance between sweet and sour, while just a ½ teaspoon of chili powder and dash or two of hot sauce add subtle heat without overpowering the other flavors. Besides being too sweet, most recipes for Sloppy Joes are also too greasy. After much trial and error, we decided that a middle-of-the-road choice—85 percent lean ground beef—was the best choice. It provided just enough fat to yield tender meat without the slick factor. Perhaps the most important discovery we made in our quest for great Sloppy Joes was the way the meat was cooked. Most recipes instruct you to brown the meat completely before adding the liquid ingredients, but this produced tough and crumbly Sloppy Joes. By cooking the meat until just pink and then adding the remaining ingredients the result is extremely soft and tender meat every time. Just 10 minutes of simmering time is all that's needed to thicken the sauce and you have a hearty and satisfying weeknight meal in no time—without resorting to a boxed mix.

    2  tablespoons vegetable oil
    1  onion, minced (about 1 cup)
    ½  teaspoon salt
    2  garlic cloves, minced
    ½  teaspoon chili powder
    1  pound 85 percent lean ground beef
       Pepper
    1  teaspoon brown sugar
    1  cup tomato puree
    ½  cup ketchup
    ¼  cup water
    ¼  teaspoon hot pepper sauce
    4  hamburger buns

**1.** Heat the oil in a large skillet over medium-high heat until shimmering. Add the onion and salt and stir until coated with oil. Reduce the heat to medium, cover, and cook, stirring occasionally, until the onion is soft, about 10 minutes (if the onion begins to burn after 5 minutes, reduce the heat to low). Add the garlic and chili powder and cook, uncovered, stirring constantly, until fragrant, about 30 seconds. Add the beef and cook, breaking up the meat with a wooden spoon, until just pink, about 3 minutes.

**2.** Add ¼ teaspoon pepper, brown sugar, tomato puree, ketchup, water, and hot sauce. Simmer until the Sloppy Joe sauce is slightly thicker than ketchup, 8 to 10 minutes. Adjust the seasonings. Spoon the meat mixture onto hamburger buns and serve with pickles, if desired.

**WHAT YOU CAN DO AHEAD OF TIME:** If you find yourself with leftover Sloppy Joes or just feel like making a double batch, the meat mixture freezes well for up to one month. To return the meat mixture to its original consistency, you may need to add a little water when it is reheated.

**WHERE THINGS CAN GO WRONG:** Be careful not to cook the meat beyond pink in step 1; if you let it brown at this point it will end up dry and crumbly. The meat will finish cooking once the liquid ingredients are added.

# SHEPHERD'S PIE

SERVES 6 TO 8

**WHAT MAKES THIS A BEST RECIPE:** This classic British comfort food gets a terrible rap on this side of the pond. Made with ground beef to suit the American palate (instead of the traditional ground lamb), more often than not, the versions of shepherd's pie in this country resemble bland, watery Sloppy Joe mix topped with a sad, sunken crown of mashed potatoes. We were determined to use ground beef but wanted to infuse it with more flavor. We also wanted a filling that was thick enough to support a handsome mashed potato topping. How did we do it? First, we added an unlikely ingredient to our filling: soy sauce. We found that the soy heightened the beefiness of the filling without calling attention to itself. And combined with a bit of tomato paste, it gave our filling an intense meatiness. Our secret ingredient, though, was O'Doul's Amber Nonalcoholic Beer (tasters were surprised that a nonalcoholic beer was more flavorful than regular beer); its slightly sweet, malt flavor acts as a complex base for the beef. As far as thickening our filling (to avoid the watery Sloppy Joe syndrome), we relied on a good amount of flour (5 tablespoons) and some heavy cream (which also adds richness and roundness). And finally, for our topping, we found that regular mashed potatoes don't cut it—they are too loose and messy. The key is to make a stiff mash using less butter and cream, which, when brushed with beaten egg, creates a beautiful golden brown crust when the pie is run under the broiler.

## FILLING

2 tablespoons unsalted butter
1 onion, minced (about 1 cup)
2 carrots, peeled and chopped fine
2 pounds 85 percent lean ground beef
 Salt and pepper
5 tablespoons unbleached all-purpose flour
1 tablespoon tomato paste
¼ cup heavy cream
1¾ cups low-sodium chicken broth
¾ cup beer
2 tablespoons soy sauce
2 teaspoons minced fresh thyme
1 cup frozen peas

To pack long-cooked flavor into a quick ground-meat filling, we added soy sauce, tomato paste, and beer.

## TOPPING

2½ pounds russet potatoes (about 5), peeled and cut into 2-inch pieces
 Salt
2 tablespoons unsalted butter, melted
⅓ cup heavy cream, warmed
 Pepper
1 large egg, beaten

**1. FOR THE FILLING:** Heat the butter in a large skillet over medium-high heat until foaming. Add the onion and carrots and cook until soft, about 8 minutes. Add the meat, ½ teaspoon salt, and ½ teaspoon pepper and cook, breaking the meat into small pieces with a wooden spoon, until browned, about 12 minutes. Add the flour and tomato paste and cook until the paste begins to darken, about 1 minute.

**2.** Add the cream and cook until it comes to a simmer and slightly thickens, about 1 minute. Add the broth, beer, soy sauce, and thyme and simmer over medium heat, stirring frequently, until the mixture is thick but still saucy, 15 to 20 minutes. Remove the skillet from the heat, stir in the peas, season the filling with salt and pepper to taste, and transfer it to a broiler-safe 2-quart casserole dish.

**3. FOR THE TOPPING:** Adjust an oven rack to the upper-middle position and heat the oven to 375 degrees. Bring the potatoes, ½ teaspoon salt, and water to cover to a boil in a large saucepan over high heat. Reduce the heat to medium-low and simmer until tender, 15 to 20 minutes. Drain the potatoes, return them to the saucepan, and mash the potatoes with the butter and cream until smooth. Season with salt and pepper.

**4.** Following the photo, spread the potatoes over the filling, using a spatula to smooth the top. Brush the top with the egg and drag a fork across the top to make ridges. Bake until the filling is bubbling, about 15 minutes. Turn on the broiler and cook until the top is golden brown, 3 to 5 minutes. Remove the pie from the oven and let cool for 10 minutes before serving.

**WHAT YOU CAN DO AHEAD OF TIME:** Make the filling through step 2, but do not add the peas. Store in an airtight container in the refrigerator for up to 2 days. When ready to proceed, reheat the filling in a large saucepan, stir in the peas, and transfer to a broiler-safe 2-quart casserole. Proceed with the recipe from step 3.

## NOTES FROM THE TEST KITCHEN

### APPLYING THE POTATO TOPPING
The mashed potato topping should seal in the filling and keep it from bubbling over the sides of the dish. Use a rubber spatula to scrape small piles of potato around the edge of the dish. Dollop more potato into the center of the dish and then spread the potato into a smooth layer flush with the edge of the dish.

### BEER OPTIONS
Although just about any mild beer will work in this recipe, we particularly enjoyed the sweet flavor of **O'Doul's Amber Nonalcoholic Beer.**

# SOFT STEAK TACOS
## WITH SALSA VERDE
SERVES 4 TO 6

**WHAT MAKES THIS A BEST RECIPE:** Nothing beats a good steak taco: juicy, well-seasoned pieces of beef tucked into a warm flour tortilla with fresh toppings—what could be better? Simply put, a good steak taco is all about the steak—the right cut, cooking technique, and seasonings make all the difference. We started developing our recipe by testing beefy cuts, such as steak tips, blade, and flank steak. With its slight chew and lean, beefy flavor, flank beat out the competition. So, what's the best way to cook the beef? First we sliced the meat, seared it, and then chopped it into bite-sized pieces. This ensures flavorful juicy pieces of meat every time. To bolster the flavor of the beef we also applied a simple spice mixture (embellished with scallions, jalapeños, and garlic) to the sliced steak before searing it. One last touch: glazing the browned meat for a final boost of flavor. A mix of tomato sauce and water reduced in the empty skillet makes a great base for a sauce, especially when tossed with the meat and its juice. Fresh lime juice and a touch of brown sugar are key to brightening the sauce. Topped with shredded cheese, lettuce, sour cream, pickled jalapeños, and salsa verde, these steak tacos will leave any store-bought taco kit in the dust.

### SALSA VERDE

- 8 tomatillos, husks removed, or 1 (11-ounce) can tomatillos, drained
- ½ onion, chopped (about ½ cup)
- 1–2 jalapeño chiles, chopped coarsely
- 2 garlic cloves
  Juice of 1 lime
- ½ cup packed fresh cilantro
- ½ teaspoon salt

### STEAK TACOS

- 1 flank steak (about 1½ pounds), sliced thin (see the photos on page 158)
- 1 tablespoon chili powder
- 1½ teaspoons ground cumin
- 1 teaspoon ground coriander
- ¾ teaspoon salt

4   garlic cloves, minced
4   scallions, green parts cut into 1-inch lengths, remaining white parts cut in half lengthwise
1–2 jalapeño chiles, minced
4   teaspoons vegetable oil
½   cup canned tomato sauce
½   cup water
2   teaspoons brown sugar
1   tablespoon fresh lime juice
8   (8-inch) flour tortillas, warmed

**1. FOR THE SALSA:** Place the tomatillos in a saucepan, cover with water, and bring to a boil over high heat (if using canned tomatillos, skip this step and simply add them drained to the food processor in step 2). Once boiling, reduce the heat to low and simmer until the tomatillos are brownish-green and soft, 5 to 7 minutes. Meanwhile, fill a large bowl with ice water. Transfer the tomatillos to the ice water and cool.

**2.** Meanwhile, pulse the onion, chiles, and garlic in a food processor until coarsely ground. Using a slotted spoon, transfer the tomatillos to the food processor along with the lime juice, cilantro, and salt. Puree until smooth, scraping down the sides of the bowl as necessary.

**3. FOR THE TACOS:** Place the sliced steak in a large bowl and sprinkle it evenly with the chili powder, cumin, coriander, and salt. Add the garlic, scallions, and chiles and toss to combine.

**4.** Heat 2 teaspoons of the oil in a large skillet over high heat until just smoking. Add half of the steak mixture and cook, turning the slices once, until they are just browned, about 1 minute per side. Transfer the meat to a bowl. Repeat this process with the remaining oil and steak and transfer it to the bowl with the first batch of meat.

**5.** Reduce the heat to medium and add the tomato sauce, water, brown sugar, and lime juice to the skillet, scraping up any browned bits from the pan bottom. Meanwhile, use a slotted spoon to transfer the browned steak mixture to a cutting board, leaving any accumulated juice in the bowl. Chop the steak into rough 1-inch pieces.

**6.** Add the reserved juice to the skillet and cook until it is reduced by half, 5 to 10 minutes. Return the steak to the skillet and cook until the meat is glazed and just cooked through, about 2 minutes. Divide the meat evenly among the tortillas and serve with the salsa.

**WHAT YOU CAN DO AHEAD OF TIME:** The salsa can be refrigerated in an airtight container for up to 4 days. The steak mixture in step 3 can be refrigerated, wrapped tightly in plastic wrap, up to 2 hours ahead of time.

## NOTES FROM THE TEST KITCHEN

### HOW TO SLICE FLANK STEAK
To make cutting the steak easier, place the whole flank in the freezer for 20 minutes to firm up.

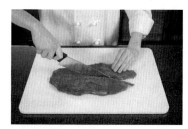

**1.** Cut the flank steak in half lengthwise.

**2.** Working with one half at a time, slice the steak on the bias into ¼-inch-thick pieces.

### WARMING THE TORTILLAS
When developing our recipe for Soft Steak Tacos, there was one small but significant detail that our tasters demanded: steaming hot tortillas. Not only are warm tortillas more pliable and less apt to tear, they also help to melt cheese and keep fillings hot. But what's the best way to heat the tortillas? The microwave works quickly but leaves the tortillas soggy and tough. Heating the tortillas over an open flame (such as a gas stovetop) worked great but required that each tortilla be heated individually. Scattering the tortillas on an oven rack enabled us to heat up to eight at a time, but they had a tendency to dry out. Ultimately, what worked best was to stack the tortillas and wrap them in aluminum foil before popping them in a 350-degree oven. After about 15 minutes they were properly heated and ready to go. What's more, when prepared this way, the tortillas would stay hot for up to 30 minutes—plenty of time to gather the family for taco night.

# VEAL SCALOPPINI
## WITH LEMON-PARSLEY SAUCE
### SERVES 4

**WHAT MAKES THIS A BEST RECIPE:** Call them what you will—scaloppini, scallops, escalopes, or even schnitzel—these thinly sliced cutlets are remarkably easy to prepare. Gently pound the cutlets, sauté them quickly, and serve with a basic pan sauce. With its tender meat and delicate flavor, veal is a natural for this preparation. It's also a more luxurious choice over the more popular substitute: chicken. Restaurants always seem to get this dish just right, pairing lightly browned veal cutlets with a bracing lemon or Marsala sauce. To avoid spending a fortune using cutlets from the pricey loin and rib section of the calf (the cut commonly used in restaurants), we turned to the inexpensive supermarket cutlets, which are a bit tough because they're cut from the shoulder or the leg (the two toughest parts of the calf). Looking for a way to tenderize them, we tried soaking them in milk (which led to steamed and burned cutlets) and then tried a hand-held tenderizer (which mangled our cutlets). Out of desperation we tried a powdered meat tenderizer and this decidedly unglamorous product was our salvation—it made supermarket cutlets every bit as tender as those found in restaurants. Not bad for a tenderizer that costs pennies per use. To get a nicely browned crust on our seasoned cutlets, we dredged them in flour. However, by the time both sides of the cutlets developed nice browning, they were overcooked. To solve this problem, we tried cooking only the first side until golden brown, then flipping each cutlet and finishing. This method prevented overcooking, but the second, quickly cooked side was pasty. Finally, we found the answer—flouring just one side of the cutlet. The floured side obtained a rich, golden brown exterior, and the other side, now without flour, was no long gummy. And after cooking three batches of veal there was plenty of fond (flavorful browned bits) in the pan to make a pan sauce. To keep the veal tender and hot though, we had to reverse the usual process and make the pan sauce in a separate saucepan before cooking the veal. Once the last batch was done, we poured the almost-finished sauce into the skillet and scraped the pan to incorporate the meaty flavors of the fond into the sauce. We finished the sauce with butter and herbs, and a minute later sauced (and tender) cutlets were on the table.

2 teaspoons plus 3 tablespoons vegetable oil
2 shallots, minced (about ⅓ cup)
1½ cups low-sodium chicken broth
1½ pounds veal cutlets, about ¼ inch thick
¾ teaspoon meat tenderizer, preferably Adolph's
    Pepper
½ cup unbleached all-purpose flour
2 tablespoons minced fresh parsley
2 tablespoons unsalted butter, cut into 4 pieces
    Salt
1–2 tablespoons fresh lemon juice

**1.** Heat 2 teaspoons of the oil in a medium saucepan over medium-high heat until shimmering. Add the shallots and cook until they begin to soften, about 1 minute. Add the broth and increase the heat to high. Simmer rapidly until the liquid is reduced to ¾ cup, about 8 minutes. Set aside.

**2.** If the cutlets are thicker than ¼ inch, place them between two sheets of plastic wrap or waxed paper and pound them to an even ¼-inch thickness with a skillet or meat pounder. Pat the cutlets dry with paper towels. Sprinkle the tenderizer and ⅛ teaspoon pepper evenly over both sides of the cutlets.

**3.** Place the flour on a rimmed baking sheet and spread it into a thin, even layer. Heat 1 tablespoon of the oil in a large nonstick skillet over high heat until just smoking. Dredge the first batch of cutlets in the flour on one side only, shake off the excess, and place them in the skillet, floured side down, making sure the cutlets do not overlap. Cook, without moving them, until the cutlets are well browned, 1 to 1½ minutes. Flip the cutlets and cook until the second sides are no longer pink and the meat feels firm when pressed, about 30 seconds. Transfer the cutlets to a platter. Repeat the process to cook the remaining cutlets in 2 batches, using the additional 1 tablespoon oil for each batch.

**4.** After transferring the last batch of cutlets to the platter, pour the reserved sauce into the empty pan and bring it to a simmer, scraping up the browned bits on the pan bottom. Off the heat, whisk in the parsley, butter, and salt, pepper, and lemon juice to taste. Pour the sauce over the cutlets and serve.

## GREAT DISCOVERIES

### DO MEAT TENDERIZERS WORK?

Using plants to tenderize meat dates back hundreds of years to the pre-Columbian Mexicans, who wrapped meat in papaya leaves. Both papaya and pineapple contain enzymes that break down collagen—the connective tissue that makes meat tough. These enzymes, papain (from papaya) and bromelain (from pineapple), are the active ingredient in meat tenderizers. Here in the test kitchen, we've dismissed these products in the past because they effectively tenderize only the outermost layer of a piece of meat—not much of an improvement for a thick tough steak. But for ultra-thin veal cutlets, I discovered that they work just fine, as no deep penetration is required.

Curious whether brand mattered, I gathered six tenderizer products (seasoned and unseasoned varieties from Adolph's, Durkee, and McCormick) and headed to the test kitchen with several pounds of tough veal cutlets. Adolph's and Durkee contain papain, while McCormick relies on bromelain to do the work. In the end, all of them worked equally—neither the brand nor the type of enzyme made any difference. Should you opt for seasoned or unseasoned? While the extra spices aren't enough to ruin dinner, we'd opted to do the seasoning ourselves.

SARAH WILSON | TEST COOK, COOK'S ILLUSTRATED

## NOTES FROM THE TEST KITCHEN

### COOKING IN BATCHES
You will need to cook the veal in three batches to avoid overcrowding the skillet; because the size of packaged cutlets varies, each batch you cook may contain as few as three cutlets or as many as six.

### TASTING: MILK-FED VS. NATURALLY RAISED VEAL
Veal calves have traditionally been fed a strict milk or formula diet, and their movement has been limited. As a result, milk-fed veal is white in color. (In general, the more muscle tissue is used, the darker it becomes.) In recent years, naturally raised veal calves, fed milk as well as grain and not given any antibiotics or hormones, have become popular. These animals are allowed more exercise, and their meat is pink.

Ethical and appearance concerns aside, we wondered if our tasters could tell the difference between milk-fed and naturally raised veal. In terms of flavor, our panel concluded that the two styles are indistinguishable. Texture is another matter. Tasters felt that the milk-fed veal was more tender, finding naturally raised veal a bit chewy. When we sprinkled the cutlets with meat tenderizer, however, the difference disappeared.

# GLAZED PORK CHOPS
## WITH GERMAN FLAVORS
### SERVES 4

**WHAT MAKES THIS A BEST RECIPE:** Over the years, we've developed strong opinions about pork chops. We've found that they should be big, brined, and bone-in: These chops cook up moist with good meaty flavor pretty much any way you cook them. Pushing these long-held beliefs aside, we decided to take another look at the inexpensive, thinner-cut boneless pork chops we often see in the supermarket—and have often found to be problematic. This quick-cooking cut curls up in the pan, hindering a good sear, which is hard to achieve anyway without the chops drying out. To solve the curling problem, we simply slashed through the fat and the silver skin, which was responsible for creating the bowing effect as it contracts. But getting a deep brown sear on both sides of these thin chops was tricky without overcooking the meat and burning the fond in the pan. The solution was to get a good sear on one side—our presentation side so to speak—and lightly sear the other side, which would lay face down on the plate. After letting the second side sear lightly (for about 1 minute), we discovered that this was the perfect time to lower the heat and add our glaze to the pan. The glaze prevented the fond from burning and helped our chops retain their moisture. For our glaze, we found that brown sugar gave us a much better texture and depth of flavors over other sweeteners, such as honey (which crystallized and became grainy). Caraway seeds, mustard, and beer are great natural pairings with pork, and give our glaze a Bavarian feel.

### GLAZE
- ¾ teaspoon caraway seeds
- ½ cup distilled white vinegar or cider vinegar
- ⅓ cup light brown sugar
- ⅓ cup beer
- 3 tablespoons whole-grain mustard
- 2 tablespoons Dijon mustard
- 1 tablespoon minced fresh thyme
- 2 teaspoons soy sauce

## CHOPS

- 4 boneless center-cut or loin pork chops, ½ to ¾ inch thick (5 to 7 ounces each)
  Salt and pepper
- 1 tablespoon vegetable oil

**1. FOR THE GLAZE:** Toast the caraway seeds in a small dry skillet over medium heat, stirring frequently, until fragrant, 3 to 5 minutes. Roughly chop the seeds and combine them with the remaining glaze ingredients in a medium bowl. Mix thoroughly and set aside.

**2. FOR THE CHOPS:** Following the photos, trim the chops and slash through the fat and silver skin with a sharp knife, making 2 cuts about 2 inches apart in each chop (do not cut into the meat of the chops). Pat the chops dry with paper towels and season with salt and pepper.

**3.** Heat the oil in a large skillet over medium-high heat until just smoking. Add the pork to the skillet and cook until well browned, 4 to 6 minutes. Flip the chops and cook for 1 minute longer. Transfer them to a plate and pour off any oil in the skillet. (Check the internal temperature of thinner chops—see note below.) Return the chops to the skillet, the browned side up, and add the glaze mixture. Cook until the center of the chops register 140 degrees on an instant-read thermometer, 5 to 8 minutes. Remove the skillet from the heat, transfer the chops to a clean platter, tent loosely with foil, and let them rest for 5 minutes.

**4.** When the chops have rested, add any accumulated juice to the skillet and set over medium heat. Simmer, whisking constantly, until the glaze is thick and the color of dark caramel (a heatproof spatula should leave a wide trail when dragged through the glaze, see the photos), 2 to 6 minutes. Return the chops to the skillet and turn to coat with the glaze. Transfer the chops back to the platter, browned side up, and spread the remaining glaze over them. Serve immediately.

**WHERE THINGS CAN GO WRONG:** If your chops are on the thinner side, check their internal temperature after the initial sear. If they are already at the 140-degree mark, remove them from the skillet and allow them to rest, loosely tented with foil, for 5 minutes, then add the platter juice and glaze ingredients to the skillet and proceed with step 4. If your chops are closer to 1 inch thick, you may need to increase the simmering time in step 3.

## NOTES FROM THE TEST KITCHEN

### PREPPING BONELESS PORK CHOPS

**1.** Trim excess fat off each chop with a sharp knife.

**2.** Cut two slits about 2 inches apart through one side of each chop—this will prevent the meat from contracting in the hot pan.

### MESSAGE IN A BUBBLE

Getting the glaze right takes some finessing—a few extra seconds can mean the difference between luxurious texture and gooey mess. Our solution? Monitor the size of the bubbles, the color of the glaze, and the amount of exposed pan surface.

**NOT YET.** Pan surface has just a few small bubbles, and a spatula makes no trails.

**JUST RIGHT.** Increased bubbles, caramel color, and a spatula just starts to make trails.

**TOO LONG.** Many large bubbles, ultra-dark glaze, and plenty of exposed pan surface.

# ROAST PORK TENDERLOIN
## WITH LOWFAT APPLE AND SAGE CREAM SAUCE
### SERVES 4

**WHAT MAKES THIS A BEST RECIPE:** Nothing is simpler (or tastier) than a juicy pork tenderloin, roasted to perfection and dressed up with a flavorful sauce. But we were looking for a lowfat cooking technique, and a quick sauce that wouldn't tip the calorie scale. To cook the pork tenderloin we used a simple technique that employed both the stovetop and the oven. Searing the meat first on the stovetop aided the development of a rich, brown crust, and then putting it in the oven for just a short time allowed it to cook through evenly without drying out. And this method requires a minimal amount of oil—just 1 tablespoon is all it takes to coat two tenderloins and facilitate an evenly browned exterior in the sauté pan. Once the meat is browned, just transfer it to a baking dish and finish it in the oven. While the tenderloin is cooking, there is plenty of time to whip up a pan sauce using the fond (the tasty browned bits) left behind in the pan. To make the sauce, the broth is added to the skillet, lightly reduced, and then finished with light cream cheese—which melts and gives the sauce a rich, velvety body without all the fat and calories of a traditional sauce finished with butter or cream. In fact, a serving of pork with sauce only has 320 calories and 11 grams of fat.

### PORK
- 2 (12-ounce) pork tenderloins, silver skin removed (see note)
- Salt and pepper
- 1 tablespoon vegetable oil

### SAUCE
- 1 Granny Smith apple, peeled, cored, and sliced into 12 wedges
- ½ onion, sliced thin (about ½ cup)
- Salt
- ⅓ cup apple cider
- 3 tablespoons applejack or brandy
- ½ cup low-sodium chicken broth
- 2 tablespoons minced fresh sage
- 3 tablespoons light cream cheese
- 2 teaspoons cider vinegar
- Pepper

**1. FOR THE PORK:** Adjust an oven rack to the lower-middle position and heat the oven to 450 degrees. Pat the tenderloins dry with paper towels, then season them with salt and pepper. Heat the oil in a large skillet over medium-high heat until just smoking. Brown the tenderloins on all sides, reducing the heat if the fat begins to smoke, about 10 minutes. Transfer the tenderloins to a 13 by 9-inch baking dish.

**2.** Roast the tenderloins until the thickest part registers 140 degrees on an instant-read thermometer, 10 to 15 minutes, flipping the tenderloins over halfway through the roasting time.

**3.** Transfer the tenderloins to a cutting board, tent loosely with foil, and let rest until the pork reaches an internal temperature of 150 degrees, about 10 minutes.

**4. FOR THE SAUCE:** Add the apple, onion, and ¼ teaspoon salt to the oil left in the skillet, return to medium-low heat, and cook, covered, until the onion has softened, 8 to 10 minutes. Stir in the cider and applejack, scraping up the browned bits. Stir in the broth and sage, bring to a simmer, and cook until the mixture measures ¾ cup, about 5 minutes.

**5.** Add any accumulated pork juice into the simmering sauce. Turn the heat to medium-low, whisk in the cream cheese, and continue to cook until the sauce has thickened, about 1 minute. Off the heat, stir in the vinegar and season with salt and pepper to taste. Slice the pork into ¼-inch-thick pieces, and spoon the sauce over the pork before serving.

## NOTES FROM THE TEST KITCHEN

**REMOVING THE SILVER SKIN FROM PORK TENDERLOIN**
The silver skin is a thin, translucent membrane that covers parts of the tenderloin. It is tough and should be removed before cooking. Slip a knife under the silver skin, angle it slightly upward, and use a gentle back-and-forth motion to remove the silver skin.

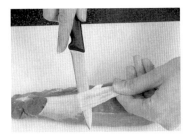

**WHERE THINGS CAN GO WRONG:** Pork tenderloins are almost always sold in pairs in vacuum-sealed packages. After buying dozens of packages for this recipe, we found that the average tenderloin weighs 12 to 16 ounces. However, we did find some packages with larger tenderloins (up to 1½ pounds) or with two tenderloins of dramatically different sizes. Larger tenderloins are fine for grilling but hard to fit into a skillet and baking dish. When shopping, pay attention to the total weight of the two tenderloins (which should be 1½ to 2 pounds) and squeeze the package to see if the tenderloins feel similar in size.

## GREAT DISCOVERIES

### A CREAMY PAN SAUCE WITHOUT CREAM?

When developing sauces for *The Best Light Recipe*, I was stumped when it came to making a creamy but lowfat pan sauce. Such a sauce is typically made by sautéing some aromatics (such as onion, garlic, or shallot), then deglazing the pan with stock or wine. The liquid is reduced and finished with heavy cream, which is then quickly cooked until the sauce has slightly thickened. What, I wondered, could possibly stand in for the ¼ cup cream normally used without turning out a sauce that was a poor facsimile of the real deal?

Turning first to half-and-half we were less than impressed with the results. We found out the hard way that half-and-half cannot be heated: it broke and turned our sauce ugly and grainy. Milk and sour cream, both full-fat and lowfat, were no better. Having exhausted all the obvious options, we turned to light cream cheese, which turned out to be perfect for making our sauce velvety and rich—and we found that a little (3 tablespoons) went a long way. When whisked in at the finish, the light cream cheese melted beautifully into the sauce, giving it good body, rich flavor, and a luxurious consistency we didn't think possible. And with only 90 calories and 6 fat grams for 3 tablespoons of light cream cheese (compared to the 200 calories and 20 fat grams in a ¼ cup of heavy cream—the typical amount added to a sauce), we were really impressed with how rich our sauce turned out.

KEITH DRESSER | ASSOCIATE EDITOR, BOOKS

# ROAST PORK LOIN
## WITH ROOT VEGETABLES
SERVES 6

**WHAT MAKES THIS A BEST RECIPE:** When it comes to making a pork roast we tend to reach for long-cooking cuts, such as those from the shoulder like Boston butt. But as great as a pork shoulder roast tastes, we don't always have 7 hours to make roast pork. We were looking for a more streamlined pork roast recipe, one that would allow us to cook some winter root vegetables alongside the roast for a complete dinner. What we did was simple. First, to ensure juicy, tender meat every time, we brined our pork roast in a solution of water, salt, and sugar for 1½ to 2 hours. As the roast sits in the brine, the meat absorbs the salt-sugar solution, which not only seasons the meat throughout, but also keeps it moist during cooking. Then, for a roast with a good brown crust, we seared the meat in a skillet on the stovetop before transferring it to a baking dish lined with a bed of vegetables (no need for a baking rack). Cooking the roast on top of the vegetables can be a bit tricky though, so we made sure to choose hardy vegetables (carrots, parsnips, red potatoes) that can withstand an hour in the oven—the time it takes the pork loin to roast. When tossed with a little oil, salt, and pepper, the vegetables cooked to perfection. Properly prepping the vegetables makes all the difference here: If cut too small, they will overcook and turn mushy, so we cut them into large even pieces that retained their shape and texture during the long roast. In the oven, the meat juice drips down to flavor the vegetables, making for an easy, tasty one-dish meal.

¼  cup salt
¼  cup sugar
1  boneless pork loin roast (2½ to 3 pounds)
1  pound carrots, peeled and cut into 1-inch pieces
1  pound parsnips, peeled and cut into 1-inch pieces
1  pound red potatoes (6 small), quartered
   Pepper
2  tablespoons vegetable oil

**1.** Dissolve the salt and sugar in 2 quarts of cold water in a container or bowl large enough to hold the brine and pork roast. Submerge the roast completely in the brine. Cover and refrigerate for 1½ to 2 hours (do not overbrine or else the meat will taste too salty). Remove the roast from the brine, rinse, and pat dry with paper towels. Tie the roast at even intervals along its length with about 5 pieces of kitchen twine. Let the roast stand at room temperature, covered loosely with plastic wrap, for 30 minutes to 1 hour.

**2.** Meanwhile, adjust an oven rack to the lower-middle position and heat the oven to 375 degrees. Toss the carrots, parsnips, potatoes, ½ teaspoon salt, and ¼ teaspoon pepper with 1 tablespoon of the oil. Spread the vegetables in a 13 by 9-inch baking dish.

**3.** Pat the roast dry with paper towels again if necessary, and season the roast with pepper. Heat the remaining 1 tablespoon oil in a large skillet over medium-high heat until just smoking. Brown the roast on all sides, reducing the heat if the fat begins to smoke, about 10 minutes. Place the roast on top of the vegetables in the baking dish.

**4.** Roast in the oven until the thickest part of the pork registers 140 degrees on an instant-read thermometer, 50 to 70 minutes, turning the roast over once halfway through the roasting time.

**5.** Transfer the roast to a cutting board, tent loosely with foil, and let it rest until the pork reaches an internal temperature of 150 degrees, about 10 minutes. While the roast rests, reduce the oven temperature to 200 degrees and return the vegetables to the oven to keep warm before serving. Remove the twine and cut the roast into ¼-inch slices.

**WHERE THINGS CAN GO WRONG:** Make sure not to brine "enhanced" pork. Before this type of pork makes its way to the supermarket meat case it is treated with a salt solution. We have made the mistake before; brining enhanced pork only intensifies its added salt solution, resulting in virtually inedible meat. If you are using enhanced pork, skip the brining step in this recipe. Also, when you're trimming the roast, make sure to leave some of the fat on the pork. This cap of fat not only adds flavor, but it also protects the pork from drying out in the oven. The flavor of the vegetables on the bottom of the pan also benefits from the fat that renders and drips down.

# OLD-FASHIONED ROAST PORK
SERVES 6 TO 8

**WHAT MAKES THIS A BEST RECIPE:** Grandma's Sunday pork roast was succulent, with a rich, almost gamey flavor. Pork today—"the other white meat"—is about 30 percent lower in fat than it was 20 years ago. Although a good sauce will help, today's pork loin will never be as flavorful or succulent as Grandma's. Because the loin is especially lean, when we have time, we prefer roasting a fattier cut like pork shoulder, which is especially flavorful and moist. We like the upper portion of the shoulder, or Boston butt: one tough cut of meat. No worries though. We found that seven hours (yes, seven hours) in a 300-degree oven produces meat that is nearly perfect. The connective tissue melts and converts to gelatin, making the meat very tender, while the melting fat keeps the roast moist. With such tender meat, getting neat slices (the meat falls apart when sliced after the typical 30-minute resting period) to place on a serving platter proved to be a challenge. Our solution? Refrigerating the unsliced roast overnight, then slicing the cold roast the next day. This technique produced beautiful clean slices, effortlessly. To warm up the pork, we simply cover the meat with a bit of liquid, and heat it in the oven before serving. The roast not only looks nice but also tastes better because the juice is completely redistributed throughout the meat; nothing is lost to the cutting board. As far as flavoring our behemoth 6-pound roast, we turned to using bold flavors. Our tasting panel agreed that the combination of garlic, rosemary, sage, and fennel seeds, along with a hefty dose of salt and freshly cracked pepper did the trick. One last note: Because we used liquid to moisten the slices of meat as they reheated, we developed a simple sauce that could be used both to flavor the meat as it reheated and to serve at the table. A classic combination of onion and apple flavors (in the form of apple cider and apple jelly mixed with cider vinegar) was a nice counterpoint to the rich flavors of the meat.

1 boneless pork shoulder roast (Boston butt) (6 pounds)

3 garlic cloves, minced

2 teaspoons pepper

1½ teaspoons salt

1 tablespoon minced fresh rosemary

1 tablespoon minced fresh sage

1 tablespoon fennel seeds, roughly chopped

2 red onions, cut into 1-inch wedges

1 cup apple cider

¼ cup apple jelly

2 tablespoons cider vinegar

**1.** Adjust an oven rack to the lower-middle position and heat the oven to 300 degrees. Trim the outer fat from the pork, leaving an ⅛-inch-thick layer. Combine the garlic, pepper, salt, rosemary, sage, and fennel seeds in a small bowl. Following the photos, tie the pork roast tightly into a uniform shape. Rub it with the herb mixture.

**2.** Transfer the roast to a deep-sided (3-inch) roasting pan and cook for 3 hours. Scatter the onion wedges around the meat, tossing the onions in the pan drippings to coat. Continue roasting until the meat is very tender and a skewer inserted into the center meets no resistance, 3½ to 4 hours. (Check the pan juices every hour to make sure that they have not evaporated. If necessary, add 2 cups water to the pan and stir browned bits into water.)

**3.** Transfer the roast to a large baking dish, place the onions in a medium bowl, and pour the pan drippings into a liquid measuring cup. Allow everything to cool for 30 minutes, cover with plastic wrap, and refrigerate overnight.

**4.** One hour before serving, adjust the oven rack to the middle position and heat the oven to 300 degrees. Cut the cold meat into ¼-inch slices and overlap them in a large baking dish. Spoon the fat layer off the drippings (discard the fat) and transfer the drippings and reserved onions to a medium saucepan. Add the cider, jelly, and vinegar and bring the mixture to a boil over medium-high heat, then reduce to a simmer. Spoon ½ cup of the simmering sauce over the pork slices and cover the baking dish with foil. Place the dish in the oven and heat until the pork is very hot, 30 to 40 minutes. Meanwhile, continue reducing the sauce until it is dark and thickened, 10 to 15 minutes (reheat the mixture just before serving the pork). Serve the pork, spooning the onion mixture over the meat or pass it at the table.

## NOTES FROM THE TEST KITCHEN

### SAVE SOME FOR SANDWICHES!
If you plan to make Cubanos (page 168), slice off and reserve a half-pound piece of the roast at the beginning of step 4. Wrapped tightly, it will keep in the refrigerator for several days.

### USING A SHALLOW BROILER PAN
A heavy, deep-sided (3-inch) roasting pan is the best choice for this recipe, but a shallow broiler pan also works well.

### THE SECRET TO OLD-FASHIONED FLAVOR
Boneless pork shoulder, or Boston butt, costs as little as $1.50 per pound, but it takes some work to transform this cheap cut into a memorable meal. This roast is usually sold in netting. Once you remove the netting at home, the roast will open up and you can start its transformation.

**TRIM AND TIE.** Trim excess fat, leaving behind an ⅛-inch-thick layer. Tie the roast into a uniform shape, with 3 pieces of butcher's twine around the width of the roast; tie one piece around its length.

**RUB WITH HERBS.** Rub a mixture of rosemary, sage, fennel seeds, garlic, salt, and pepper over the roast.

**COOK FOR A LONG TIME.** Roast the pork for 3 hours, add red onion wedges, and continue to roast until the meat is extremely tender, 3½ to 4 hours more.

# CUBANOS
## SERVES 4

**WHAT MAKES THIS A BEST RECIPE:** Leftover Old-Fashioned Roast Pork (page 165) is perfect for making south Florida's most popular sandwich-shop special, the Cubano, at home. Made with a combination of roast pork, ham, Swiss cheese, and pickles, and sometimes mustard and mayonnaise, the Cubano is brushed with melted butter, pressed, and grilled. The bread should be golden brown and crisp and the filling hot, its ingredients melded together. Cubanos are traditionally made with Cuban bread; submarine shaped and often made with lard, this bread browns and crisps beautifully. Here in the test kitchen, in hopes of finding a suitable substitute, we tested every type of sub roll and baguette-style bread sold in local supermarkets. Unfortunately, they were either too dense and bready, even when compressed, or too light and airy, in which case they turned crackery when pressed and grilled. Forgoing the traditional shape, we tried round rolls and had more success. The best was the slightly sweet potato roll (we liked Arnold or Freihofer's rolls best), but kaiser rolls can be used in a pinch. The potato rolls crisped up beautifully while still maintaining some of their thick, bready chew. Once the rolls were selected, assembling the sandwiches was easy. We split the rolls in half and spread the top half with mayonnaise and the bottom half with mustard—tasters liked both the creaminess of the mayonnaise and the tang of yellow mustard, so we used both. Then we simply layered the ham and roast pork with a mixture of diced dill pickles and jarred banana peppers (not traditional, but welcomed by tasters for their pickly sweetness and crunch), and finally the Swiss cheese. All that was left to do was to cook the sandwiches, but what if you don't have a sandwich press? No problem. To mimic the effects of a sandwich press, we found that using a preheated heavy pot or Dutch oven to weight the sandwiches worked best to crisp up the buttered rolls superbly. One last note: To ensure very thin slices of pork roast, slice the leftover meat straight from the refrigerator.

⅓ cup diced dill pickles
⅓ cup diced jarred banana peppers
4 potato sandwich rolls
2 tablespoons mayonnaise
1½ tablespoons yellow mustard
¼ pound deli ham, sliced thin
½ pound cold roast pork, sliced thin
¼ pound Swiss cheese, sliced thin
3 tablespoons unsalted butter, melted

**1.** Combine the pickles and peppers in a small bowl. Split the rolls in half and spread the top half with mayonnaise and the bottom half with mustard. Layer the ham, roast pork, pickle mixture, and cheese onto the bottom half, finishing with the cheese on top. Set the tops of the rolls in place and press down to flatten the sandwiches.

**2.** Heat a large nonstick skillet over medium-low heat for 4 minutes. Meanwhile, heat a large pot or Dutch oven on a separate burner over medium-low heat for 4 minutes. Brush the tops of the sandwiches with melted butter and place them in the skillet buttered side down. Brush the rolls with the remaining butter and use the preheated pot to compress the sandwiches for 15 to 20 seconds following the photo. Cook (keeping the pot on the sandwiches but not pressing down) until the first side is golden brown, 4 to 5 minutes. Remove the pot, flip the sandwiches over, replace the pot on top of the sandwiches, and cook until they are golden brown, 3 to 4 minutes.

## NOTES FROM THE TEST KITCHEN

### NO PRESS, NO PROBLEM
Cubanos are traditionally cooked under a heavy cast-iron sandwich press that heats the sandwich from the top as it compresses the contents. To get the effects of a press, we weight the sandwiches with a preheated heavy Dutch oven.

# GRILL-SMOKED PORK CHOPS
## WITH APPLE CHUTNEY
### SERVES 6

**WHAT MAKES THIS A BEST RECIPE:** Here's a great way to use a simple kettle grill to smoke pork chops while avoiding the usual pitfall of dry meat that's been poorly smoked (either not enough smoke, or way too much). The key is to use center-cut pork chops that are evenly cut and about 2 inches thick. These chops are a tender and deeply flavored cut and their size ensures that they will stay plenty moist while cooking. To emulate the indirect cooking effect of a smoker, we banked a moderate amount of coals on one side of the grill, placing the chops on the cool side of the grill. The low-temperature indirect cooking created moist chops and allowed enough time for the smoke to permeate the chops. As far as what to use to smoke our chops: 2 wood chunks soaked in water for an hour created the perfect amount of smoke. The chunks smolder at a good, slow rate, whereas chips (even when soaked) burn too quickly (leaving the chops thin on smoke flavor). And when the vents are positioned opposite the coals—directly over the chops—the smoke circulates across the chops and is pulled up and out, thereby lending a much fuller flavor to the meat. One last technique—an important one for evenly cooked/smoked chops—is standing the chops up on the grill, bone-side down. The heat-resistant bone, a wide base, provides firm footing and shields the meat from uneven heating. And while our chops are great on their own, they pair extremely well with our spicy-sweet apple chutney. Our trick for great apple chutney is to cook the apples separately from the base to ensure that they retain some of their texture.

### PORK CHOPS

2    (3-inch) wood chunks

6    center-cut pork chops, about 2 inches thick
     (14 ounces each)
     Salt and pepper

### APPLE CHUTNEY

3    tablespoons vegetable oil

1    red bell pepper, stemmed, seeded, and cut into ½-inch
     pieces

½    small onion, minced (about ¼ cup)

2    tablespoons minced fresh ginger

2    garlic cloves, minced

1    cup cider vinegar

1    cup packed light brown sugar

1    tablespoon mustard seeds

½    teaspoon ground allspice

⅛    teaspoon cayenne pepper

3    Granny Smith apples, peeled, cored,
     and cut into ½-inch cubes

**1.** FOR THE PORK CHOPS: Soak the wood chunks in cold water to cover for 1 hour and then drain. Meanwhile, let the pork chops come to room temperature, about 1 hour.

**2.** Open the bottom vents on the grill. Light a large chimney starter filled halfway with hardwood charcoal (3 quarts, or about 50 briquettes) and allow it to burn until all the charcoal is covered with a layer of fine gray ash, about 20 minutes. Spread the coals out over half of the grill bottom, leaving the other half with no coals. Place the soaked wood chunks on top of the coals. Set the cooking grate in place and let it heat up for 5 minutes. Use a grill brush to scrape the cooking grate clean. Cover the grill and open the lid vents two-thirds of way.

## NOTES FROM THE TEST KITCHEN

### GAS GRILL–SMOKED PORK CHOPS
Wood chips are the only option on a gas grill, which produces chops that are not as smoky as those cooked on a charcoal grill.

Follow the recipe for Grill-Smoked Pork Chops, making the following changes. Cover 2 cups of wood chips with water and soak them for 30 minutes, then drain and place them in a foil tray following the photo. Place the foil tray with the soaked chips over a burner that will remain on. Light all the burners and turn the heat to high, close the lid, and heat the grill until the chips smoke heavily, about 20 minutes. (If the chips ignite, extinguish the flames with water from a squirt bottle.) Turn off the burner(s) without the wood chips. Arrange the pork chops (seasoned generously with salt and pepper) bone-side down on the cool side of the grill and cover (the grill temperature should register about 275 degrees). Proceed with the recipe.

A novel cooking technique yields juicy, smoky, restaurant-style pork chops.

**3.** Season the chops generously with salt and pepper. Arrange them bone-side down on the cool side of the grill. Cover the grill, positioning the lid so that the vents are opposite the wood chunks to draw smoke through the grill (the grill temperature should register about 350 degrees initially, but will soon start dropping). Cook until an instant-read thermometer inserted into the side of the chop away from the bone registers 145 degrees, 30 to 45 minutes. Let the chops rest 10 minutes before serving.

**4. FOR THE APPLE CHUTNEY:** While the pork chops are cooking, heat 1 tablespoon of the oil in a medium saucepan over medium-high heat until shimmering. Add the bell pepper, onion, ginger, and garlic. Cover, reduce the heat to medium, and cook until the vegetables have softened, about 5 minutes. Stir in the vinegar, brown sugar, mustard seeds, allspice, and cayenne and bring to a simmer over medium-high heat. Cook, adjusting the heat as necessary to maintain a simmer, until the mixture is thick and syrupy and has reduced to 1¼ cups, about 10 minutes. Remove the saucepan from the heat, transfer the mixture to a medium bowl, and cool.

**5.** Heat 1 tablespoon of the remaining vegetable oil in a large nonstick skillet over medium-high heat until it is just smoking. Add half of the apples and cook, stirring frequently, until they are golden brown on all sides, about 4 minutes. Transfer the apples to the bowl with the syrupy vinegar reduction. Repeat the process with the remaining 1 tablespoon of oil and remaining apples. Toss the chutney gently to combine and serve.

**WHAT YOU CAN DO AHEAD OF TIME:** The chutney may be made 1 day ahead, kept refrigerated, and reheated before serving in a small heavy-bottomed saucepan over low heat.

## NOTES FROM THE TEST KITCHEN

### BUY THE RIGHT PORK CHOP
Supermarket chops are often cut thick at the bone and thinner at the outer edge, like the one on the left. With such chops, the thinner edge will overcook before the thicker meat near the bone is finished. Make sure you buy chops that are of even thickness, like the one on the right.

### MEASURING THE TEMPERATURE OF A PORK CHOP
When you think the chop might be done, use a pair of tongs to hold the chop and then slide an instant-read thermometer through the edge of the chop and deep into the meat, making sure to avoid the bone.

### USING WOOD CHIPS ON A GAS GRILL
Place the soaked and drained wood chips in a disposable aluminum tray. Place the aluminum tray underneath the cooking grate directly on top of the primary burner. The primary burner is the one that lights first and can stay lit even when the other burners have been turned off.

# A GUIDE TO ESSENTIAL COOKWARE

In any cluttered kitchen (ours included), there are pots and pans that gather dust and others that rarely get put away. After a decade of careful testing, we've identified the "must-have" pots and pans that we reach for time and again. We think every cook should own these eight pieces of cookware.

## SAUTÉ PAN

**WHAT WE USE IT FOR:** A good choice for pan-frying. Also good for dishes in which you want to brown meat and vegetables and then add liquid, such as smothered chops, fricassees, and meaty pasta sauces.
**WHY WE LIKE IT:** With its high, straight sides, this pan has a greater capacity for liquid than a skillet and a slightly wider cooking surface. Does well in the oven, too.

**TEST KITCHEN TIPS**
- Handles should be long, comfortable, and ovensafe, and they should stay cool on the stovetop—some phenolic (heat-resistant plastic) handles are oven-worthy only to about 350 degrees.
- A 3-quart pan, 10 to 11 inches in diameter, is best.

**TEST KITCHEN FAVORITE**
★ ALL-CLAD Stainless 3-Quart Covered Sauté Pan, $184
BEST BUY: Gourmet Standard Tri-Ply 10-Inch Sauté Pan, $73

### COOKWARE 101
"Fully clad" pieces have a complete core of conductive material (aluminum or copper) that extends up the sides of the pan. In a "disk-bottom" pan, a conductive disk of aluminum is added to the bottom of the pan. Disk-bottom pans often perform just as well as fully clad pans: The thickness of the core is usually more important than whether or not it covers the sides of the pan.

## TRADITIONAL SKILLET

**WHAT WE USE IT FOR:** This is the pan we reach for when pan-searing steaks, chops, and cutlets and when pan-roasting chicken parts. The traditional (that is, not nonstick) finish develops fond—the crusty, browned bits that collect on the pan bottom and are deglazed to make pan sauces.
**WHY WE LIKE IT:** The flared, shallow sides encourage the rapid evaporation of moisture, so pan sauces reduce quickly and foods sear rather than steam.

**TEST KITCHEN TIPS**
- Consider weight carefully. The pan should be heavy enough to retain heat, but it also needs to be easily maneuverable (even when loaded with 3 pounds of chicken parts).
- Look for a comfortable handle that can safely go under the broiler.
- A 12-inch diameter (measured across the top) is the best choice to accommodate four large chops or a whole, cut-up chicken.

**TEST KITCHEN FAVORITE**
★ ALL-CLAD Stainless 12-Inch Frypan, $125
BEST BUY: WOLFGANG PUCK Bistro 12-Inch Open Omelet Pan, $30

## CAST-IRON SKILLET

**WHAT WE USE IT FOR:** Cast iron is just the thing for searing or blackening food quickly over very high heat. When we're after a really dark, even crust on steaks, chops, or even cornbread, there's nothing better.
**WHY WE LIKE IT:** In our lineup of winning pans, this is the placekicker. We may not use it every day, but it's almost essential to have on hand when the right recipe comes along. Why? For the simple reason that no other metal in the cookware arena retains heat as well as cast iron. With its slow response time and tremendous heft, this pan is the wrong choice for delicate sauté work, but it's dirt cheap and will outlast any other pan.

**TEST KITCHEN TIPS**
- This pan's tiny, scorching-hot handle tells you something: It's not designed to be moved around while in use. So heavier is better, within reason.
- Look for a pouring lip for easier disposal of used oil.
- A 12-inch skillet is the best all-purpose size.

**TEST KITCHEN FAVORITE**
★ LODGE 12-Inch Skillet, $20

## NONSTICK SKILLET

**WHAT WE USE IT FOR:** This is our favorite pan for searing delicate items, such as fish fillets, omelets, and other egg dishes. We also use it for stir-fries and pancakes.
**WHY WE LIKE IT:** The nonstick finish means no fond for pan sauces, but the foods themselves still get nicely browned provided the pan is large enough to avoid overcrowding. The flared sides allow for the quick redistribution of food by jerking and sliding the pan over the burner. Easy cleanup, of course.

**TEST KITCHEN TIPS**
- Nonstick bonding technology has improved by leaps and bounds, meaning that it's worth investing in a nonstick skillet with a thick base that distributes heat evenly.
- A 12-inch nonstick skillet can handle a batch of fish fillets or a stir-fry serving four. Smaller nonstick skillets (8 or 10 inches) are a good choice for omelets and snacks like quesadillas or grilled-cheese sandwiches.

**TEST KITCHEN FAVORITE**
★ ALL-CLAD Stainless Nonstick 12-Inch Frypan, $125
BEST BUY: Wolfgang Puck Bistro 12-Inch Nonstick Omelet Pan, $35

## SAUCIER

**WHAT WE USE IT FOR:** Does anything a saucepan can do—and does a few things better. A good choice for sauces, risotto, pastry cream, or anything else that requires constant attention and frequent stirring.

**WHY WE LIKE IT:** A saucier's wide mouth and rounded, flared sides easily accommodate whisks and spatulas and eliminate tight corners where food can stick and burn.

### TEST KITCHEN TIPS
- We like the wider, shallower pans in this category for easy access and visibility. A saucier should be weighty enough to distribute heat evenly yet still be maneuverable. Its bottom should be wide enough to cover the burner and prevent excess heat from wafting up the sides.
- Also look for a stay-cool handle that's long enough to keep hands clear of heat during constant stirring.
- Avoid "disk-bottom" sauciers, which are prone to burning.

### TEST KITCHEN FAVORITE
★ ALL-CLAD Stainless 3-Quart Saucier, $145

## SAUCEPAN

**WHAT WE USE IT FOR:** Rice, sauces, vegetables, gravy, pastry cream, and poached fruit, to list just a few.

**WHY WE LIKE IT:** Just the right size and shape for a thousand and one common kitchen tasks. A true workhorse: It's easy to maneuver and stays out of your way on a crowded cooktop.

### TEST KITCHEN TIPS
- A comfortable, stay-cool handle is a must, and the handle should also be long enough for two-handed carrying when the pan is full.
- Larger saucepans should be able to handle some sauté work, so good heat conduction is a must.
- Every kitchen should be equipped with a large saucepan with a capacity of 3 to 4 quarts.
- Consider a nonstick finish when choosing smaller saucepans, which are useful for cooking oatmeal and reheating leftovers.

### TEST KITCHEN FAVORITE
★ ALL-CLAD Stainless 3-Quart Saucepan, $150
**BEST BUY:** Sitram Profiserie 3.3-Quart Sauce Pan, $50

## DUTCH OVEN

**WHAT WE USE IT FOR:** Our choice for soups and stocks; ideal for frying, stewing, and braising.

**WHY WE LIKE IT:** Built for both oven and stovetop use, it's wider and shallower than a conventional stockpot. This makes it easy to reach and see into and provides a wider surface area for browning (at least a 2 to 1 ratio of diameter to height is ideal). Its tremendous heft translates into plenty of heat retention, which is perfect for keeping frying oil hot or maintaining a very low simmer.

### TEST KITCHEN TIPS
- Looping handles should be extremely sturdy and wide enough to grab with thick oven mitts.
- Lids should be tight fitting and heavy enough not to clatter when the pot contents are simmering below.
- We find the most useful sizes to be 6 to 8 quarts.

### TEST KITCHEN FAVORITE
★ LE CREUSET 7¼-Quart Round French Oven, $215
**BEST BUY:** Tramontina Sterling II 7-Quart Dutch Oven, $59

## ROASTING PAN

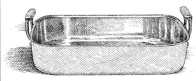

**WHAT WE USE IT FOR:** This pan is for roasting poultry and other large cuts of meat. It can also be used to deglaze drippings for gravies and sauces on the stovetop.

**WHY WE LIKE IT:** This pan's low sides and open design promotes even browning. (High-sided covered roasters cook faster and hotter but cause meat to steam and inhibit browning.)

### TEST KITCHEN TIPS
- A roaster should be heavy enough to handle large birds and roasts without buckling but not so heavy as to be backbreaking.
- Look for handles that are sturdy, upright, and large enough to accommodate thick oven mitts.
- A light-colored interior finish makes it easier to spot burning drippings.
- Oval-shaped models may not accommodate roasting racks.
- Measure your oven before shopping for a roasting pan; it should fit with about 2 inches of clearance on all sides. Most of the large roasters are between 16 and 18 inches long and accommodate a 25-pound turkey.

### TEST KITCHEN FAVORITE
★ CALPHALON Contemporary Stainless Steel Roasting Pan, $100

## THE BIG FOUR METALS

**COPPER** conducts heat extremely well, but is reactive, heavy, and expensive. **Not worth the expense.**

**ALUMINUM** conducts heat well and is inexpensive but reactive. **Best used in combination with other metals** (unless anodized, which makes it less reactive).

**CAST IRON** heats up slowly but retains heat well. Requires seasoning; is mildly reactive. **Useful in limited applications.**

**STAINLESS STEEL** is a poor heat conductor and prone to hot spots; warps over high heat. However, it is nonreactive, durable, and attractive. **Great with other metals.**

# POULTRY

# CHICKEN
# FRANCESE
SERVES 4

**WHAT MAKES THIS A BEST RECIPE:** We love this dish because it's simple, it's quick, and it's chicken—three things almost every home cook appreciates. A humble dish with a refined name, Chicken Francese features pan-fried chicken cutlets with a soft, rich eggy coating and a bright lemony sauce. Many recipes combine egg and flour (and sometimes water or milk) to create a batter for the cutlets, but the result is usually tough and rubbery chicken and a coating that is too thin. Our recipe guarantees that the coating will stay put by dredging the cutlets in flour, dipping them in egg, and then a second layer of flour. The second layer of flour ensures that the cutlets remain delicate and soft, while adding just a couple tablespoons of milk to the egg further ensures a tender exterior. We sautéed the cutlets in a combination of butter and oil—the butter added flavor and the oil, with its higher smoking point, kept the chicken from burning. Initially, we were transferring the cutlets to a low oven to keep warm while we focused on the sauce—fresh lemon juice (whole lemon slices were unbearably bitter), wine, and chicken broth thickened with a buttery roux. We quickly discovered that by the time the sauce was done, the cutlets in the oven had dried out. The solution was switching the recipe around and starting with the sauce, then cooking the chicken. Though not traditional, this produced the best fresh chicken cutlets and a generous amount of silky, well-balanced lemon sauce that was thick enough to cling to (but not penetrate) the coating we had worked so hard to achieve.

## SAUCE
- 3 tablespoons unsalted butter
- ⅓ cup minced onion
- 1 tablespoon unbleached all-purpose flour
- ½ cup dry white wine or vermouth
- ⅓ cup fresh lemon juice from 2 lemons
- 2¼ cups low-sodium chicken broth
- Salt and pepper

## CHICKEN
- 1 cup unbleached all-purpose flour
  Salt and pepper
- 2 large eggs
- 2 tablespoons milk
- 4 boneless, skinless chicken breasts (6 to 8 ounces each), tenderloins removed, breasts halved horizontally and pounded to a ¼-inch thickness (see page 177)
- 2 tablespoons unsalted butter
- 2 tablespoons olive oil
- 2 tablespoons minced fresh parsley

**1.** Adjust an oven rack to the middle position and heat the oven to 200 degrees. Set a wire rack on a rimmed baking sheet and place the sheet in the oven.

## NOTES FROM THE TEST KITCHEN

### TIPS FOR BUYING BONELESS CHICKEN BREASTS
There's more than one way to buy boneless chicken breasts at the supermarket. Here are the options you are likely to encounter along with instructions on cutting them into cutlets. Prices for all of the options are similar.

**WHOLE BONELESS CHICKEN BREASTS:** 12 to 16 ounces each
**WHAT IT IS.** The entire breast in one piece. Although some heavy butchering at home will be required, some premium brands are sold this way and are worth the effort.
**HOW TO PREPARE.** Cut the breast in half, remove the cartilage that connects the breast halves, remove the tenderloins, trim the fat, slice each piece horizontally, and pound lightly.

**BONELESS CHICKEN BREAST HALVES:** 6 to 8 ounces each
**WHAT IT IS.** Half of a whole chicken breast. The most widely available choice, breast halves require a modest amount of work.
**HOW TO PREPARE.** Remove the tenderloin, trim the fat, slice in half horizontally, and pound lightly.

**CHICKEN FILLETS:** 4 to 6 ounces each
**WHAT IT IS.** Breast halves with the tenderloins and fat removed (sometimes called chef's trim). The easiest choice, buy them if they are available.
**HOW TO PREPARE.** At home, just slice each piece horizontally and pound lightly.

**CHICKEN CUTLETS:** 2 to 3 ounces each
**WHAT IT IS.** Breast halves that have been trimmed and sliced for you. Usually ragged and poorly butchered, cutlets are ready to use but cook very unevenly.
**HOW TO PREPARE.** Not worth buying.

**2. FOR THE SAUCE:** Melt 1 tablespoon of the butter in a medium saucepan over medium heat. Add the onion and cook, stirring occasionally, until translucent, 2 to 3 minutes. Add the flour and stir until light golden brown, about 1 minute. Whisk in the wine, lemon juice, and broth. Increase the heat to high and bring to a boil, whisking constantly. Lower the heat to medium-high and cook, whisking occasionally, until the mixture is reduced to 1½ cups, 10 to 15 minutes. Strain the sauce through a mesh strainer and set aside.

**3. FOR THE CHICKEN:** Set a second wire rack on a second rimmed baking sheet on the counter. Whisk together the flour, 1 teaspoon salt, and ¼ teaspoon pepper in a shallow dish. In a second shallow dish, whisk the eggs and milk. Pat the chicken dry with paper towels and season with salt and pepper. Coat the cutlets in the seasoned flour; shake off the excess flour. Transfer the cutlets to the egg mixture; coat evenly and let the excess run off. Return the cutlets to the seasoned flour; coat evenly and shake off the excess flour. Place the coated cutlets on the wire rack on the counter.

**4.** Heat 1 tablespoon each of the butter and oil in a large nonstick skillet over medium-high heat. When the foaming subsides, place 4 cutlets in the skillet. Cook until well browned, 1½ to 2 minutes. Carefully flip the cutlets and continue to cook until lightly browned on the second sides, 30 to 60 seconds. Transfer the chicken to the wire rack in the oven. Wipe out the skillet with paper towels. Repeat, using the remaining 1 tablespoon each butter and oil to cook the remaining cutlets. After transferring the chicken to the oven, wipe out the skillet with paper towels.

**5. TO FINISH THE SAUCE AND SERVE:** Transfer the sauce to the now-empty skillet. Cook over low heat until heated through, about 1 minute. Whisk in the remaining 2 tablespoons butter and season with salt and pepper to taste. Transfer 4 of the cutlets to the skillet, turn to coat with the sauce, then transfer each serving (2 cutlets) to individual plates. Repeat with the remaining cutlets. Spoon 2 tablespoons of additional sauce over each serving and sprinkle with the parsley. Serve immediately, passing the extra sauce separately.

**WHERE THINGS CAN GO WRONG:** Don't use store-bought cutlets. They can be ragged and uneven, causing the edges of the cutlets and the coating to dry out by the time the chicken cooks through. Instead, buy boneless chicken breasts and take 5 minutes to halve and pound them to create thin cutlets. Note that just 1 tablespoon of the butter for the sauce is used in step 2; the remaining 2 tablespoons are used in step 5.

## NOTES FROM THE TEST KITCHEN

### HOW TO SLICE YOUR OWN CUTLETS
The chicken breasts will be easier to slice into cutlets if you freeze them for about 15 minutes until they are firm but not fully frozen.

**1.** Sometimes, a small strip of meat (the tenderloin) is loosely attached to the underside of the breast. Simply pull it off to remove.

**2.** Lay the chicken smooth side up on a cutting board. Holding one hand on top of the chicken, carefully slice the chicken in half horizontally to yield two pieces.

**3.** The two pieces should each be between ¼ and ½ inch thick. If necessary, pound the cutlets to desired thickness.

### THE PERFECT COATING
A dusting of flour and a dip in beaten egg made a coating that was too thin (top). A batter coating (made by mixing flour and eggs) was too thick and rubbery (center). We obtained the best results by dusting cutlets with flour, dipping them in eggs beaten with milk, and coating them again with flour (bottom). This coating remained soft and tender but was sturdy enough to stand up to the lemon sauce.

**THIN AND INSUBSTANTIAL**

**THICK AND EGGY**

**JUST RIGHT**

# CHICKEN BREASTS
## WITH BACON, ROSEMARY, AND LEMON
SERVES 4

**WHAT MAKES THIS A BEST RECIPE:** Sautéed chicken breasts are an obvious choice for a quick and easy dinner, but they're usually not something to get excited about. We have come across many recipes for sautéed chicken breasts that offer up flavorless, dried-out chicken with a tough, pale exterior, and we knew we could do better. We also wanted to develop a pan sauce that would jazz up a weeknight meal. To begin, we investigated different pan choices and we found that a large traditional skillet was absolutely necessary to fit four chicken breasts comfortably, and to promote the best browning. Unlike a nonstick surface, the traditional skillet left fond (browned bits) behind to flavor the sauce. Dredging the chicken in flour resulted in a more evenly browned exterior; more importantly, however, the flour prevented the crust from turning tough and stringy. Initially, we were cooking the chicken in vegetable oil, but this contributed little to the sauce in terms of flavor. Instead, we cooked some bacon until crispy, and removed it from the pan and held it aside for garnish, leaving its flavorful fat in the skillet. We cooked the chicken and then set it aside while we made our quick sauce. Lightly browned, thinly sliced garlic added a mellow background flavor, while at the same time acting as a garnish in the sauce. Fresh rosemary imparted a woodsy earthiness, and red pepper flakes provided a touch of heat. Chicken broth was the obvious choice for the base of the sauce, but we supplemented it with a touch of lemon juice to brighten the flavors. We stirred in the crispy, smoky bacon just before serving, and returned the cooked chicken breasts to the pan to coat them with the tasty sauce.

5 slices bacon, chopped

¼ cup unbleached all-purpose flour

4 boneless, skinless chicken breasts
(6 to 8 ounces each)
Salt and pepper

1 tablespoon unsalted butter

4 garlic cloves, sliced thin

1 tablespoon chopped fresh rosemary

⅛ teaspoon red pepper flakes

1 cup low-sodium chicken broth

2 tablespoons fresh lemon juice

**1.** Fry the bacon in a large skillet over medium-high heat until crispy, about 5 minutes. Transfer the bacon with a slotted spoon to a paper towel–lined plate. Spoon off all but 2 tablespoons of the bacon fat.

**2.** Meanwhile, place the flour in a shallow dish. Pat the chicken dry with paper towels and season with salt and pepper. Dredge the chicken in the flour, and shake to remove the excess. Melt the butter with the reserved bacon fat in the skillet over high heat. When the foaming subsides, reduce the heat to medium-high and cook the chicken until browned on both sides and the thickest part of the chicken registers 160 degrees on an instant-read thermometer, 3 to 4 minutes per side. Transfer the chicken to a plate (leaving the fat in the skillet) and tent loosely with foil.

**3.** Reduce the heat to medium and add the garlic, rosemary, and pepper flakes. Cook until the garlic is browned and crisp, about 2 minutes. Stir in the broth and lemon juice and simmer, scraping up the browned bits, until slightly thickened, about 4 minutes.

**4.** Return the chicken and bacon to the pan and simmer, turning the chicken once or twice, until the sauce is thick and glossy, 2 to 3 minutes. Season with salt and pepper to taste and serve.

## NOTES FROM THE TEST KITCHEN

### OUR FAVORITE BONELESS CHICKEN BREASTS
Boneless chicken breasts are a lowfat, no-fuss, virtually ready-to-use product, which makes them standard fare in many homes. Considering their popularity, we were curious to know if there was a difference in flavor among the confusing array of options in the markets. We also wondered if terms like "all natural," "organic," "free range," and "kosher" have any real bearing on the quality and flavor of the meat. To find out, we gathered six brands of boneless, skinless chicken breasts and tried them in casseroles and sautéed with a pan sauce. When it came to the casseroles, most tasters agreed that there was very little noticeable difference from brand to brand. However, on their own, we found that the kosher and all-natural breasts had flavor and texture that were superior to the average supermarket brands. In the end, we preferred **Bell & Evans**, a naturally raised brand, for its "clean, rich" flavor and good texture.

CHICKEN BREASTS WITH BACON, ROSEMARY, AND LEMON

# CHICKEN KIEV

### SERVES 4

**WHAT MAKES THIS A BEST RECIPE:** Crisply breaded and packed with herbed butter, Chicken Kiev was a star of the 1960s American restaurant scene. Today, the typical version of this Russian transplant, commonly found on airplanes, in banquet halls, and at catered events, is a greasy bundle of flavorless poultry with a sandy, disconcertingly peelable exterior and a greasy, leaky center—definitely a dish in need of a revival. Chicken Kiev has three distinct parts: the chicken, the butter, and the coating. The butter is stuffed inside the boneless chicken breast, and the whole thing is rolled in a coating, then fried up crisp. For our recipe we started with the butter, which we flavored with shallots, fresh parsley and tarragon, and lemon juice, and then chilled completely to facilitate rolling it up in the chicken. For the chicken, we butterflied the boneless, skinless breasts and pounded them thin. We then put a chilled piece of butter on top, and rolled the chicken around it to form a compact package that encased the butter completely—no leaking. Now, with four chicken bundles at the ready, we focused on the exterior. No matter what type of crumbs we used—fresh or dried, coarse or fine—we found that deep-frying gave the Kievs a thin, homogenous, corndog-like quality, and while pan-frying browned the tops and bottoms of the chicken nicely, it was hard to get the sides evenly colored without manhandling the Kievs, which often resulted in unraveling. That's when we made the decision that would finally and effectively transform our chicken Kiev from greasy banquet food to elegant dinner showpiece: toasting the breadcrumbs first. We found that dredging the Kievs in seasoned flour, dipping them in egg, coating them with toasted homemade breadcrumbs, and baking them in the oven yielded a perfectly crisp (but not oily) crust.

### HERB BUTTER

8  tablespoons (1 stick) unsalted butter, softened
1  shallot, minced (3 tablespoons)
1  tablespoon minced fresh parsley
½  teaspoon minced fresh tarragon
1  tablespoon fresh lemon juice
⅜  teaspoon salt
⅛  teaspoon pepper

### CHICKEN

4  slices high-quality sandwich bread, torn into quarters
2  tablespoons vegetable oil
   Salt and pepper
4  boneless, skinless chicken breasts (6 to 8 ounces each), tenderloins removed, breasts halved horizontally and pounded to a ¼-inch thickness (see page 177)
1  cup unbleached all-purpose flour
3  large eggs, beaten
1  teaspoon Dijon mustard

## NOTES FROM THE TEST KITCHEN

### TROUBLESHOOTING CHICKEN KIEV

**"CORNDOGGY"**
**PROBLEM.** Homogenized crust that is reminiscent of a corndog.
**SOLUTION.** We had better results using coarse (not ultra-fine) crumbs and baking, not frying.

**LEAKY**
**PROBLEM.** Compound butter leaks.
**SOLUTION.** Pounding the chicken thin (and thinner at the edges) and refrigerating to let the seams set produced butter-tight Kievs.

**SPOTTY**
**PROBLEM.** Pan-fried coating browns unevenly, and the sides remain pale.
**SOLUTION.** Browning the breadcrumbs before coating the chicken yielded a uniform crust.

### THE BEST MEAT POUNDER
In our testing, the best meat pounders were lightweight, with a large surface, preferably disk-shaped (no sharp edges to poke into the meat). The winning meat pounder was the **Norpro Offset Pounder** ($14.99), which efficiently transformed breasts into cutlets, and its offset handle meant no more bruised knuckles.

**1. FOR THE HERB BUTTER:** Mix the butter, shallot, herbs, lemon juice, salt, and pepper together in a medium bowl. Form the mixture into a 3-inch square, wrap tightly in plastic wrap, and refrigerate until firm, about 1 hour.

**2. FOR THE CHICKEN:** Adjust an oven rack to the lower-middle position and heat the oven to 300 degrees. Pulse the bread in a food processor to coarse crumbs, about 8 pulses. Toss the breadcrumbs with the oil and ⅛ teaspoon each salt and pepper until evenly coated. Bake the crumbs on a rimmed baking sheet until golden brown and dry, about 25 minutes, stirring twice during the baking time. Let the crumbs cool to room temperature (you should have about 2½ cups).

**3.** Cut the butter into 4 rectangular pieces. Pat the chicken dry with paper towels, season with salt and pepper, and place the breast cut side up on the work surface. Place 1 piece of the butter in the center of the bottom half of each breast. Roll the bottom edge of the chicken over the butter, then fold in the sides and continue rolling to form a neat, tight package, pressing on the seam to seal. Refrigerate the chicken, uncovered, for about 1 hour

**4.** Adjust an oven rack to the middle position and heat the oven to 350 degrees. Place the flour, eggs, and breadcrumbs in separate shallow dishes. Season the flour with ¼ teaspoon salt and ⅛ teaspoon pepper. Season the breadcrumbs with ½ teaspoon salt and ¼ teaspoon pepper. Add the mustard to the eggs and whisk to combine. Dredge each stuffed chicken breast in flour, shaking off the excess, then coat with the egg mixture, allowing the excess to drip off. Coat the chicken with the breadcrumbs, pressing gently so that the crumbs adhere. Place on a wire rack set over a rimmed baking sheet.

**5.** Bake until an instant-read thermometer inserted into the center of the chicken (from the top) registers 160 degrees, 40 to 45 minutes. Let the chicken rest for 5 minutes on the wire rack before serving.

**WHERE THINGS CAN GO WRONG:** Do not skip refrigerating the stuffed chicken breasts before breading them or the entire package will became less compact and the seam will open up, causing the butter to leak out.

**WHAT YOU CAN DO AHEAD OF TIME:** Unbaked, breaded chicken Kievs can be refrigerated overnight and baked the next day or frozen for up to 1 month. To cook frozen chicken Kievs, increase the baking time to 50 to 55 minutes (do not thaw the chicken).

# CHEESY BASIL-STUFFED CHICKEN BREASTS
SERVES 4

**WHAT MAKES THIS A BEST RECIPE:** Pounding, rolling, and stuffing chicken breasts is great for when the in-laws are coming, but for everyday eating we prefer a simpler approach. Here, we just cut a pocket in the thick part of the chicken breast, spoon in a filling, and thread the opening shut with a skewer or toothpick. For the filling, we've always been partial to mozzarella for its terrifically gooey texture. Our tasters liked the pronounced milky flavor of fresh mozzarella, but it didn't melt as well as block mozzarella. For the best of both worlds, we added a touch of heavy cream to the plain old block mozzarella. It infused the supermarket cheese with a dairy-fresh flavor to go along with its superb meltability. The flavors of fresh basil, garlic, lemon juice, and black pepper complemented the cheese nicely. In our opinion, stuffed chicken needs a crunchy breadcrumb coating—as long as the coating stays put and doesn't fall off in the baking dish. To help the breadcrumbs adhere, we brushed the chicken with mayonnaise (stickier than the other options we tried, including butter) before sprinkling it with crumbs. After 25 minutes in a 425-degree oven, the chicken was cooked, the cheese melted, and the breadcrumbs crisped. Our dish was good, but tasters wanted tomato sauce, too. We eventually came up with a simple solution: We nestled halved cherry tomatoes around the chicken breasts as they cooked. Once roasted, the sweet-tart tomatoes served as both sauce and vegetable side dish.

4   ounces whole milk mozzarella cheese, shredded
    (about 1 cup)
¼   cup minced fresh basil
2   tablespoons heavy cream
1   tablespoon fresh lemon juice
3   garlic cloves, minced
    Salt and pepper
4   boneless, skinless chicken breasts (6 to 8 ounces each)
3   tablespoons mayonnaise
1   slice high-quality sandwich bread, torn into quarters
2   tablespoons extra-virgin olive oil
1   pint cherry tomatoes, halved

**1.** Adjust an oven rack to the middle position and heat the oven to 425 degrees. Combine the cheese, 2 tablespoons of the basil, cream, lemon juice, 2 teaspoons of the garlic, ½ teaspoon salt, and pepper to taste in a medium bowl.

**2.** Pat the chicken dry with paper towels. Following the photos, cut a pocket in each chicken breast, stuff with the cheese mixture, and seal. Transfer the stuffed breasts to a 13 by 9-inch baking dish and spread the tops evenly with mayonnaise.

**3.** Pulse the bread in a food processor to coarse crumbs, about 8 pulses. Toss the breadcrumbs with the remaining 1 teaspoon garlic, remaining 2 tablespoons basil, and 1 tablespoon of the oil. Sprinkle the crumb mixture over the chicken, pressing lightly to adhere.

**4.** Toss the tomatoes with the remaining 1 tablespoon oil, ½ teaspoon salt, and pepper to taste. Arrange in the baking dish around the chicken. Bake until the crumbs are golden brown and the thickest part of the chicken registers 160 degrees on an instant-read thermometer, about 25 minutes. Serve.

**WHERE THINGS CAN GO WRONG:** Avoid thin chicken breasts for this recipe; they are difficult to stuff without tearing. Preshredded or part-skim mozzarella will also work in the filling, but it will be grainy.

## NOTES FROM THE TEST KITCHEN

### HOW TO STUFF CHICKEN BREASTS

**1.** Use a sharp paring knife to cut a pocket in the thickest part of the chicken breast. Gently work the knife back and forth until the pocket extends down into most of the breast.

**2.** Scoop one-quarter of the filling into each chicken breast.

**3.** Seal in the filling by threading a toothpick or wooden skewer through the chicken about ¼ inch from the opening.

# LIGHT CHICKEN PARMESAN
SERVES 6

**WHAT MAKES THIS A BEST RECIPE:** The best part of chicken Parmesan—breaded, fried chicken cutlets topped with tomato sauce, Parmesan cheese, and melted mozzarella—is the crisp, golden coating on the cutlets. Unfortunately, this terrific breaded coating is the result of frying the cutlets in a good amount of oil. Sure, there are lots of recipes for low-fat, or "un-fried," chicken Parmesan that bake the breaded cutlets rather than frying them, but none that we tried for *The Best Light Recipe* even came close to the flavor, color, or crispness of a traditional fried recipe. Setting the issue of the sauce and cheese aside, we started with how to cook the breaded cutlets. Obviously deep-frying and pan-frying the chicken were both out—these methods simply used too much oil to be healthy. That left us with the oven, but simply breading the cutlets (using the classic breading of flour, then egg—in this case egg whites—then breadcrumbs) and baking them on a baking sheet didn't work. The bottoms were soggy and the coating was pale and flavorless. Our solution was to bake the chicken on a wire rack set over a baking sheet to keep the bottom from becoming soggy, and to spray the tops with vegetable oil spray to help the breading on top of the cutlets crisp up nicely. To give the breadcrumbs "fried" flavor without the fat, we toasted them in a skillet over medium heat until golden with a little olive oil, then tossed them with some grated Parmesan cheese before breading the cutlets. These cutlets were a big improvement, with an even golden color and crisp fried texture. Testing the difference between store-bought dried breadcrumbs, fresh breadcrumbs, and panko (Japanese-style breadcrumbs), the test kitchen universally disliked the "old," "ground cardboard" flavor of the store-bought dried breadcrumbs. Not surprisingly, we preferred the neutral flavor and ultra-crisp texture of panko, though fresh breadcrumbs can be used if panko is unavailable. We then layered our golden brown and crispy cutlets with tomato sauce and lowfat shredded mozzarella, but we quickly found out that any bit of breading that touched the sauce, cheese, or other cutlets lost its crispness in the oven. To remedy this, we decided to leave the cutlets right on the rack and spoon just a small portion of the sauce

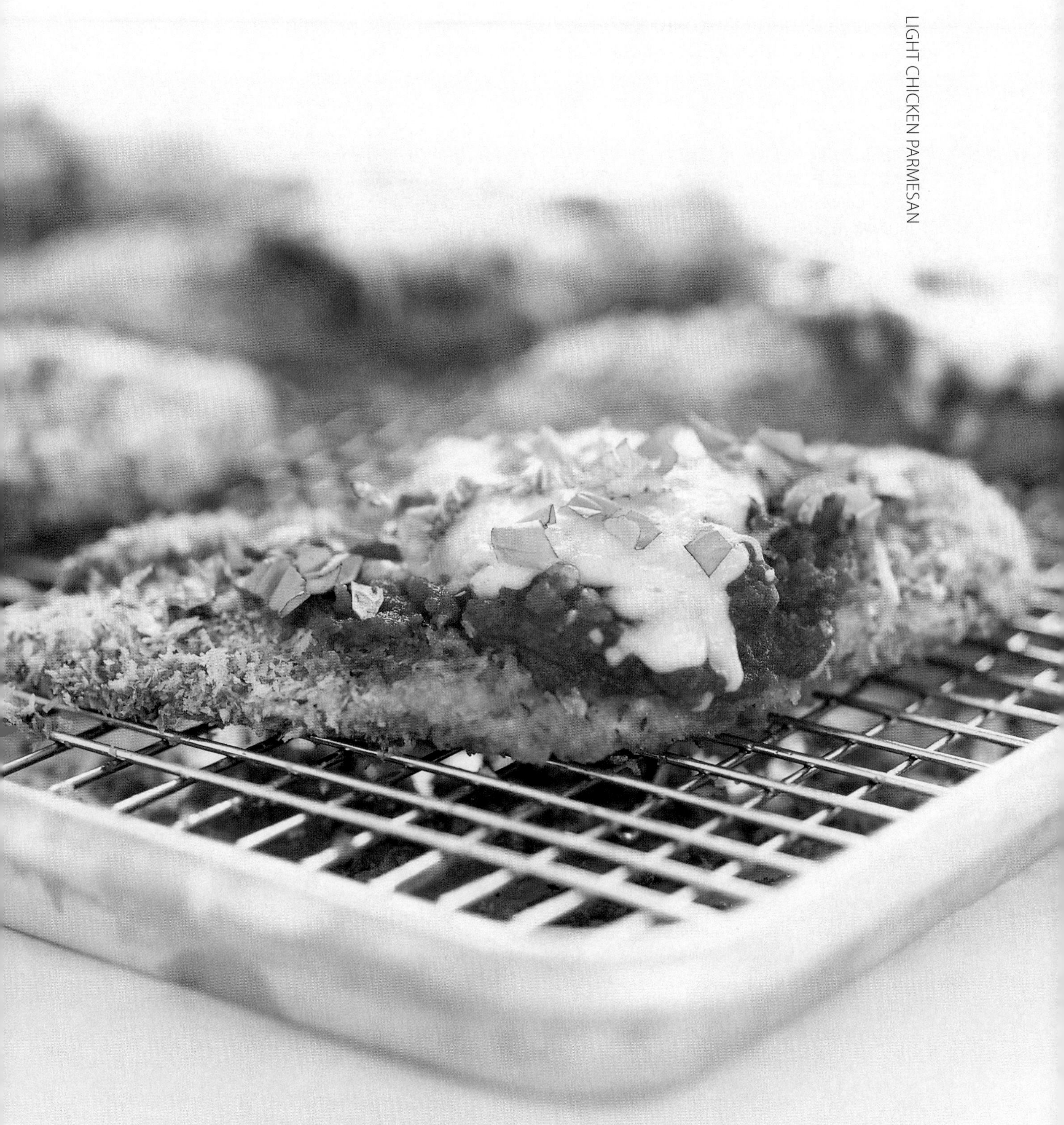

LIGHT CHICKEN PARMESAN

and mozzarella onto the center of each piece of chicken, leaving the edges clean. Bingo! Served with extra sauce and grated Parmesan on the side, these oven-baked chicken Parmesan cutlets knock the calories down from 410 to 310 and the fat grams from 22 to 8, and they taste every bit as good as the full-fat version.

### SAUCE

- 1 (28-ounce) can diced tomatoes
- 4 garlic cloves, minced
- 1 tablespoon tomato paste
- 1 teaspoon olive oil
- ⅛ teaspoon red pepper flakes
- 1 tablespoon minced fresh basil
  Salt and pepper

### CHICKEN

- 1½ cups panko (Japanese-style breadcrumbs) or 2 cups fresh breadcrumbs
- 1 tablespoon olive oil
- 1 ounce Parmesan cheese, grated (about ½ cup), plus extra for serving
- ½ cup unbleached all-purpose flour
- 1½ teaspoons garlic powder
  Salt and pepper
- 3 large egg whites
- 1 tablespoon water
  Vegetable oil spray
- 3 boneless, skinless chicken breasts (6 to 8 ounces each), tenderloins removed, breasts halved horizontally and pounded to a ¼-inch thickness (see page 177)
- 3 ounces lowfat mozzarella, shredded (about ¾ cup)
- 1 tablespoon minced fresh basil

**1.** Adjust an oven rack to the middle position and heat the oven to 475 degrees.

**2. FOR THE SAUCE:** Pulse the tomatoes with their juice in a food processor until mostly smooth, about ten 1-second pulses; set aside. Cook the garlic, tomato paste, oil, and pepper flakes in a medium saucepan over medium heat until the tomato paste begins to brown, about 2 minutes. Stir in the pureed tomatoes and cook until the sauce is thickened and measures 2 cups, about 20 minutes. Off the heat, stir in the basil and season with salt and pepper to taste; set aside until needed.

**3. FOR THE CHICKEN:** Meanwhile, combine the breadcrumbs and oil in a large skillet and toast over medium heat, stirring often, until golden, about 10 minutes. Spread the breadcrumbs in a shallow dish and cool slightly; when cool, stir in the Parmesan.

**4.** In a second shallow dish, combine the flour, garlic powder, 1 tablespoon salt, and ½ teaspoon pepper. In a third shallow dish, whisk the egg whites and water together.

**5.** Line a rimmed baking sheet with foil, place a wire rack on top, and coat the rack with vegetable oil spray. Pat the chicken dry with paper towels and season with salt and pepper. Following the photos, lightly dredge the cutlets in the flour, shaking off the excess, then dip into the egg whites, and finally coat with the breadcrumbs. Press on the breadcrumbs to make sure they adhere. Lay the chicken on the prepared wire rack.

## NOTES FROM THE TEST KITCHEN

### HOW TO BREAD CUTLETS

**1.** Lightly dredge the cutlets thoroughly in flour, shaking off the excess.

**2.** Using tongs, coat both sides of the cutlets in the egg mixture, allowing the excess to drip back into the dish.

**3.** Dip both sides of the cutlets in the breadcrumbs, pressing the crumbs on with your fingers to form an even, cohesive coat.

**4.** Place the breaded cutlets in a single layer on a wire rack set over a foil-lined baking sheet—this prevents the bottom of the cutlets from becoming soggy.

**6.** Spray the tops of the chicken with vegetable oil spray. Bake until the meat is no longer pink in the center and feels firm when pressed with a finger, about 15 minutes.

**7.** Remove the chicken from the oven. Spoon 2 tablespoons of the sauce onto the center of each cutlet and top the sauce with 2 tablespoons of the mozzarella. Return the chicken to the oven and continue to bake until the cheese has melted, about 5 minutes. Sprinkle with the basil and serve, passing the remaining sauce and Parmesan separately.

**WHERE THINGS CAN GO WRONG:** Because these cutlets are breaded, we found that one cutlet per person was plenty, but buy the largest chicken breasts you can find to ensure good-size portions.

**WHAT YOU CAN DO AHEAD OF TIME:** The tomato sauce can be refrigerated in an airtight container for up to 4 days or frozen for up to 1 month.

---

## GREAT DISCOVERIES

### CREATE THAT DEEP-FRIED CRUST WITHOUT FRYING

It's hard enough to create a great deep-fried crust when there's no limit on fat or calories so we all (myself included) had some misgivings about mimicking it in the oven. Oven-frying breaded foods, rather than frying them in oil, is an obvious way to cut lots of calories and fat. And after oven-frying numerous batches of chicken for *The Best Light Recipe*, I learned a few tricks that can be used anytime you want to oven-fry something breaded. First, toast the breadcrumbs in a skillet with a little oil before you bread the food. Second, always bake the breaded food on a greased wire rack (set over a baking sheet to catch crumbs) so that the hot air of the oven can circulate all around the food and make the breading crisp—this eliminates soggy bottoms. And finally, spray the tops of the breaded food with vegetable oil spray to make the top crumbs extra-crisp (this adds negligible fat). This small amount of oil adds that "fried" flavor to the crumbs, giving the food the illusion of being truly fried without making it greasy or adding too much fat, and ensures that it will emerge from the oven gorgeously golden.

JULIA COLLIN DAVISON | SENIOR FOOD EDITOR, BOOKS

# FAST CHICKEN TERIYAKI
### SERVES 4

**WHAT MAKES THIS A BEST RECIPE:** When the fish isn't so fresh and the soba's just so-so, you can usually count on chicken teriyaki as a reliable standby at most Japanese restaurants. But after sorting through lots of misguided, Americanized recipes—including everything from over-marinated, preformed chicken breast patties to skewered chicken chunks shellacked in a corn-syrupy sauce—we decided it was time to make this classic recipe taste good again. We'd had our fill of food-court chicken teriyaki wannabes—we wanted a simple, authentic recipe that could be on the table in thirty minutes. Teriyaki consists of pan-fried, grilled, or broiled meat with the sauce added during the final stages of cooking. Figuring out the fundamentals—which cut of chicken to use and how to get super crisp skin—was our first step. After trying numerous methods, we found it easiest to use bone-in, skin-on thighs, and to cook them in a non-stick pan under the weight of a heavy pot. The thighs cooked up tender, providing a nice meaty foil to the salty sauce, and the nonstick surface promoted a crisp, browned skin that stuck to the chicken rather than the pan, and the heavy pot pressed the skin of chicken onto the skillet for a serious sear.

With the chicken set, we moved on to the sauce. The test kitchen unanimously rejected bottled teriyaki sauce in favor of a homemade sauce, which consists of a handful of ingredients and takes just five minutes to prepare. Tinkering with various amounts of soy sauce, sugar, and mirin (the core ingredients in a traditional teriyaki), we found that the best balance of sweetness and saltiness was achieved with near equal amounts of soy sauce and sugar flavored by a smaller amount of mirin (Japanese cooking wine), garlic, fresh ginger, and red pepper flakes. In terms of consistency, we found the ideal texture hard to attain without the help of a little cornstarch. After the chicken was cooked, we simmered the sauce in the skillet until thick and glossy, and a garnish of scallions added the perfect finishing touch.

CHICKEN

8 small bone-in, skin-on chicken thighs

Pepper

1 tablespoon vegetable oil

SAUCE

½ cup soy sauce

½ cup sugar

2 tablespoons mirin, sherry, or white wine

2 teaspoons grated fresh ginger

1 garlic clove, minced

½ teaspoon cornstarch

⅛ teaspoon red pepper flakes

2 scallions, sliced thin

**1. FOR THE CHICKEN:** Pat the chicken dry with paper towels and season with pepper. Heat the oil in a large non-stick skillet over medium-high heat until shimmering. Add the chicken skin-side down. Following the photos, weight the chicken with a heavy pot. Cook until the skin is a deep mahogany brown and very crisp, about 15 minutes. (The chicken should be moderately brown after 10 minutes. Reduce the heat if very brown, or increase the heat if pale.)

**2.** Flip the chicken over and continue to cook, without replacing the weight, until the chicken registers 175 degrees on an instant-read thermometer, 5 to 10 minutes.

**3. FOR THE SAUCE:** While the chicken cooks, whisk the soy sauce, sugar, mirin, ginger, garlic, cornstarch, and pepper flakes together.

**4.** Transfer the chicken to a plate. Pour off all the fat from the skillet. Whisk the sauce to recombine, then add to the skillet and return to medium heat. Return the chicken to the skillet, skin-side up, and spoon the sauce over the top. Continue to simmer until the sauce is thick and glossy, about 2 minutes longer. Transfer the chicken and sauce to a plate. Sprinkle with the scallions before serving.

**WHERE THINGS CAN GO WRONG:** Small thighs work best here. If the thighs are large, you might need to extend the browning time in step 1. There is a fair amount of soy sauce used in this dish, so do not season it with extra salt or it could become inedible.

## NOTES FROM THE TEST KITCHEN

### THE SECRET TO CRISP SKIN

The challenge in this recipe was getting the chicken skin deeply browned with as much of the fat rendered out as possible. To that end, we discovered that setting a weight on top of the chicken as it cooked (we used a heavy Dutch oven) helped to brown a greater surface area of chicken evenly, as well as aid in pressing out most of the fat.

**1.** To crisp up the skin, set a heavy pot on top of the chicken thighs as they cook.

**2.** After the first side has browned nicely, remove the pot, flip the chicken over, and continue to cook the second side (without the weight) until browned.

### SKIP BOTTLED TERIYAKI SAUCE

Considering that a great teriyaki sauce can be had in a mere four minutes with just a few not terribly exotic ingredients, a bottled sauce can hardly boast convenience. But how do they taste? We sampled eight leading brands to find out. Our 19 tasters had difficulty identifying many of these sauces as teriyaki. Several brands resembled hoisin, oyster, or even barbecue sauce. Of the three that met tasters' standards for teriyaki sauce, Annie Chun's All Natural received top marks. A second tasting pitted Annie Chun's against our homemade teriyaki sauce. Our judges deemed Annie Chun's harsh in comparison to the brighter-tasting and better-balanced teriyaki we had made ourselves.

# OVEN-FRIED CHICKEN

## SERVES 8

**WHAT MAKES THIS A BEST RECIPE:** One of our favorite dinners is crispy, crunchy deep-fried chicken. Let's be honest, while classic fried chicken is tasty, it is also unspeakably high in calories (a whopping 552 per piece) and fat (34 grams to be exact). Fried chicken is definitely a treat—not suited for everyday eating. But before subjecting our friends and family to grilled chicken-breast dinners, we decided to try our hand at a lowfat, oven-fried version. Could Southern-style deep-fried chicken be slimmed down without sacrificing flavor, crunch, or happiness?

Many of the recipes we found called for boneless, skinless chicken breasts, but no self-respecting fried-chicken lover would dream of using anything other than bone-in chicken parts. Our first concessions were to use bone-in breasts (which have fewer calories and less fat than dark meat) and to remove the skin. We knew that removing the skin would cost us flavor and moistness, so we borrowed a tried-and-true fried-chicken trick and soaked the parts in robustly seasoned (and naturally lowfat) buttermilk. In search of an appealing coating, we tested some "creative" options offered by writers of "healthy" recipes, including grated Parmesan cheese, dry Cream of Wheat, pulverized shredded wheat, bran flakes, Weetabix cereal, crushed pretzels, packaged stuffing mix, and even ground-up lowfat popcorn. A cornflake chicken bake, though somewhat lacking in terms of flavor and texture, was the best of the lot, making us wonder if cornflakes might be at least part of the equation. Luckily, a mixture of crushed cornflakes and fresh breadcrumbs was pretty close to perfect. The bottom of each piece was a little soggy, but we solved this problem by baking the chicken on a wire rack, which ensured even crispness and eliminated the need for turning. Because the coating was still a bit dry, we mixed in a modest 2 tablespoons oil, which gave the baked chicken a genuine "fried" texture. Our coating now had great crunch, but it needed more flavor. We seasoned the crumbs with the obvious salt, pepper, and garlic powder, but also added cayenne for heat, paprika for color, and ground

No fryer needed for this extra-crisp chicken.

poultry seasoning (a humble mixture of ground sage, thyme, and bay leaves) for even more depth. Our gamble had paid off. The flavorful, craggy, deeply golden brown coating of this batch was a far cry from the lackluster coating found on most "oven-fried" recipes. Better still, it satisfied our craving for the full-fat stuff.

2 cups buttermilk
2 tablespoons Dijon mustard
  Salt
1½ teaspoons garlic powder
  Pepper
1 teaspoon hot pepper sauce
8 bone-in, skin-on split chicken breasts (10 to 12 ounces each), skin removed and ribs trimmed
1 slice high-quality sandwich bread, torn into quarters
2½ cups crushed cornflakes
½ teaspoon ground poultry seasoning
½ teaspoon paprika
⅛ teaspoon cayenne pepper
2 tablespoons vegetable oil

**1.** Whisk the buttermilk, mustard, 2 teaspoons salt, 1 teaspoon of the garlic powder, 1 teaspoon black pepper, and the hot sauce together in a large bowl. Add the chicken, turn to coat well, cover, and refrigerate at least 1 hour.

**2.** Adjust an oven rack to the upper-middle position and heat the oven to 400 degrees. Line a rimmed baking sheet with foil, place a wire rack on top, and coat the rack with vegetable oil spray. Pulse the bread in a food processor to coarse crumbs, about 8 pulses.

**3.** Gently toss the cornflakes, breadcrumbs, remaining ½ teaspoon garlic powder, ½ teaspoon black pepper, ¼ teaspoon salt, poultry seasoning, paprika, and cayenne in a shallow dish until combined. Drizzle the oil over the crumbs and toss until well coated. Working with one piece at a time, remove the chicken from the marinade and dredge in the crumb mixture, firmly pressing the crumbs onto all sides of the chicken. Place the chicken on the prepared wire rack, leaving ½ inch of space between each piece. Bake until the chicken is deep golden brown and the thickest part registers 160 degrees on an instant-read thermometer, 35 to 45 minutes.

**WHAT YOU CAN DO AHEAD OF TIME:** The chicken can be marinated in the buttermilk mixture and refrigerated for up to 24 hours. The dry ingredients can be combined in a zipper-lock bag. When ready to cook the chicken, toss the crumb mixture with the oil, coat the chicken, and bake.

## NOTES FROM THE TEST KITCHEN

### THE CRUNCHIEST CHOICE
After testing dozens of options, tasters decided that cornflakes made the crispiest coating for our oven-fried chicken. Although at first glance it may seem easier to buy a box of ready-made cornflake crumbs, their texture was too fine for this dish. We got better results when we crushed regular cornflakes cereal ourselves. To crush the flakes, place them in a plastic bag and use a rolling pin to break them into pieces no smaller than ½ inch.

# FREEZER CHICKEN ENCHILADAS
SERVES 4 TO 6

**WHAT MAKES THIS A BEST RECIPE:** Saucy and cheesy, chicken enchiladas are popular here in the test kitchen. The problem is that they require a long list of steps: browning onions, toasting spices, cooking chicken, making sauce, straining, shredding, dipping, filling, rolling, baking—the works. Our goal was simple: Streamline the recipe and make it freezer-worthy, so we could have enchiladas whenever the mood struck. We started with the sauce. We simply pureed the sauce ingredients (canned tomato sauce, garlic, cumin, onion, and coriander) in a blender and then concentrated the flavors by simmering the mixture for 10 minutes. Smoky chipotle chiles were an important addition to our sauce; they added deep, complex flavor, and all we had to do was open a can. As for the filling, we used rotisserie (or leftover) chicken and boosted its flavor by mixing it with some of our sauce and a little cheese. The traditional method of dipping each corn tortilla in oil and sauce so that it becomes soft enough to fill and roll is tedious. Even more important, tortillas treated this way turn to mush once frozen, thawed, and baked. After trial and error, we found that a light coating of vegetable oil spray and 2 minutes in a moderate oven softened the tortillas enough for rolling and helped to prevent sogginess. The step of saucing the bottom of the baking dish and the tops of the tortillas before freezing was also a no-no. After chilling down the filled enchiladas, we wrapped them in bundles—well protected with plastic wrap and foil—and froze the sauce separately. Essentially, we now had an enchilada "kit" in the freezer. With no time to wait for the enchiladas to thaw for dinner, we arranged them, still stone-cold frozen, in a baking dish, coated them with vegetable oil spray, and baked them "naked" for 20 minutes before slathering on the sauce (which was defrosting in the microwave). This allowed the tortillas to crisp before they absorbed any sauce. And not given the chance to thaw and absorb moisture, these straight-from-the-freezer enchiladas were hot and cheesy on the inside but nowhere near mushy. Along with extra sauce, we like to serve these enchiladas with chopped avocado, pickled jalapeños, shredded lettuce, and/or sour cream.

1 (29-ounce) can tomato sauce
½ onion, chopped (about ½ cup)
3 garlic cloves, minced
1 canned chipotle chile in adobo sauce
1 teaspoon ground cumin
1 teaspoon ground coriander
¼ teaspoon salt
½ cup low-sodium chicken broth
1 tablespoon vegetable oil
3 cups shredded cooked chicken
10 ounces shredded Monterey Jack cheese (2½ cups)
⅓ cup chopped fresh cilantro
2 tablespoons minced canned pickled jalapeño chiles
10 (6-inch) corn tortillas
   Vegetable oil spray

**1.** Blend the tomato sauce, onion, garlic, chipotle, cumin, coriander, salt, and broth in a blender until smooth. Heat the oil in a large nonstick skillet over medium heat until shimmering. Add the tomato mixture, bring to a boil, reduce the heat to medium-low, and simmer until the mixture is reduced to 3½ cups, 8 to 10 minutes. Transfer to a bowl and refrigerate until cool, about 1 hour.

**2.** Adjust an oven rack to the middle position and heat the oven to 300 degrees. Toss ¾ cup of the sauce with the chicken, 1 cup of the cheese, cilantro, and jalapeños.

**3.** Place 5 tortillas on a baking sheet and lightly coat both sides with vegetable oil spray. Bake the tortillas until just pliable, about 2 minutes. Working quickly, transfer one tortilla at a time to a work surface, fill with ⅓ cup of the chicken mixture, and roll tightly. Transfer, seam-side down, to a large plate. Repeat the warming and rolling process with the remaining 5 tortillas. Place the plate in the freezer until the enchiladas are frozen, at least 1 hour.

**4.** Place the remaining sauce in a freezer-safe container and press 2 layers of plastic wrap directly onto the surface of the sauce. Tightly wrap the enchiladas in bundles of 5, first in plastic wrap and then in foil. Freeze for up to 2 months.

**5.** WHEN READY TO SERVE: Adjust an oven rack to the middle position and heat the oven to 350 degrees. Defrost the enchilada sauce in the microwave on the defrost setting, about 12 minutes.

**6.** Coat a 13 by 9-inch baking dish with vegetable oil spray. Arrange the frozen enchiladas in a single layer in the prepared baking dish and coat the tops with vegetable oil spray. Bake until the tops of the tortillas are just beginning to flake, about 20 minutes. Remove the dish from the oven, top the

enchiladas with 1½ cups of the sauce, and bake 10 minutes longer. Sprinkle the enchiladas with the remaining 1½ cups cheese and bake until the cheese melts and the center of the casserole is hot and bubbling, 3 to 5 minutes. Serve, passing the remaining sauce separately.

**WHERE THINGS CAN GO WRONG:** Note that you won't need 1½ cups of the cheese until you bake the enchiladas.

## NOTES FROM THE TEST KITCHEN

### HOW TO FREEZE AND BAKE ENCHILADAS

**1.** Tightly wrap the enchiladas in bundles of five, first in plastic and then in foil. Freeze the sauce separately.

**2.** When ready to cook them, arrange the frozen enchiladas in a single layer in a greased baking dish and coat with vegetable oil spray.

**3.** Pour the defrosted sauce over the enchiladas after they have baked for about 20 minutes (when the tortillas are starting to flake).

### WHAT ABOUT CANNED ENCHILADA SAUCE?

Curious as to how canned enchilada sauces would stack up against our homemade version, we tried six supermarket brands: Old El Paso, La Victoria, Hatch, La Preferida, Comida Mexicana, and Las Palmas. None could compete with our recipe. Tasters compared one sauce to "canned tomato soup" and another to "spicy Chef Boyardee." Some comments were even more scathing, likening the supermarket sauces to "burnt coffee grounds" and "salty and bitter tomato paste." So if you're taking the time to make our enchiladas, why spoil their flavor with a sub-par sauce? Ours can be ready in less than 15 minutes.

# 30-MINUTE
# CHICKEN FRICASSEE
## WITH MUSHROOMS
### SERVES 4

**WHAT MAKES THIS A BEST RECIPE:** These days it seems that hardly anyone thinks about making a simple chicken fricassee, perhaps because most of us mistake it for some outdated Cordon Bleu preparation. In fact, a chicken fricassee is nothing more than chicken poached in stock, after which a simple sauce is made from the liquid. It's simple, it's flavorful, and it's easy. So why is it also forgotten? The truth is that many versions of this recipe are either too time consuming or too heavy. Could we streamline it and capture the essence of this wonderful braise?

For a traditional chicken fricassee, bone-in, skin-on chicken parts are sautéed until a deep golden brown and then simmered in either broth or wine (or a mixture of both) until cooked through. Aromatics and vegetables are cooked in a skillet, and then a sauce is built with cream and the liquid used to cook the chicken. The result is a rich and complex dish with moist and tender chicken. We knew right away that our key challenge would be what kind of chicken to use: neither bone-in thighs nor boneless thighs could be properly braised in a 30-minute time limit (and certainly bone-in breasts would be tricky too) so we decided to do something radical. We turned to the microwave for help thinking that if we could jump-start the cooking process there, we would be able to have more time to actually braise and tenderize the meat. We couldn't simmer the meat more briskly—it would toughen if we did so. And we didn't have time to brown the meat either which is why we decided to use skinless thighs. By not browning the meat and using that time instead to jump-start the braising of the thighs in the microwave, we were able to make this dish work in 30 minutes. After trying a variety of powers and cooking times, we found that 50% power for 15 minutes did the trick. There was, however, one drawback to using the microwave: we missed the depth of flavor that resulted from browning. The finished dish just did not capture the essence of the original. The solution turned out to be fairly easy though. To replace this flavor we browned a slice of diced bacon with the aromatics (onion and garlic).

Once the chicken was out of the microwave, it was time for the actual braise. For the cooking liquid we chose both wine and chicken broth, which together produced the most concentrated flavor. A little flour helped thicken the liquid into a savory sauce that clung to the chicken. To add more earthiness and depth to our recipe, we took the lead of many fricassees and added mushrooms, in addition to the aromatics. No one will ever suspect the shortcuts here—this fast chicken fricassee is every bit as good as its French precursor.

2 pounds boneless, skinless chicken thighs
   Salt and pepper
1 slice bacon, minced
1 tablespoon vegetable oil
1 onion, minced (about 1 cup)
10 ounces white mushrooms, quartered
4 garlic cloves, minced
2 tablespoons unbleached all-purpose flour
½ cup dry white wine
¾ cup low-sodium chicken broth
½ cup heavy cream
2 tablespoons minced fresh parsley

**1.** Season the chicken with salt and pepper and arrange in a single layer in a microwave-safe casserole dish. Cover tightly with plastic wrap and microwave on 50 percent power for 15 minutes.

**2.** While the chicken cooks, cook the bacon and oil in a large Dutch oven over medium-high heat until the bacon fat begins to render, about 2 minutes. Stir in the onion, mushrooms, and ¼ teaspoon salt and cook until lightly browned, 8 to 10 minutes. Stir in the garlic and cook until fragrant, about 30 seconds.

**3.** Stir in the flour and cook until lightly browned, about 1 minute. Slowly stir in the wine, scraping up any browned bits. Stir in the broth and bring to a simmer.

**4.** Reduce the heat to low and add the microwaved chicken with any accumulated juice. Cover and continue to cook until the chicken is tender, about 10 minutes.

**5.** Stir in the cream and parsley and return to a brief simmer. Season with salt and pepper to taste. Serve.

**WHERE THINGS CAN GO WRONG:** It is important to cover the chicken with plastic wrap in the microwave so that the meat doesn't dry out. Be careful when taking the chicken out of the microwave as it will be very hot.

# MOROCCAN CHICKEN

## WITH OLIVES AND LEMON

### SERVES 4

**WHAT MAKES THIS A BEST RECIPE:** Tagines are exotically spiced, assertively flavored Moroccan stews slow-cooked in earthenware vessels of the same name. They can include all manner of meats, vegetables, and fruit, though our favorite combines chicken with olives and lemon. While we love tagine, it's a dish that usually requires time-consuming, labor-intensive cooking methods, a special pot (the tagine), and hard-to-find ingredients (preserved lemon). This recipe is a simplified version of the classic. For our recipe, we preferred a whole chicken, cut into pieces. Batches made entirely with white meat lacked the depth and character of those made with a blend of dark and white. However, when we cooked the white and dark meat in the same way—simmered partially submerged in broth until fork-tender—the white meat turned dry and stringy. We solved this by piling sliced carrots (cut ½ inch thick so that they wouldn't overcook) into the bottom of the pot around the dark meat pieces and setting the white meat on top. In this fashion, both dark meat and white meat pieces were perfectly cooked—and ready at the same time. The cooking technique in place, we felt ready to address the defining ingredients of the tagine: spices, olives, and lemon. We experimented with a broad range of spices in batch after batch until we arrived at a blend of cumin, ginger, cinnamon, cayenne, coriander, and paprika, which we toasted to maximize flavor. The lemon flavor in authentic tagines comes from preserved lemon, a long-cured Moroccan condiment that's hard to find outside of specialty stores. Part tart citrus, part pickled brine, preserved lemon has a unique flavor that's impossible to imitate. So we chose not to try; instead, we aimed to add a rich citrus backnote to the dish. We added a few broad ribbons of lemon zest along with the onions, and a lemon's worth of juice just before serving reinforced the bright flavor. A spoonful of honey further balanced things, and chopped cilantro freshened the flavors, but we felt the stew still lacked a certain spark. A last-minute addition of raw garlic and finely chopped lemon zest seemed to clinch it, as the sharpness brought out the best in each of the stew's components. This stew is great on its own, but we like to serve it with couscous.

1¼ teaspoons sweet paprika
½ teaspoon ground cumin
¼ teaspoon cayenne pepper
¼ teaspoon ground ginger
¼ teaspoon ground coriander
¼ teaspoon ground cinnamon
3 strips lemon zest (each about 2 inches by ¾ inch)
5 garlic cloves, minced
1 whole chicken (3½ to 4 pounds), giblets discarded and cut into 8 pieces (4 breast pieces, 2 thighs, 2 drumsticks; wings reserved for another use) following the photos on page 196
  Salt and pepper
1 tablespoon olive oil
1 onion, halved and cut into ¼-inch slices
1¾ cups low-sodium chicken broth
1 tablespoon honey
2 carrots, peeled and cut crosswise into ½-inch-thick coins, cut into half moons if pieces are quite large
1 cup Greek cracked green olives, pitted and halved
2 tablespoons chopped fresh cilantro
3 tablespoons fresh lemon juice

## NOTES FROM THE TEST KITCHEN

**THE BEST GREEN OLIVES FOR MOROCCAN CHICKEN**
Until we began developing our recipe for Moroccan chicken, we were unaware of just how many green olive varietals were out there—from the $1.99-a-jar cocktail garnish to the $12.99-per-pound French import. Our curiosity (and taste buds) piqued, we scoured local supermarkets and returned with nearly two dozen jars and deli containers of the green fruits. We first tried all of the olives plain, then we tasted them cooked in our Moroccan chicken.

Straight from the container, the hands-down favorites were the imported (and somewhat expensive) French samples—Lucques and Picholines—for their buttery, bright flavor and al dente texture. When incorporated into a cooked dish, however, the cracked, salt-brined Conservoleas (Divina was our favorite brand) topped the charts for being "bright" and "snappy"—and which, at $3.79 a jar, left a little green in our wallets.

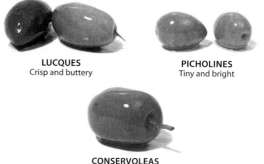

**LUCQUES**
Crisp and buttery

**PICHOLINES**
Tiny and bright

**CONSERVOLEAS**
Bright and snappy, the best choice for Moroccan chicken

**1.** Combine the spices in a small bowl and set aside. Mince 1 strip of lemon zest. Combine the minced zest with 1 teaspoon of minced garlic and mince together until reduced to a fine paste; set aside.

**2.** Pat the chicken dry with paper towels and season with salt and pepper. Heat the oil in a large heavy-bottomed Dutch oven over medium-high heat until beginning to smoke. Brown the chicken pieces skin-side down in a single layer until deep golden, about 5 minutes. Using tongs, turn the chicken pieces and brown until golden on the second side, about 4 minutes longer. Transfer the chicken to a large plate. When cool enough to handle, peel off the skin and discard. Pour off and discard all but 1 tablespoon fat from the pot.

**3.** Add the onion and the remaining lemon zest strips to the pot and cook, stirring occasionally, until the onion pieces have browned at the edges but still retain a slight bite, 5 to 7 minutes (add 1 tablespoon water if the pan gets too dark). Add the remaining 4 teaspoons garlic and cook, stirring, until fragrant, about 30 seconds. Add the spice combination and cook, stirring constantly, until darkened and very fragrant, about 1 minute. Stir in the broth and honey, scraping the bottom of the pot with a wooden spoon to loosen any browned bits. Add the thighs and drumsticks, reduce the heat to medium, and simmer for 5 minutes.

**4.** Add the carrots and breast pieces (with any accumulated juice) to the pot, arranging the breast pieces in a single layer on top of the carrots. Cover, reduce the heat to medium-low, and simmer until the thickest part of the breast registers 160 degrees on an instant-read thermometer, 10 to 15 minutes.

**5.** Transfer the chicken to a plate and tent with foil. Add the olives to the pot. Increase the heat to medium-high and simmer until the liquid has thickened slightly and the carrots are tender, 4 to 6 minutes. Return the chicken to the pot and stir in the garlic/zest mixture, cilantro, and lemon juice. Season with salt and pepper to taste. Serve immediately.

**WHERE THINGS CAN GO WRONG:** If the olives are particularly salty, give them a rinse so they don't overpower the tagine. Use a vegetable peeler to remove wide strips of zest from the lemon before juicing it, but make sure to trim any white pith from the zest, as it can impart bitter flavor.

## NOTES FROM THE TEST KITCHEN

### HOW TO CUT UP A WHOLE CHICKEN

Every cook is confronted a few times at least with having to cut up a whole chicken. Don't sweat it—it only takes a few minutes and is easy to do with a decent pair of kitchen shears (see page 213) and a sharp chef's knife. Plus, because whole chickens are usually cheaper, you'll wind up saving money.

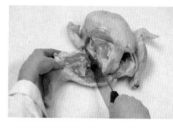

**1.** Using a chef's knife, cut off the legs, one at a time, by severing the joint between the leg and the body.

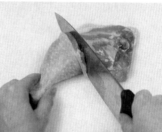

**2.** Cut each leg into 2 pieces—the drumstick and the thigh—by slicing through the joint that connects them (marked by a thick white line of fat). Your knife should glide right through.

**3.** Flip the chicken over and remove the wings by slicing through each wing joint.

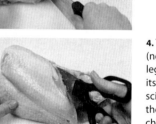

**4.** Turn the chicken (now without its legs and wings) on its side and, using scissors, remove the back from the chicken breast. (The back can be saved for stock, if desired.)

**5.** Flip the breast skin-side down and, using a chef's knife, cut it in half through the breast plate (marked by a thin white line of cartilage).

# ONE-POT SOUTHWESTERN CHICKEN AND RICE

### SERVES 4

**WHAT MAKES THIS A BEST RECIPE:** Although there is no specific American tradition for a dish called "chicken and rice," its appeal is obvious: It's a one-dish supper, it's easy, and it's eminently variable. Yet after having made a dozen attempts at perfecting this recipe, we found two major problems: The chicken tends to dry out, and the rice is often unevenly cooked and crunchy. And even when we get the basics right, the dish can be pretty bland. Tackling the problem of overcooked chicken was easy. Many recipes call for both dark and white meat, which cook at different rates. We kept it simple and chose all bone-in breasts, which we lightly browned to develop flavor, then set aside and eventually returned to the pot to cook through and flavor the rice. The texture of the rice was a more vexing issue. To cook rice successfully, we usually use less than twice as much liquid as rice. We discovered that rice needs additional liquid when other ingredients are cooking alongside it in the pot. For the 1½ cups rice called for in this recipe, it took a whopping 4 cups of liquid in order for the rice to turn out completely tender. Next, we focused on jazzing up the flavors. Instead of plain old chicken and rice, we took a Southwestern route. For a backbone of flavor, we cooked the rice in chicken broth and white wine, which we fortified with onion, garlic, and red pepper flakes. We also added black beans and sweet yellow corn, not only for flavor but also for their contrast in texture and color. Before serving, we stirred in cheddar cheese, which melted and made the rice slightly creamy, and, last, a little cilantro for freshness.

4   bone-in, skin-on split chicken breasts
    (10 to 12 ounces each)
    Salt and pepper
2   tablespoons vegetable oil
1   onion, chopped (about 1 cup)
¼   teaspoon red pepper flakes
4   garlic cloves, minced
1½  cups long-grain white rice
3½  cups low-sodium chicken broth
½   cup dry white wine

1   (15.5-ounce) can black beans, drained and rinsed
1   (10-ounce) package frozen corn, thawed and patted dry
4   ounces cheddar cheese, shredded (about 1 cup)
2   tablespoons minced fresh cilantro
    Salsa, for serving

**1.** Pat the chicken dry with paper towels and season with salt and pepper. Heat the oil in a large Dutch oven over medium-high heat until just smoking. Add the chicken skin-side down and cook until golden, about 5 minutes. Transfer the chicken to a plate, leaving the fat in the pot.

**2.** Add the onion, pepper flakes, and ½ teaspoon salt to the fat in the pot and place over medium heat. Cook, scraping up any browned bits on the pan bottom, until the onion is softened, about 5 minutes.

**3.** Stir in the garlic and cook until fragrant, about 15 seconds. Stir in the rice and cook until the edges turn translucent, about 3 minutes. Stir in the broth and wine and bring to a simmer.

**4.** Return the chicken to the pot, skin-side up. Cover, reduce the heat to low, and cook until the thickest part of the breast registers 160 degrees on an instant-read thermometer, about 25 minutes.

**5.** Transfer the chicken to a serving platter. Stir the black beans, corn, cheddar, and cilantro into the rice. Let the cheddar melt for 1 minute. Season the rice mixture with salt and pepper to taste. Serve with the salsa.

## NOTES FROM THE TEST KITCHEN

### THE BEST SUPERMARKET CHEDDAR CHEESE
White or orange, mild or sharp, different types of cheddar dominate the cheese case. We wanted to find out how different brands faced off against each other.

In a side-by-side taste test of different brands of supermarket cheddar, we limited the choice to sharp. We tested them both raw and melted in grilled cheese sandwiches. One of the great surprises of our tasting was the success of Cracker Barrel, which at a bargain-priced $3.29 for 10 ounces, outranked cheeses costing three times as much. Cracker Barrel finished in third place overall, bested by Vermont-made **Cabot,** which sells for about $6 a pound, and Oregon-made Tillamook, which sells for about $7 a pound. All three shared a rich, tangy flavor and melted smoothly.

# SKILLET-ROASTED TARRAGON CHICKEN
### SERVES 4

**WHAT MAKES THIS A BEST RECIPE:** Cooking bone-in, skin-on chicken breasts can be a challenge. They are difficult to sauté or cook through on the stovetop because they have great girth on one end and are thin and tapered on the other, and oven-roasting whole breasts fails to impress us because the delicate white meat cooks through well before the skin can crisp. Our solution was to try pan-roasting, a restaurant technique in which food is browned in a skillet on the stovetop and then placed in a hot oven to finish cooking. An added bonus of pan-roasting is that the skillet is left with caramelized drippings, or fond, just the essence of flavor you want for making a rich pan sauce. When it came to browning the chicken, all it took was a mere teaspoon of vegetable oil heated in the skillet until it was smoking. We then added the chicken breasts to the skillet, skin-side down, and browned them on both sides before transferring them to a baking dish on the lowest rack in the oven. We tried a range of oven temperatures and found that at 450 degrees the skin was handsomely browned and crackling crisp, and the chicken cooked swiftly to the internal temperature of 160 degrees, which translated to about 15 to 20 minutes for 10- to 12-ounce breasts. While the chicken rested we made the pan sauce using shallots, wine, chicken broth, tarragon, and butter. The sauce added flavor interest and made these crisp-skinned, skillet-roasted chicken breasts the perfect weeknight dinner.

### CHICKEN
- 4 bone-in, skin-on split chicken breasts (10 to 12 ounces each)
  Salt and pepper
- 1 teaspoon vegetable oil

### SAUCE
- 2 teaspoons vegetable oil
- 1 shallot, minced (3 tablespoons)
  Salt
- ¾ cup low-sodium chicken broth

- ½ cup dry white wine or vermouth
- 3 tablespoons unsalted butter, cut into 3 pieces and chilled
- 2 teaspoons minced fresh tarragon or 1 teaspoon dried
  Pepper

**1. FOR THE CHICKEN:** Adjust an oven rack to the lowest position, place a 13 by 9-inch baking dish on the rack, and heat the oven to 450 degrees.

**2.** Pat the chicken dry with paper towels and season with salt and pepper. Heat the oil in a large skillet over high heat until just smoking. Add the chicken skin-side down and cook until golden brown on both sides, about 10 minutes.

**3.** Transfer the chicken to the preheated baking dish in the oven, skin-side up. (Do not wash the skillet.) Bake until the thickest part of the breast registers 160 degrees on an instant-read thermometer, 15 to 20 minutes. Remove from the oven, tent with foil, and let rest while making the sauce.

**4. FOR THE SAUCE:** While the chicken rests, add the oil to the skillet and return to medium-high heat until shimmering. Add the shallot and ¼ teaspoon salt and cook until softened, about 2 minutes. Stir in the broth and wine, scraping up any browned bits on the pan bottom, and simmer until reduced and slightly syrupy, about 8 minutes.

**5.** Stir in any accumulated chicken juice. Turn the heat to low and whisk in the butter, one piece at a time. Off the heat, stir in the tarragon and season with salt and pepper to taste. Spoon the sauce over the chicken before serving.

## NOTES FROM THE TEST KITCHEN

### HOW TO KNOW WHEN YOUR SKILLET IS HOT ENOUGH
Is your skillet properly preheated? The oil—the smoking oil, to be exact—will tell you. Measured into a cold skillet and heated for a few minutes, oil gives off wisps of smoke that serve as a visual cue that the skillet is sufficiently heated and ready for cooking. A properly heated pan also helps to reduce the chance that the added food will stick. To further reduce the chances of sticking, pat the food dry with paper towels just before adding it to the skillet (unless the ingredient is floured).

This sticky mess is what will happen if you attempt to cook chicken in a skillet that is not hot enough.

# CRISPY ROAST CHICKEN AND POTATOES
### SERVES 4

**WHAT MAKES THIS A BEST RECIPE:** At first glance, roasting chicken and potatoes together seems easy enough. All too often, though, the potatoes wind up soggy and the breast meat is overcooked. Having roasted thousands of chickens over the years, we had come up with a slightly fussy method (calling for a very hot oven, a V-rack, and three turns in the oven) that keeps the breast meat from overcooking. This method also produces fairly crisp skin, but we wanted the crispiest skin ever. We found that poking holes in the chicken's skin released the fat that was bubbling underneath it as the chicken roasted. When combined with a sprinkling of cornstarch, a trick used in many Asian stir-fry recipes, these steps created an extra-crunchy coating. We also discovered that roasting the chicken in a super-hot oven (475 degrees) made for an even more superior bird—with deeply browned and crisp skin and moist and tender meat. With the chicken perfected, we turned to solving the problem of soggy and greasy potatoes. Instead of starting the potatoes along with the chicken, we added them to the roasting pan when we turned the chicken for the third (and last) time. Since we had lined the roasting pan with foil, just before we added the potatoes we gathered the corners of the foil and discarded the rendered fat. We then spread the potatoes cut side down in the bottom of the hot roasting pan, replaced the V-rack (with the chicken breast side up), and returned the pan to the oven. By the time the chicken was done, the potatoes were tender, but they lacked the chicken flavor and the golden brown color we were after. To add chicken flavor to the potatoes without the fat, we simply poured the juice from the cavity of the chicken onto the potatoes (as we were moving it for resting) and popped them back in the oven to color and crisp up. Ten minutes later they were a deep brown and infused with chicken flavor, minus the fat. Not the simplest roast chicken and potatoes in the world perhaps, but by far the best we had ever tasted!

2 teaspoons cornstarch
  Salt
1 (3½ to 4-pound) whole chicken, giblets discarded
2 pounds small red potatoes, scrubbed and halved
2 teaspoons vegetable oil

**1.** Line a roasting pan with foil, letting the foil come up the sides of the pan. Adjust an oven rack to the middle position (8 to 10 inches from the broiler element), place the roasting pan on the rack, and heat the oven to 475 degrees. Coat a V-rack with vegetable oil spray.

**2.** Combine the cornstarch and 2 teaspoons salt in a small bowl. Use a skewer to poke holes all over the chicken skin. Pat the chicken dry with paper towels and rub the cornstarch mixture evenly over the chicken.

## NOTES FROM THE TEST KITCHEN

### ROASTING SECRETS
For perfectly crisp skin and juicy meat, you've got to flip the bird. Rotating the chicken also ensures that the white meat, which cooks more quickly than the dark meat, will not over-cook while you're waiting for the thighs to reach an internal temperature of 170 degrees.

**1.** Place the chicken, wing-side up in a greased V-rack. Place the V-rack in a preheated roasting pan lined with foil and roast for 15 minutes. Flip the chicken so that the other wing faces up and roast for another 15 minutes.

**2.** Remove the V-rack from the roasting pan, discard the foil and grease, add the potatoes to the empty roasting pan, turn the chicken breast-side up, and return the V-rack to the pan. Roast for another 20 minutes or until done.

**3.** Remove the roasting rack and chicken, tipping the juice from the cavity back into the roasting pan. Toss the potatoes with the chicken juice and return to the oven to finish cooking.

**3.** Remove the roasting pan from the oven. Following the photo on page 199, place the chicken wing-side up in the V-rack, then place the V-rack in the preheated roasting pan. Roast the chicken 15 minutes. Remove the roasting pan from oven and, using a wad of paper towels, flip the chicken so that the other wing is facing up. Roast for 15 minutes.

**4.** Meanwhile, toss the potatoes, oil, and ½ teaspoon salt in a medium bowl. Remove the roasting pan from the oven and, with a potholder, carefully transfer the V-rack with the chicken to a rimmed baking sheet. Gather up the foil by its corners, capturing any fat and juice, and discard. Arrange the potatoes cut side down in the roasting pan. Using a wad of paper towels, flip the chicken breast side up in the V-rack. Place the V-rack back in the roasting pan and roast the chicken until the thickest part of the thigh registers 170 degrees on an instant-read thermometer, about 20 minutes.

**5.** Using a wad of paper towels, remove the chicken from the V-rack and pour the juice from the cavity into the roasting pan with the potatoes. Place the chicken on an angel-food-cake pan insert or an empty soda can to rest upright for 10 to 15 minutes. Meanwhile, toss the potatoes in the chicken juice, return to the oven, and cook until well browned and crisp, 10 to 15 minutes. Carve the chicken following the photos and serve with the potatoes.

**WHERE THINGS CAN GO WRONG:** If using a chicken larger than 4 pounds, the oven time will need to be lengthened slightly.

## GREAT DISCOVERIES
### STARCH MAKES IT CRISPY

After searching in vain for a foolproof recipe for crispy roast chicken, I stumbled upon a secret ingredient: plain old cornstarch. Sprinkling just 2 teaspoons of cornstarch over the chicken before putting it into the oven helped to form a crispy, golden crust. How does this work? Before sprinkling the bird with cornstarch, I used a skewer to poke holes in the skin. In the oven, the fat escapes through these holes, mixes with the starch, and creates an extra-crisp coating.

JEREMY SAUER | ASSOCIATE EDITOR, COOK'S COUNTRY

## NOTES FROM THE TEST KITCHEN
### HOW TO CARVE A ROASTED CHICKEN

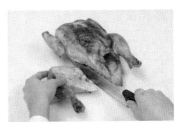

**1.** Cut the chicken where the leg meets the breast.

**2.** Pull the leg quarter away from the carcass. Separate the joint by gently pressing the leg out to the side and pushing up on the joint.

**3.** Carefully cut through the joint to remove the leg quarter.

**4.** Cut through the joint that connects the drumstick to the thigh. Repeat on the second side to remove the other leg.

**5.** Cut down along one side of the breastbone, pulling the breast meat away from you as you cut.

**6.** Remove the wing from the breast by cutting through the wing joint. Slice the breast into attractive slices.

# STUFFED TURKEY BREAST

SERVES 6 TO 8

**WHAT MAKES THIS A BEST RECIPE:** After you make this flavorful stuffed turkey breast for the first time, we bet that you will think twice about automatically planning to make that 20-pound bird the centerpiece of your next Thanksgiving meal. And whether or not you make this recipe a new holiday tradition, we're certain that you'll want to make it more than once a year. This is a recipe with a lot going for it in the convenience department: It's much easier than it looks to put together, it can be stuffed and rolled ahead of time, it goes well with a multitude of side dishes, and the fragrant and tasty spinach and cheese filling turns turkey into something special. In short, although it makes a great Sunday night dinner with family, it is perfect for a buffet table or any occasion when you have guests. Boneless, skinless turkey breast, now widely available in supermarkets, weighs just 3 to 4 pounds and is a top contender for a family meal: It's easily stuffed and won't leave behind a week's worth of leftovers. Being without skin, bones, or dark meat, however, this ultra-lean cut can be a challenge to prepare well, often ending up flavorless, overcooked, and dry. When it comes to flavor, most recipes go wrong by depending on a bland bread stuffing. For a boneless, skinless breast, the stuffing—not the turkey—must provide the flavor. With that in mind, we opted for a potent vegetable-and-cheese-based stuffing in place of the typical plain bread one. Spinach and assertively flavored ingredients such as onion, garlic, fontina cheese, and lemon zest seasoned the white meat from the inside out. While this stuffing remedied a lack of flavor, our turkey breast tests continued to come out of the oven awfully dry. One reason, we figured, was their uneven shape, as the tapered end cooked (and turned dry) long before the broad end was done. To remedy this, we first cut the breast open (or butterflied it). This is not hard, you just need a sharp chef's knife and must pay attention and not cut too deeply as you slice into the meat. After some careful pounding the turkey was ready

A turkey breast can be butterflied, stuffed, rolled, and roasted. When sliced, this method yields spirals of turkey and filling that are attractive and flavorful.

for the filling. We spread the stuffing over the flattened meat, rolled it into a cylinder, and tied it with twine. The football-shaped cylinder cooked evenly and, when sliced, yielded a spiraling combination of turkey and filling, but even still, the interior of the turkey was dry and the exterior pale. We found that the way to guarantee juicy turkey was one, to keep the oven temperature at 325 degrees and, two, to make up for the turkey's pallid and flavorless exterior by coating the cylinder with a light sprinkling of sugar (along with salt and pepper). The sugared turkey displayed a golden exterior, but, even better, it was the tastiest bird yet. For a perfectly browned exterior (and beautiful spirals on your platter), you must turn the turkey every 30 minutes until done. This turkey breast was now as moist and flavorful as a bone-in bird—and a whole lot easier to manage.

1  boneless, skinless turkey breast (3 to 4 pounds)
4  tablespoons extra-virgin olive oil
1  onion, minced (about 1 cup)

1  (8-ounce) package frozen spinach, thawed, squeezed dry, and chopped

3  garlic cloves, minced

¼  teaspoon grated lemon zest

8  ounces fontina cheese, shredded (about 2 cups)
   Salt and pepper

1  tablespoon sugar

**1.** Adjust an oven rack to the middle position and heat the oven to 325 degrees. Following the photos, butterfly the turkey breast, cover with plastic wrap, and pound lightly with a meat mallet until about ½ inch thick.

**2.** Heat 2 tablespoons of the oil in a large skillet over medium-high heat until shimmering. Add the onion and cook until softened, about 5 minutes. Stir in the spinach, garlic, and zest and cook until fragrant, 30 seconds. Remove from the heat and cool 10 minutes. Stir in the fontina and season with salt and pepper.

**3.** Spread the stuffing in an even layer over the turkey. Starting with the short side nearest you, roll up the turkey and tie at 1-inch intervals with butcher's twine. Rub the turkey with the remaining 2 tablespoons oil and sprinkle evenly with the sugar, 2 teaspoons pepper, and 1 teaspoon salt. Place on a wire rack set over a rimmed baking sheet and roast, turning every 30 minutes, until the turkey registers 160 degrees on an instant-read thermometer, about 2 hours. Transfer the turkey to a cutting board, cover loosely with foil, and let rest for 15 minutes. Remove the twine and slice crosswise into ½-inch-thick slices. Serve.

**WHERE THINGS CAN GO WRONG:** When shopping for the turkey breast, make sure to buy a turkey breast half, not an entire breast with two lobes of meat—a whole breast is too large for this recipe. Soggy spinach can make for a watery filling. To prevent this, place the thawed spinach in the center of a clean kitchen towel and twist the ends of the towel to wring out excess moisture.

**WHAT YOU CAN DO AHEAD OF TIME:** Once stuffed and tied, the turkey breast can be refrigerated for up to 2 days before roasting. Or just the stuffing can be made in advance; refrigerate it in an airtight container for up to 3 days.

## NOTES FROM THE TEST KITCHEN

### HOW TO STUFF A TURKEY BREAST

To prepare this recipe, you must first butterfly the turkey breast. It sounds hard, but it's actually quite simple. Once butterflied, the turkey breast is pounded, stuffed, rolled, and tied. The entire process takes less than 10 minutes.

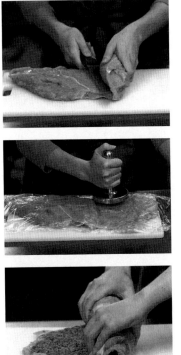

**1.** With the turkey smooth side down, slice into the thickest part, keeping the knife ½ inch above the cutting board and stopping ½ inch from the edge of the breast. Open it like a book.

**2.** Place a sheet of plastic wrap over the turkey and pound lightly with a meat mallet until the turkey breast is an even ½-inch thickness throughout.

**3.** Remove the plastic wrap and spread the filling evenly over the turkey, stopping ½ inch from the sides. Starting with the shorter side nearest you, roll the turkey into a tight cylinder.

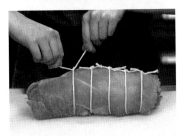

**4.** Use butcher's twine to tie the turkey breast at 1-inch intervals. Tuck in the ends of the turkey and loop a piece of twine around the ends to keep the stuffing from falling out.

# CHICKEN FAJITAS

SERVES 4 TO 6

**WHAT MAKES THIS A BEST RECIPE:** With or without the sizzling cast-iron skillet, what passes for chicken fajitas in most restaurants these days is about as authentic as Belgian toaster waffles. Guacamole, sour cream, and salsa do most of the heavy lifting to mask the bland, soggy flavors of the underlying ingredients. For this recipe, we wanted to go back to the basics, a simple combination of smoky grilled vegetables and strips of chicken, wrapped up tableside in warm flour tortillas. Boneless, skinless chicken breasts were the most appropriate and traditional choice for chicken fajitas, but we found they greatly benefited from a marinade. A high-acid marinade of lime juice and vegetable oil added fresh citrus flavor notes and also reduced the marinating time to a mere 15 minutes. For smokiness and depth, we added Worcestershire sauce, a bit of brown sugar helped round out the salty flavors, and some minced jalapeño chile and cilantro added freshness. Next we turned our attention to the vegetables. Both green and red bell peppers gave the fajitas contrast in terms of color and in their bitter and sweet flavors, and onions were a no-brainer. We quickly discovered that whereas the chicken needed blazing-hot coals, the vegetables, which are more prone to burning, required more moderate heat. To allow the chicken and vegetables to cook side by side at slightly different heat levels, we created a simple two-level fire. To add a burst of flavor to the chicken and vegetables, we tossed a small amount of unused reserved marinade back in with the chicken and vegetables after we sliced them into strips. Although the chicken and vegetables have enough flavor to stand on their own, guacamole, salsa, sour cream, shredded cheddar or Monterey Jack cheese, and lime wedges are always welcome accompaniments at the table.

⅓ cup fresh lime juice (2 to 3 limes)

6 tablespoons vegetable oil

3 garlic cloves, minced

1 tablespoon Worcestershire sauce

1½ teaspoons brown sugar

1 jalapeño chile, seeds and ribs removed, minced

1½ tablespoons minced fresh cilantro

Salt and pepper

3 boneless, skinless chicken breasts (6 to 8 ounces each), tenderloins removed and breasts pounded to ½-inch thickness (see page 177)

1 red onion, peeled and cut into ½-inch-thick rounds (do not separate rings)

1 red bell pepper, quartered, stemmed, and seeded

1 green bell pepper, quartered, stemmed, and seeded

8–12 (6-inch) flour tortillas

**1.** Whisk the lime juice, 4 tablespoons of the oil, garlic, Worcestershire, brown sugar, jalapeño, cilantro, 1 teaspoon salt, and ¾ teaspoon pepper together in a medium bowl. Reserve ¼ cup of the marinade and set aside. Add 1 more teaspoon salt to the remaining marinade and add the chicken. Cover with plastic wrap and refrigerate for 15 minutes. Brush the onion rounds and peppers with the remaining 2 tablespoons oil and season with salt and pepper.

**2.** Meanwhile, light a large chimney starter filled with charcoal briquettes (about 100 pieces) and allow it to burn until all the charcoal is covered with a layer of fine gray ash, about 20 minutes. Spread the coals out over the grill bottom, placing an additional 20 unlit coals over the lit coals on one side

## NOTES FROM THE TEST KITCHEN

### THE BEST SUPERMARKET FLOUR TORTILLAS

It's no surprise that the best flour tortillas are freshly made to order. But those of us without a local tortilleria must make do with the packaged offerings at the local supermarket. To find out which ones taste best, we rounded up every 6-inch flour tortilla we could find (usually labeled "fajita size") and headed into the test kitchen to taste them.

Tasters immediately zeroed in on texture, which varied dramatically from "doughy and stale" to "thin and flaky." The thinner brands were the hands-down winners: Most brands had a mild, pleasantly wheaty flavor, but two of the doughier brands, Olé and La Banderita (both made by the same company), were panned for off, sour notes. Our advice is simple: Buy the thinnest tortillas you can find at your local market.

### CHICKEN FAJITAS ON A GAS GRILL

Follow the recipe through step 1. Light all the burners on a gas grill and turn the heat to high. Cover and heat the grill until hot, about 15 minutes; scrape the cooking grate clean with a grill brush. Leave one burner on high heat while turning the remaining burner(s) down to medium. Continue with the recipe from step 3, cooking the chicken and vegetables covered. When the grill is empty, set all burners to medium. Working in batches, if necessary, place the tortillas in a single layer on the grate and grill until warm and lightly browned, about 20 seconds per side. As they are done, wrap the tortillas in a kitchen towel or a large sheet of foil. Proceed as directed in step 5 of the recipe.

of the grill. Set the cooking grate in place, cover, and let the grill heat up for 5 minutes. Use a grill brush to scrape the cooking grate clean.

**3.** Place the chicken breasts smooth side down on the hotter side of the grill, discarding the remaining marinade. Place the onion rounds and peppers (skin-side down) on the cooler side of the grill. Cook the chicken until well browned, 4 to 5 minutes. Flip the chicken and continue cooking until the thickest part of the breast registers 160 degrees on an instant-read thermometer, 4 to 5 minutes longer. Meanwhile, cook the peppers until spottily charred and crisp-tender, 8 to 10 minutes, turning once or twice as needed. Cook the onions until tender and charred on both sides, 10 to 12 minutes, turning every 3 to 4 minutes. When the chicken and vegetables are done, transfer them to a large plate and tent with foil to keep warm.

**4.** Working in batches, place the tortillas in a single layer on the cooler side of the now-empty grill and cook until warm and lightly browned, about 20 seconds per side. As the tortillas are done, wrap them in a clean kitchen towel or a large sheet of foil.

**5.** Separate the onions into rings and slice the bell peppers lengthwise into ¼-inch strips. Toss the vegetables with 2 tablespoons of the reserved marinade. Slice the chicken into ¼-inch strips and toss with the remaining 2 tablespoons reserved marinade. Arrange the chicken and vegetables on a large platter and serve with the warmed tortillas.

**WHERE THINGS CAN GO WRONG:** Do not grill the tortillas too long or they will become brittle.

## NOTES FROM THE TEST KITCHEN

### KEYS TO A BETTER MARINADE
Our marinade transforms bland chicken in just 15 minutes. We found that a generous dose of lime juice and a shot of Worcestershire sauce were key. The lime juice adds bracing acidity, while the Worcestershire (made with molasses, anchovies, tamarind, onion, garlic, and other seasonings) lends smoky, salty depth.

# EASY JERK CHICKEN
## WITH GRILLED BANANA AND RED ONION SALSA
### SERVES 4

**WHAT MAKES THIS A BEST RECIPE:** Jerk chicken, with its marriage of hot chiles, warm spices, and smoky grilled chicken, along with a cool Red Stripe beer, is our vision of island paradise. We created this recipe because, as much as we would like to, we can't hop on a plane to Jamaica anytime we get a hankering for the stuff. The challenge with jerk chicken turned out to be creating a jerk paste that wasn't too spicy, harsh tasting, or bland, and figuring out how to apply the paste so that it flavored the chicken, not just the skin. We made our jerk paste using habanero chiles (which we liked for their great flavor and slow, steady heat), allspice, garlic, thyme, and scallions. To temper the heat and spice, we added vegetable oil and dark, smoky molasses, both of which had the added benefit of making the paste smoother and more cohesive—perfect for adhering to the chicken. In our research, we found that many recipes call for marinating the chicken for days—a step we wanted to skip. After much trial and error with "quick" marinating techniques, we realized that if we wanted the jerk seasonings to flavor the meat more quickly, we would have to rub the paste directly on the meat. This technique produced dramatic results, cutting the minimum marinating time from 24 hours to 2. Now we were ready to fire up the grill. To keep the skin from burning before the meat near the bone was cooked through, we built a two-level fire on the grill. We began by placing the chicken skin-side down over the hot part of the grill (with more coals) to crisp the skin. This caused the jerk paste on the exterior of the bird to char slightly—just enough to create an authentic smoky flavor. After flipping the chicken to cook it skin-side up for a few minutes, we slid the chicken pieces over to the cooler side of the grill (with fewer coals) to finish cooking. When serving the chicken, we passed around some lime wedges and a grilled fruit and red onion salsa. The tart addition of the lime along with the sweetness of the salsa mingled with the jerk beautifully, proving that with great jerk the whole is greater than the sum of its parts.

CHICKEN

- 1 bunch scallions, chopped
- 3 garlic cloves, peeled
- 2 teaspoons ground allspice
- 1 tablespoon dried thyme
- 2 teaspoons salt
- 2 tablespoons mild or robust molasses
- 2 habanero chiles, stemmed and halved
- ¼ cup vegetable oil
- 3 pounds bone-in, skin-on chicken thighs, legs, or breasts

SALSA

- 1 red onion, peeled and cut crosswise into ½-inch rounds
- 3 bananas, peeled and halved lengthwise
- 2 tablespoons vegetable oil
- ½ teaspoon ground cumin
  Salt and pepper
- 2 tablespoons fresh lime juice
- 2 tablespoons chopped fresh mint
- 1 tablespoon light brown sugar
- 1 tablespoon dark rum (optional)
  Lime wedges, for serving

**1. FOR THE CHICKEN:** Puree the scallions, garlic, allspice, thyme, salt, molasses, chiles, and oil in a food processor or blender until almost smooth, scraping down the sides, if necessary. Wearing latex gloves and working with one piece of chicken at a time, slide your fingers between the skin and the meat to loosen the skin, then rub 1 tablespoon of the spice mixture under the skin of each piece and transfer the chicken to a gallon-sized zipper-lock bag. Pour the remaining spice mixture over the chicken, seal the bag, and use your hands to squeeze and turn the bag so that the chicken pieces are covered with the mixture. Refrigerate for at least 2 hours.

**2.** Light a large chimney starter filled with charcoal briquettes (about 100 pieces) and allow it to burn until all the charcoal is covered with a layer of fine gray ash, about 20 minutes. Stack the briquettes 2 to 3 high on one side of grill and in a single layer on the other side. Set the cooking grate in place, cover, and let the grill heat up for 5 minutes. Use a grill brush to scrape the cooking grate clean.

**3.** Remove the chicken from the bag and arrange it skin-side down over the hot part of the grill. Cover the grill and cook the chicken until well browned on both sides, 3 to 5 minutes per side. Transfer the chicken to the cooler part of the grill, cover, and continue to cook, turning occasionally, until very

dark and the thickest part of the breast registers 160 degrees and the thighs register 170 degrees on an instant-read thermometer, 15 to 22 minutes.

**4. FOR THE SALSA:** Meanwhile, brush both sides of the onion rounds and banana halves with the oil and sprinkle with the cumin and salt and pepper to taste. Grill the onion over the hottest part of the grill, covered, until well browned, 3 to 4 minutes per side. Transfer the onion to the cooler part of the grill and place the bananas, cut-side down, over the hottest part of the grill. Grill the bananas, covered, until browned in spots, about 2 minutes per side.

**5.** Transfer the onion and bananas to a cutting board and cool slightly. Whisk the lime juice, mint, brown sugar, and rum (if using) together in a medium bowl until the sugar has dissolved. Roughly chop the onion and bananas, add them to the bowl, and toss to coat. Season the salsa with salt and pepper to taste. Serve the chicken with the lime wedges and salsa.

**WHERE THINGS CAN GO WRONG:** Your mouth may love the rush you get from eating spicy foods but, as anyone who's ever rubbed his or her eyes after handling hot chiles will tell you, don't push your luck. Be sure to wear latex gloves when handling the habaneros—they are among the hottest chiles in the world.

**WHAT YOU CAN DO AHEAD OF TIME:** The chicken can be prepared through step 1 and refrigerated for up to 36 hours. The salsa can be refrigerated in an airtight container for up to 2 days. Bring the salsa to room temperature before serving and adjust the consistency and seasoning with lime juice and rum (if using).

## NOTES FROM THE TEST KITCHEN

### YOU CAN DOUBLE IT
This recipe can easily be doubled, but, depending on the size of your cooking grate, you may have to grill the chicken in two batches.

### JERK CHICKEN ON A GAS GRILL
Follow the recipe through step 1. Light all the burners on a gas grill and turn the heat to high. Cover and heat the grill until hot, about 15 minutes; use a grill brush to scrape the cooking grate clean. Leave one burner on high heat while turning the remaining burner(s) down to low. Continue with the recipe from step 3, cooking the chicken covered. Proceed as directed in steps 4 and 5 of the recipe.

A simple blend of spices and a quick yogurt sauce give this chicken complex, exotic flavor.

# TANDOORI-STYLE CHICKEN BREASTS
## WITH RAITA
### SERVES 4

**WHAT MAKES THIS A BEST RECIPE:** Tandoori chicken is a favorite among children on Indian restaurant menus, luring them in with its preternaturally bright red hue. Typically marinated in a spicy yogurt mixture and then grilled in a tandoor oven, well-made tandoori chicken is complex, tangy, and deeply charred from an intense fire. Yet adults tend to avoid this dish. It's not the flavors, it's how dried out and tired the chicken usually is. Perhaps it's the blistering heat of the tandoor oven or an inattentive cook in the kitchen, but the meat is inevitably dry and stringy. We hoped to do better. Tandoori is more a style of cooking than a particular dish, as it refers to a tandoor, a type of Indian oven. Typically made from clay, tandoors are beehive-shaped and heated with charcoal or gas to very high temperatures. We don't have a tandoor in the test kitchen, but we did have a grill on which we hoped to mimic the tandoor's high, dry heat. Our research produced recipes that suggested that just about any cut of chicken can be pressed into service, though we found that bone-in, skin-on chicken breasts were the best suited. The skin shielded the top of the breast and the bone shielded the interior from the grill's hot, dry heat. In addition, there was plenty of surface area to which spices could cling. Temperatures in a tandoor can easily exceed 500 degrees. A grill can do that too, though not successfully, as we found out after several batches of burnt and blackened chicken. As with many of our other grilling recipes, we found that a two-level fire was the way to go. We first browned and crisped the chicken over the hot coals, then slid the meat over to the cooler side to finish. In addition, we covered the breasts—while on the cool side—with a disposable aluminum pan to trap heat and speed up the cooking process while keeping the meat tender and juicy. Foods to be cooked "tandoori-style" are typically soaked for a day or two in a spiced yogurt marinade, which adds both flavor and moisture. After trying a few classic recipes, we found the marinade's impact slight and the time involved significant, so we opted to skip it in favor of a dry rub, a winning combination of fresh ginger, coriander, cinnamon, and cumin,

and turmeric (for color). We then decided to add the tangy yogurt flavor, which tasters missed, after grilling with a raita, an herb and garlic dipping sauce as familiar to most Indian tables as ketchup is in the United States. Our tandoori-style chicken wasn't quite as colorful as the restaurant variety, but it wasn't dry or tough either. It was moist and tender and had all the full, rich flavors that define tandoori.

RAITA

1 cup whole milk yogurt
2 tablespoons minced fresh cilantro
1 garlic clove, minced
  Salt
  Cayenne pepper

CHICKEN

1 tablespoon minced fresh ginger
1 tablespoon ground coriander
1½ teaspoons ground cumin
1 teaspoon ground turmeric
½ teaspoon ground cinnamon
½ teaspoon salt
¼ teaspoon cayenne pepper
4 bone-in, skin-on split chicken breasts
  (10 to 12 ounces each)

**1.** FOR THE RAITA: Mix the yogurt, cilantro, and garlic together in a medium bowl. Season with salt and cayenne to taste and refrigerate until needed.

**2. FOR THE CHICKEN:** Light a large chimney starter filled with charcoal briquettes (about 100 pieces) and allow it to burn until all the charcoal is covered with a layer of fine gray ash, about 20 minutes. Spread the coals out over half of the grill bottom, leaving the other half with no coals. Set the cooking grate in place, cover, and let the grill heat up for 5 minutes. Use a grill brush to scrape the cooking grate clean.

**3.** Mix the ginger, coriander, cumin, turmeric, cinnamon, salt, and cayenne together in a small bowl. Pat the chicken dry with paper towels and coat both sides of the chicken breasts with the spice mixture. Arrange the chicken skin-side down over the hotter part of the grill and cook, uncovered, until well browned on both sides, 2 to 3 minutes per side. Move the chicken skin-side up to the cooler side of the grill and cover with a disposable aluminum roasting pan; continue to cook for 10 minutes. Turn and continue to cook until the thickest part of the breasts register 160 degrees on an instant-read thermometer, about 5 minutes longer. Transfer to a serving platter and serve immediately with the raita.

**WHERE THINGS CAN GO WRONG:** Do not use nonfat yogurt in the raita; the sauce will taste hollow and bland.

**WHAT YOU CAN DO AHEAD OF TIME:** The raita can be refrigerated in an airtight container for up to 3 days.

## NOTES FROM THE TEST KITCHEN

### HOW TO PEEL AND MINCE GINGER
Because of its shape, a knob of fresh ginger can be difficult to peel and mince. These techniques work best.
**1.** Use the bowl of a teaspoon to scrape off the knotty skin from the ginger. The spoon moves easily around the curves in the ginger, so you remove just the skin.
**2.** Slice the peeled knob of ginger into thin rounds, then fan the rounds out and cut them into thin matchstick-like strips.
**3.** Chop the matchsticks crosswise into a fine mince.

### TANDOORI-STYLE CHICKEN BREASTS ON A GAS GRILL
With the lid down on a gas grill, there's no need to cook the chicken under a disposable aluminum roasting pan. If the fire flares because of dripping fat or a gust of wind, move the chicken to the cooler side of the grill until the flames die down. Follow the recipe for Tandoori-Style Chicken Breasts with Raita through step 1. Light all the burners and turn the heat to high, close the lid, and heat the grill until very hot, about 15 minutes. Scrape the cooking grate clean with a grill brush. Leave one burner on high heat, while turning the other burner(s) down to medium-low. Continue with the recipe from step 3, cooking the chicken covered.

# BBQ BEER-CAN CHICKEN
SERVES 6 TO 8

**WHAT MAKES THIS A BEST RECIPE:** Beer-can chicken is a barbecue-circuit trick that's been around for years. The beer can is placed inside the cavity of the chicken and acts as both stand and steamer. The dry heat of the grill attacks the chicken from all sides, rendering the skin to a crackly crunch. Meanwhile, the beer steams happily away on the inside, ensuring especially moist meat. The key to this recipe was to place the upright bird in the center of the grill and bank the coals on the sides, creating an empty space below the chicken and radiant heat to brown the bird front and back. To catch the chicken drippings and hold the coals securely in place, we placed a disposable aluminum roasting pan beneath the chicken. After adding some soaked wood chips to the coals (a must for any barbecue), we had even heat, lots of smoke, and enough room on the grill to cook two small chickens at once. With the fire under wraps, it was time to start piling on the flavor. We saw the beer can as our workhorse, capable of pulling triple duty, not only as stand and steamer but as flavor container as well. By itself, the beer didn't provide much more flavor than plain water, but a few crumbled bay leaves added to the can infused the meat with its strong herbal aroma. Now that we had the smoke from the grill and the flavorful steam from the can, it was time to spice things up. We made a spice rub of black pepper, cayenne pepper, paprika, salt, and light brown sugar that had the perfect mix of heat and sweetness. For cracklin' crisp chicken skin, we patted the chicken dry with paper towels before rubbing on the spices, and then we used a skewer to poke holes all over the skin. This worked perfectly, rendering out the fat in those hard-to-reach places and leaving an extra-crispy skin. Our final step was to make a quick glaze with beer, ketchup, vinegar, brown sugar, some of the spice rub, and a couple of dashes of hot sauce. We applied the glaze about 20 minutes before the chickens were finished cooking (any earlier and it might char), and when we lifted the lid of the grill, the birds looked amazing—and tasted even better.

## SPICE RUB

- 2 tablespoons packed light brown sugar
- 2 tablespoons paprika
- 1 tablespoon salt
- 1 tablespoon black pepper
- 1 teaspoon cayenne pepper

## CHICKEN

- 2 (12-ounce) cans beer
- 4 bay leaves, crumbled
- 2 (3 to 3½-pound) whole chickens, giblets discarded
- 4 cups wood chips

## GLAZE

- 2 tablespoons packed light brown sugar
- 2 tablespoons ketchup
- 2 tablespoons white vinegar
- 1 teaspoon hot sauce

Disposable aluminum roasting pan

## NOTES FROM THE TEST KITCHEN

### DISPOSABLE ALUMINUM PANS

Whether large enough to hold a 20-pound turkey or small enough to cover a single sausage link, disposable aluminum pans are a grill-cook's best friend. We routinely use these inexpensive trays to cover meats (and retain heat) on windy days, to hold our grilling tools, and to transfer food from kitchen to grill and back. Recently, we found another use for them: as a drip pan. When preparing many of our recipes, we like to place a 13 by 9-inch disposable aluminum roasting pan in the center of the grill before adding the lit charcoal. Once the charcoal in the starter is lit and covered with light gray ash, we pour the coals into equal piles on either side of the pan. The pan ensures that the coals stay in place for even heating and makes cleanup a cinch—all of the rendered chicken fat (which can be quite a bit) collects in the disposable pan, not on the bottom of the grill. If you're barbecuing on a gas grill, you won't need the 13 by 9-inch pan, but you'll want to use a smaller disposable pan to hold the wood chips.

**1. FOR THE SPICE RUB:** Mix the brown sugar, paprika, salt, black pepper, and cayenne together. Remove 1 tablespoon and set aside for the glaze.

**2. FOR THE CHICKEN:** Measure out 1 cup of beer from each can. Remove 2 tablespoons from the measured beer and set aside for the glaze. Following the photos on page 211, punch holes in the tops of the beer cans using a church key and add 2 crumbled bay leaves to each can.

**3. FOR THE GLAZE:** Stir the brown sugar, ketchup, vinegar, and hot sauce together in a medium bowl. Add the reserved 2 tablespoons beer and 1 tablespoon spice rub.

**4.** Loosen the skin on the breasts and thighs of the chicken. Massage the spice mixture on the skin, under the skin, and inside the cavity. Using a skewer, poke the skin all over.

**5.** Soak the wood chips in a bowl of water to cover for 15 minutes. Light a large chimney starter filled with charcoal briquettes (about 100 pieces) and allow it to burn until all the charcoal is covered with a layer of fine gray ash, about 20 minutes. Place a 13 by 9-inch disposable aluminum roasting pan in the center of the grill. Stack half of the coals into a pile on each side of the grill, leaving the pan in the center. Scatter the wood chips evenly over the coals. Set the cooking grate in place, cover, and let the grill heat up for 5 minutes. Use a grill brush to scrape the cooking grate clean.

**6.** Place the chickens on the beer cans on the center of the grate, using the drumsticks to stabilize them. Cover and grill until the skin is well browned and very crisp, 40 to 60 minutes. Brush with the ketchup glaze and grill, covered, until the thigh meat registers 170 degrees on an instant-read thermometer, about 20 minutes longer. Wearing oven mitts or using a wad of paper towels, transfer the chickens (still on the cans) from the grill to a cutting board and let rest for 10 minutes. Hold the base of the can with an oven mitt or wad of paper towels, insert tongs into the neck cavity of the chicken, and pull the chicken off the can. Carve and serve.

**WHERE THINGS CAN GO WRONG:** Look for chickens that weigh between 3 and 3½ pounds; if they are significantly larger, you may have trouble fitting the lid on the grill.

# NOTES FROM THE TEST KITCHEN

### FLAVOR THAT'S MORE THAN SKIN DEEP
From its crisp, spiced skin, to its moist meat, beer-can chicken is flavored through and through. Here's how to get the ultimate beer-can chicken experience from your grill.

**1.** Use a church key can opener to punch holes in the top of the can; this will allow the maximum amount of steam to escape.

**2.** Loosen the skin on the breasts and thighs of the chicken by sliding your fingers between the skin and the meat.

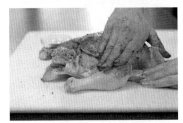

**3.** Massage the spice rub on the skin, under the skin, and inside the cavity.

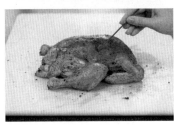

**4.** Using a skewer, poke the skin all over to render as much fat as possible.

### BBQ BEER-CAN CHICKEN ON A GAS GRILL
To hold the wood chips, you will need a small disposable aluminum pan. Prepare the recipe for BBQ Beer-Can Chicken through step 4. Soak the wood chips in bowl of water to cover for 15 minutes, then place the chips in a small aluminum tray and place the tray directly on the primary burner. Light all the burners and turn the heat to high and close the lid, keeping the grill covered until the wood chips begin to smoke, about 15 minutes. Leave the primary burner on high and turn off all the other burners. Place the chickens on the cans on the cool part of the grill and proceed with the recipe from step 6.

# ALABAMA BBQ CHICKEN
SERVES 6 TO 8

**WHAT MAKES THIS A BEST RECIPE:** While most people think of barbecue sauce as red, sweet, and tomatoey, there are dozens of regional barbecue sauces that don't contain either tomato or a lot of sugar. For example, the mayonnaise-based sauce that is a specialty in northern Alabama. While the origins of many recipes can be hazy, it's easy to trace the history of Alabama chicken and white barbecue sauce to just one place: the Big Bob Gibson Bar-B-Q restaurant in Decatur, which has been around since 1925. Before developing our own recipe for white sauce, we wanted to figure out the best way to smoke the chickens (we wanted to cook two). Taking a cue from our BBQ Beer-Can Chicken (page 209), we banked the charcoal on either side of the grill and placed the birds right in the center, with a drip pan underneath. Hickory is the classic choice at Big Bob's, and we saw no reason to change this part of the recipe. We found that 2 cups of hickory chips placed directly on the coals gave the chickens a nice smoky flavor. Unfortunately, it took nearly two hours to grill two whole chickens, and our fire was beginning to peter out. We didn't want to add more coals, so we looked for ways to reduce the cooking time. The solution was to split the chickens in half, which cut the barbecue time to less than an hour and exposed more of the meat to the smoke. It was time to work on the sauce. We started by tasting the sauce from Big Bob's. It was creamy and tart, with a hint of sweetness and decent heat. Clearly, the sauce started with mayonnaise that was thinned out with vinegar to reach a loose consistency, not unlike that of salad dressing. For our sauce, tasters preferred the sweet-tart flavor of cider vinegar to bland white vinegar, and a little granulated sugar reinforced the subtle sweetness in the sauce. For heat, we relied on black pepper, just like Big Bob, but tasters wanted more heat. A little cayenne and horseradish punched up the sauce without making the heat too overpowering. While at Big Bob's, each smoked chicken is "baptized" by being dunked in a two-gallon vat of white sauce that is replenished throughout the day, but we didn't want to make gallons of sauce. Fortunately, we found that brushing the chickens with the sauce twice—once when they came off the grill and then again 10 minutes later—was sufficient.

ALABAMA BBQ CHICKEN

## SAUCE

- ¾ cup mayonnaise
- 2 tablespoons cider vinegar
- 2 teaspoons sugar
- ½ teaspoon prepared horseradish
- ½ teaspoon salt
- ½ teaspoon black pepper
- ¼ teaspoon cayenne pepper

## CHICKEN

- 1 teaspoon salt
- 1 teaspoon black pepper
- ½ teaspoon cayenne pepper
- 2 (3½ to 4-pound) whole chickens, giblets discarded and split following the photos
- 2 cups hickory wood chips
  Disposable aluminum roasting pan
  Vegetable oil for the grill

**1. FOR THE SAUCE:** Puree all of the ingredients in a blender until smooth, about 1 minute. Refrigerate the sauce in an airtight container for at least 1 hour.

**2. FOR THE CHICKEN:** Mix the salt, black pepper, and cayenne together in a small bowl. Pat the chicken dry with paper towels and rub the spice mixture all over the chickens.

**3.** Soak the wood chips in a bowl of water to cover for 15 minutes. Meanwhile, open the bottom grill vents completely. Light a large chimney starter filled with charcoal briquettes (about 100 pieces) and allow it to burn until all the charcoal is covered with a layer of fine gray ash, about 20 minutes. Place a 13 by 9-inch disposable aluminum roasting pan in the center of the grill (see page 210). Stack half of the coals into a pile on each side of the grill, leaving the pan in the center. Scatter the wood chips evenly over the coals. Set the cooking grate in place, cover, with the lid vents positioned over the center of the grill and opened halfway, and let the grill heat up for 5 minutes. Use a grill brush to scrape the cooking grate clean.

**4.** Dip a wad of paper towels in the oil and oil the grate, holding the paper towels with long-handled tongs. Place the chickens skin-side down on the center of the grill. Cover (with half-opened lid vents over the chicken halves) and grill until the skin is well browned, 35 to 45 minutes. Flip the chickens skin-side up and grill, covered, until the breast meat registers 165 degrees on an instant-read thermometer, 15 to 20 minutes longer.

**5.** Transfer the chickens to a cutting board, brush with 2 tablespoons of the sauce, tent with foil, and let rest for 10 minutes. Remove the foil and brush the chickens with 1 tablespoon of the sauce. Carve and serve, passing the remaining sauce at the table.

**WHAT YOU CAN DO AHEAD OF TIME:** The sauce can be refrigerated in an airtight container for up to 2 days.

## NOTES FROM THE TEST KITCHEN

### AN EASY WAY TO SPLIT A CHICKEN

**1.** Using kitchen shears, cut along both sides of the backbone to remove it.

**2.** Using a chef's knife, split the breastbone to separate the chicken into two halves.

### HOW TO FIT THE CHICKEN ON THE GRILL

To get as much smoke flavor into the chicken as possible, arrange the coals on opposite sides of the grill and put the chicken in the middle, away from direct heat. Arrange each chicken half so that the legs are on opposite sides of each other.

### ALABAMA BBQ CHICKEN ON A GAS GRILL

To hold the wood chips, you will need a small disposable aluminum pan. Prepare the recipe for Alabama BBQ Chicken through step 2. Soak the wood chips in a bowl of water to cover for 15 minutes, place the chips in a small aluminum tray, and place the tray directly over the primary burner. Light all the burners and turn the heat to high and close the lid, keeping the grill covered until the wood chips begin to smoke, about 15 minutes. Oil the cooking grate and turn all of the burners to medium-low. Place the chicken skin-side down on the grill and proceed with the recipe from step 4.

### OUR FAVORITE KITCHEN SHEARS

When you need to trim or butterfly a chicken, there is no better tool for the job than a pair of kitchen shears. Our top choice was the **Wüsthof Kitchen Shears** ($27.99), which made easy, smooth cuts, even through small chicken bones. Plus, they boasted heft, solid construction, and textured handles that were comfortable, even when wet and greasy. Coming in a close second were the Messermeister TakeApart Kitchen Shears ($17.95).

# GRILL-ROASTED CHINESE-STYLE DUCK

### SERVES 3 TO 4

**WHAT MAKES THIS A BEST RECIPE:** Without a doubt, the best duck is one of those mahogany-colored beauties hanging by the neck in markets throughout any Chinatown in the United States. The skin is paper thin, crisp, and well seasoned with a salty-sweet glaze; the meat is moist, juicy, and largely free of the excessive fattiness that mars most duck we have had. We wanted to try cooking a duck like this at home, but the one time we had tried ended in disaster—smoke, flames, a fire extinguisher. After that experience, the last thing we wanted to do was cook another one indoors. Grill-roasting, however, was another option that made a great deal of sense. Any smoke generated by the dripping fat could billow away harmlessly, and it's hard to beat the rich savor lent to poultry through live-fire cooking. The trick, we discovered, was to steam the duck first to render its fat, and grill it second to crisp the skin. As important to steaming the duck for fat removal was lancing its skin to allow for drainage of the fat; otherwise it just pooled in the gaps between meat and skin. For the grill-roasting stage, we followed many of our other recipes for whole chickens and configured the coals in small piles on either side of the grill, with the duck set in between. In this fashion, the bird cooked most evenly and didn't require turning or flipping. And the rendering fat didn't drip onto hot coals, lessening the chance of scorching flare-ups that would burn the bird. With the cooking technique perfect, we moved on to flavor. The ducks in Chinatown are slicked with a lightly spiced, fairly sweet, deeply flavored glaze. We mimicked this using a mixture of honey, soy sauce, five-spice powder, and sesame oil, but a problem quickly arose. The honey in the glaze burned black as the bird cooked. When we tried omitting sweetener, however, the duck didn't taste nearly as good. Our solution was to make a sugar-free glaze to flavor the bird as it cooked, then once the bird was cooked through, we brushed on a sweet second glaze. In just a couple minutes on the grill, it dried and darkened to a deep mahogany color very similar to that of the ducks in Chinatown. For even more flavor, we stuffed a few scallions and coins of

ginger into the duck just before we transferred it to the grill. The heat released the flavors and the duck picked up the unmistakable sharpness of the scallions and piquancy of the ginger. This bird was finally every bit as good as our Chinatown paradigm, just minus the neck and head.

2  (3-inch) wood chunks, or 2 cups wood chips
1  whole Pekin duck (about 4½ pounds), neck and giblets discarded, excess skin and fat removed (see the photos)
2½  tablespoons soy sauce
2  teaspoons five-spice powder
1  teaspoon Asian sesame oil
3  scallions, root end trimmed, cut into thirds
1  (1½-inch) piece fresh ginger, sliced into thin coins
   Disposable aluminum roasting pan
2  tablespoons honey
2  tablespoons rice vinegar

## NOTES FROM THE TEST KITCHEN

### OUR FAVORITE SOY SAUCE

Soy sauce consists of simple ingredients transformed by the process of fermentation. Soybeans and sometimes roasted wheat are inoculated with a mold and matured in vats for three days, and then the resulting culture is transferred to fermentation tanks where it is mixed with salt and water to produce a mash. The mash ferments, or "brews," for as little as several months or as long as several years. The liquid element of the mash is then filtered out and bottled as soy sauce. Soy sauce comes in two styles: shoyu and tamari. Shoyu is relatively thin; tamari is thicker and is made from soybeans only (not roasted wheat). They are largely interchangeable.

We bought a dozen nationally available brands and tasted them raw—on plain rice and silken tofu—and cooked in a simple chicken stir-fry. In general, the sauces that fared best were pleasingly distinct and balanced in flavor. Saltiness was acceptable as long as it was not the only flavor characteristic. One thing's for certain: You should avoid any soy sauce that lists hydrolyzed vegetable protein on the label; it's indicative of inferior, cheaply made soy sauce. Tasters decisively ranked **Eden Selected Shoyu Soy Sauce** ($2.59 for 10 ounces) number one in both taste tests. The flavor was "toasty, caramel-y, and complex," not wimpy. The salt flavor was tangible but not overpowering.

1. Soak the wood chunks in cold water to cover for 1 hour and drain, or place the wood chips on an 18-inch square of heavy-duty aluminum foil, seal to make a packet, and use a fork to create about 6 holes to allow the smoke to escape.

2. Meanwhile, following the photos, using the tip of a paring knife, make many pricks in the skin over the entire body of the duck. Set a V-rack inside a large roasting pan and place the duck breast-side up on the rack. Place the roasting pan over 2 burners and add enough water to come just below the bottom of the duck. Bring the water to a boil over high heat, cover tightly with aluminum foil, and adjust the heat to medium. Steam, adding more hot water to maintain the water level, if necessary, until the fat beads on the pores of the duck and the bird is partially cooked, about 30 minutes. Lift the duck from the rack, pat the skin gently with paper towels, so as not to break it, to remove excess fat and moisture.

3. Mix 1½ tablespoons of soy sauce, five-spice powder, and sesame oil together in a small bowl. Brush the mixture onto all sides of the duck, being careful not to tear the skin. Place the scallions and ginger into the cavity of the duck.

4. Light a large chimney starter filled with charcoal briquettes (about 100 pieces) and allow it to burn until all the charcoal is covered with a layer of fine gray ash, about 20 minutes. Place a 13 by 9-inch disposable aluminum roasting pan in the center of the grill (see page 210). Stack half of the coals into a pile on each side of the grill, leaving the pan in the center. Add one soaked wood chunk to each pile, or place the chip packet on one pile. Set the cooking grate in place, cover, with the lid vents positioned over the center of the grill and opened halfway, and let the grill heat up for 5 minutes. Use a grill brush to scrape the cooking grate clean.

5. Position the duck breast-side up in the middle of the cooking grate between the two piles of charcoal. Cover the grill, turning the lid so the vents are between the two piles of coals. Grill-roast until the skin is crisp, thin, and richly browned, about 1 hour. (The initial temperature inside the grill should be about 425 degrees. It will drop to about 375 degrees by the time the duck is done.)

6. Combine the honey, vinegar, and remaining 1 tablespoon soy sauce in a small bowl, then brush the duck generously with the mixture. Cover the grill and cook until the glaze heats through, 3 to 5 minutes. (Be careful that the glaze does not burn.)

7. Transfer the duck to a cutting board and let rest for 10 minutes. Carve and serve.

**WHERE THINGS CAN GO WRONG:** When grilling, keep a squirt bottle handy in case of flare-ups.

## NOTES FROM THE TEST KITCHEN

### KEY STEPS TO GRILL-ROASTED DUCK

The excessive amount of fat under the skin of the duck is removed by careful trimming and two cooking processes: steaming and grill-roasting.

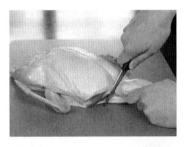

**TRIM.** Trim away any skin that is not directly above the meat or bone. Pull back the skin in the neck cavity and cut away pieces of fat on the underside of the skin to expose the wing joints.

**PIERCE.** To help the fat to escape, prick the entire skin of the duck with the tip of a paring knife, making sure not to cut into the meat.

**STEAM.** Steam the duck on a rack set over simmering water before grill-roasting to render its fat. To trap the steam, cover the pan with aluminum foil.

### GAS GRILL–ROASTED CHINESE-STYLE DUCK

Follow the recipe for Grill-Roasted Chinese-Style Duck. In step 1, soak the wood chips in cold water for 30 minutes, drain, and place in a foil tray. Proceed with steps 2 and 3 of the recipe. While the duck steams, place the foil tray with soaked wood chips on top of the primary burner (see the photo on page 171). Place a drip pan over the secondary burner(s). Light all the burners and turn the heat to high and preheat with the lid down until the chips are smoking heavily, about 20 minutes. Use a grill brush to scrape the cooking grate clean. Open the grill and turn off all but the primary burner, which should be left on high. Position the duck breast-side up directly over the drip pan. Cover and grill-roast until the duck just begins to brown, about 30 minutes. The average temperature should be between 325 and 350 degrees; regulate the lit burner as necessary to maintain the temperature. Turn a secondary burner(s) to low and grill-roast until the skin is dark brown and crisp, 40 to 50 minutes. (The average temperature will be between 425 and 450 degrees during this period.) Proceed with step 6.

# RECIPE RESCUE

## TROUBLESHOOTING AT THE STOVETOP

When certain things burn there is no going back. Scorched oil and garlic, for example, will contribute a burnt, bitter flavor to the finished dish. In this case, it's best to wipe the pan clean and start over. And most such problems can be avoided by choosing the proper pan, cooking fat, and burner setting for the job. That said, here's what to do if . . .

**MELTING BUTTER STARTS TO BURN:** Blackened butter will impart a bitter flavor to a finished dish and should be thrown away. However, slightly browned butter is no problem—in fact, it has a pleasantly nutty flavor. To keep it from browning further, add a small amount of vegetable oil to the pan. With its higher smoke point, vegetable oil is more resistant to burning and will help keep the butter from burning.

**FOOD STICKS TO THE PAN:** Food that initially sticks to the pan usually releases on its own after a crust begins to form. As long as the food is not burning, wait a minute or two and then try again. For stubbornly stuck pieces of meat or fish, dip a thin, flexible spatula into cold water and slide the inverted spatula blade underneath the food.

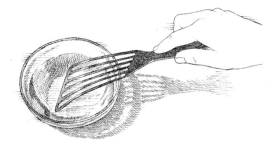

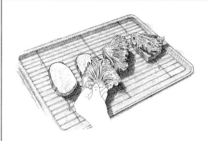

**MEAT IS UNDERCOOKED:** The meat has rested and been sliced, and it's underdone in the center. Simply putting the slices in the oven to finish cooking is not a good idea—the slices will dry out and quickly turn gray. Boston chef Gordon Hamersley has the solution: Place the sliced meat on a wire rack set over a baking sheet, then cover the meat with lettuce leaves before putting it in the oven. The meat will gently steam under the lettuce, without drying out.

**THE FOOD WON'T SIMMER SLOWLY:** If it's hard to get your stovetop burners to maintain a very low flame (necessary when trying to cook soups or stews at a bare simmer), improvise a flame tamer out of a thick ring of aluminum foil. Set the foil ring on the burner, then place the pot on top.

**THE PAN GETS TOO DARK:** Searing meat in a pan produces a crusty, brown "fond," which is the key to great flavor in many soups, stews, and sauces. But when those dark brown bits begin to turn black, you've got a good thing gone bad. When searing cutlets over high heat, for example, it's often the areas of the pan between the pieces of meat that are the first to blacken. To guard against this, shift the position of the food to cover the darker spots. The juices released from the meat will help to deglaze the pan. When searing a large quantity of meat in batches, it may be necessary to deglaze the empty pan with water, wine, or stock between batches.

### WHEN SEASONINGS GO AWRY

If you've added too much salt, sugar, or spice to a dish, the damage is done. In mild cases, however, the overpowering ingredient can sometimes be masked by the addition of another from the opposite end of the flavor spectrum. Consult our chart for ideas. And remember to account for the reduction of liquids when seasoning a dish—a perfectly seasoned stew will likely taste too salty after several hours of simmering. Your best bet: Season with a light hand during the cooking process, then adjust the seasoning just before serving.

| IF YOUR FOOD IS . . . | ADD . . . | SUCH AS . . . |
| --- | --- | --- |
| Too salty | An acid or sweetener | vinegar, lemon, or lime juice; canned, unsalted tomatoes; sugar, honey, or maple syrup |
| Too sweet | An acid or seasonings | vinegar or citrus juice; chopped fresh herb; dash of cayenne; or, for sweet dishes, a bit of liqueur or espresso powder |
| Too spicy or acidic | A fat or sweetener | butter, cream, sour cream, cheese, or olive oil; sugar, honey, or maple syrup |

# SMART FIXES FOR BAKED GOODS

Here's how to fix common problems that arise when baking.

**CREAM WON'T WHIP:** Check to make sure that your bowl and whisk (not to mention the cream) are very cold. Place the bowl and whisk in the freezer or fill the bowl with ice water.

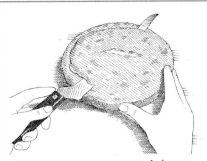

**CAKE LAYERS BAKE UNEVENLY:** As long as the damage will be covered with icing, use a serrated bread knife to remove the domed portion of the cake layer.

**BAKED GOODS BURN:** Badly burnt baked goods are usually not worth salvaging, but a few burnt corners can be easily removed with a Microplane grater. If the scarring is noticeable, brush the grated areas with an egg wash and return to the oven until just browned, no more than five minutes.

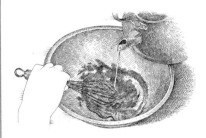

**CHOCOLATE SEIZES:** If chocolate is melted over a burner that's too hot, it will "seize," taking on a greasy, curdled appearance. Provided the problem is not too severe, it can be corrected by adding boiling water to the chocolate, a tablespoon at a time, and stirring vigorously after each addition.

**BREAD DOUGH RISES TOO SLOWLY:** Place the dough in a warm, draft-free, and preferably humid place. The inside of a turned-off oven is ideal. To maximize the effect, place a baking pan filled with boiling water on the oven rack beneath the dough.

**MUFFINS STICK TO THE TIN:** Pass the bottom of the muffin tin over a medium-low burner several times to heat the pan and try again to shake the muffins loose. Also try using a grapefruit knife to gently dig down under the muffin and set it free.

**GELATINS AND CUSTARDS STICK:** If your crème caramel (or another custard or a gelatin dessert) won't slip out of its ramekin, dip the mold in hot water for about 15 seconds. As a last-ditch measure, run a small paring knife around the inside of the mold to loosen the contents.

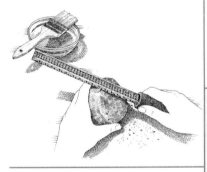

## FROM TOO THICK OR THIN TO JUST RIGHT

Soups, stews, and sauces often need some last-minute adjustments, even if the recipe was followed to the letter. Why? The moisture and fat content of foods can vary a great deal.

**IF YOUR SAUCE IS TOO THIN:** Simmering the liquid until the desired consistency is reached is the simplest option but not necessarily the best one. Time will not always permit a lengthy simmer, which may also overcook any meat or vegetables in the dish. Here are some better options:

**CORNSTARCH.** Soups and stews can be thickened with cornstarch, provided it is first dissolved in a small amount of cold water to prevent lumps.

**BREAD.** Many vegetable and bean soups are thickened by pureeing some of the soup, then adding it back to the pot.

When that's not an option, use bread to thicken a watery soup. Soak several pieces of crusty bread in some of the broth, then puree in a blender or food processor until smooth, adding more broth if necessary. Add the mixture back to the soup and stir to combine.

**BUTTER.** Whisking cold butter into a sauce just before serving adds richness and body.

**IF YOUR SAUCE IS TOO THICK:** Gradually add more water, broth, canned tomatoes, or whatever liquid is appropriate. Remember to correct the seasoning before serving.

SEARED SALMON WITH BALSAMIC GLAZE

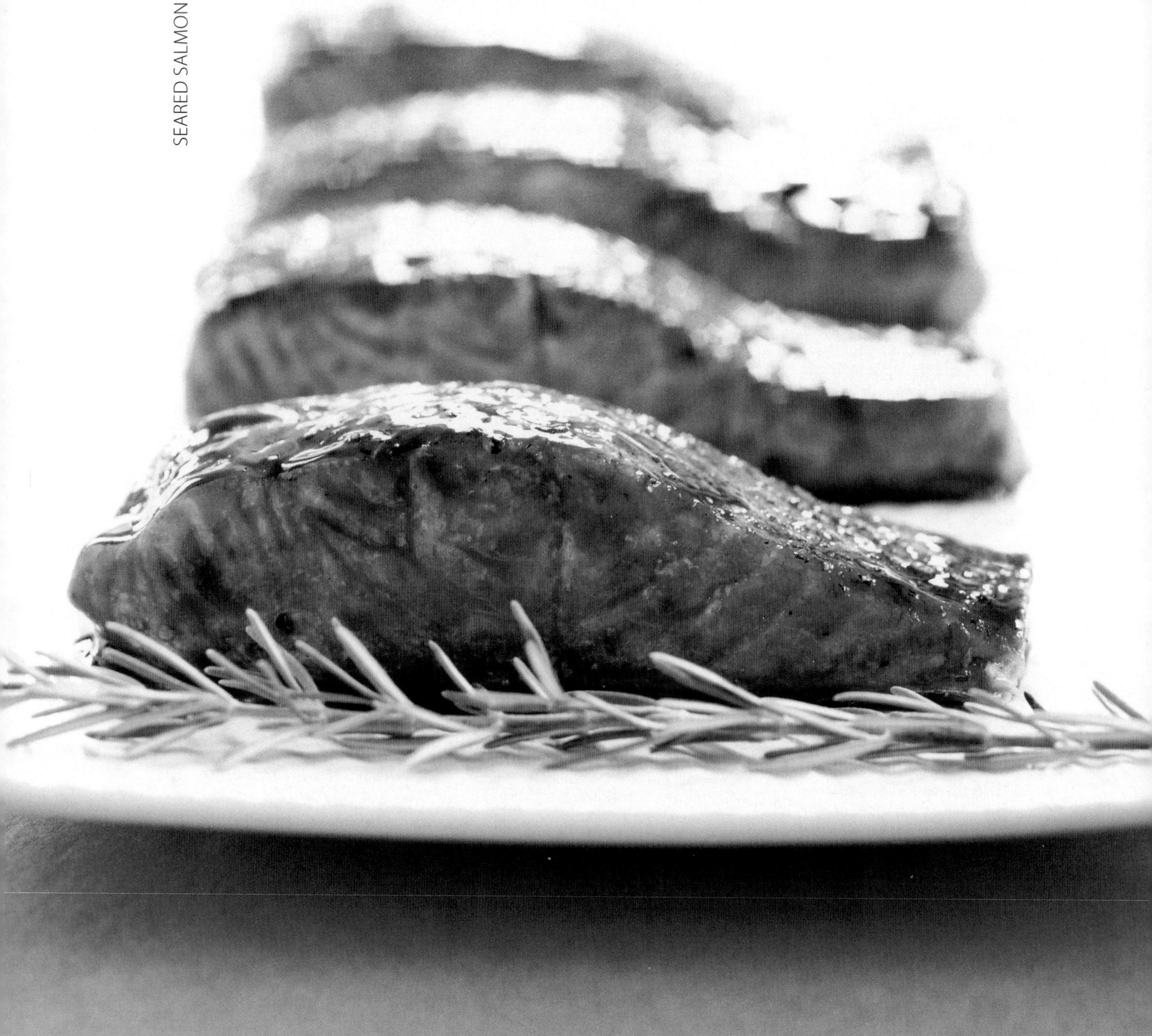

# SEAFOOD

# FISH AND CHIPS

SERVES 4

**WHAT MAKES THIS A BEST RECIPE:** If you've ever crossed the Atlantic and sampled the addictive fish and chips available at even the humblest British pub, you'll understand why we were willing to spend weeks in our test kitchen trying to duplicate them—from the crisp and tender batter that coated the fish to the thick-cut fries, served up crispy with soft interiors. But the challenges to replicating this in a home kitchen were many—from coordinating the frying of both the fish and the chips to constructing a batter that would be light and crisp—we knew that this would be no easy task. Focusing first on the batter, we followed the lead of most cookbooks and used a 50/50 mix of flour and beer. To our dismay, our coating was thick and bready. The obvious culprit behind the bready texture was gluten, the protein that gives bread its structure and is produced when any wheat flour is mixed with water. What if we replaced some of the all-purpose flour with a starch that doesn't develop gluten? Sure enough, testing various amounts and combinations of rice flour, cornmeal, and cornstarch led us to a 3 to 1 ratio of flour to cornstarch. And to make the batter lighter and airier, we added a teaspoon of baking powder, which created tiny bubbles in the batter. To keep the batter from sliding off the fish, we dredged the pieces of fish in flour both before and after they went into the batter. The resulting coating had a slightly crumbly, irregular texture that clung tightly to the fish. With the fish set, we turned our attention to the chips. From previous testing, we knew that the best fries are cooked twice. They're "blanched" in relatively low-temperature oil, to cook the centers evenly, then finished in hotter oil just before serving to crisp the outsides to a golden brown. But this created a logistical nightmare: To serve four people, we would have to cook a fairly large number of potatoes, which meant blanching them in several batches, and then frying them again. Plus, we also had to cook the fish. All in all, this took almost an hour, leaving the kitchen a splattered mess, not to mention the oil, which degrades with each use, absorbing water from the food and losing its ability to make things crisp. To avoid excessive time spent hovering over a pot of bubbling oil, we parcooked the fries in the microwave. This

We achieved the ideal contrast of light, crisp exterior and moist interior by carefully constructing our batter—and our cooking sequence.

simple technique cut the frying time by more than half. And to keep spent oil from ruining our fish and chips, we added an additional quart of fresh oil after the fries were blanched. We fried the fish until golden brown, moist, and, tender, and then the blanched, cooled fries went back into the oil while the fried fish spent five minutes draining. The fries emerged hot and crispy just a few minutes later. Served with traditional malt vinegar or tartar sauce, this recipe will satisfy anyone's longing for the real deal.

- 3 pounds russet potatoes (about 4 large potatoes), peeled, ends and sides squared off, and cut lengthwise into ½ inch by ½-inch chips
- 3 quarts plus ¼ cup vegetable oil
- 1½ cups unbleached all-purpose flour
- ½ cup cornstarch
- ½ teaspoon cayenne pepper
- ½ teaspoon paprika
- ⅛ teaspoon pepper
- Salt
- 1 teaspoon baking powder
- 1½ cups (12 ounces) cold beer
- 1½ pounds cod or other thick white fish fillet, patted dry and cut into eight 3-ounce pieces about 1 inch thick

**1.** Place the fries in a large, microwaveable bowl, toss with ¼ cup of the oil, and cover tightly with plastic wrap. Microwave on high power until the potatoes are partially translucent and pliable but still offer some resistance when pierced with the tip of a paring knife, 6 to 8 minutes, stirring them halfway through the cooking time. Carefully pull back the plastic wrap and drain the potatoes into a large mesh strainer. Rinse well under cold running water. Spread the potatoes onto kitchen towels and pat dry. Let rest until room temperature, at least 10 minutes or up to 1 hour.

**2.** While the fries cool, whisk the flour, cornstarch, cayenne, paprika, pepper, and 2 teaspoons salt together in a large bowl; transfer ¾ cup of the mixture to a rimmed baking sheet. Add the baking powder to the bowl and whisk to combine.

**3.** In a heavy-bottomed Dutch oven, heat 2 quarts of the oil over medium heat to 350 degrees. Add the fries to the hot oil and increase the heat to high. Fry, stirring with a mesh spider or slotted metal spoon, until the potatoes turn light golden and just begin to brown at the corners, 6 to 8 minutes. Transfer the fries to a thick paper bag or paper towels to drain.

**4.** Reduce the heat to medium-high, add the remaining 1 quart oil, and heat the oil to 375 degrees. Meanwhile, thoroughly dry the fish with paper towels and dredge each piece of fish in the flour mixture on the baking sheet; transfer the pieces to a wire rack, shaking off the excess flour. Add 1¼ cups of the beer to the flour mixture in the large bowl and stir until just combined (the batter will be lumpy). Add the remaining beer, 1 tablespoon at a time, whisking after each addition, until the batter falls from the whisk in a thin, steady stream and leaves a faint trail across the surface of the batter. Using tongs, dip 1 piece of fish in the batter and let the excess drain off. Place the battered fish back onto the baking sheet with the flour mixture and turn to coat both sides. Repeat with the remaining fish, keeping the pieces in a single layer on the baking sheet.

**5.** When the oil reaches 375 degrees, increase the heat to high and, gently shaking off the excess flour, add the battered fish to the oil with tongs. Fry, stirring occasionally, until golden brown, 7 to 8 minutes. Transfer the fish to a thick paper bag or paper towels to drain. Allow the oil to return to 375 degrees.

**6.** Add the fries back to the oil and fry until golden brown and crisp, 3 to 5 minutes. Transfer to a fresh paper bag or paper towels to drain. Season the fries with salt and serve immediately with the fish.

**WHERE THINGS CAN GO WRONG:** The oil will bubble up when you add the fries, so be sure you have at least 5 inches of room at the top of the pot. Any beer will work in this recipe, even nonalcoholic beers, with the exception of dark stouts and porters. In order for the batter to adhere, the fish must be very dry. If you have room in your refrigerator, air-dry the fish pieces, uncovered, on a wire rack set over a rimmed baking sheet while you prepare the batter and parcook the potatoes in the microwave. Otherwise, make sure to pat the fish dry just before dredging and battering.

## NOTES FROM THE TEST KITCHEN

### HOW TO GET THE FISH AND CHIPS IN SYNC
It's fish and chips, not fish then chips. To avoid the latter, follow this sequence of steps.

**1.** Microwave the oil-tossed potatoes until softened and pliable.
**2.** Rinse the potatoes under cold running water and pat dry.
**3.** Fry the potatoes in 350-degree oil until just beginning to brown.
**4.** Add more oil to the pot, heat the oil to 375 degrees, and fry the fish until golden brown.
**5.** Return the fries to the oil and cook until crisp and golden.

### THE BEST HIGH-END DEEP FRYERS
From past tests, we know a decent deep fryer can be had for less than $80. Spend more and you'll get fancy features like oil filtration systems. But what about basic performance? To find out, we embarked on a french-fry marathon with six high-end models—Masterbuilt Turk'N'Surf ($150), Deni Multi-Fryer ($99.99), DeLonghi Dual Zone ($99.95), Waring Professional ($129.95), T-Fal Ultimate EZ Clean ($119.95), and DeLonghi Cool Touch ($129.95)—plus our favorite inexpensive model, the **Oster Immersion** ($79.95).

All the models turned out tasty fries—eventually. The difference between good performance and great hinged on oil capacity. The more capacity, the less severe the temperature drop once the food hit the oil, which allowed for fewer batches and quicker recovery between batches. For instance, the Masterbuilt, which holds 2 gallons of oil (enough to fry a 14-pound turkey), dropped 34 degrees when we added a pound of fries. In contrast, the DeLonghi Cool Touch, which uses a mere 1.3 quarts (it rotates food into and out of the oil), lost a whopping 114 degrees. What that means in practical terms is that the Masterbuilt can effectively cook an entire batch of fries; by the time the smallest model finished its fourth batch, the other batches were soggy and limp. Every model was equipped with a built-in thermostat—an essential feature to our minds. But other "deluxe" features seemed extraneous.

Ideally, we'd fry our fries in one batch, but pouring 2 gallons of oil into the Masterbuilt seems excessive. If you don't often fry fish and chips, the Oster—the cheap model—is all you really need.

# CREOLE CRAB CAKES
## WITH QUICK RÉMOULADE SAUCE
### SERVES 4

**WHAT MAKES THIS A BEST RECIPE:** We developed this recipe because we were sick and tired of crab-flecked dough balls being passed off as crab cakes. Not surprisingly, we found that to make crab cakes that actually taste like crab, we had to start with a healthy dose of lump crabmeat and keep the binder to a minimum. For our binder, we chose saltine crackers, which added more flavor than other binders we tried, and didn't make our crab cakes pasty, as breadcrumbs did. Instead of the traditional crab cake flavorings (like Old Bay Seasoning), we gave ours a Creole twist. In Louisiana, most dishes, including the crab cakes, are flavored with green bell pepper, onion, and celery. We included that classic trio, along with plenty of fresh garlic, dry mustard, and cayenne, and a little heavy cream for richness (because a true Louisiana dish *is* rich). These are great with just a squeeze of lemon, but for an added Creole kick, try them with our quick version of classic *rémoulade* (a mayonnaise-based sauce).

### CRAB CAKES

- 2 teaspoons plus 3 tablespoons vegetable oil
- ½ onion, minced (about ½ cup)
- ½ green bell pepper, stemmed, seeded, and chopped fine
- 1 celery rib, chopped fine
- 3 garlic cloves, minced
- 1½ pounds lump crabmeat, picked over for any shells
- 30 saltine crackers, crushed into fine crumbs (about 1¼ cups)
- ¼ cup mayonnaise
- 1 large egg
- 2 tablespoons heavy cream
- 1 tablespoon dry mustard
- ¼ teaspoon cayenne pepper
- 1 tablespoon Worcestershire sauce

### RÉMOULADE SAUCE

- 1 cup mayonnaise
- 1 tablespoon whole-grain mustard
- ¼ cup chopped dill pickles
- 1 scallion, sliced thin
- 1 tablespoon fresh lemon juice
- ¼ teaspoon cayenne pepper
  Salt and pepper
  Lemon wedges, for serving

**1. FOR THE CRAB CAKES:** Heat 2 teaspoons of the oil in a medium skillet over medium heat. Add the onion, bell pepper, celery, and garlic and cook until soft, about 5 minutes. Transfer to a plate and refrigerate for 5 minutes.

**2.** Transfer the vegetables to a large bowl. Stir in the crabmeat and ¾ cup of the cracker crumbs, being careful not to break up large pieces of crab. Whisk the mayonnaise, egg, heavy cream, mustard, cayenne, and Worcestershire together in a small bowl. Using a rubber spatula, fold the mayonnaise mixture into the crab mixture. Divide into 8 portions and shape each into a 1¼-inch-thick cake. Transfer to a plate, cover, and refrigerate until well chilled, at least 30 minutes.

**3. FOR THE SAUCE:** Meanwhile, mix all the ingredients together in a small bowl and season with salt and pepper to taste. Cover with plastic wrap and chill until the flavors blend, at least 10 minutes.

**4.** Heat the remaining 3 tablespoons oil in a 12-inch nonstick skillet over medium-high heat until shimmering. Meanwhile, dredge the crab cakes in the remaining ½ cup cracker crumbs and press to adhere the crumbs to the cakes. Cook 4 of the crab cakes until well browned on both sides, about 5 minutes per side. Transfer to a paper towel–lined plate and repeat with the remaining crab cakes. Serve immediately with the lemon wedges and rémoulade sauce.

**WHERE THINGS CAN GO WRONG:** Though you might be tempted to fry up these crab cakes right after shaping them, it is important to let them chill for at least 30 minutes so that they do not fall apart when you dredge them in the cracker crumbs and fry them.

**WHAT YOU CAN DO AHEAD OF TIME:** The rémoulade sauce can be refrigerated in an airtight container for up to 3 days. The crab cakes can be shaped, wrapped tightly in plastic wrap, and refrigerated for up to 1 day before cooking.

# BRAISED COD PROVENÇAL

## SERVES 4

**WHAT MAKES THIS A BEST RECIPE:** For *The America's Test Kitchen Family Cookbook,* we wanted to create a fish dish that was fast, fresh, and easy enough for a weeknight dinner, but also adequately flavorful and complex to serve to guests. Using cod because it is so widely available (halibut, snapper, tilapia, monkfish, or sea bass fillets are all good substitutions), we tried a number of different cooking methods, from baking to broiling, and finally settled on braising the fish. While braising is usually reserved for cooking tough pieces of meat over a long period of time, we found it to be a great way to add complexity to mild-flavored fish (like cod). To braise the fish, we first built a tomato-based sauce in a skillet with full-flavored ingredients, including onion, fennel, garlic, thyme, and white wine. We then nestled pieces of fish in this sauce, covered the pan, and let the fish braise. This method traps the heat so the fish partially steamed and partially simmered in this aromatic stew of vegetables and herbs. The smell was delightful, not fishy, and the result was tender, moist, flavor-packed fish that took less than 30 minutes to get on the table. Garnished with a sprinkling of fresh parsley and a drizzle of extra-virgin olive oil, this dish is excellent served with a loaf of crusty bread to sop up the extra sauce.

- 2  tablespoons extra-virgin olive oil, plus more for drizzling (optional)
- 1  onion, halved and sliced thin
- 1  fennel bulb, halved, cored, and sliced ¼ inch thick
   Salt and pepper
- 4  garlic cloves, minced
- 1  (14.5-ounce) can diced tomatoes, drained
- ½  cup dry white wine or vermouth
- 1  teaspoon minced fresh thyme or ½ teaspoon dried
- 4  skinless cod fillets (8 ounces each)
- 2  tablespoons minced fresh parsley

**1.** Heat the oil in a 12-inch nonstick skillet over medium-high heat until shimmering. Add the onion, fennel, and ½ teaspoon salt. Cook until the vegetables have softened, about 5 minutes. Stir in the garlic and cook until fragrant, about

30 seconds. Add the tomatoes, wine, thyme, and ¼ teaspoon pepper. Bring to a boil.

**2.** Pat the cod dry with paper towels and season with salt and pepper. Nestle the cod into the sauce and spoon some of the sauce over the fish. Cover and reduce the heat to medium-low. Cook until the fish flakes apart when gently prodded with a paring knife (see the photos), about 10 minutes.

**3.** Transfer the fish to individual plates. Stir the parsley into the sauce and season with salt and pepper to taste. Spoon the sauce over the fish and drizzle with a little oil (if desired).

**WHERE THINGS CAN GO WRONG:** This method of cooking fish is much gentler than most and reduces (but does not eliminate) the risk of overcooking. Watch the clock, but, more important, check the fish, cooking it just to the point that it flakes when prodded with a paring knife.

## NOTES FROM THE TEST KITCHEN

### HOW TO KNOW WHEN FISH IS DONE

Overcooked fish is tough, dry, and flavorless. Unfortunately, overcooking fish is also one of the most common cooking mistakes. The trick to perfectly cooked fish—fish that is cooked all the way through but not dried out—is knowing when to remove it from the oven (or pan) so that it is just slightly underdone, and then allowing the residual heat to finish the cooking. This is easy to do with salmon because the change in color is so obvious. With white fish, however, the change in the color is much more subtle and harder to see. To make sure that the fish is cooked just right, use a paring knife to peek inside.

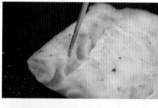

**HALF-COOKED FISH**
The flesh is still translucent.

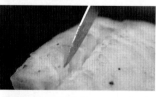

**PERFECTLY COOKED FISH**
The flesh is opaque and flaky but still juicy.

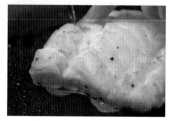

**OVERCOOKED FISH**
The flesh is dry and falling apart.

# BAKED COD
## WITH CRUNCHY LEMON-HERB TOPPING
### SERVES 4

**WHAT MAKES THIS A BEST RECIPE:** Many recipes for simple baked cod are nothing more than fish fillets that have been brushed with butter and rolled in dry and flavorless store-bought breadcrumbs—hardly better than the frozen variety. For this recipe, we wanted bolder flavor and crunchier texture, but we still wanted to keep things quick and easy. Our major challenge was to find a coating that would remain crunchy even after the fish was baked. We tinkered with cracker crumbs, fresh breadcrumbs, and even potato chips. The buttery, rich flavor of Ritz cracker crumbs won us over, especially when tossed with fresh herbs. Coarsely crushed crumbs were preferred to finely ground; not only were they easier to make, but they baked to a nice golden brown, and provided a super-crunchy contrast to the tender fish. Still, we were having trouble getting enough of the crumbs to stick to the butter-coated fish. Turning to mayonnaise instead of butter as a coating, we found our solution—now more crumbs adhered to the fish. We also found that we could mix the mayonnaise with fresh herbs, garlic, and lemon, which further boosted the flavor of the fish.

24 Ritz crackers, crushed into coarse crumbs (about 1 cup)
2 tablespoons minced fresh parsley, dill, or basil
3 tablespoons mayonnaise
2 garlic cloves, minced
1 teaspoon grated lemon zest
1 tablespoon fresh lemon juice
4 skinless cod fillets (8 ounces each)
 Salt and pepper
 Lemon wedges, for serving

**1.** Adjust an oven rack to the middle position and heat the oven to 450 degrees. Coat a baking sheet with vegetable oil spray. Toss the cracker crumbs and 1 tablespoon of the parsley together in a medium bowl. Mix the remaining 1 tablespoon parsley, mayonnaise, garlic, and lemon zest and juice together in a small bowl.

**2.** Pat the fish dry with paper towels and season with salt and pepper. Place on the baking sheet, spacing the pieces

about ½ inch apart. Brush the tops and sides of the fish with the mayonnaise mixture, then press the cracker crumbs into the mayonnaise.

**3.** Bake until the crumbs are golden brown and the fish flakes apart when gently prodded with a paring knife (see the photos on page 224), about 15 minutes. Serve with the lemon wedges.

**WHERE THINGS CAN GO WRONG:** The crackers should be crushed into crumbs about the size of peas. If you grind the crackers too fine, they will not become crunchy in the oven.

## NOTES FROM THE TEST KITCHEN

### THE BEST WAY TO ENSURE EVEN COOKING
Cod is most often sold skinless, in 8-ounce pieces. Sometimes, however, it is sold in larger odd-shaped pieces that can weigh up to 2 pounds. Faced with such a big piece of cod, simply cut it crosswise into 8-ounce pieces. One of these pieces (from the tail end) will be much thinner and wider than the others. Be sure to tuck the thinner tail piece under before cooking (to make it thicker) so that it will cook at the same rate as the other pieces.

### BUYING FISH
Buying top-quality fish is just as important as employing the proper cooking technique. Here are a few general points to keep in mind when purchasing fish:

- Always buy from a trusted source (preferably one with high volume to help ensure freshness). The store, and the fish in it, should smell like the sea, not fishy or sour. And all the fish should be on ice or be properly refrigerated.
- Make sure the fish you buy is fresh. The flesh of the fish should look bright, shiny, and firm, not dull or mushy. Whole fish should have moist, taut skin, clear eyes, and bright red gills.
- When possible, have your fishmonger slice steaks and fillets to order rather than buying precut pieces that may have been sitting.
- Keep your fish cold. If you have a long ride home, ask your fishmonger for a plastic bag of ice to lay the fish on. At home, store the fish in the coldest part of your refrigerator (in a sealed bag over a bowl of ice is best).
- Cook your fish the day you buy it.

# ASIAN-FLAVORED STEAMED FISH BUNDLES

SERVES 4

**WHAT MAKES THIS A BEST RECIPE:** Steamed fish is a spa-cuisine staple. Not only is it healthful, it is also quick and easy to prepare, and when steamed properly, the fish is moist and pure in flavor. The problem with most steamed fish is that all too often it's bland and overcooked. For this recipe, we coated small sole fillets with a zesty orange-ginger butter for flavor, and to add interest we then rolled them into bundles around a medley of brightly colored, tasty vegetables, including asparagus, carrots, and red onion. Because the vegetables took longer to cook than the fish, we steamed them first, which allowed us to focus on cooking the fish until perfectly moist and tender. To impart the fish bundles with even more flavor, we steamed them over orange slices, which had the added advantage of preventing the fish from sticking to the steamer basket.

## NOTES FROM THE TEST KITCHEN

### STEAMER BASKET OPTIONS
All you really need for steaming is a pot with a lid and a perforated steamer basket that sits above the water. Don't have a steamer basket? Consider using a perforated pasta-pot insert or just a sturdy wire rack that fits inside one of your larger pots or saucepans.

**A.** Collapsible steamer baskets like this one are cheap and perfect for steaming fish.

**B.** If you have a perforated pasta-pot insert, it can also come in handy for steaming fish.

1 pound thin asparagus, tough ends discarded
2 carrots, peeled and cut into 2-inch matchsticks (see page 227)
1 red onion, halved and sliced thin
3 tablespoons unsalted butter, softened
½ shallot, minced (1½ tablespoons)
1 garlic clove, minced
1 teaspoon soy sauce
1 teaspoon grated orange zest
½ teaspoon grated fresh ginger
Salt and pepper
8 small skinless sole fillets (3 ounces each)
2 oranges, sliced thin
1 teaspoon sesame seeds, toasted

**1.** Fit a large Dutch oven with a steamer basket. Fill the pot with water until it just touches the bottom of the basket. Bring to a boil. Add the asparagus, carrots, and onion to the basket, cover, and steam until just tender, about 5 minutes. Remove the steamer basket with the vegetables from the pot. Rinse the vegetables until cool, then pat dry. Cover the pot to keep the steaming liquid warm.

**2.** Meanwhile, mix the butter, shallot, garlic, soy sauce, orange zest, ginger, and a pinch of pepper together.

**3.** Pat the sole dry with paper towels, then season with salt and pepper. Following the photos, spread 1 teaspoon of the butter mixture over each fillet. Lay some of the vegetables across the wider end of each piece of fish. Roll the fish up around the vegetables into tidy bundles.

**4.** Line the steamer basket with 8 orange slices. Lay a fish bundle, seam-side down, on top of each slice. Lay an orange slice on top of each bundle.

**5.** Bring the water in the Dutch oven to a boil and gently lower the steamer basket with the fish into the pot. Cover and steam the fish until it flakes apart when gently prodded with a paring knife (see page 224), about 7 minutes. Using a spatula, gently transfer the fish bundles to individual plates, discarding the orange slices and steaming liquid. Dot each fish bundle with some of the remaining butter mixture and sprinkle with the sesame seeds before serving.

**WHERE THINGS CAN GO WRONG:** Take care to place the fish bundles in the steamer basket seam-side down to prevent them from opening during steaming.

**WHAT YOU CAN DO AHEAD OF TIME:** The fish bundles can be filled and rolled through step 3, wrapped tightly in plastic wrap, and refrigerated for up to 4 hours before steaming.

# NOTES FROM THE TEST KITCHEN

## HOW TO CUT CARROTS INTO MATCHSTICKS

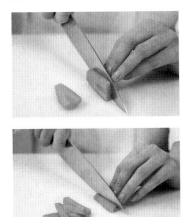

**1.** After peeling the carrots, cut each carrot into 2-inch lengths, then slice each length into ¼-inch planks.

**2.** Laying each plank flat on the cutting board, slice it into ¼-inch matchsticks.

## HOW TO MAKE FISH BUNDLES

For this recipe, we found that the smaller sole fillets were easier to roll into tidy bundles than larger fillets.

**1.** Spread 1 teaspoon of the butter mixture over each fillet.

**2.** Gather the vegetables into a neat pile and lay them across the wider end of the fish.

**3.** Roll the fillet up snugly around the vegetables, forming a bundle.

**4.** Place the bundles on the citrus slices, seam-side down, to keep them from opening during steaming.

# BAKED SOLE FLORENTINE
### SERVES 4

**WHAT MAKES THIS A BEST RECIPE:** Stuffed sole is an elegant way to serve fish for dinner and is usually reserved for a special occasion. Friends and family will think you've spent hours in the kitchen, and with most recipes, they'd be right. It's a multicomponent recipe starting first with the spinach, the ingredient from which the recipe gets its name. The spinach needs to be washed, dried, sautéed, and laboriously squeezed dry. Then you must make the filling. To finish the process, the fish needs to be carefully stuffed and rolled. And then (as if that weren't enough), a white sauce needs to be prepared, slowly simmered, and poured over the fish before it goes into the oven.

For *The Best 30-Minute Recipe*, we wanted to find a way to make sole Florentine hassle free for the cook, yet still impressive (and tasty). We turned to frozen spinach to save time on the filling prep. Using frozen, prechopped spinach cut out most of the painstaking spinach preparation; all we had to do was make sure it was thawed and thoroughly squeezed dry. As for the sauce, most recipes start with a roux, a combination of butter and flour. The problem we found was that after cream was added to the roux the sauce needed to be simmered in order to cook out the starch and allow the flour sufficient time to lose its raw flavor, a 10-minute time luxury we couldn't afford. To solve this, we turned to cornstarch. It thickens nicely and its raw flavor cooks out in only 2 minutes, a great time-saver. Finished with a quick, buttery cracker topping, this sole Florentine tastes and looks complicated, but isn't.

2  tablespoons unsalted butter
1  shallot, minced (about 3 tablespoons)
1  garlic clove, minced
2  cups half-and-half
2  teaspoons minced fresh thyme
4  teaspoons cornstarch
   Salt and pepper
½  cup grated Parmesan cheese
2  (10-ounce) packages frozen chopped spinach, thawed and squeezed dry

8  small skinless sole fillets (3 ounces each)
15 Ritz crackers, crushed fine (¾ cup)
   Lemon wedges, for serving

**1.** Adjust an oven rack to the middle position and heat the oven to 475 degrees. Coat a 13 by 9-inch baking dish with 1 tablespoon of the butter.

**2.** Melt the remaining 1 tablespoon butter in a medium saucepan over medium-high heat. Add the shallot and cook until softened, about 2 minutes. Stir in the garlic and cook until fragrant, about 30 seconds. Stir in 1¾ cups of the half-and-half and the thyme and bring to a simmer. Whisk the remaining ¼ cup half-and-half and the cornstarch together to dissolve the cornstarch, then stir into the saucepan. Continue to simmer until the sauce is thickened, about 2 minutes. Season with salt and pepper to taste.

**3.** Stir 1 cup of the sauce and the Parmesan into the spinach and season with salt and pepper to taste. Pat the fish dry with paper towels, and season with salt and pepper.

**4.** Following the photos, lay the fish on a cutting board, skinned side up. Divide the spinach filling among the fish fillets, mounding it in the middle of each fillet. Fold the tail end of the fillet tightly over the filling, then fold the thicker end of the fillet over the top (this should make a tidy bundle).

**5.** Arrange the fish bundles, seam-side down (leaving space between each roll) in the prepared baking dish. Pour the remaining sauce evenly over the fish, then sprinkle with the Ritz crumbs. Bake until all but the very center of the fish turns from translucent to opaque, 12 to 15 minutes. Serve with the lemon wedges.

**WHERE THINGS CAN GO WRONG:** Be sure to squeeze as much moisture out of the frozen spinach as possible or the filling will be too watery.

**WHAT YOU CAN DO AHEAD OF TIME:** The sauce can be made a day in advance and refrigerated in an airtight container. The fish bundles can be filled and rolled through step 4, arranged in the baking dish, wrapped tightly in plastic wrap, and refrigerated for up to 4 hours before baking. Store the remaining sauce in an airtight container in the refrigerator. Pour the sauce over the fish before baking and increase the baking time by 5 minutes.

## NOTES FROM THE TEST KITCHEN

### HOW TO STUFF FISH FILLETS

**1.** Lay the fillets on a cutting board, skinned side up. Divide the spinach filling evenly among the fillets, mounding it in the center of each fillet. Tightly fold the tapered end of the fillet over the filling, then fold the thicker end of the fillet over the top.

**2.** Flip the bundles over, transfer them to the baking dish, and press on them lightly to flatten, leaving a small space between each bundle. Pour the sauce evenly over the fish, then sprinkle with the Ritz crumbs.

### A FISH FILLET'S BEST SIDE

Flat fish fillets have two distinct sides—a "skinned" side and a "boned" side. The boned side has rounded indentations that run along the length of the fillet (where the bones once were), and a clean, white color. The skinned side has spots or stripes of darker-colored flesh that is less attractive (and doesn't brown as well when sautéed). In restaurants, therefore, the boned side of the fillet is considered the presentation side and is always laid on the plate facing up. Similarly, for fish rolls or bundles, the boned side should face out because it is visually more appealing.

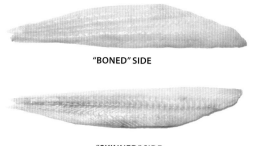

**"BONED" SIDE**

**"SKINNED" SIDE**

# SEARED SALMON
## WITH BALSAMIC GLAZE
### SERVES 4

**WHAT MAKES THIS A BEST RECIPE:** Searing salmon until it has a crisp, even, deeply golden crust and a moist interior is an effortless technique that heightens the flavor of the fish and produces an appealing contrast in texture. Add to that a sweet and sour balsamic glaze, and you have the perfect weeknight meal for family and guests. In the past, however, we have struggled to attain the perfect sear and degree of doneness on our salmon fillets. Our fish was often over-cooked to the point of being dry and chalky as we tried to create a healthy crust, or, in an effort to protect against over-cooking, we ended up with a wimpy crust.

For this recipe, we perfected the cooking technique, determining that a nonstick skillet was the best pan for the job—the fish formed a deep, even crust, it didn't stick to the pan, and cleanup was a cinch. We also found that salmon fillets, as with many cuts of meat, have enough residual heat to continue cooking briefly after they come out of the pan. In fact, we removed the fish from the pan when all but the very center was opaque, tented it with foil, and let it sit to cook through. Cooking the fish this way had an added bonus—it freed up the skillet for our simple glaze.

| | |
|---|---|
| ¼ | cup balsamic vinegar |
| ¼ | cup orange juice |
| 2 | tablespoons honey |
| ⅛ | teaspoon red pepper flakes |
| 2 | teaspoons vegetable oil |
| 4 | skin-on salmon fillets (6 ounces each) |
| | Salt and pepper |
| 2 | tablespoons unsalted butter |

**1.** Whisk the vinegar, juice, honey, and pepper flakes together in a small bowl. Heat the oil in a 12-inch nonstick skillet over medium-high heat until smoking. Season the salmon with salt and pepper and cook, skin-side up, without moving, until well browned, 4 to 5 minutes. Flip the fish skin side-down and cook until all but the very center of the fish is opaque, 2 to 3 minutes. Transfer to a platter and tent with foil.

**2.** Wipe out the pan with paper towels and lower the heat to medium. Carefully pour the balsamic mixture into the pan (it will splatter). Simmer until thick and syrupy, about 5 minutes. Whisk in the butter, season the sauce with salt and pepper to taste, and pour over the salmon. Serve.

**WHERE THINGS CAN GO WRONG:** Be sure to wipe out the pan after you sear the salmon, otherwise your glaze will be strongly flavored with the oils from the fish.

## NOTES FROM THE TEST KITCHEN

### HOW TO FLIP SALMON
Start the fish skin-side up, then use tongs or a fish spatula to gently flip the fish after it has developed a nice crust.

### PLASTIC FISH SPATULAS ARE BEST
While they may be called fish spatulas, these flexible, thin spatulas are equally good at flipping chicken cutlets and steaks. Priced around $7, the **Matfer Slotted Pelton Spatula** was our favorite, outperforming spatulas costing eight times as much. The Matfer received raves for its comfortable handle, long blade, and exceptional performance. Because of its smooth, slippery plastic surface, the spatula nimbly flipped fish without scarring the delicate flesh (as the metal spatulas did), and it is completely safe for nonstick skillets. We recommend fish spatulas with one caveat: They are designed for righthanded cooks. Some companies make lefthanded versions as well, but Matfer does not.

# OVEN-POACHED SIDE OF SALMON
## WITH CREAMY DILL SAUCE
### SERVES 8 TO 10

**WHAT MAKES THIS A BEST RECIPE:** A whole poached side of salmon, served with a creamy dill sauce, is a perennial favorite and the perfect dish to make ahead for a party or Sunday brunch. But most recipes we found required the use of a fish poacher (a piece of equipment we didn't own or want to fork over $80 for). Our challenge, then, was to find an alternative way to poach a whole side of salmon. Our solution was to oven "poach" the salmon. The trick, we discovered, was to create a substantial enough way to wrap the salmon in heavy-duty foil so that we could place it directly on the oven rack for even cooking. We began by folding two long sheets of heavy-duty foil together to create a tight seam, then piled a third sheet on top for further reinforcement. We plopped the side of salmon down the middle of them, wrapped it up, and proceeded to bake the packet directly on the oven rack; this kept the bottom from cooking more rapidly than the top. Because the tail end of the salmon is quite thin, we undercooked the thickest part slightly to keep the tail end palatable. All we needed to do to spark the flavor before baking was give the salmon a splash of vinegar and the hint of fresh herbs and lemon. For added appeal, we served our salmon with lemon wedges and a cool creamy dill sauce.

## SALMON

- 1 (4-pound) side of salmon, skin on
  Salt
- 2 tablespoons cider or white wine vinegar
- 6 sprigs fresh dill or tarragon
- 2 lemons, sliced thin

## SAUCE

- 1 cup sour cream
- 3 tablespoons minced fresh dill
- 1½ teaspoons fresh lemon juice
- 1 garlic clove, minced
  Salt and pepper

Lemon wedges, for serving

**1. FOR THE SALMON:** Adjust an oven rack to the middle position and heat the oven to 250 degrees. Following the photos, assemble three sheets of foil and spray with vegetable oil spray.

**2.** Remove any pinbones from the salmon. Pat the salmon dry with paper towels, then season with salt. Following the photos, lay the salmon, skin-side down, on top of the prepared foil. Sprinkle with the vinegar and lay the herb sprigs on top. Arrange the lemon slices on top of the herbs. Crimp the foil down over the fish.

**3.** Lay the foil-wrapped fish directly on the baking rack (without a baking sheet) and cook until the color of the flesh has turned from pink to orange and the thickest part measures 135 to 140 degrees on an instant-read thermometer, 45 to 60 minutes.

**4.** Remove the fish from the oven and open the foil. Let the salmon cool at room temperature for 30 minutes.

**5.** Pour off any accumulated liquid. Reseal the salmon in the foil and refrigerate until cold, about 1 hour.

**6. FOR THE SAUCE:** Meanwhile, mix the sour cream, 1 tablespoon minced dill, lemon juice, and garlic together in a small bowl. Season with salt and pepper to taste, cover, and refrigerate until needed.

**7.** To serve, unwrap the salmon. Brush away the lemon, herbs, and any solidified poaching liquid. Transfer the fish to a serving platter. Sprinkle the salmon with the remaining minced dill and serve with the sauce and lemon wedges.

**WHERE THINGS CAN GO WRONG:** Oven-poaching salmon is easy, but the tricky part is telling when the fish is done. Looks can be deceiving here because this slow-cooking method often produces salmon with a strange, semitranslucent orange hue, like that of smoked salmon, even though it is fully cooked (the normal color returns after it's chilled). The best way to avoid dry and chalky overcooked salmon is to take its temperature with an instant-read thermometer—the thickest part should measure 135 to 140 degrees.

**WHAT YOU CAN DO AHEAD OF TIME:** The poached salmon can be refrigerated for up to 2 days. Let the salmon sit at room temperature for 30 minutes before serving. The sauce can be refrigerated in an airtight container for up to 4 days.

## NOTES FROM THE TEST KITCHEN

### HOW TO WRAP THE SALMON FOR OVEN-POACHING

**1.** Cut two pieces of heavy-duty foil about a foot longer than the fish. Fold up one long side of each piece of foil by 3 inches.

**2.** Lay the pieces side by side, folded sides together; overlap the edges and fold to create a 1-inch seam.

**3.** Using your fingers, firmly press the seam flat.

**4.** Lay a third sheet of foil over the seam and spray with vegetable oil spray.

**5.** Lay the salmon down the center of the foil and fold the edges up over the salmon.

**6.** Fold the edges of the foil to create a seam on top of the salmon. Fold the ends to secure the seam, but do not crimp too tightly.

# CHARCOAL-GRILLED TUNA BURGERS
## WITH WASABI MAYONNAISE
### SERVES 4

**WHAT MAKES THIS A BEST RECIPE:** We developed this recipe for grilled fish burgers as an alternative to the usual summertime backyard fare. Our research turned up recipes for fish burgers that were dried-out and broke apart into a mess of crumbly pieces on the grill. These burgers are just the opposite—compact, with a moist, tender interior and a crusty exterior. The key was to use tuna, a rich, oily fish with lots of flavor, and to hand chop it into ⅛-inch pieces. Chopped this small, the fish packed into tight burgers that stayed that way on the grill. Any coarser, and they fell apart. While many recipes treat fish burgers in the same way as hamburgers, cooking them over high heat, we found that reducing the grill temperature to medium-hot helped the burgers retain their moisture. We also learned that burgers made with fresh fish are best cooked just to medium-rare, so that they are still pink in the center. Cooked any longer, they will certainly be dry. Lastly, to prevent our burgers from falling apart on the grill, we oiled both the spatula and the cooking grate, and refrigerated the burgers before grilling; these few simple steps saved us a lot of headaches. We like these burgers served with wasabi mayonnaise, either plain or on a toasted bun.

### TUNA BURGERS

| | |
|---|---|
| 1¼ | pounds high-quality tuna steaks |
| 1 | garlic clove, minced |
| 1 | teaspoon minced fresh ginger |
| ½ | teaspoon salt |
| | Pepper |

### WASABI MAYONNAISE

| | |
|---|---|
| ¼ | cup mayonnaise |
| 1 | teaspoon soy sauce |
| 1 | teaspoon wasabi powder |

Vegetable oil for the cooking grate

Hand chopping and diligent grilling are the keys to successful fish burgers.

**1. FOR THE BURGERS:** Chop the tuna into ¼- to ⅓-inch pieces. Using a rocking motion with the knife, chop the tuna until it is coarsely ground into ⅛-inch pieces. Mix with the garlic, ginger, salt, and pepper to taste. Divide the mixture into 4 equal portions and use your hands to press each into a compact patty about 1 inch thick. Place the patties on a parchment-lined baking sheet and refrigerate for at least 15 minutes.

**2. FOR THE MAYONNAISE:** Mix all of the ingredients for the wasabi mayonnaise together in a small bowl. Cover with plastic wrap and chill until the flavors blend, at least 10 minutes.

**3.** Meanwhile, light a large chimney starter filled with charcoal (6 quarts or about 100 briquettes) and allow it to burn until all of the charcoal is covered with a layer of fine gray ash, about 15 minutes. Spread the coals evenly over the grill bottom. Set the cooking grate in place, cover, and let the grill heat up for 5 minutes. Use a grill brush to scrape the cooking grate clean.

**4.** Following the photo, lightly dip a large wad of paper towels in the vegetable oil; holding the wad with long-handled tongs, wipe the cooking grate. Grill the burgers until browned on one side, about 3 minutes. Flip the burgers with a greased metal spatula. Continue grilling, uncovered, to the desired doneness, about 2 minutes for medium-rare or 3 minutes for medium. Serve immediately with wasabi mayonnaise.

**WHERE THINGS CAN GO WRONG:** Do not let these burgers overcook; tuna becomes very dry when cooked for too long.

**WHAT YOU CAN DO AHEAD OF TIME:** The wasabi mayonnaise can be refrigerated in an airtight container for up to 3 days.

## NOTES FROM THE TEST KITCHEN

### TUNA BUYING GUIDE
You might think tuna is, well, tuna, but there's a big difference in the flavor and texture of the four varieties commonly sold in the United States. We tasted all four, simply sautéed and lightly salted. Here are our impressions.

**YELLOWFIN.** The favorite. The flavor was the "most complex," not fishy, and "almost sweet." "Best texture," wrote one taster, and others agreed. Tender and smooth, with a melt-in-your-mouth quality.

**BIGEYE.** The most intensely flavored of all four varieties, with an "almost meaty flavor" and the deepest red color. The texture was tender but "very wet and moist." The high water content prevented the formation of a crust when pan-searing.

**BLUEFIN.** Many tasters noticed an odd, "almost metallic" aftertaste, and the texture was thought to be "chewy," "slippery," and "mushy." Bluefin was even wetter than bigeye. The liquid seeped out of the fish both during pan-searing and while it sat sliced on the serving plate.

**ALBACORE.** The only variety that can legally be sold in cans labeled "white-meat" tuna. Most found it bland and somewhat dry. The texture was firm but not tough. Unlike other varieties, albacore does not have a brilliant red color, even when raw.

### HOW TO OIL THE COOKING GRATE
Just before placing the burgers on the grill, dip a large wad of paper towels in vegetable oil, grab it with tongs, and wipe the grate thoroughly to lubricate and prevent sticking. This will also clean off any remaining residue from previous grilling. This step works well with other foods that stick, including fish fillets and burgers.

### FOR GAS-GRILLED TUNA BURGERS
Follow steps 1 and 2 of the recipe for Charcoal-Grilled Tuna Burgers. Light all the burners, turn the heat to high, close the lid, and heat the grill until very hot, about 15 minutes. Leave all the burners on high. Continue as directed from step 3, grilling the tuna burgers with the lid down, until well browned on one side, about 3 minutes. Flip the burgers with a greased metal spatula. Continue grilling, covered, to desired doneness, about 3 minutes for medium-rare or 4 minutes for medium. Serve immediately.

# OVEN-BAKED
# SHRIMP AND ORZO

### SERVES 6

**WHAT MAKES THIS A BEST RECIPE:** The classic Greek-style baked shrimp with orzo is an excellent casserole to make for company. Unfortunately, rubbery overcooked shrimp, or bland orzo that is either undercooked or mushy, often ruins this dish. For this recipe, we cooked the orzo "pilaf style," or sautéed it briefly in oil with flavorings before adding the liquid, which made it toasty brown and deeply flavored. Instead of cooking the orzo on the stovetop until completely tender as many recipes do, we left it slightly undercooked in the center. We then transferred the orzo to a baking dish and embedded the raw shrimp in the mix before baking. The orzo became tender in the oven, while at the same time it shielded the shrimp from the oven's direct heat, effectively preventing them from drying out and toughening. For a finishing touch we topped the baking dish with salty, briny feta cheese, which complemented the sweetness of the shrimp.

1½  pounds large shrimp (31 to 40 per pound), peeled and
    deveined
    Salt and pepper
1   red onion, minced
1   red bell pepper, stemmed, seeded, and cut into ½-inch
    pieces
1   teaspoon extra-virgin olive oil
6   garlic cloves, minced
1   pound orzo
    Pinch saffron
4   cups low-sodium chicken broth
1   cup water
1   (28-ounce) can diced tomatoes, drained
1   cup frozen peas (optional)
4   teaspoons minced fresh oregano
4   ounces feta cheese, crumbled (about 1 cup)
4   scallions, sliced thin
    Lemon wedges, for serving

**1.** Adjust an oven rack to the middle position and heat the oven to 400 degrees. Pat the shrimp dry with paper towels and season them with salt and pepper; set aside.

**2.** Combine the onion, bell pepper, oil, and ½ teaspoon salt together in a large Dutch oven. Cover and cook over medium-low heat until the vegetables have softened, 8 to 10 minutes. Stir in the garlic and cook until fragrant, about 30 seconds. Stir in the orzo and saffron and cook, stirring frequently, until the orzo is coated with oil and lightly browned, about 4 minutes.

**3.** Stir in the broth and water and continue to cook, stirring occasionally, until the grains of orzo are mostly tender yet still slightly firm at the center, about 12 minutes. Stir in the tomatoes, peas (if using), oregano, and shrimp.

**4.** Pour into a 13 by 9-inch baking dish and sprinkle the feta evenly over the top. Bake until the shrimp are cooked through and the cheese is lightly browned, about 20 minutes. Sprinkle with the scallions and serve with the lemon wedges.

**WHERE THINGS CAN GO WRONG:** The orzo should be slightly firm to the bite when transferred to the baking dish in step 4; otherwise it may overcook in the oven. If you are tempted to use a large (12-inch) skillet to make this recipe, don't; the pan will overflow.

## NOTES FROM THE TEST KITCHEN

### HOW TO BUY SHRIMP

Virtually all of the shrimp sold today in supermarkets has been previously frozen, either in large blocks of ice or with a method called "individually quick frozen," IQF for short. Supermarkets simply defrost the shrimp before displaying them on ice at the fish counter, where they look as though they are freshly plucked from the sea. As a general rule, we highly recommend purchasing bags of still-frozen, shell-on IQF shrimp and defrosting them as needed at home, since there is no telling how long "fresh" shrimp may have been kept on ice at the market. IQF shrimp also have a better flavor and texture than shrimp frozen in blocks. IQF shrimp are available both with and without their shells, but we find the shell-on shrimp to be firmer and sweeter. Also, shrimp should be the only ingredient listed on the bag. Some packagers add sodium-based chemicals as preservatives, but we find these shrimp have a strange translucency and unpleasant texture. Shrimp are sold by size (small, medium, large, and extra large) as well as by the number needed to make 1 pound, usually given in a range. Choosing shrimp by the numerical rating per pound is more accurate than choosing them by the size label, because that varies from store to store. Here's how the two sizing systems generally compare:

**Small:** 51 to 60 per pound
**Medium:** 41 to 50 per pound
**Large:** 31 to 40 per pound
**Extra large:** 21 to 25 per pound

# SESAME-GINGER SHRIMP

SERVES 4

**WHAT MAKES THIS A BEST RECIPE:** Marry tender shrimp with sesame, ginger, scallions, soy sauce, and vegetables, and you have a classic stir-fry. Stir-frying is a naturally quick and easy cooking technique. However, it does require that you pay attention to the details, plus it pays to be organized (and have all of your ingredients prepped) before you begin. Many stir-fry recipes err by throwing everything into the pan at one time, and the ingredients steam and stew, not stir-fry. Here in the test kitchen, we find that the key to stir-frying is to cook everything quickly in batches over high heat. For this recipe, we first cooked thin strips of red bell peppers and scallions, then shrimp, which we briefly marinated in a little soy sauce to improve their flavor. Another mistake many recipes make is adding the aromatics (garlic and ginger) too early, causing them to burn and become harsh-tasting. When we stir-fry, we like to push the cooked shrimp to the sides of the pan, and then add the aromatics with a little oil to the center and mash them with a spoon just until fragrant. We then stir the aromatics into the shrimp and add a sauce. For this recipe, we paired the shrimp and vegetables with a zesty combination of soy sauce, toasted sesame oil, and oyster sauce. We like to serve this dish with rice, though Asian noodles are tasty as well.

1 pound extra-large shrimp (21 to 25 per pound), peeled and deveined
4 teaspoons soy sauce
2 garlic cloves, minced
2 teaspoons minced fresh ginger
¼ teaspoon red pepper flakes
2 tablespoons plus 1 teaspoon peanut or vegetable oil
½ cup water

1 tablespoon toasted sesame oil
1 tablespoon oyster sauce
1 teaspoon cornstarch
1 red bell pepper, stemmed, seeded, and cut into thin 2-inch-long strips
5 scallions, cut into 2-inch pieces
1 teaspoon fresh lemon juice
1 tablespoon sesame seeds, toasted

**1.** Toss the shrimp and 2 teaspoons of the soy sauce together in a medium bowl. Mix the garlic, ginger, pepper flakes, and 1 teaspoon of the peanut oil together in a small bowl. Stir the water, sesame oil, oyster sauce, remaining 2 teaspoons soy sauce, and cornstarch together in a small bowl.

**2.** Heat 1 tablespoon of the peanut oil in a 12-inch nonstick skillet over high heat until smoking. Add the bell pepper and scallions and cook until browned in spots, about 5 minutes. Transfer to a bowl. Add the remaining tablespoon peanut oil and the shrimp to the now-empty skillet and cook, tossing until just opaque, about 30 seconds.

**3.** Push the shrimp to the sides of the skillet, add the garlic mixture to the center of the pan, and mash with a spoon until fragrant, 10 to 15 seconds. Stir the mixture into the shrimp. Add the water mixture and cook until thickened, about 1½ minutes. Return the vegetables to the pan, add the lemon juice, and toss until heated through. Sprinkle with the sesame seeds before serving.

## NOTES FROM THE TEST KITCHEN

### HOW TO GRATE GINGER
Peel a small section of a large piece of ginger. Grate the peeled portion, using the rest of the ginger as a handle to keep fingers safely away from the grater.

# SPICY
# BAKED SHRIMP

### SERVES 4

**WHAT MAKES THIS A BEST RECIPE:** When a craving for crunchy breaded shrimp strikes, most of us head to our favorite seaside restaurant. This recipe, however, is a great, easy alternative; and while it isn't true fried shrimp, it will satisfy that craving. Spicy, crispy, buttery, and plump, these shrimp make a great dinner when served with a small salad or crusty roll. And if you're looking for an alternative to shrimp cocktail, these shrimp are a welcome and hot alternative.

When developing this recipe, we knew that we wanted our shrimp to have a crunchy exterior, but we didn't feel like breaking out the deep fryer for the task. Instead, we coated the shrimp with melted butter and fresh breadcrumbs (dried breadcrumbs were too gritty), followed by a quick spritz of vegetable oil spray for even browning. We then baked the shrimp in a very hot oven until just cooked through. The breadcrumbs on the top of the shrimp crisped beautifully, but the underside became soggy from contact with the baking sheet. We solved this problem by breading the shrimp on only one side—the top. The shrimp were light and crunchy, and not at all greasy, but they needed a little spice. Before coating the shrimp with the breadcrumbs, we tossed them, along with the butter, in a zesty mix of paprika, cayenne, and Dijon mustard. This not only elevated the flavor of the shrimp, but it gave the breadcrumbs a surface to adhere to, and kept the shrimp juicy in the oven. For added heat and bite, we seasoned the melted butter liberally with garlic, lemon juice, and hot pepper sauce. This butter mixture was so tasty that we made a little extra to serve as a dipping sauce alongside the shrimp.

Vegetable oil spray
6   tablespoons unsalted butter
4   garlic cloves, minced
2   teaspoons fresh lemon juice
4½  teaspoons hot pepper sauce
    Salt and pepper
2   pounds extra-large shrimp (21 to 25 per pound), peeled and deveined, tails intact
2   teaspoons paprika
⅛   teaspoon cayenne pepper

2   teaspoons Dijon mustard
1   cup breadcrumbs, preferably fresh (see page 7)
2   tablespoons chopped fresh parsley
    Lemon wedges, for serving

**1.** Adjust an oven rack to the middle position and heat the oven to 500 degrees. Coat a baking sheet with vegetable oil spray.

**2.** Melt the butter in a small saucepan over medium heat. Add the garlic and cook until fragrant, about 30 seconds. Stir in the lemon juice and hot sauce and season with salt and pepper. Remove from the heat.

**3.** Toss the shrimp, paprika, cayenne, mustard, ¼ teaspoon salt, and ⅛ teaspoon pepper together in a large bowl. Add 2 tablespoons of the butter mixture. Place the breadcrumbs in a shallow bowl.

**4.** Dip one side of each shrimp in the breadcrumbs, pressing to adhere them. Place the shrimp breaded side up on the prepared baking sheet, spacing them slightly apart. Spray the shrimp with the vegetable oil spray and bake until just cooked through and the breadcrumbs are golden and crisp, 8 to 9 minutes. Rewarm the butter mixture and stir in the parsley. Serve the shrimp with the butter mixture and lemon wedges.

**WHERE THINGS CAN GO WRONG:** Use your hands to really press the breadcrumbs onto the shrimp in step 4. If the shrimp are not sufficiently coated in the breadcrumbs, they will not become crispy in the oven.

## NOTES FROM THE TEST KITCHEN

### THE BEST HOT SAUCE

Since most hot sauces are made from a basic combination of red peppers, vinegar, and salt, we'd never given much thought to brand. But curious about whether it mattered, we rounded up eight supermarket samples to find out, sprinkling each atop a portion of steamed white rice. Across the board, tasters deemed one sauce a knockout: **Frank's RedHot** won points for its potent heat and "bright" and "tangy" notes. Surprisingly, Tabasco came in last; its searing heat masked any other flavor in the sauce and tasters disliked it's bitter taste and thin consistency. Wondering if Tabasco would fare better in a cooked application, we pitted it against Frank's in a breakfast strata but here the results were split. One taster put it succinctly: "Tabasco is an ingredient, while Frank's is a condiment."

# SHRIMP JAMBALAYA

SERVES 4 TO 6

**WHAT MAKES THIS A BEST RECIPE:** Packed to the gills with shrimp, sausage, rice, and vegetables, jambalaya is the cream of the one-pot crop. But what makes it so attractive—its hodge-podge of textures and flavors—is also what makes it such a challenge to prepare. Often, the rice is too crunchy, the shrimp too bland and chewy, or everything is just plain overcooked—it can be tough to juggle all these ingredients in just one pot. After experimenting with various cooking techniques, we found that cooking the ingredients separately, and then marrying them before serving, was the best way to ensure that each would have optimal flavor and texture. We started by browning andouille sausage (if you cannot find andouille, substitute chorizo), then we pumped up the flavor of the shrimp by browning it in the fat that the sausage left behind. To prevent the shrimp from being dry and rubbery, we seared them before peeling them. In addition, the shells lent a more complex shrimp flavor to the jambalaya, and they protected the flesh of the shrimp from scorching in the pan. To further fortify the flavor of the rice, we chose clam juice as the cooking liquid. And to avoid crunchy bits of unevenly cooked rice, we transferred the jambalaya to the oven where heat attacks the pot from all sides, not just the bottom, and covered the pot with a piece aluminum foil, pressed flush to the surface of the rice, as well as the lid. The combination of the foil and the lid really trapped in steam and heat, resulting in perfectly cooked rice every time.

| | |
|---|---|
| 2 | teaspoons vegetable oil |
| 8 | ounces andouille sausage, halved lengthwise and cut crosswise into ¼-inch half-moons |
| 1 | pound large shell-on shrimp (31 to 40 per pound) |
| 1 | onion, minced (about 1 cup) |
| 1 | celery rib, chopped fine |
| 1 | green bell pepper, stemmed, seeded, and chopped fine |
| 5 | garlic cloves, minced |
| 1½ | cups long-grain white rice |
| 1 | tablespoon tomato paste |
| 1 | teaspoon salt |
| ½ | teaspoon minced fresh thyme |
| 1 | (14.5-ounce) can diced tomatoes, drained, with ¼ cup juice reserved |
| 2 | (8-ounce) bottles clam juice |
| 1 | bay leaf |
| 2 | scallions, sliced thin |

**1.** Adjust an oven rack to the middle position and heat the oven to 325 degrees.

**2.** Heat the oil in a large Dutch oven over medium-high heat until shimmering. Add the sausage and cook until browned, 3 to 5 minutes. Using a slotted spoon, transfer the sausage to a plate lined with paper towels. Add the shrimp to the pot and cook until the shells are lightly browned on both sides, about 1 minute per side. Transfer the shrimp to a large bowl and refrigerate.

**3.** Reduce the heat to medium and add the onion, celery, bell pepper, and garlic to the pot. Cook, stirring occasionally, until the vegetables have softened, 5 to 10 minutes. Add the rice, tomato paste, salt, and thyme and cook until the rice is coated with fat, about 1 minute. Stir in the tomatoes, reserved tomato juice, clam juice, bay leaf, and sausage. Place a square of aluminum foil directly on the surface of the rice. Bring to a boil, cover the pot, transfer to the oven, and bake until the rice is almost tender and most of the liquid is absorbed, about 20 minutes.

**4.** Meanwhile, peel the shrimp (devein if desired, see page 10) and discard the shells. Remove the pot from the oven, lift off the aluminum foil, and gently stir in the peeled shrimp and any accumulated juice. Replace the foil and lid, return the pot to the oven, and cook until the rice is fully tender and the shrimp are cooked through, about 5 minutes. Remove from the oven, discard the foil and bay leaf, fold in the scallions, and serve immediately.

**WHERE THINGS CAN GO WRONG:** To ensure perfectly plump shrimp, not dry and rubbery ones, only cook the shrimp in step 2 for a minute per side, and then refrigerate them immediately after they come out of the pan.

## NOTES FROM THE TEST KITCHEN

### FOR EVENLY COOKED RICE

Baking the jambalaya in the oven ensures that the rice won't scorch, as often happens when this dish is prepared on top of the stove. Place a sheet of aluminum foil directly on the surface of the rice (and pressed against the sides of the Dutch oven) before the jambalaya goes into the oven. The foil holds in steam and heat far more effectively than the lid alone, ensuring that every grain of rice cooks perfectly.

SHRIMP JAMBALAYA

# DESSERTS

# DEEP-DISH APPLE PIE

SERVES 8 TO 10

**WHAT MAKES THIS A BEST RECIPE:** First of all, we love this pie because it delivers on its name—no wimpy slice of apple pie here but rather a nearly impossibly high wedge of pie packed from the bottom crust to the top with a mix of tart-sweet apples. And unlike most recipes we tried, this one delivered apples that held their shape without being crunchy or floating in an overabundance of juice (that also made the crust soggy). Add to this a butter-rich and flaky pie pastry that was easy to work with, and we had a pie that was worth all the effort. Our secrets? Cook the apples first in a large Dutch oven and use at least 5 pounds of them (so they'll be no gaping hole between the apples and the top crust). And use both butter and sour cream in the pie dough (see page 245 for our Foolproof All-Butter Pie Pastry).

½ cup (3½ ounces) plus 1 teaspoon granulated sugar

¼ cup (1¾ ounces) packed light brown sugar

¼ teaspoon salt

½ teaspoon grated lemon zest plus 1 tablespoon fresh lemon juice

⅛ teaspoon ground cinnamon

2½ pounds firm tart apples (about 5 medium), peeled and cut into ¼-inch-thick slices

2½ pounds firm sweet apples (about 5 medium), peeled and cut into ¼-inch-thick slices

1 recipe Foolproof All-Butter Pie Pastry (page 245)

1 large egg white, beaten lightly

**1.** Mix ½ cup of the granulated sugar, brown sugar, salt, zest, and cinnamon in a large bowl; add the apples and toss to combine. Transfer the apples to a Dutch oven (do not wash the bowl) and cook, covered, over medium heat, stirring frequently, until the apples are tender when poked with a fork but still hold their shape, 15 to 20 minutes. (The apples and their juice should gently simmer during cooking.) Transfer the apples and juice to a rimmed baking sheet and cool to room temperature, about 30 minutes.

**2.** Remove 1 disk of the dough from the refrigerator and following the photos on page 247, roll it out on a lightly floured surface or between 2 large sheets of parchment paper

or plastic wrap to a 12-inch circle, about ⅛ inch thick. (If the dough becomes soft and/or sticky, return it to the refrigerator until firm.) Transfer the dough to a 9-inch pie plate. Working around the circumference, ease the dough into the plate by gently lifting the edge of dough with one hand while pressing it into the plate bottom with the other hand. Leave the dough that overhangs the plate in place; refrigerate until the dough is firm, about 30 minutes.

**3.** Meanwhile, roll the second disk of dough out on a lightly floured surface or between 2 large sheets of parchment paper or plastic wrap to a 12-inch circle, about ⅛ inch thick. Refrigerate until firm, about 30 minutes.

**4.** Meanwhile, adjust an oven rack to the lowest position, place an empty rimmed baking sheet on the rack, and heat the oven to 425 degrees. Set a large colander over the now-empty bowl; transfer the cooled apples to the colander. Shake the colander to drain off as much juice as possible (the cooked apples should measure about 8 cups); discard the juice. Transfer the apples to the dough-lined pie plate and sprinkle with the lemon juice.

**5.** Flip the remaining dough onto the apples. Pinch the edges of the top and bottom dough rounds firmly together. Trim and seal the edges of dough, then cut four 2-inch slits in the top of the dough. Brush the surface with beaten egg white and sprinkle evenly with the remaining teaspoon sugar.

**6.** Set the pie on the preheated baking sheet. Bake until the crust is dark golden brown, 45 to 55 minutes. Transfer the pie to a wire rack and cool for at least 1½ hours. Cut into wedges and serve.

## NOTES FROM THE TEST KITCHEN

### A BETTER WAY TO PEEL APPLES

If there was ever a recipe on which to test apple-processing gadgets, our Deep-Dish Apple Pie was it. So we rounded up five models—and a bushel of apples—and headed into the test kitchen. The winner? **The Back to Basics Apple Peeler** ($24.95)—with its sharp blade and enough length to mount even extra-large apples. And it allowed us to peel 5 pounds of apples in under 4 minutes (while it took the test kitchen's best peeler 12 minutes to do the same—manually).

DEEP-DISH APPLE PIE

**WHERE THINGS CAN GO WRONG:** If you precook the apples over heat that is too high, the apples will disintegrate (which will defeat the entire purpose of this step). But if the apples are gently heated, their pectin (which gives them structure) is converted to a heat-stable form that prevents them from becoming mushy when cooked further in the oven. The key is to keep the temperature of the apples below 140 degrees during this step. This is why it's best to heat them gently in a large, covered Dutch oven. If you use a skillet, you're much more apt to overheat them.

**WHAT YOU CAN DO AHEAD OF TIME:** The pie can be assembled (but do not brush with egg wash) and frozen for up to 2 weeks. Freeze the pie for 2 to 3 hours, then wrap tightly in a double layer of plastic wrap, then foil, and freeze for up to 2 weeks. To bake, remove the pie from the freezer, brush it with the egg wash, sprinkle with the sugar, cut slits in the top crust, and place directly on the baking sheet in the preheated oven. Bake for 5 to 10 minutes longer than normal. The apples can be cooked up to 1 day ahead; cool them completely on the baking sheet, then wrap tightly in plastic wrap, and refrigerate.

## NOTES FROM THE TEST KITCHEN

### CHOOSE A MIX OF APPLES
A combination of sweet and tart apples works best in pie so choose a mix of apples (see our lineup) and stay away from McIntosh apples, which break down easily, turning to mush.

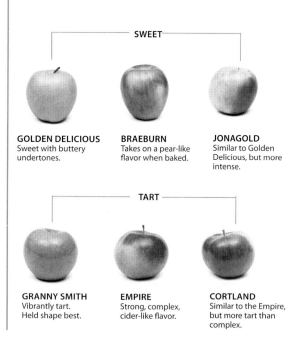

**SWEET**

**GOLDEN DELICIOUS**
Sweet with buttery undertones.

**BRAEBURN**
Takes on a pear-like flavor when baked.

**JONAGOLD**
Similar to Golden Delicious, but more intense.

**TART**

**GRANNY SMITH**
Vibrantly tart. Held shape best.

**EMPIRE**
Strong, complex, cider-like flavor.

**CORTLAND**
Similar to the Empire, but more tart than complex.

## GREAT DISCOVERIES
### COOK THE APPLES TWICE

During research for my deep-dish apple pie story, I had come across recipes that called for sautéing the apples before assembling them in the pie, the idea being to both extract juice and cook the apples more evenly. Although this logic seemed counterintuitive (how could cooking the apples twice cause them to become anything but insipid and mushy?), I went ahead and tested the improbable. Every test with raw apples had been an utter failure—producing a flood of juice and soggy crust—so what did I have to lose? After browning the apples in a hot skillet (in two batches to accommodate the large volume), I made yet another pie, then held my breath and crossed my fingers. The apples were disappointingly mealy and soft, especially the exteriors, which had been seared in the hot pan. But this pie delivered on more than one count: Aside from the absence of juice flooding the bottom of the pie plate, it offered a nicely browned bottom crust.

Could I try this cooking method with a gentler hand to keep the apples from disintegrating? For a more moderate approach, I dumped the whole mound into a large Dutch oven along with some granulated sugar (to flavor the apples and extract moisture), then covered the pan to promote more even cooking. With frequent stirring over medium heat for 15 to 20 minutes, the apples were tender yet still held their shape. After cooling and draining the apples (so the butter in the crust would not melt), I baked off the pie, which was again free of excess juice and sported the same browned bottom as before. And this time the apples weren't mealy or blown out but instead miraculously tender.

After talking with some apple scientists, I discovered that apples undergo a significant structural change when held at low-to-moderate temperatures for several minutes. Between 120 and 140 degrees Fahrenheit, pectin is converted to a more heat-stable form. (While pectin provides structure in the raw fruit, it breaks down under the high heat of sautéing.) Once an adequate amount of pectin has been stabilized at low heat (as it apparently was on the stovetop), the apples can tolerate the heat from additional cooking (in the oven) without breaking down and becoming excessively soft. To top it off, because the apples were shrinking before going into the pie rather than after, I had inadvertently solved the problem of the maddening gap! The top crust now remained united with the rest of the pie, and slicing was a breeze.

ERIKA BRUCE | ASSOCIATE EDITOR, COOK'S ILLUSTRATED

# FOOLPROOF ALL-BUTTER PIE PASTRY

MAKES ONE 9-INCH DOUBLE-CRUST PIE SHELL

**WHAT MAKES THIS A BEST RECIPE:** We love the rich flavor that all-butter pie doughs deliver, but they often fail to be flaky and are notoriously difficult to work with. In the past, we have made sure that our pie crusts would turn out both tender and flaky by using a combination of butter and vegetable shortening. The shortening, with a fat content of 100 percent (butter has an 80 percent fat content), tenderizes pie crusts, and its melting point, well-above body temperature—makes it easy to work with. For our Deep-Dish Apple Pie (page 242) we wanted it all: a dough that was easy to work with, a tender, flaky crust, and the rich taste that only an all-butter crust could offer. In addition to the butter, we tried other forms of fat to tenderize the dough and make it easier to manage. Sour cream, with its slightly nutty tang, beat out the competition (heavy cream and cream cheese) in terms of flavor and tenderness. Because acid slows or reduces the formation of gluten (the structure-forming protein in flour), it made sense that a more acidic dough would lead to a more tender crust.

2½ cups (12½ ounces) unbleached all-purpose flour
1 teaspoon salt
1 tablespoon sugar
16 tablespoons (2 sticks) unsalted butter, cut into ½-inch pieces and frozen for 10 minutes
3 tablespoons sour cream
⅓ cup ice water, plus more as needed

**1.** Process the flour, salt, and sugar in a food processor until combined. Add the butter and pulse until the butter is the size of large peas, about ten 1-second pulses.
**2.** Mix the sour cream and ⅓ cup ice water in a small bowl until combined. Add half of the sour cream mixture to the flour mixture; pulse for three 1-second pulses. Repeat with the remaining sour cream mixture. If the dough does not come together, add more water, 1 tablespoon at a time, and process until the dough forms large clumps and no dry flour remains, four 1-second pulses.

Sour cream gives our all-butter pie dough good flavor and tender crust (and helps make it easier to manage).

**3.** Turn the dough out onto the counter. Divide the dough into 2 balls and flatten each into a 4-inch disk. Wrap each disk in plastic wrap and refrigerate for at least 1 hour before rolling.

**WHERE THINGS CAN GO WRONG:** If your kitchen is very warm, refrigerating all of the ingredients for 30 minutes before making the recipe will help to keep the dough cool during preparation. A common mistake among home bakers is not processing the butter and flour properly (see page 246). While some pieces of butter ought to remain intact, it is better to overprocess the butter than to leave large chunks in the mix, which will make the dough difficult to roll out. After adding the sour cream and water mixture, if the dough doesn't form large clumps, it needs more water (a dry dough is impossible to roll out). If the dough is too warm, the butter will melt and make a soft, sticky dough. Firm it by chilling it rather than by rolling it in flour, which will only toughen the dough. (See page 246 for more information on making pie dough.)

**WHAT YOU CAN DO AHEAD OF TIME:** The disks of dough can be wrapped tightly in plastic wrap and refrigerated for up to 2 days, or frozen for up to 1 month. Thaw frozen dough in the refrigerator. Before rolling, let the dough stand at room temperature for 15 minutes to soften.

# PIE PASTRY 101: PREPARING THE DOUGH

## 1. COMBINE THE FLOUR AND FAT

Small lumps of butter should be evenly distributed throughout the dough to promote the formation of flaky layers. If the butter pieces are too large, the dough will be difficult to roll out. If they are completely incorporated into the flour, the crust will be crumbly and cookie-like. The largest pieces should be about the size of a pea.

**BUTTER IS TOO LUMPY:** Dough will be hard to roll out

**BUTTER IS TOO SMALL:** Crust will be crumbly

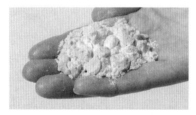

**BUTTER IS JUST RIGHT:** Pearl-sized pieces are ideal

## 2. ADD JUST ENOUGH WATER

Our recipe begins with a minimum amount of water. You will probably need to add more water, depending on the brand of flour and the humidity in your kitchen. Take a small handful of dough out of the food processor and pinch it together. If the dough seems at all floury or won't hold together, it needs more water. When the dough is properly hydrated, it will form large clumps and no dry flour will remain.

**DOUGH IS TOO DRY:** Add more water as needed

**PERFECTLY MOISTENED:** The dough can be very tacky but not sticky or gluey

## FRENCH PINS ROLL OVER AMERICAN PINS

Once upon a time, rolling pins fell into two camps: standard wooden pins with dowel-style, ball-bearing handles and French rolling pins, also wooden, which are basically solid cylinders with tapered ends. Not anymore. These days, the old standbys compete for space in the bakeware aisle with newfangled models. Made from fancy materials and souped up with ergonomic designs and "deluxe" features, do these new pins make traditional wooden rolling pins passé? We rolled out pie crust and pizza and tart doughs with 10 different pins to find out.

Dough has a tendency to stick to rolling pins, an issue usually blamed on overwarm dough. Marble and metal pins (refrigerated before rolling) and a hollow pin made of laboratory glass (filled with ice) try to tackle the problem from a temperature perspective. A nylon pin (and one of the metal designs) opt for the non-stick surface approach.

But at the end of the day, we hold that gimmick-free wooden pins are the way to go. Dirt cheap and durable (unlike the accidentally smashed glass pin), they will also handle any task. Tapered pins should be around 20-inches long, with a diameter of at least 1½ inches—otherwise, there's not enough flat surface to ensure a level roll. You handled-pin fans should look for pins at least 12 inches long with the largest diameter you can manage.

**OUR WINNER**
Fante's French rolling pin with tapered ends ($7.99) is easy to use and offers maximum control.

**RUNNER-UP**
Fante's handled maple rolling pin ($11.99) is great for bakers who want a little extra leverage.

## 3. GETTING THAT PERFECT CIRCLE

Here are some key points to help you roll the dough into a perfect circle that will be easy to fit in the pie plate:

**KEEP IT COLD:** If the dough is too warm, the butter will melt and cause sticking. Chill the dough thoroughly (at least 1 hour) before attempting to roll it out. If the dough is chilled for several hours, let it warm slightly before rolling it out.
**KEEP IT COVERED:** A floured counter will keep dough from sticking, but the extra flour can make the dough tough. We prefer to roll the dough between sheets of parchment paper or plastic wrap.

**KEEP IT TURNING:** Misshapen dough is hard to fit into a pie plate and often has thinner edges. For a perfectly round dough of even thickness, don't keep rolling over the same spot or in the same direction. Starting at the center of the dough, roll away from yourself two or three times, then rotate the disk one quarter turn and repeat.

# ROLLING OUT AND FITTING THE DOUGH

## HOW TO ROLL AND FIT THE DOUGH

**1.** Laying the disk of dough on a lightly floured surface (or between sheets of parchment paper or plastic wrap), roll the dough outward from its center into a 12-inch circle.

**2.** As you roll the dough, give it a quarter turn every few strokes, adding more flour as needed to keep the dough from sticking to the counter.

**3.** Loosely roll the dough around the rolling pin. Then gently unroll the dough over the pie plate.

**4.** Gently press the dough into the corners of the pie plate. Leave any dough that overhangs and refrigerate until needed.

## MAKING A DECORATIVE EDGE ON A SINGLE-CRUST PIE

**1.** After fitting the dough into the pan, trim the dough to within ½ inch of the outer lip of the pie plate. Tuck the trimmed dough underneath itself to form a doubled rim that sits above the lip of the pie plate.

**2.** For a fluted edge, use the index finger of one hand and the thumb and index finger of the other to create fluted edges perpendicular to the edge of the pie plate.

## HOW TO ASSEMBLE A TOP CRUST

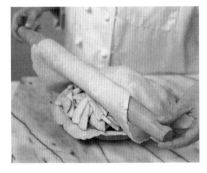

**1.** After rolling out the top crust, loosely roll it around the rolling pin, then gently unroll it over the filled pie crust bottom.

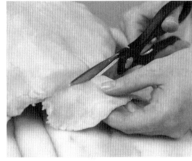

**2.** Trim all but ½ inch of the dough overhanging the edge of the pie plate with scissors. Press the top and bottom crust together, then tuck the edges underneath.

**3.** Crimp the dough evenly around the edge of the pie, using your fingers.

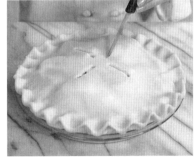

**4.** Cut four 2-inch slits attractively in the center of the top crust with a paring knife. Then brush the surface with beaten egg white and sprinkle evenly with sugar.

# MODERN MINCEMEAT PIE

SERVES 10 TO 12

**WHAT MAKES THIS A BEST RECIPE:** Most of the mincemeat pies we have tried have been murky tasting and overly rich; more than a bite or two is too much. We love the complex fruit flavors of mincemeat, but wanted to bring it into the modern age by making it cleaner and lighter. A traditional mincemeat pie involves boiling a lean cut of beef until it falls apart, then cooking this meat with apples, dried fruit, spices, suet, sugar, and brandy or whiskey for hours. Our goal: a more modern recipe, one that dropped the beef and the suet and, while we were at it, we wanted to maximize the fruit flavor.

To avoid a pie filling that more closely resembled applesauce, we used equal amounts of McIntosh apples, which fell apart to form the base of the filling, and Granny Smith apples, which maintained a bit of texture and tartness to punctuate the filling's sweetness. A simple blend of golden raisins, tiny currants, and candied orange peel, and a little restraint with the spices (cinnamon, allspice, ginger, and cloves), gave our pie its complex fruit flavors. To prevent the filling from reeking of booze, which is fairly common in the world of mincemeat, and to keep it bright and fresh, we simmered the fruit in apple cider and added just ⅓ cup of rum or brandy—two distinctly different options that both tasted good—in the final 10 minutes of cooking. We like to serve this pie with whipped cream or vanilla ice cream.

### FILLING

- 3 large Granny Smith apples (about 1½ pounds), peeled, cored, and cut into ¼-inch dice
- 3 large McIntosh apples (about 1½ pounds), peeled, cored, and cut into ¼-inch dice
- 1 cup golden raisins
- 1 cup currants
- ¾ cup (5¼ ounces) packed dark brown sugar
- 8 tablespoons (1 stick) unsalted butter
- ¼ cup diced candied orange peel (optional)
  Grated zest and juice from 1 orange
- Grated zest and juice from 1 lemon
- 1 teaspoon ground cinnamon
- ½ teaspoon ground allspice
- ½ teaspoon ground ginger
- ¼ teaspoon ground cloves
- ¼ teaspoon salt
- 1½ cups apple cider, plus more as needed
- ⅓ cup rum or brandy
- 1 recipe Foolproof All-Butter Pie Pastry (page 245)
- 1 large egg white, beaten lightly
- 1 tablespoon sugar

**1.** Bring all of the filling ingredients except ½ cup of the cider and the rum to a simmer in a large saucepan over medium-low heat. Cook, stirring occasionally, until the mixture thickens and darkens in color, about 3 hours, adding more cider as necessary to prevent scorching. Continue cooking, stirring frequently, until the mixture has a jam-like consistency, about 20 minutes. Stir in the remaining ½ cup apple cider and rum and cook until the liquid in the pan is thick and syrupy, about 10 minutes; cool the mixture.

**2.** Remove 1 disk of the dough from the refrigerator and following the photos on page 247, roll it out on a lightly floured surface or between 2 large sheets of parchment paper or plastic wrap to a 12-inch circle, about ⅛ inch thick. (If the dough becomes soft and/or sticky, return it to the refrigerator until firm.) Transfer the dough to a 9-inch pie plate. Working around the circumference, ease the dough into the plate by gently lifting the edge of the dough with one hand while pressing it into the plate bottom with the other hand. Leave the dough that overhangs the plate in place; refrigerate until the dough is firm, about 30 minutes.

**3.** Meanwhile, roll the second disk of dough out on a lightly floured surface or between 2 large sheets of parchment paper or plastic wrap to a 12-inch circle about ⅛ inch thick. Refrigerate until firm, about 30 minutes.

**4.** Meanwhile, adjust an oven rack to the middle position and heat the oven to 400 degrees. Transfer the mincemeat to the dough-lined pie plate. Flip the remaining dough onto the mincemeat. Pinch the edges of the top and bottom dough rounds firmly together. Trim and seal the edges of dough, then cut four 2-inch slits in the top of the dough. Brush the surface with beaten egg white and sprinkle evenly with sugar.

**5.** Bake until the crust is light golden brown, about 25 minutes. Reduce the oven temperature to 350 degrees and continue to bake until the juices bubble and the crust is dark golden brown, about 35 minutes. Transfer the pie to a wire rack and cool to room temperature. Cut into wedges and serve.

**WHERE THINGS CAN GO WRONG:** It's easy to scorch this filling as you're simmering it, so be sure to stir it occasionally and add enough cider to keep the mixture from drying out. Also, it is critical to reduce the oven temperature in step 5, or the pie will burn.

**WHAT YOU CAN DO AHEAD OF TIME:** The pie can be assembled (but do not brush with egg wash) and frozen for up to 2 weeks. Freeze the pie for 2 to 3 hours, then wrap tightly in a double layer of plastic wrap, then foil, and freeze for up to 2 weeks. To bake, remove the pie from the freezer, cut slits in the top crust, brush it with egg wash, sprinkle with sugar, and bake in the preheated oven. Bake for 5 to 10 minutes longer than normal. The disks of dough can be wrapped tightly in plastic wrap and refrigerated for up to 2 days, or frozen for up to 1 month. Thaw frozen dough in the refrigerator. Before rolling, let the dough stand at room temperature for 15 minutes to soften. The mincemeat filling can be cooked up to 3 days ahead; cool completely and refrigerate in an airtight container.

## NOTES FROM THE TEST KITCHEN

### WHAT TO LOOK FOR IN A PIE PLATE
A pie plate's rim should be wide and sturdy enough to support a fluted edge. We found that pie plates with rims narrower than ½ inch were not up to the task. Of all the pie plates we have tested, the classic **Corning Pyrex Original** ($4.95) was our favorite, delivering a solid performance across the board, a budget price, and a see-through bottom.

# SOUTHERN PECAN PRALINE PIE
SERVES 8 TO 10

**WHAT MAKES THIS A BEST RECIPE:** This Southern Pecan Praline Pie is buttery, dark, and rich, nothing like the gritty, taffy-like, boozy pie that many recipes try to pass off as the classic Southern dessert. Our pie packs praline flavor right down to its crust, which is made with dark brown sugar and all butter. For the filling, after making several hard and chewy renditions following the candy-making technique for making praline, we decided to follow a pecan pie approach. We cooked butter, brown sugar, corn syrup, eggs, and vanilla in a saucepan until glossy, and then stirred in toasted pecans. Dark corn syrup delivered candy-like flavor, and the eggs ensured that the filling set up in the oven while still remaining soft enough to slice. A little salt kept the filling from being too cloying, while butter and bourbon added richness. We like to serve this pie topped with whipped cream or vanilla ice cream.

### CRUST
- 1¼ cups (6¼ ounces) unbleached all-purpose flour
- 2 tablespoons dark brown sugar
- ½ teaspoon salt
- 8 tablespoons (1 stick) unsalted butter, cut into ¼-inch pieces and chilled
- 3–4 tablespoons ice water

### FILLING
- 8 tablespoons (1 stick) unsalted butter, cut into 1-inch pieces
- ¾ cup (5 ounces) packed dark brown sugar
- 1 teaspoon salt
- 3 large eggs
- ¾ cup dark corn syrup
- 1 tablespoon vanilla extract
- 2 tablespoons bourbon
- 2 cups whole pecans, toasted, cooled, and broken into small pieces

**1. FOR THE CRUST:** Process the flour, brown sugar, and salt in a food processor until combined. Add the butter and

pulse until the mixture resembles coarse cornmeal, about ten 1-second pulses. Turn the mixture into a medium bowl.

**2.** Sprinkle 3 tablespoons of the ice water over the mixture. Stir and press the dough together using a stiff rubber spatula until the dough sticks together. If the dough does not come together, stir in the remaining 1 tablespoon water until the dough forms large clumps and no dry flour remains. Turn the dough out onto the counter and flatten into a 4-inch disk. Wrap the disk in plastic wrap and refrigerate for at least 1 hour before rolling.

**3.** Remove the disk of dough from the refrigerator and following the photos on page 247, roll it out on a lightly floured surface or between 2 large sheets of parchment paper or plastic wrap to a 12-inch circle ⅛ inch thick. (If the dough becomes soft and/or sticky, return it to the refrigerator until firm.) Transfer the dough to a 9-inch pie plate. Working around the circumference, ease the dough into the plate by gently lifting the edge of the dough with one hand while pressing it into the plate bottom with the other hand. Trim and flute the edges; refrigerate until the dough is firm, about 30 minutes, then freeze for 20 minutes.

**4.** Meanwhile, adjust an oven rack to the middle position and heat the oven to 375 degrees. Following the photos, line the chilled dough-lined pie plate with a double layer of aluminum foil and fill with pie weights. Bake until the pie dough dries out, 20 to 25 minutes. Carefully remove the pie weights and foil and continue to bake until the crust is firmly set and lightly browned, 10 to 15 minutes. Transfer to a wire rack.

**5. FOR THE FILLING:** Lower the oven temperature to 275 degrees. Place the pie shell in the oven if not still warm.

**6.** Cook the butter, brown sugar, and salt together in a medium saucepan over medium heat until the sugar is melted and the butter is absorbed, about 2 minutes. Remove from the heat and whisk in the eggs, one at a time; whisk in the corn syrup, vanilla, and bourbon. Return the pan to medium heat and cook, stirring constantly, until the mixture is glossy and warm to the touch, about 4 minutes. (Do not overheat; remove the pan from the heat if the mixture starts to steam or bubble. The temperature should be about 130 degrees.) Remove the pan from the heat and stir in the pecans.

**7.** Pour the filling into the warm shell and bake until the center feels set yet soft, like gelatin, when gently pressed, 45 to 60 minutes. Transfer the pie to a wire rack to cool completely, at least 4 hours. Cut into wedges and serve. (The pie can also be warmed briefly in the oven before serving.)

**WHERE THINGS CAN GO WRONG:** Chopping the pecans with a knife will produce a fine dust that can cloud the resulting pie. Instead, use a rolling pin to gently break the pecans into ½-inch pieces. Also, be sure to remove the pie from the oven when the center is set but still wobbly; residual heat will finish cooking the filling and prevent it from becoming rubbery (a risk if the pie is overcooked).

**WHAT YOU CAN DO AHEAD OF TIME:** The pie can be wrapped tightly in plastic wrap and refrigerated for up to 1 day. Be sure to let the pie come to room temperature (or warm it briefly in the oven) before serving. The baked pie shell can be cooled, wrapped tightly in plastic wrap, and stored at room temperature for up to 1 day. The disk of dough can be wrapped tightly in plastic wrap and refrigerated for up to 2 days, or frozen for up to 1 month. Thaw frozen dough in the refrigerator. Before rolling, let the dough stand at room temperature for 15 minutes to soften.

## NOTES FROM THE TEST KITCHEN

### HOW TO BLIND BAKE A PIE CRUST

The crusts for many pies and tarts are baked before filling (this is called blind baking) so that they are golden brown, crisp, and flaky. Here are instructions for successful blind baking.

**1.** Line the chilled pie crust with a double layer of aluminum foil, covering the edges to prevent burning.

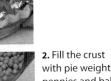

**2.** Fill the crust with pie weights or pennies and bake for 20 to 25 minutes.

**3.** After baking, carefully remove the pie weights and foil and either let the crust cool (for a partially baked crust) or continue to bake for 10 to 15 minutes (for a fully baked crust).

# CHOCOLATE TRUFFLE TART
SERVES 12 TO 14

**WHAT MAKES THIS A BEST RECIPE:** For a holiday party, it's hard to beat the impression a chocolate tart can make. And, as an added bonus, it serves a crowd; a thin sliver is satisfying. Many chocolate tart recipes require complicated steps and fine pastry skills to pull them off, or they lack sophistication, tasting and looking little better than a fudgy brownie. Not this one. We created a crisp, cookie-like European-style crust with a rich chocolatey flavor and deep color. (Many similar recipes use a plain crust and miss the opportunity to add more chocolate flavor to this tart.) And for the filling, we made a straightforward ganache—a blend of chocolate and heavy cream. Ganache recipes vary in their ratios of cream to chocolate. After numerous tests, we found that 1 part cream to 1½ parts chocolate, by weight, gave us the flavor and texture we were looking for. To further enhance the texture of the filling, making it both smoother and denser, we added a generous amount of butter. For flavor, a splash of cognac augmented the filling's deep chocolate notes, elevating this dessert to all-star status. Simple, smooth, and elegant—what more can you ask from a dessert? This tart is very rich and benefits from an accompaniment such as whipped cream, fresh berries, or both.

### CRUST
- 1 large egg yolk
- 2 tablespoons heavy cream
- ½ teaspoon vanilla extract
- 1¼ cups (6¼ ounces) unbleached all-purpose flour, plus more as needed
- ¾ cup (3 ounces) confectioners' sugar
- ¼ cup (¾ ounce) Dutch-processed cocoa powder
- ¼ teaspoon salt
- 10 tablespoons (1¼ sticks) unsalted butter, cut into ½-inch pieces and chilled

### FILLING
- 2 cups heavy cream
- 1½ pounds bittersweet chocolate, chopped

A creamy bittersweet chocolate ganache spiked with a shot of cognac makes this easy tart the star of the holiday dessert table.

- 12 tablespoons (1½ sticks) unsalted butter, at room temperature and cut into ½-inch pieces
- 2 tablespoons cognac

**1. FOR THE CRUST:** Whisk together the yolk, cream, and vanilla in a small bowl. Process the flour, sugar, cocoa, and salt in a food processor until combined. Add the butter and pulse until the mixture resembles coarse cornmeal, about twenty 1-second pulses. With the machine running, add the egg mixture and process until the dough comes together, about 12 seconds. Turn the dough out onto the counter and flatten into a 6-inch disk. Wrap the disk in plastic wrap and refrigerate for at least 1 hour before rolling.

**2.** Remove the disk of dough from the refrigerator and following the photos on page 247, roll it out on a lightly floured surface or between 2 lightly floured large sheets of parchment paper or plastic wrap (or piece 4 small sheets together to form 2 large sheets) to a 15-inch circle. (If the dough becomes soft and/or sticky, return it to the refrigerator until firm.) Transfer the dough to an 11-inch tart pan with a removable bottom. Working around the circumference, ease the dough into the pan by gently lifting the edge of the dough with one hand while pressing it into the pan bottom with the other hand. Press the dough against the fluted sides of pan, patching breaks or cracks if necessary. (If some sections of the edge are too thin, reinforce them by folding excess dough back on itself.) Run a rolling pin over the top of the tart pan to remove excess dough. Set the dough-lined tart pan on a baking sheet or a large plate and freeze for 30 minutes.

**3.** Meanwhile, adjust an oven rack to the middle position and heat the oven to 375 degrees. Set the chilled dough-lined tart pan on a baking sheet. Line the chilled dough-lined tart pan with a double layer of aluminum foil and fill with pie weights. Bake until the tart dough dries out and blisters, about 30 minutes. Carefully remove the pie weights and foil and continue to bake for an additional 5 minutes. Transfer the baking sheet with the tart shell to a wire rack and cool to room temperature, about 30 minutes.

**4. FOR THE FILLING:** Meanwhile, bring the cream to a simmer in a saucepan over medium-high heat. Pour the hot cream over the chocolate in a medium bowl and set aside for 1 minute. Using a whisk, slowly stir the chocolate and cream until smooth, being careful to avoid aerating the mixture. Slowly stir in the butter until combined. Stir in the cognac.

**5.** Pour the filling into the cooled tart shell. (The filling should reach just below the top of the tart shell. If the sides of the tart shell slumped a bit when baked, you will have a little extra filling.) Use an offset spatula to spread the filling to the sides of the shell and smooth the top. Refrigerate until firm, at least 2 hours. Cut into thin wedges and serve.

**WHERE THINGS CAN GO WRONG:** If you stir the chocolate mixture too much, you won't end up with a wonderful satiny ganache but rather a filling that has air bubbles throughout.

**WHAT YOU CAN DO AHEAD OF TIME:** The tart can be wrapped tightly in plastic wrap and refrigerated for up 2 days. The baked tart shell can be cooled, wrapped tightly in plastic wrap, and stored at room temperature for up to 1 day. The disk of dough can be wrapped tightly in plastic wrap and refrigerated for up to 2 days, or frozen for up to 1 month. Thaw frozen dough in the refrigerator. Before rolling, let the dough stand at room temperature for 15 minutes to soften.

## NOTES FROM THE TEST KITCHEN

### HOW TO FIT TART DOUGH INTO THE PAN

**1.** After rolling the dough out and wrapping it loosely around the rolling pin (see page 247), unroll the dough over an 11-inch tart pan with a removable bottom.

**2.** Lifting the edges of the dough, gently ease the dough into the pan.

**3.** Press the dough into the fluted sides of the pan and into the corners, forming a small seam.

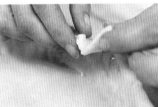

**4.** If any part of the edge is too thin, reinforce it by folding some of the excess dough that overhangs the tart pan back on itself.

**5.** Run the rolling pin over the top of the tart pan to remove any excess dough and make a clean edge.

**6.** The finished edge should be ¼ inch thick. If it is too thick, press some of the dough up over the edge of the pan and trim it away.

# FREE-FORM
# SUMMER FRUIT TART
### SERVES 6

**WHAT MAKES THIS A BEST RECIPE:** Here we created a free-form tart that tastes every bit as good as a hard-to-prepare pie, with a single layer of buttery, flaky pastry folded up around juicy summer fruit. Without the support of a pie plate, tender crusts are prone to leak juice, and this results in soggy bottoms. Therefore, our challenge was to create a sturdy crust to support the fruit. We used a high proportion of butter to flour for a crust with a great buttery flavor and tender texture, but to save the crust from frailty, we added sour cream and cornmeal. Once rolled out and filled with fruit, the dough was then easily lifted up and back over the fruit (the center of the tart remains exposed), which needed only the simple addition of sugar and a little butter.

### DOUGH

- 1 cup (5 ounces) unbleached all-purpose flour
- ¼ cup (1 ounce) fine-ground cornmeal
- 2 teaspoons sugar
- ½ teaspoon salt
- 7 tablespoons unsalted butter, cut into ½-inch pieces and chilled
- 2 tablespoons sour cream
- 2 tablespoons ice water

### FILLING

- 3 cups mixed berries (15 ounces), or pitted stone fruit, cut into ¼-inch slices
- 2–3 tablespoons sugar
- 2 tablespoons unsalted butter, cut into ¼-inch pieces
- 1 tablespoon water

**1. FOR THE DOUGH:** Process the flour, cornmeal, sugar, and salt in a food processor until combined. Add half of the butter and pulse until the butter is the size of small peas, about four 1-second pulses. Add the remaining butter and pulse until the butter is the size of small peas, about 4 pulses.

**2.** Mix the sour cream and water in a small bowl until combined. Add half of the sour cream mixture to the flour mixture; pulse for three 1-second pulses. Repeat with the remaining sour cream mixture until the dough just comes together, about five 1-second pulses. Turn the dough out onto the counter and flatten into a 6-inch disk. Wrap the disk in plastic wrap and refrigerate for at least 1 hour before rolling.

**3.** When ready to roll and bake the tart, adjust an oven rack to the middle position and heat the oven to 400 degrees. Remove the disk of dough from the refrigerator and following the photos on page 247, roll it out between 2 large sheets of parchment paper or plastic wrap to a 13-inch circle. (If the dough becomes soft and/or sticky, return it to the refrigerator until firm.) Slide the dough, still between the sheets of parchment paper, onto a baking sheet and refrigerate until firm, about 20 minutes.

**4. FOR THE FILLING:** Discard the top sheet of parchment paper. Following the photos, pile the fruit in the center of the dough, leaving a 2- to 3-inch border. Sprinkle 1 to 2 tablespoons of the sugar over the fruit and dot with the butter.

**5.** Fold the edges of the dough over the fruit. Brush the top of the tart with the water and sprinkle with the remaining 1 tablespoon sugar. Bake until the crust is golden brown and crisp and the fruit is bubbling, about 40 minutes. Transfer the baking sheet with the tart to a wire rack and cool for 10 minutes. Slide the tart off the baking sheet and cool on the rack until warm or room temperature before serving.

**WHAT YOU CAN DO AHEAD OF TIME:** This tart is best eaten on the day it is baked, but the disk of dough can be wrapped tightly in plastic wrap and refrigerated for up to 2 days, or frozen for up to 1 month. Thaw frozen dough in the refrigerator. Before rolling, let the dough stand at room temperature for 15 minutes to soften.

## NOTES FROM THE TEST KITCHEN

**SHAPING A FREE-FORM TART**

**1.** Place the fruit in the center of the rolled-out dough, leaving a 2- to 3-inch border. Sprinkle sugar over the fruit and dot with butter.

**2.** Fold the edges of the dough up over the filling, using the underlying parchment paper to help you lift and pleat the dough to fit snugly around the fruit.

# LEMON POUND CAKE

SERVES 8

**WHAT MAKES THIS A BEST RECIPE:** Pound cake has been around for a long time (it was popular in Colonial America), but that doesn't mean that most recipes for it are reliable. It often turns out heavy, leaden, and dry, when it should be rich, buttery, and moist. We found that the secrets to a great pound cake were pretty straightforward. We lightened the cake with a little baking powder, kept it moist and rich by adding sour cream, and pumped up the flavor with lots of lemon. Beating lemon zest with the sugar helped to release the flavorful oils in the zest, and lemon syrup (nothing more than lemon juice simmered with sugar) brushed over the cake once it emerged from the oven added additional lemony goodness. Last, we added more lemon zing by replacing the milk, typically used in the white glaze drizzled over the cooled cake, with lemon juice.

### CAKE

- 16 tablespoons (2 sticks) unsalted butter, softened but still cool, plus more for the pan
- 1¾ cups (8¾ ounces) unbleached all-purpose flour, plus more for the pan
- ½ teaspoon baking powder
- ½ teaspoon salt
- ¼ cup sour cream
- 1½ tablespoons fresh lemon juice
- 1½ tablespoons grated lemon zest
- 1 cup (7 ounces) plus 2 tablespoons granulated sugar
- 5 large eggs, at room temperature, beaten lightly

### SYRUP

- ¼ cup sugar
- ¼ cup fresh lemon juice from 2 lemons

### GLAZE

- ½ cup (2 ounces) confectioners' sugar, sifted
- 1 tablespoon fresh lemon juice

**1. FOR THE CAKE:** Adjust an oven rack to the middle position and heat the oven to 325 degrees. Grease a 9 by 5-inch loaf pan with butter; dust the pan with flour, then tap out the excess. Sift the flour, baking powder, and salt into a bowl. Stir the sour cream and lemon juice together in a second bowl.

**2.** Using your fingers, toss the zest and sugar together in a large bowl until the clumps are gone. Add the butter and beat with an electric mixer at medium-high speed until smooth and light, about 3 minutes. Scrape down the sides of the bowl. Add the beaten eggs in three additions, mixing until smooth and scraping down the bowl after each addition (mixture will begin to look curdled). With the mixer on low, add one-third of the flour mixture, followed by half of the sour cream mixture, scraping down the bowl as needed. Repeat, ending with the flour mixture. Scrape down the sides of the bowl, then mix on low until smooth, about 30 seconds. Use a rubber spatula to give the batter a final stir.

**3.** Pour the batter into the prepared loaf pan and smooth with a spatula. Gently tap the pan on the counter to release air bubbles. Bake until golden brown and a toothpick inserted into the center comes out with a few crumbs attached, 55 to 70 minutes.

**4. FOR THE SYRUP:** Meanwhile, stir the sugar and lemon juice together in a saucepan over medium-high heat until the sugar dissolves. Simmer for 2 minutes, remove from the heat, and set aside while the cake is baking.

**5.** Cool the cake in the pan on a wire rack for 10 minutes, then turn it out onto the rack.

**6.** Brush the top and sides of the still-warm cake with the syrup and cool completely, about 2 hours.

**7. FOR THE GLAZE:** Whisk the confectioners' sugar and lemon juice in a bowl until smooth. Spread the glaze over the cake, allowing some to drip down the sides. Let the glaze set for at least 15 minutes before serving.

**WHAT YOU CAN DO AHEAD OF TIME:** The test kitchen found this cake to be more moist the day after it was baked. The cake (brushed with the syrup and glazed) can be cooled completely, wrapped tightly in plastic wrap, and stored at room temperature for up to 5 days. It can also be frozen unglazed for up to 1 month. Brush the cake with the syrup, cool completely, and wrap tightly in plastic wrap. Thaw the cake, still wrapped, at room temperature, remove the plastic wrap, and proceed with glazing the cake as directed in step 7.

# NOTES FROM THE TEST KITCHEN

### ROOM TEMPERATURE IS THE RIGHT TEMPERATURE

Baking usually requires softened butter and room-temperature eggs and milk. Using those key ingredients at the correct temperature is vital to the success of your cakes. Softened butter creams easily and room-temperature eggs and milk are more readily incorporated into the batter than when they are cold. Here are some tips on knowing when your butter is properly softened and how to bring your eggs to room temperature quickly.

Properly softened butter should bend with little resistance, without cracking or breaking.

Properly softened butter should also give slightly when pressed but still hold its shape. If the butter is too soft, your cakes (or other baked goods) will be greasy and won't rise properly.

To bring eggs to room temperature quickly, place whole raw eggs in a bowl and cover them with hot (not boiling) tap water. Allow them to stand for about 10 minutes.

### YOU CAN DOUBLE IT

Since pound cake freezes so well and can be dressed up in so many ways, it's nice to have a loaf in the freezer. So while you're at it, you may as well bake two loaves. Just double all ingredients except the eggs, using 9 eggs (instead of 10). Cream the butter and sugar in step 2 for 6 minutes (rather than 3 minutes) and add the eggs in four additions (rather than three). Divide the batter between two buttered and floured loaf pans and bake as directed, rotating the pans halfway through the baking time.

# LIGHT CARROT CAKE
## WITH LIGHT CREAM CHEESE FROSTING
### SERVES 16

**WHAT MAKES THIS A BEST RECIPE:** A relic of the health food craze, carrot cake was once heralded for its use of vegetable oil in place of butter and of carrots as a natural sweetener. But with most carrot cakes tipping the scales at 500 calories and 31 grams of fat per slice, it was never really a healthy cake—until now. For *The Best Light Recipe,* we created a formula where the natural sweetness of the carrots takes center stage, and the cake is moist and rich, but not fatty. To save on fat grams, we reduced the amount of oil from 1½ cups to ½ cup. We also reduced the number of eggs from 5 to 3, and whipped air into them to keep the cake from being too dense and leaden. This cake is tasty with a dusting of confectioners' sugar, but we like it best with our Light Cream Cheese Frosting; we replaced the cream cheese and butter with Neufchâtel reduced-fat cheese and mixed it by hand to prevent it from becoming runny. Each slice (with frosting) has just 350 calories and 12.5 grams of fat.

### CAKE
- 2½ cups (12½ ounces) unbleached all-purpose flour
- 1¼ teaspoons baking powder
- 1 teaspoon baking soda
- 1¼ teaspoons ground cinnamon
- ½ teaspoon ground nutmeg
- ⅛ teaspoon ground cloves
- ½ teaspoon salt
- 3 large eggs
- 1 cup (7 ounces) packed light brown sugar
- 1 cup (7 ounces) granulated sugar
- ½ cup vegetable oil
- 1 pound carrots (about 6 medium), peeled and grated (about 3 cups)

### FROSTING
- 12 ounces Neufchâtel (⅓ less fat) cream cheese, softened but still cool
- 1 teaspoon vanilla extract
- 1½ cups (6 ounces) confectioners' sugar

For our Light Carrot Cake, we cut way back on the amount of oil, and reduced the number of eggs to create a moist, rich, but substantially lighter cake.

**1.** Adjust an oven rack to the middle position and heat the oven to 350 degrees. Lightly coat a 13 by 9-inch metal baking pan with vegetable oil spray, then line the bottom with parchment paper.

**2. FOR THE CAKE:** Whisk the flour, baking powder, baking soda, spices, and salt together in a medium bowl; set aside. With an electric mixer, beat the eggs and sugars in a medium bowl until thick and creamy, 1 to 3 minutes. Turn the mixer to low and slowly whip in the oil until thoroughly combined and emulsified, 30 to 60 seconds. Sift half of the flour mixture over the batter and gently mix in. Repeat once more with the remaining flour mixture and continue to whisk the batter gently until most of the lumps are gone (do not overmix). Using a rubber spatula, gently stir in the carrots.

**3.** Pour the batter into the prepared pan and bake until a toothpick inserted into the center comes out with a few moist crumbs attached, 35 to 40 minutes, rotating the pan halfway through baking (do not overbake). Cool the cake in the pan for 10 minutes, then invert the cake onto a wire rack and remove the parchment paper. Flip the cake right-side up, and cool completely on a wire rack, about 2 hours, before frosting.

**4. FOR THE FROSTING:** Mix the Neufchâtel and vanilla together in a large bowl with a rubber spatula. Add the confectioners' sugar and stir until thoroughly combined and smooth. Place the cake on a serving platter and spread the frosting evenly across the top of the cake with a spatula. Serve.

**WHERE THINGS CAN GO WRONG:** Your cake will not be as brown if you use a glass pan so be sure to use a metal cake pan which is better at conducting heat. Also, it is best to mix the frosting by hand—an electric mixer or food processor will yield a soupy frosting that it is thin and unspreadable.

**WHAT YOU CAN DO AHEAD OF TIME:** The unfrosted cake can be stored at room temperature, wrapped tightly in plastic wrap, for up to 2 days, or frozen, wrapped in an additional layer of foil, for up to 1 month. Thaw at room temperature for about 4 hours before frosting or serving.

## NOTES FROM THE TEST KITCHEN

### THE LOWDOWN ON CREAM CHEESE
The creamy texture and tangy flavor of cream cheese is welcome on bagels and in many baked goods, but at 5 grams of fat and 50 calories per tablespoon, we needed to explore the possibility of using its lowfat cousins. Here's what we found:

Fat-free cream cheese, with 15 calories per tablespoon, was awful across the board. It produced a rubbery, tacky cheesecake with a vinyl-like top, and a gummy frosting. Light cream cheese (with 2 grams of fat and 30 calories per tablespoon) makes soupy frosting, but is excellent for finishing pan sauces. And the cheesecake made with light cream cheese (in combination with yogurt cheese and lowfat cottage cheese) rivaled a traditional cheesecake, with its smooth and creamy texture and characteristically tangy flavor.

American Neufchâtel cheese is marketed as reduced-fat cream cheese, having one-third less fat than cream cheese. It is strikingly similar to regular cream cheese, but with 3 grams of fat and 35 calories per tablespoon it was a little too high in fat for most of our light recipes. Neufchâtel did, however, make great cream cheese frosting. Mixed by hand, the frosting had the consistency and flavor of its full-fat counterpart.

**FAT-FREE CREAM CHEESE**
Rubbery and gummy

**LIGHT CREAM CHEESE**
Excellent in cheesecake and pan sauces

**NEUFCHÂTEL CHEESE**
Great in cream cheese frosting

# CHOCOLATE-ORANGE ANGEL FOOD CAKE

### SERVES 12

**WHAT MAKES THIS A BEST RECIPE:** When we compiled the dessert chapter for *The Best Light Recipe*, we knew we'd want to include angel food cake along with a few twists on the classic recipe—since who wants angel food cake with strawberries every time? This chocolate-orange version was a hit in the test kitchen (and a far cry from those dense and chewy cakes that come from a mix). To give this cake its flavorful punch, we added finely grated bittersweet chocolate, which is an easy way to infuse the entire cake with serious chocolate flavor without adding a significant amount of fat. Add to that a little Grand Marnier and orange zest, and we had an angel food cake we could be proud to serve to guests.

| | |
|---|---|
| 1 | cup (4 ounces) cake flour |
| 1½ | cups (10½ ounces) sugar |
| 12 | large egg whites, at room temperature |
| 1 | teaspoon cream of tartar |
| ¼ | teaspoon salt |
| 1 | tablespoon Grand Marnier |
| 2 | teaspoons grated orange zest |
| ½ | teaspoon vanilla extract |
| 2 | ounces bittersweet chocolate, grated fine |

**1.** Adjust an oven rack to the lower-middle position and heat the oven to 325 degrees. Have ready an ungreased large tube pan (9-inch diameter, 16-cup capacity), preferably with a removable bottom. (If the pan bottom is not removable, line it with parchment paper or waxed paper.)

**2.** Whisk the flour and ¾ cup of the sugar in a small bowl; set aside. With an electric mixer, beat the egg whites on low speed until just broken up and foamy. Add the cream of tartar and salt and increase the speed to medium-high. Continue to beat, adding the remaining ¾ cup sugar, 1 tablespoon at a time, until all the sugar is added and the whites are shiny and form soft peaks. Beat in the Grand Marnier, zest, and vanilla until just blended.

**3.** Sift the flour mixture over the whites, about ¼ cup at a time, and gently fold it in using a large rubber spatula. Gently fold the grated chocolate into the batter. Carefully scrape

## NOTES FROM THE TEST KITCHEN

### THE IMPORTANCE OF BEATING EGG WHITES

This recipe requires that the whites be beaten to soft peaks (so that they have the structure to properly support the batter) while other recipes require that you beat whites until stiff peaks form. For the best results, use room-temperature eggs and make sure that your bowl, beater, and scraper are clean and free of grease. For perfectly whipped whites, start with a low mixer speed and increase the mixer speed and add the cream of tartar and a little sugar once the whites have developed some structure and turned foamy. Whipped egg whites can be finicky and require a keen eye and close attention; when they are beaten to soft peaks, they will droop slightly downward from the tip of the whisk or beater; stiff peaks will stand tall.

**SOFT PEAKS**          **STIFF PEAKS**

### LIQUID EGG WHITES: DO THEY WORK?

When making recipes that call for only egg whites, we often feel guilty throwing away the yolks. To see if we could avoid being wasteful, we purchased three widely available brands of pasteurized liquid egg whites—Papetti Foods All Whites, Eggology 100% Egg Whites, and Egg Beaters Egg Whites—and tested them against regular egg whites in four recipes: angel food cake, baked meringues, Italian meringue frosting, and scrambled eggs whites.

In all four applications, the Papetti Foods and Egg Beaters products failed to perform as well as Eggology. The Papetti Foods All Whites almost always deflated into a soupy mess after other ingredients were whipped or folded in, rendering any application except the scrambled egg whites an abject failure. The Egg Beaters Egg Whites produced decent meringues but when scrambled had a slightly chemical aftertaste.

Overall, Eggology was the closest to real egg whites. The meringues and scrambled eggs whites were identical to the real thing. The frosting was slightly less fluffy and more sticky and slick than the original but still acceptable. The angel food cake, however, failed miserably. Although only about ½ inch shy of the 3-inch-high cake made with fresh whites, the cake made with Eggology had a sunken center, sizeable slimy air pockets throughout, and a dense, gummy bottom half.

**EGGOLOGY 100% EGG WHITES**
Closest to real egg whites, but don't try them in angel food cake

the batter into the pan and smooth the top with the spatula. Give the pan a couple of raps on the counter to release any large air bubbles. Bake until golden brown and the top springs back when pressed firmly, 55 to 60 minutes.

**4.** If the cake pan has prongs around the rim for elevating the cake, invert the pan onto them. If the pan does not have prongs, invert the pan onto the neck of a bottle or funnel (see the photo). Let the cake cool completely upside down, 2 to 3 hours.

**5.** To unmold, run a knife around the edge of the cake pan, being careful not to separate the golden crust from the cake. Loosen the cake from the center tube using a wire cake tester or skewer. Slide the cake with the removable cake bottom out of the pan. Run a knife between the cake and the pan bottom to loosen, then gently flip the cake out onto a platter, bottom side facing up (the bottom is the presentation side). (If the pan bottom is not removable, loosen the cake from the edges and center tube as described, then flip it out onto a platter and remove the parchment paper.) Cut slices by sawing gently with a large, serrated knife. This cake tastes best when served the same day it is made.

**WHERE THINGS CAN GO WRONG:** Angel food cakes rely on beaten egg whites for their delicate, airy structure and leavening, so it is critical to separate the eggs properly, and beat the whites correctly (see page 259). Also, if you don't sift the flour mixture into the batter, it can clump and won't dissolve. The result? You'll be left with pockets of flour in your cake, the batter will be runny, and the cake will turn out flat and rubbery.

**WHAT YOU CAN DO AHEAD OF TIME:** The cake can be cooled completely, wrapped tightly in plastic wrap, and stored at room temperature for up to 3 days.

## NOTES FROM THE TEST KITCHEN

### USE A BOTTLE TO COOL THE CAKE
Immediately after removing the cake from the oven, insert the neck of a heavy-bottomed bottle (like a wine bottle) or a standard kitchen funnel into the tube and invert the pan so that it is hanging upside down. Let the cake cool like this for 2 to 3 hours before removing from the pan and serving.

# INDIVIDUAL BLUEBERRY-PECAN BUCKLES
### SERVES 6

**WHAT MAKES THIS A BEST RECIPE:** We were inspired to develop this surprisingly easy recipe by an editor clamoring for a truly simple but party-worthy fruit dessert that made the most of the summer's fresh blueberries. Nothing could be simpler than this rich and nutty batter, made entirely in the food processor. When the buckles are baked, the berries, which are just scattered over the top, sink into the buttery cake, but remain intact. We like to serve these warm in their ramekins, but you can also run a paring knife around the edges of the ramekins to loosen the buckles and flip them out onto individual plates (flip them right-side up again before serving). For an added treat, serve with Crème Anglaise (page 270), vanilla ice cream, or whipped cream.

- ¾ cup (5¼ ounces) sugar
- ¼ cup pecans
- ¼ teaspoon salt
- 4 tablespoons (½ stick) unsalted butter, at room temperature
- 2 large eggs
- 1 teaspoon vanilla extract
- ½ cup (2½ ounces) unbleached all-purpose flour
- ½ teaspoon baking powder
- 1½ cups fresh blueberries (7½ ounces)

**1.** Adjust an oven rack to the middle position and heat the oven to 375 degrees. Lightly coat six 6-ounce ramekins with vegetable oil spray and place on a rimmed baking sheet.

**2.** Process the sugar, pecans, and salt in a food processor until finely ground, 10 to 15 seconds. Add the butter, eggs, and vanilla and process until smooth, about 5 seconds. Add the flour and baking powder and pulse until just incorporated, about 5 pulses. Divide the batter among the prepared ramekins. Sprinkle the berries over the batter (the berries will sink into the batter during baking).

**3.** Bake until golden brown and the buckles begin to pull away from the sides of the ramekins, 25 to 30 minutes. Let cool on a wire rack for about 10 minutes before serving.

**WHAT YOU CAN DO AHEAD OF TIME:** The baked buckles can be cooled completely, covered with plastic wrap, and stored at room temperature for up to 6 hours. Serve at room temperature or microwave until warm before serving, checking the progress every 30 seconds.

## NOTES FROM THE TEST KITCHEN

### USE FROZEN BERRIES

You can substitute 2 cups frozen blueberries, thawed, drained, and patted dry, for the fresh berries. **Wyman's Frozen Wild Blueberries** are our favorite, with intense color and flavor, a pleasing balance of sweetness and tanginess, and a clean, fresh berry finish.

### AN EASY WAY TO WASH BERRIES

While it is important to wash berries to rid them of any dirt and debris, they can break under the pressure of the water or drying. We figured out a two-step method that treats berries gently.

**1.** Place the berries in a colander and place under running water for about 30 seconds.

**2.** Line a salad spinner with a couple of layers of paper towels and carefully disperse the berries. Spin until the berries are dry, about 20 spins.

# PECAN–SOUR CREAM COFFEECAKE
## WITH TROPICAL ORANGE GLAZE
### SERVES 12 TO 16

**WHAT MAKES THIS A BEST RECIPE:** Most coffeecakes are not much more than fluffy yellow cake lurking beneath a buttery crumb topping, or leaden pound cake with a few measly nuts strewn throughout. We have created the ultimate coffeecake—moist and rich with an intensely nutty flavor and an array of flavored glaze options. Instead of using plain old sugar to sweeten the cake, we added complexity in the form of maple syrup. The syrup was the perfect complement to the pecans, which pull double duty as an ingredient in both the cake (finely ground and added with the flour) and the swirl of sweet streusel (paired with a little brown sugar, flour, and cinnamon). To further intensify the flavor of the cake and the streusel, we toasted the nuts (a step omitted in most other coffeecake recipes). And for the perfect finishing touch, we created orange, maple, coffee, and cinnamon glazes.

### STREUSEL

- ½ cup pecans, toasted, cooled, and ground fine
- 3 tablespoons dark brown sugar
- 1 tablespoon unbleached all-purpose flour
- 1 teaspoon ground cinnamon

### CAKE

- 16 tablespoons (2 sticks) unsalted butter, at room temperature and cut into ½-inch pieces, plus more for the pan
- 6 large eggs
- 1¾ cups sour cream
- ¼ cup maple syrup
- 1½ tablespoons vanilla extract
- 3 cups (15 ounces) unbleached all-purpose flour
- ½ cup pecans, toasted, cooled, and ground fine
- 1¼ cups (8¾ ounces) granulated sugar
- 1½ tablespoons baking powder
- 1¼ teaspoons baking soda
- 1 teaspoon salt

GLAZE

  1  cup (4 ounces) confectioners' sugar
  2  tablespoons orange juice
  1  teaspoon grated orange zest

**1. FOR THE STREUSEL:** Combine the pecans, brown sugar, flour, and cinnamon in a small bowl and set aside.

**2. FOR THE CAKE:** Adjust an oven rack to the lowest position and heat the oven to 350 degrees. Grease a 12-cup nonstick Bundt pan. Whisk the eggs, sour cream, maple syrup, and vanilla together in a medium bowl.

**3.** With an electric mixer, mix the flour, pecans, granulated sugar, baking powder, baking soda, and salt on low speed in a large bowl until combined. Add the butter and half of the egg mixture and beat on low speed, taking care not to splatter the ingredients, until the mixture starts to come together, about 15 seconds. Scrape down the sides of the bowl, add the remaining egg mixture, and beat on medium speed until the batter is light and fluffy, about 2 minutes (scrape down the sides of the bowl again after 1 minute).

**4.** Pour 5 cups of the batter into the prepared Bundt pan, using a rubber spatula to smooth out the surface. Sprinkle the streusel evenly over the batter and then cover with the remaining batter, spreading it evenly.

**5.** Bake until a skewer inserted into the middle comes out with a few crumbs attached, about 60 minutes. Cool the cake in the pan on a wire rack for 30 minutes, then invert onto the rack to cool completely before glazing, about 1 hour.

**6. FOR THE GLAZE:** Whisk the confectioners' sugar, orange juice, and zest together in a medium bowl. Using a fork or whisk, drizzle the glaze over the top and sides of the cake. Serve.

**WHERE THINGS CAN GO WRONG:** Because some nuts are added directly to the cake batter, you must grind them very finely, but do not overprocess them either, or they will form a paste and clump together. Use a food processor to grind the toasted and cooled nuts until they are sandy.

**WHAT YOU CAN DO AHEAD OF TIME:** The cake can be cooled completely (unglazed), wrapped tightly in plastic wrap, and stored at room temperature for up to 3 days, or frozen for up to 1 month. Thaw the cake, still wrapped, at room temperature, then remove the plastic wrap and glaze.

## NOTES FROM THE TEST KITCHEN

### ALL ABOUT NUTS
Toasting nuts helps release their essential oils, bringing out their full flavor and aroma. Toast nuts in a skillet (without any oil) over medium heat, shaking the pan occasionally to prevent scorching, until they begin to darken slightly in color, generally 3 to 5 minutes.

### DRESSING UP COFFEECAKE WITH EASY GLAZES
This coffeecake is rich enough to eat as is, but it looks and tastes even better with a drizzle of sweet glaze running down its sides. Here are some other easy glazes to try:
**MUST BE MAPLE GLAZE:** Whisk together 1 cup confectioners' sugar, 2 tablespoons milk, and 1 tablespoon maple syrup.
**JAVA JOLT GLAZE:** Whisk together 1 cup confectioners' sugar and 1 teaspoon instant espresso or coffee dissolved in 2 tablespoons milk.
**CINNAMON TOAST GLAZE:** Whisk together 1 cup confectioners' sugar, 2 tablespoons milk, and ½ teaspoon ground cinnamon.

### A TIP FOR TESTING FOR DONENESS
Determining when a cake is done is not easy. Common sense will tell you that your cake is not fully baked when a skewer (or toothpick) comes out with raw batter clinging to it. On the other hand, a completely clean skewer signifies an overdone cake. As a rule of thumb, we pull our cakes out of the oven when there are just a few crumbs still clinging to the skewer. The carryover heat will continue to bake the cakes during the time they rest in the pans before being turned out to cool. Also, we found it best to use a wooden skewer or toothpick, rather than a metal cake tester, because crumbs cling better to wood.

**UNDERDONE.** When your skewer comes out of the cake with streaks of wet batter, your cake is underdone.

**PERFECTLY DONE.** When your skewer comes out of the cake with just a few crumbs attached, your cake is perfectly done.

# OLD-FASHIONED CHOCOLATE LAYER CAKE

SERVES 10 TO 12

**WHAT MAKES THIS A BEST RECIPE:** While most everything has been super-sized in recent years, chocolate cakes have moved in the opposite direction, becoming denser, richer, and squatter. We were inspired to create an old-fashioned chocolate cake, one that reminded us of childhood birthdays—the tall, sweet, chocolatey cakes our mothers set before us once a year. The secret to creating a moist cake with deep, dark chocolate flavor was to mix melted unsweetened chocolate together with cocoa powder and hot water, a mixture called a chocolate "pudding" in many older cookbooks. Buttermilk, though not traditional, further contributed to the cake's moistness and added a welcome tang. We then created a silky and billowy frosting with good chocolate flavor. The key was to combine melted butter with melted chocolate and cold heavy cream, and then cool the mixture to 70 degrees before whipping it into a light and fluffy frosting to adorn our cake.

## CAKE

- 12 tablespoons (1½ sticks) unsalted butter, very soft, plus more for the pans
- 1¾ cups (8¾ ounces) unbleached all-purpose flour, plus more for the pans
- 4 ounces unsweetened chocolate, chopped
- ¼ cup (¾ ounce) Dutch-processed cocoa powder
- ½ cup hot water
- 1¾ cups (12¼ ounces) sugar
- 1½ teaspoons baking soda
- 1 teaspoon salt
- 1 cup buttermilk
- 2 teaspoons vanilla extract
- 4 large eggs, plus 2 large egg yolks

## FROSTING

- 16 ounces semisweet chocolate, chopped
- 8 tablespoons (1 stick) unsalted butter
- ⅓ cup (2⅓ ounces) sugar
- 2 tablespoons light corn syrup
- 2 teaspoons vanilla extract

- ¼ teaspoon salt
- 1¼ cups chilled heavy cream

**1. FOR THE CAKE:** Adjust an oven rack to the middle position and heat the oven to 350 degrees. Grease and flour two 9-inch-round by 2-inch-high cake pans, knocking out the excess flour. Combine the chocolate, cocoa, and hot water in a medium heatproof bowl; set the bowl over a saucepan containing 1 inch of simmering water and stir with a rubber spatula until the chocolate is melted, about 2 minutes. Add ½ cup of the sugar to the chocolate mixture and stir until thick and glossy, 1 to 2 minutes. Remove the bowl from the heat and set aside to cool.

**2.** Whisk the flour, baking soda, and salt in a medium bowl. Combine the buttermilk and vanilla in a small bowl. With an electric mixer, beat the eggs and yolks on medium-low speed in a large bowl until combined, about 10 seconds. Add the remaining 1¼ cups sugar, increase the speed to high, and beat until fluffy and lightened in color, 2 to 3 minutes. Add the cooled chocolate mixture to the egg-sugar mixture and mix on medium speed until thoroughly incorporated, 30 to 45 seconds. Scrape down the sides of the bowl as needed. Add the butter one tablespoon at a time, mixing about 10 seconds after each addition. Add about one-third of the flour mixture followed by half of the buttermilk mixture, mixing until incorporated after each addition (about 15 seconds). Repeat using half of the remaining flour mixture and all of the remaining buttermilk mixture (the batter may appear separated). Scrape down the sides of the bowl and add the remaining flour mixture; mix at medium-low speed until the batter is thoroughly combined, about 15 seconds. Fold the batter once or twice with a rubber spatula to incorporate any remaining flour. Divide the batter evenly between the prepared cake pans; smooth the batter to the edges of the pan with a spatula.

**3.** Bake until a toothpick inserted into the center comes out with a few crumbs attached, 25 to 30 minutes. Cool the cakes in the pans for 15 minutes, then invert onto a wire rack. Cool the cakes to room temperature before frosting, 45 to 60 minutes.

**4. FOR THE FROSTING:** Melt the chocolate in the microwave (see page 267) and stir until smooth. Meanwhile, melt the butter in a small saucepan over medium-low heat. Increase the heat to medium; add the sugar, corn syrup, vanilla, and salt and stir with a heatproof rubber spatula until the sugar is dissolved, 4 to 5 minutes. Combine the melted chocolate, butter mixture, and cream in a large bowl.

**5.** Place the bowl over an ice bath and stir the mixture constantly with a rubber spatula until the frosting is thick and just beginning to harden against the sides of the bowl, 1 to 2 minutes (the frosting should be 70 degrees). With an electric mixer, beat the mixture on medium-high speed until the frosting is light and fluffy, 1 to 2 minutes. Stir with a rubber spatula until completely smooth.

**6. TO FROST THE CAKE:** Place one cake layer on a cake plate or cardboard round. Spread 1½ cups of the frosting evenly across the top of the cake with a spatula. Place the second cake layer on top, then spread the remaining frosting evenly over the top and sides of the cake. Serve.

**WHERE THINGS CAN GO WRONG:** Making this frosting isn't hard but it is a little tricky. Cool it to exactly 70 degrees otherwise it will not whip properly, or it will break when whipped. For best results, don't make the frosting until the cakes are cooled, and use the frosting as soon as it is ready. If the frosting gets too cold it will become stiff and difficult to spread. When frosting the cake, wrap the bowl with a towel soaked in hot water and mix on low speed until the frosting appears creamy and smooth.

**WHAT YOU CAN DO AHEAD OF TIME:** The cakes can be cooled completely (unfrosted), wrapped tightly in plastic wrap, and frozen for up to 1 month. Thaw the cakes, still wrapped, at room temperature, then remove the plastic wrap and frost.

## NOTES FROM THE TEST KITCHEN

### GETTING THE FROSTING JUST RIGHT
The frostings below were made with exactly the same ingredients. The only difference was how soon the mixture was removed from the ice bath and whipped.

**STILL TOO WARM**
At 75 degrees, the frosting won't set up properly once whipped.

**JUST RIGHT**
At 70 degrees, the frosting whips up to a billowy, creamy consistency.

**TOO COOL**
At 65 degrees, the mixture has cooled too much and seizes once whipped.

## GREAT DISCOVERIES
### THE "PUDDING" MAKES IT PERFECT

After making nearly 130 chocolate layer cakes, trying just about every technique from traditional creaming to reverse creaming to the genoise method of ribboning the eggs, I had come very close to our ideal cake. Yet, somehow I hadn't come far enough. How, I wondered, could I infuse even more chocolate flavor and boost the moistness of the crumb? Recalling some turn-of-the-century cookbooks I had read through at the start of this marathon baking project, I realized there was one thing I had overlooked—the mysterious "pudding" that many of them added to the batter.

This wasn't pudding in the classic sense (chocolate, milk, eggs, sugar, cornstarch) but a simpler concoction of chocolate, water, and sugar. Probably taken up to keep the chocolate from burning, this technique was popular in the early 1900s. I found recipes using this technique in *The Settlement Cookbook* (1901)—one of the most important American cookbooks of its era—and in the first edition of *Joy of Cooking* (1931). Although I could find few modern references to this method, I was reminded of the supermarket cake mixes that include powdered "pudding" for extra moisture. I'd always assumed this was just a gimmick, but maybe these cake-mix makers were onto something.

So following the method described in these century-old books, I melted the unsweetened chocolate and cocoa powder in hot water in a double boiler, then stirred in sugar until it dissolved. Sure enough, when added to my batter, this "pudding" delivered the moistest chocolate cake yet, with a pronounced yet subtle chocolate flavor and a rich brown color. This was the cake I had been searching for!

What was going on? Further research revealed that as soon as I dissolved the sugar in the pudding mixture, the sugar molecules bonded tightly with the water molecules, leaving the flavorful cocoa solids free to dissolve in the cocoa butter (the fat)—a better medium than water for conveying chocolate flavor. (Chocolate flavor molecules are more soluble in fat than in water.) Additionally, when the sugar is dissolved in the pudding mixture, it bonds with the water and reduces the amount of evaporation that occurs during baking. This translates to a moister cake. So a nearly forgotten technique proved to be the secret to a great old-fashioned chocolate cake. Skip the pudding and you'll have a cake that's diminished in chocolate flavor.

DAVID PAZMIÑO | TEST COOK, COOK'S ILLUSTRATED

# CHOCOLATE 101

## CHOCOLATE BASICS

Chocolate liquor, a dark, pasty liquid made by grinding the nibs extracted from dried, fermented, roasted cacao beans, is pure, unsweetened chocolate, the base ingredient for all other processed chocolates. About 55 percent of chocolate liquor is cocoa butter, a natural fat responsible for chocolate's unique texture. Its melting point is close to body temperature, which explains why chocolate melts so smoothly in your mouth but stays solid and shelf-stable at room temperature. Suspended in the cocoa butter are particles of ground cocoa solids, which carry the chocolate flavor.

## UNSWEETENED CHOCOLATE

**WHAT IT IS:** Pure chocolate liquor that has been cooled and formed into bars.
**COOKING TIP:** Because most unsweetened chocolates are starchy and unrefined, unsweetened chocolate is the traditional choice for recipes in which a bold chocolate flavor is more important than a smooth texture (think brownies).
**SUBSTITUTION:** Replace 1 ounce unsweetened chocolate with 3 tablespoons cocoa powder plus 1 tablespoon butter or oil.
**CAUTION:** This substitution is best for small quantity substitutions. A pan of fudgy brownies made with cocoa powder and butter will usually turn out cakelike and dry.

**TEST KITCHEN FAVORITE**
★ SCHARFFEN BERGER Unsweetened Chocolate, $11 for 9.7 ounces

## COCOA POWDER

**WHAT IT IS:** Chocolate liquor fed through a press to remove all but 10 to 24 percent of the cocoa butter. To counter the harsh, acidic flavor of natural cocoa, the powder is sometimes treated with an alkaline solution, or "Dutched." Cookbooks often claim that Dutching "mellows" chocolate flavor, but our tasters disagreed. Without the distraction of natural cocoa's harsh acidity, the more subtle, complex chocolate flavors came to the fore. We think Dutched cocoa tastes best, although it is interchangeable with natural cocoa.
**COOKING TIP:** Cocoa powder contributes a lot of chocolate flavor with little additional fat, making it perfect for hot beverages or recipes that already contain plenty of butter, such as cakes and cookies. In the test kitchen, we often "bloom" cocoa powder in a hot liquid such as water or coffee. This dissolves the remaining cocoa butter and disperses water-soluble flavor compounds. The result? A deeper, stronger chocolate flavor.
**SUBSTITUTION:** None. Chocolates have too much fat to take the place of cocoa.

**TEST KITCHEN FAVORITE**
★ CALLEBAUT, $20 for 2.2 pounds (mail order)
**BEST SUPERMARKET BRAND:** DROSTE Cocoa, $5.49 for 8.8 ounces

## SWEET CHOCOLATE

**WHAT IT IS:** Think milk chocolate without the milk. Also called sweet dark chocolate, it is just that—extremely sweet. While it must contain at least 15 percent chocolate liquor, it is often more than 60 percent sugar. Sweet chocolate is sold by the Baker's company as German's Sweet Chocolate Bar.
**COOKING TIP:** We have little use for the stuff, even in our German Chocolate Cake recipe.

## WHITE CHOCOLATE

**WHAT IT IS:** Technically not chocolate because it contains no cocoa solids. To meet government standards for "white chocolate," this product must contain at least 20 percent cocoa butter, which is usually de-odorized to remove any naturally occurring flavors that might overwhelm white chocolate's mild flavors of milk, sugar, and vanilla.

**TEST KITCHEN FAVORITE**
★ CALLEBAUT, $8 for 1 pound

## WHITE CHOCOLATE CHIPS

**WHAT IT IS:** Many "white chips" contain palm oil in addition to (or instead of) cocoa butter and do not qualify as "white chocolate." We prefer the brands with the most fat, be it cocoa butter or palm oil, for their softer texture, especially in cookies or brownies eaten straight from the oven.

**TEST KITCHEN FAVORITE**
★ GUITTARD Choc-Au-Lait White Chips, $2.79 for 12 ounces

## MILK CHOCOLATE

**WHAT IT IS:** Candy bar chocolate. Milk chocolate must contain at least 10 percent chocolate liquor and 12 percent milk solids.
**COOKING TIP:** Because of its relatively weak chocolate flavor (milk chocolate is usually more than 50 percent sugar), it's best for nibbling, not baking.

**TEST KITCHEN FAVORITE**
★ PERUGINA Milk Chocolate, $2.59 for 4 ounces

## CHOCOLATE CHIPS

**WHAT IT IS:** Real semisweet or bittersweet chocolate, only with a slightly lower fat content (about 27 percent), which improves the chips' stability.
**COOKING TIP:** While we don't recommend using chips in chocolate sauces or puddings, you can use them instead of bittersweet or semisweet chocolate in a simple brownie recipe.
**SUBSTITUTION:** Chopped up bar chocolate (for cookies).

## BITTERSWEET/SEMISWEET CHOCOLATE

**WHAT IT IS:** The government makes no distinction between "bittersweet" and "semisweet" chocolates. Both must contain at least 35 percent chocolate liquor, though most contain closer to 50 percent and many "high-percentage" chocolates have 70 percent chocolate liquor or more. If comparing chocolates made by the same company, it is fairly safe to assume that the bittersweet variety contains more chocolate liquor than the semisweet; otherwise, the terms are of little value.
**COOKING TIPS:** Use for sauces, frostings, custards, and icings. For cooking, we preferred the chocolates that were proportionally higher in sugar. **Ghirardelli Bittersweet,** our test kitchen favorite, is 44 percent sugar, while most of the high-percentage entrants in our tasting were 30 to 35 percent sugar.
**SUBSTITUTION:** Replace 1 ounce bittersweet or semisweet chocolate with ⅔ ounce unsweetened chocolate plus 2 teaspoons granulated sugar.
CAUTION: Will not provide the same smooth creamy texture.

# WORKING WITH CHOCOLATE

## CHOPPING CHOCOLATE

**A.** Hold a large knife at a 45-degree angle to one of the corners and bear down evenly. After cutting about an inch from the corner, repeat with the other corners.

**B.** Alternatively, use a sharp two-tined meat fork to break the chocolate into smaller pieces.

## MELTING CHOCOLATE

**A. DOUBLE BOILER:** Place the chopped chocolate in a heatproof bowl set over a pot of barely simmering water. Stir occasionally.

**B. MICROWAVE:** Microwave chopped chocolate at 50 percent power for 2 minutes. Stir chocolate and continue heating until melted, stirring once every additional minute. If melting butter with chocolate, add the butter at the 2-minute mark when stirring the chocolate.

## DECORATING WITH CHOCOLATE

To create chocolate curls for cake decorating, scrape a block of chocolate with a sharp paring knife, anchoring the block carefully with your other hand. Pick up the shavings with a toothpick or tweezers.

To write with chocolate, put chopped semisweet or bittersweet chocolate in a zipper-lock bag and melt, either in a microwave or by submerging in hot water. Snip off a tiny piece from one corner. Holding the bag in one hand, gently squeeze out the chocolate as you write.

## STORING CHOCOLATE

Never store chocolate in the refrigerator or freezer, as cocoa butter can easily pick up off flavors from other foods. If chocolate is exposed to rapid changes in humidity or temperature. sugar or fat may dissolve and migrate, discoloring the surface. This cosmetic condition, known as *bloom,* is not harmful—bloomed chocolate is safe to eat and cook with. To extend the life of chocolate, wrap it tightly in plastic wrap and store it in a cool, dry place. Milk and white chocolates should last for six months to a year; dark chocolates will last for several years.

# TIPSY SQUIRE

SERVES 10 TO 12

**WHAT MAKES THIS A BEST RECIPE:** Trifle, that familiar tower of cake, cream, custard, and fruit, is quite the looker on the holiday buffet, but beneath that fragile facade is usually soggy cake, grainy custard, and fruit strewn about helter-skelter. This version, with its origins in the South, is different. The simple secret to our recipe: stale sponge cake. It produced a dessert with distinct components, whereas most trifles that we tried, made with fresh cake, turned into a spongy, gloppy mess. It's not worth making your own sponge cakes for this recipe—most bakeries sell plain sponge cake that works perfectly here. To stale the cakes, leave them uncovered on the counter overnight or place them on a wire rack over a baking sheet in a 300-degree oven for 3 hours.

### CUSTARD

 2 cups heavy cream
 ½ cup (3½ ounces) sugar
   Pinch salt
 5 large egg yolks
 3 tablespoons cornstarch
 4 tablespoons (½ stick) cold unsalted butter, cut into 4 pieces
1½ teaspoons vanilla extract

### TRIFLE

 2 (8-inch) round stale store-bought sponge cakes (each about 1½ inches thick)
1½ cups cream sherry
 1 cup seedless raspberry jam
 2 cups heavy cream
40 small almond macaroons or amaretti cookies
 1 cup fresh raspberries (5 ounces)

**1. FOR THE CUSTARD:** Heat the cream, 6 tablespoons of the sugar, and salt in a heavy saucepan over medium heat until simmering, stirring occasionally to dissolve the sugar. Meanwhile, whisk the egg yolks in a medium bowl until thoroughly combined. Whisk in the remaining 2 tablespoons sugar until the sugar begins to dissolve. Whisk in the cornstarch until the mixture is pale yellow and thick, about 30 seconds.

**2.** When the cream mixture reaches a full simmer, gradually whisk half of it into the yolk mixture to temper. Return the mixture to the saucepan, scraping down the bowl with a rubber spatula; return to a simmer over medium heat, whisking constantly, until 3 or 4 bubbles burst on the surface and the mixture is thickened, about 1 minute. Off the heat, whisk in the butter and vanilla. Transfer the mixture to a bowl, press plastic wrap flush against the surface, and refrigerate until set, at least 3 hours (or up to 2 days).

**3. FOR THE TRIFLE:** Slice each cake round in half horizontally. Brush each cut side of one cake with ¼ cup of the sherry, then spread with ¼ cup of the jam. Stack the 2 cut sides together (resulting in a jam sandwich). Repeat with the second cake to make a second jam sandwich. Cut each cake into 5 long slices, then cut 5 more slices crosswise. (Reserve the small jam cakes for nibbling; you will need 30 to 40 of the larger jam cakes for step 5.)

**4.** With an electric mixer, beat the cream and ¼ cup of the sherry on medium-high speed to soft peaks. Reduce the speed to low, gradually add the custard, and mix well, about 1 minute. Toss the macaroons with the remaining ¼ cup sherry in a large bowl.

**5. TO ASSEMBLE:** Arrange 12 to 14 (depending on the size) macaroons in a single layer to cover the bottom of a 3-quart trifle bowl. Spoon 2 cups of the custard mixture evenly over the macaroons. Arrange 15 to 20 jam cakes in a single layer on the custard. Top with 2 cups of the custard mixture. Repeat the layering of cookies, custard mixture, jam cakes, and the custard mixture once more. Arrange remaining 12 to 16 macaroons in a circle midway between the rim of the bowl and the center of the trifle, so that they stick up slightly like a crown. Cover tightly with plastic wrap and refrigerate at least 12 hours. When ready to serve, pile the raspberries inside the circle of macaroons.

**WHERE THINGS CAN GO WRONG:** The success of this dessert depends on getting the consistency of the custard just right (so don't over- or undercook it or it will either be too runny or will curdle) and using stale sponge cake (if it is too fresh, it will disintegrate).

**WHAT YOU CAN DO AHEAD OF TIME:** This trifle actually improves in flavor and consistency after an overnight stay in the fridge. Store the fully assembled trifle, wrapped tightly in plastic wrap, in the refrigerator for up to 2 days.

# INDIVIDUAL STICKY TOFFEE PUDDING CAKES
## WITH CRÈME ANGLAISE
### SERVES 8

**WHAT MAKES THIS A BEST RECIPE:** Sticky toffee pudding cake is a member of the pudding family, a hodgepodge of steamed and baked desserts, that sport such colorful names as "cabinet pudding," "spotted dick," and "roly-poly." Most "pudds" haven't traveled far beyond Britain's shores, but sticky toffee pudding is an exception. After looking at a slew of recipes, we realized that there was nothing complicated about this pudding cake; no separated eggs, sifted flour or whipped anything. It is a simple batter of flour, butter, sweetener, and eggs to which dates are added. At its best, it's a moist cake, laced with dates, richly flavored with brown sugar, and served afloat a bed of crème anglaise. Unlike most versions that have a dense texture and unapologetic sweetness, this recipe packs a full date flavor, has a tolerable sweetness level, and a moist, tender crumb. Our secret was to first soak some of the dates to soften their skins, then process the remaining dates with brown sugar. To keep the cake light, we used a combination of baking soda and baking powder. For the toffee, we made a light-tasting, smooth sauce and added a splash of rum, a not uncommon flavoring, which cut through the sticky richness. While sticky toffee pudding is traditionally served with crème anglaise, vanilla ice cream also serves as a suitable foil to its sweetness.

### CRÈME ANGLAISE
½    vanilla bean, halved lengthwise
1½   cups whole milk
5    large egg yolks
¼    cup sugar
     Pinch salt

### PUDDING CAKES
4    tablespoons (½ stick) unsalted butter, melted, plus more for the ramekins
1¼   cups (6¼ ounces) unbleached all-purpose flour, plus more for the ramekins

1¼   cups pitted dates, cut crosswise into ¼-inch slices
¾    cup warm water
½    teaspoon baking soda
½    teaspoon baking powder
½    teaspoon salt
¾    cup (5¼ ounces) packed light or dark brown sugar
2    large eggs
1½   teaspoons vanilla extract

### TOFFEE SAUCE
8    tablespoons (1 stick) unsalted butter
1    cup (7 ounces) packed light or dark brown sugar
⅔    cup heavy cream
1    tablespoon rum

**1.** FOR THE CREME ANGLAISE: With a paring knife, scrape the vanilla seeds free from the pod. Place the seeds, bean pod, and milk in a medium saucepan and heat the mixture over medium heat until steaming, about 3 minutes. Remove from the heat, cover, and steep for 20 minutes. Uncover, return the mixture to medium heat, and heat until steaming, about 1 minute.

**2.** Meanwhile, whisk the yolks, sugar, and salt together in a medium bowl until pale yellow in color, about 1 minute. Slowly pour ½ cup of the hot milk into the yolk mixture to temper, whisking constantly. Return the mixture to the saucepan and cook over low heat, stirring constantly with a wooden spoon, until the mixture thickens slightly, coats the back of a spoon with a thin film, and registers 175 to 180 degrees on an instant-read thermometer, 5 to 8 minutes. Immediately pour the mixture through a fine-mesh strainer into a medium bowl.

**3.** FOR THE PUDDING CAKES: Adjust an oven rack to the middle position and heat the oven to 350 degrees. Grease and flour eight 4-ounce ramekins, knocking out the excess flour, and line the bottom of each with a round of parchment paper cut to fit. Set the ramekins in a large roasting pan lined with a clean dish towel. Bring a kettle or a large saucepan of water to a boil over high heat.

**4.** Combine half of the dates with the water and baking soda in a glass measuring cup (the dates should be submerged in the water) and soak for 5 minutes. Drain the dates, reserving the liquid, and transfer to a medium bowl. Whisk the flour, baking powder, and salt together in another medium bowl.

Laced with soft dates and richly flavored with brown sugar, sticky toffee pudding is an easy alternative to fancy cakes or pies.

occasionally, until the mixture looks puffy, 3 to 4 minutes. Slowly pour in the cream and rum, whisk just to combine, reduce the heat, and simmer until frothy, about 3 minutes. Remove from the heat, cover to keep warm, and set aside.

**8.** To serve, invert each ramekin onto a plate or shallow bowl, remove the ramekin, and peel off the parchment paper lining. Divide the toffee sauce evenly among the cakes and serve immediately, accompanied by crème anglaise or vanilla ice cream.

**WHAT YOU CAN DO AHEAD OF TIME:** The baked pudding can be cooled completely, wrapped tightly in plastic wrap, and stored at room temperature for up to 2 days. Microwave until warm before serving, checking progress every 30 seconds. The crème anglaise can also be made up to 2 days ahead. Transfer to a clean, airtight container, pressing a piece of plastic wrap flush against the surface to prevent the sauce from forming a skin. Cover and refrigerate.

**5.** Process the remaining dates and brown sugar in a food processor until just blended, about five 1-second pulses. Add the reserved soaking liquid, eggs, and vanilla and process until smooth, about 5 seconds. With the machine running, pour the melted butter through the feed tube in a steady stream. Transfer the mixture to the bowl with the dates.

**6.** Gently stir the dry mixture into the wet mixture until just combined and the date pieces are evenly dispersed. Distribute the batter evenly among the prepared ramekins. Fill the roasting pan with enough boiling water to come halfway up the sides of the ramekins, making sure not to splash water into the ramekins. Cover the pan tightly with aluminum foil, crimping the edges to seal. Bake the pudding cakes until puffed and small holes appear on the surface, about 40 minutes. Immediately remove the ramekins from the water bath and cool on a wire rack for 10 minutes.

**7. FOR THE TOFFEE SAUCE:** Meanwhile, melt the butter in a medium saucepan over medium heat. Whisk in the brown sugar until smooth. Continue to cook, stirring

## NOTES FROM THE TEST KITCHEN

### AN EASIER WATER BATH
Though the pudding cakes can be baked directly on an oven rack, tasters much preferred the moister, softer cakes baked partially submerged in an insulating water bath. Water baths take a little extra effort, but we think they are well worth it in this case. Most recipes, ours included, recommend lining the water pan with a clean dish towel to insulate the ramekins. Unfortunately, this method leaves you with a sopping wet towel. If you own a nonstick baking liner (such as a Silpat), use it instead of the towel.

### LARGE STICKY TOFFEE PUDDING CAKE
If you don't have individual ramekins, you can bake the pudding in an 8-inch-square baking dish. The texture will be cakier. Grease and flour an 8-inch-square baking dish and set it in a large roasting pan lined with a clean dish towel. Follow the recipe for Individual Sticky Toffee Pudding Cakes, pouring the batter into the prepared baking dish. Add enough boiling water to reach halfway up the sides of the baking dish and cover the pan tightly with aluminum foil. Bake until the outer 2 inches develop small holes and the center has puffed and is firm to the touch, about 40 minutes. Immediately remove the dish from the water bath and set it on a wire rack. Liberally poke the top of the pudding with the tip of a paring knife or wooden skewer; pour the toffee sauce over the pudding and spread it evenly with a rubber spatula. Cool for 10 minutes, cut into squares, and serve accompanied by crème anglaise or vanilla ice cream.

# STRAWBERRY CREAM CAKE

### SERVES 8 TO 10

**WHAT MAKES THIS A BEST RECIPE:** Strawberry cream cake is one of our favorite summer desserts, yet most versions are nothing more than soggy cake, bland berries, and squishy cream. We created an elegant rendition with three layers of sturdy cake, a firm filling, and, most of all, enough strawberry flavor to give it a starring role. The cake has the structure of a sponge cake, married with the moistness and richness of a butter cake. And unlike most strawberry cream cakes, which contain a mere two pints of berries, we were able to squeeze four pints into ours. We arranged half of the lushest berries, cut in half, around the edges of the filling layers for visual appeal, and the remainder we macerated in sugar, then pulsed in a food processor. To prevent the processed berries from exuding too much juice and making the cake soggy, we strained off the excess liquid, boiled it until syrupy, and added the syrup back to the berries, which helped concentrate and round out the berry flavor. For the cream layer, we whipped cream cheese with the heavy cream, which produced a stiff yet silky smooth blend that served to anchor the cake layers in place, so that even when sliced, the cake remained intact.

## CAKE

1¼  cups (5 ounces) cake flour
1½  teaspoons baking powder
¼  teaspoon salt
1  cup (7 ounces) sugar
5  large eggs (2 whole and 3 separated), at room temperature
6  tablespoons (¾ stick) unsalted butter, melted and cooled slightly
2  tablespoons water
2  teaspoons vanilla extract

## STRAWBERRY FILLING

2  pounds strawberries (about 2 quarts), washed, dried, and hulled
4–6  tablespoons sugar
2  tablespoons kirsch
   Salt

## WHIPPED CREAM

8  ounces cream cheese, at room temperature
½  cup (3½ ounces) sugar
⅛  teaspoon salt
1  teaspoon vanilla extract
2  cups heavy cream

**1.** FOR THE CAKE: Adjust an oven rack to the lower-middle position and heat the oven to 325 degrees. Grease and flour a round 9 by 2-inch cake pan or a 9-inch springform pan and line with a circle of parchment paper. Whisk the flour, baking powder, salt, and all but 3 tablespoons of the sugar in a large mixing bowl. Whisk in 2 whole eggs and 3 yolks (reserving the whites), butter, water, and vanilla; whisk just until the batter is smooth.

**2.** With an electric mixer, beat the remaining 3 egg whites on medium-low speed in a large bowl until frothy, 1 to 2 minutes. Gradually add the remaining 3 tablespoons sugar, increase the speed to medium-high, and beat until soft peaks form, 60 to 90 seconds. Stir one-third of the whites into the batter to lighten; add the remaining whites and gently fold them into the batter until no white streaks remain. Pour the batter into the prepared pan and bake until a toothpick inserted into the center comes out clean, 30 to 40 minutes. Cool in the pan for 10 minutes, then invert the cake onto a greased wire rack; peel off and discard the parchment round. Invert the cake again and cool completely before assembling, about 2 hours.

**3.** FOR THE STRAWBERRY FILLING: Halve 24 of the best-looking berries (roughly 1 quart) and reserve. Quarter the remaining berries; toss with 4 to 6 tablespoons of sugar (depending on the sweetness of the berries) in a medium bowl and let sit for 1 hour, stirring occasionally. Strain the juice from the berries and reserve (you should have about ½ cup). Pulse the macerated berries in a food processor until they form a chunky puree, about five 1-second pulses (you should have about 1½ cups). Simmer the reserved juice and kirsch in a small saucepan over medium-high heat until syrupy and reduced to about 3 tablespoons, 3 to 5 minutes. Pour the reduced syrup over the macerated berries, add a pinch of salt, and toss to combine. Set aside until the cake is cooled.

**4.** FOR THE WHIPPED CREAM: When the cake has cooled, beat the cream cheese, sugar, and salt with an electric mixer on medium-high speed in a large bowl until light and fluffy, 1 to 2 minutes, scraping down the sides of the bowl as needed. Add the vanilla and beat at medium speed until combined, about 30 seconds; scrape down the sides of the bowl. With the mixer on low speed, gradually add the heavy cream in a slow steady stream; when almost fully combined, increase the speed to medium-high and beat until the mixture holds stiff peaks, 2 to 2½ minutes more, scraping down the bowl as needed (you should have about 4½ cups).

**5.** TO ASSEMBLE THE CAKE: Using a large serrated knife, slice the cake into three even layers. Place the bottom layer on a cake plate or cardboard round and arrange a ring of 20 strawberry halves, cut sides down and stem ends facing out, around the perimeter of the cake layer. Pour half of the pureed berry mixture (about ¾ cup) in the center, then spread to cover any exposed cake. Gently spread about one-third of the whipped cream (about 1½ cups) over the berry layer, leaving a ½-inch border from the edge. Place the middle cake layer on top and press down gently (the whipped cream layer should become flush with the cake edge). Repeat with 20 additional strawberry halves, the remaining berry mixture, and half of the remaining whipped cream; gently press the last cake layer on top. Spread the remaining whipped cream over the top; decorate with the remaining cut strawberries. Serve immediately or chill for up to 4 hours.

**WHERE THINGS CAN GO WRONG:** It is important that you assemble this cake as close to serving time as possible, so that the whipped topping stays fresh and the cake layers don't become soggy.

**WHAT YOU CAN DO AHEAD OF TIME:** The cake layer can be cooled completely, wrapped tightly in plastic wrap, and frozen for up to 1 month. Thaw the cake, still wrapped, at room temperature, then remove the plastic wrap and proceed with the recipe.

## GREAT DISCOVERIES

### A BETTER CREAM LAYER

I love billowy whipped cream dolloped on cake or berries, but as the filling for a layer cake, it is problematic—it just isn't firm enough to stay put or hold the berries in place. Pastry cream was an obvious solution but that meant more steps in the recipe, so I turned to easier options. Sour cream and yogurt both added a nice tang but didn't help the consistency. I found the solution with cream cheese, which when whipped with heavy cream, made a sturdy and tangy filling.

ERIKA BRUCE | ASSOCIATE EDITOR, COOK'S ILLUSTRATED

## NOTES FROM THE TEST KITCHEN

### USE A STRAW TO HULL STRAWBERRIES

If you don't own a strawberry huller (and almost no one does), you can improvise with a plastic drinking straw. Push the straw through the bottom of the berry and up through the leafy stem end. The straw will remove the core as well as the leafy top.

### HOW TO BUILD THE BEST STRAWBERRY CREAM CAKE

**1.** With a serrated knife, use a sawing motion to cut the cake into 3 layers, rotating the cake as you go.

**2.** Place halved berries evenly around the edges (they will be visible once the layers are assembled).

**3.** Cover the center of the cake completely with half of the mashed strawberries.

**4.** Spread one-third of the whipped cream over the berries, leaving a ½-inch border from the cake edge. Repeat the layering of cake, berries, and cream.

**5.** Press the last layer into place, spread with the remaining cream, and decorate with the remaining berries.

# GRASSHOPPER PIE

SERVES 8

**WHAT MAKES THIS A BEST RECIPE:** A true grasshopper pie should have a creamy, billowy chiffon filling, and more mint-chocolate flavor than a peppermint patty. Unlike other grasshopper pies that have a filling of mint chocolate chip ice cream, or whipped egg whites, this one gets its fluffy volume and creaminess from whipped cream. Similar to most chiffon-style pies, we used gelatin to stabilize the filling; however, instead of softening the gelatin in water, which is commonplace, we softened ours in heavy cream for added silky softness. The secret to our grasshopper pie was to get big mint and chocolate flavor from several sources. The filling got a serious chocolate mint punch from green crème de menthe and white crème de cacao, and the crust, which is normally made from chocolate wafer cookies, got the same from Mint 'n Creme Oreo Cookies.

### CRUST
- 16 Mint 'n Creme Oreo Cookies (with filling), broken into rough pieces and processed in a food processor to fine, even crumbs
- 3 tablespoons unsalted butter, melted and cooled

### FILLING
- 3 large egg yolks
- 1 envelope unflavored gelatin
- ½ cup (3½ ounces) sugar
- 2½ cups heavy cream
  Pinch salt
- ¼ cup green crème de menthe
- ¼ cup white crème de cacao

**1. FOR THE CRUST:** Adjust an oven rack to the middle position and heat the oven to 350 degrees. In a medium bowl, stir together the cookie crumbs and melted butter until combined. Transfer the mixture to a 9-inch pie plate and press evenly into the pan bottom and sides. Refrigerate the crust until firm, about 20 minutes. Bake until fragrant and set, 8 to 10 minutes. Cool on a wire rack.

**2. FOR THE FILLING:** Beat the egg yolks in a medium bowl. Combine the gelatin, sugar, ½ cup of the cream, and salt

in a medium saucepan and let sit until the gelatin softens, about 5 minutes. Cook over medium heat until the gelatin dissolves and the mixture is very hot but not boiling, about 2 minutes. Whisking vigorously, slowly add the gelatin mixture to the egg yolks. Return the mixture to the saucepan and cook, stirring constantly, until slightly thickened, about 2 minutes. Remove from the heat and add the crème de menthe and crème de cacao. Pour into a clean bowl and refrigerate until just starting to become wobbly but not set, about 20 minutes.

**3.** With an electric mixer, beat the remaining 2 cups cream on high speed to stiff peaks. Whisk 1 cup of the whipped cream into the gelatin mixture until completely incorporated. Using a rubber spatula, fold the remaining whipped cream into the gelatin mixture until no streaks of white remain. Scrape the mixture into the cooled pie shell, smooth the top, and refrigerate until firm, at least 6 hours or preferably overnight. Serve, topped with chocolate curls (see page 267), if desired.

**WHERE THINGS CAN GO WRONG:** If you don't press the crumbs firmly into the pie plate, the crust will be crumbly. It is important to refrigerate the gelatin mixture just until it is wobbly but not set. If the gelatin is too firm, it will be impossible to incorporate the whipped cream.

**WHAT YOU CAN DO AHEAD OF TIME:** The assembled pie can be wrapped tightly in plastic wrap and refrigerated for up to 2 days.

## NOTES FROM THE TEST KITCHEN

### SMOOTHING THINGS OVER
Here's how the test kitchen makes even, mess-free crumb crusts every time.

Use your hands to distribute the crumbs in an even layer over the bottom and up the sides of the pie plate. Press down lightly, then place a piece of plastic wrap on top of the crust. Run the back of a dinner spoon over the crumbs, smoothing them into the bottom, curves, and sides of the pan.

# BOSTON CREAM CUPCAKES
### MAKES 12 CUPCAKES

**WHAT MAKES THIS A BEST RECIPE:** Inspired by Boston cream pie, these decadent (and decidedly grown-up) cupcakes feature the same irresistible layers of cake, custard, and deep chocolate glaze. But making all these elements work in proportion in cupcake form proved harder than we had imagined. Turning first to the cake, we knew that the traditional sponge cake wouldn't work in cupcake form so we developed a fine-textured yellow cake using the reverse-creaming method. The traditional creaming method, which relies on aerating the butter with the sugar, creates large air pockets that result in a coarser crumb. In the reverse creaming method, the butter coats the flour before the batter is aerated, keeping the cake tender and fine-crumbed. With the cake in place, we moved on to the filling and the glaze. We then made a simple pastry cream filling that was stiff enough to hold its shape inside the cupcake but still gooey enough to ooze slightly when you bit into it. For the glaze, we added corn syrup to provide sheen and used bittersweet chocolate for its rich flavor. Now that we had assembled all of the components, the real challenge began—how were we to get the pastry cream inside the cupcake? At first, we piped the filling in through a small hole in the bottom of the cupcake, but when tasters took a bite they scowled and demanded more filling. It was clear that some of the cake would have to go to make room for more pastry cream. By removing a cone-shaped section of cake from each cupcake (reserving the tops for reassembly), we were able to fit a whopping 2 tablespoons of pastry cream inside (see page 278). We then returned the tops and applied the shiny chocolate glaze, making the incisions invisible.

## PASTRY CREAM

- 1⅓ cups heavy cream
- 3 large egg yolks
- ⅓ cup (2⅓ ounces) sugar
  Pinch salt
- 4 teaspoons cornstarch
- 2 tablespoons cold unsalted butter, cut into 2 pieces
- 1½ teaspoons vanilla extract

## CUPCAKES

- 1¾ cups (8¾ ounces) unbleached all-purpose flour, plus extra for muffin tin
- 1½ teaspoons baking powder
- ¾ teaspoon salt
- 1 cup (7 ounces) sugar
- 12 tablespoons (1½ sticks) unsalted butter, softened but still cool, cut into 12 pieces
- 3 large eggs
- ¾ cup milk
- 1½ teaspoons vanilla extract

## CHOCOLATE GLAZE

- ¾ cup heavy cream
- ¼ cup light corn syrup
- 8 ounces bittersweet chocolate, chopped
- ½ teaspoon vanilla extract

**1. FOR THE PASTRY CREAM:** Bring the cream to a simmer in a medium saucepan over medium heat, stirring occasionally. Meanwhile, whisk the egg yolks, sugar, and salt together in a medium bowl. Add the cornstarch and whisk until the mixture is pale yellow and thick, about 15 seconds.

**2.** When the cream reaches a full simmer, slowly whisk it into the yolk mixture. Return the mixture to the saucepan and cook over medium heat, whisking constantly, until thick and glossy, about 1½ minutes. Off the heat, whisk in the butter and vanilla. Transfer the pastry cream to a small bowl and refrigerate, with plastic wrap pressed flush against its surface, until cold and set, at least 2 hours or up to 2 days.

**3. FOR THE CUPCAKES:** Adjust an oven rack to the middle position and heat the oven to 350 degrees. Coat a standard muffin tin with vegetable oil spray, flour generously, and tap the pan to remove the excess flour.

**4.** With an electric mixer on low speed, combine the flour, baking powder, salt, and sugar in a large bowl. Add the butter, one piece at a time, and combine until the mixture resembles coarse sand. Add the eggs, one at a time, and mix until combined. Add the milk and vanilla, increase the speed to medium, and mix until light and fluffy and no lumps remain, about 3 minutes.

**5.** Fill the muffin cups three-quarters full (do not overfill). Bake until a toothpick inserted in the center of a cupcake comes out clean, 18 to 20 minutes. Cool the cupcakes in the pan for 5 minutes, then transfer to a wire rack to cool completely.

**6. FOR THE GLAZE:** Cook the cream, corn syrup, chocolate, and vanilla in a small saucepan over medium heat, stirring constantly, until smooth. Set aside to cool and thicken for 30 minutes.

**7. TO ASSEMBLE THE CUPCAKES:** Following the photos, insert the tip of a small knife at a 45-degree angle about ⅛ inch from the edge of each cupcake and cut all the way around, removing a cone of cake. Cut away all but the top ¼ inch of the cone, leaving only a small disk of cake. Fill each cupcake with 2 tablespoons pastry cream and top with the disk of cake. Set the filled cupcakes on a wire rack set over parchment paper. Spoon 2 tablespoons of glaze over each cupcake, allowing it to drip down the sides. Refrigerate until just set, about 10 minutes.

**WHERE THINGS CAN GO WRONG:** Don't be tempted to bake these cupcakes in paper cupcake liners. Baking them, as directed, in a greased and floured muffin tin allows the chocolate glaze to run down the sides of the cooled cakes.

**WHAT YOU CAN DO AHEAD OF TIME:** The cupcakes can be refrigerated in an airtight container for 2 days. Bring the cupcakes to room temperature before serving.

## NOTES FROM THE TEST KITCHEN

### HOW TO MAKE BOSTON CREAM CUPCAKES

**1.** Insert the tip of a small knife at a 45-degree angle about ⅛ inch from the edge of the cupcake and cut all the way around, removing a cone of cake.

**2.** Cut away all but the top ¼ inch of the cone, leaving only a small disk of cake.

**3.** Fill the cupcake with 2 tablespoons pastry cream and top with the disk of cake. Spoon 2 tablespoons of glaze over each cupcake, allowing it to drip down the sides.

# INDIVIDUAL MOCHACCINO BREAD PUDDINGS
#### SERVES 4

**WHAT MAKES THIS A BEST RECIPE:** Bread pudding should be a simple affair, but by no means plain. Unlike many of the modern cookbooks, which call for specialty breads such as brioche or challah, our version uses firm, hearty white bread from your local supermarket. Other recipes let the bread sit out to stale overnight, soak it in custard for up to 2 hours, and then bake the pudding in a roasting pan filled with steaming hot water. We soaked our fresh bread in custard for just 20 minutes, and we found that a water bath is definitely not necessary—the pudding bakes up nice and creamy in a low oven. Inspired by the oversized cappuccinos served in big white porcelain mugs at our local coffee shop, we jazzed up the flavors of our easy bread pudding with coffee and chopped bittersweet chocolate, baked them in individual coffee cups, and just before serving, topped them with fluffy whipped cream and a dusting of cocoa.

> Unsalted butter for greasing coffee cups
> 2   large eggs
> ⅓   cup (2⅓ ounces) sugar, plus 1½ tablespoons for topping
> 1   cup milk
> 1   cup heavy cream, plus ¾ cup for topping
> 1½   tablespoons instant espresso powder
> 1   teaspoon vanilla extract
> 4–5   slices firm white bread, cut into 1½-inch squares (5 cups)
> 4   ounces bittersweet chocolate, chopped
> Cocoa powder for dusting tops

**1.** Adjust an oven rack to the middle position and heat the oven to 325 degrees. Grease four 1-cup ovensafe coffee cups or ramekins.

**2.** Whisk the eggs and ⅓ cup of the sugar together in a large bowl. Whisk in the milk, 1 cup of the heavy cream, instant espresso, and vanilla. Transfer the custard to a large measuring cup.

**3.** Arrange 4 bread squares in the bottom of each prepared coffee cup, overlapping the pieces so they fit snugly. Sprinkle

Bake and serve these mocha-flavored bread puddings in large coffee cups.

1 heaping tablespoon of the chocolate on top of the bread in each cup. Make a second layer using 4 bread pieces, then top with the remaining chocolate. Pour the custard over the bread and chocolate. Transfer the coffee cups to a rimmed baking sheet and set aside for 20 minutes.

**4.** Bake until the puddings are set but still a bit wobbly when shaken, 25 to 30 minutes. Cool for at least 30 minutes (we like to serve these warm) or to room temperature.

**5.** With an electric mixer, beat the remaining ¾ cup cream and 1½ tablespoons sugar to soft peaks. Spoon the whipped cream over each pudding. Sprinkle with cocoa and serve immediately.

**WHERE THINGS CAN GO WRONG:** Be sure to use a wide, hearty loaf of sandwich bread—a smaller loaf may not provide enough bread. Our favorites are Arnold Country Classics White and Pepperidge Farm Farmhouse Hearty White.

**WHAT YOU CAN DO AHEAD OF TIME:** The baked puddings can be cooled completely, covered with plastic wrap, and refrigerated for up to 1 day. Bring to room temperature, then microwave until warm before serving, checking the progress every 30 seconds.

# ULTIMATE TURTLE BROWNIES
MAKES TWENTY-FIVE 1½-INCH BROWNIES

**WHAT MAKES THIS A BEST RECIPE:** With this recipe, we created a brownie reminiscent of a candy turtle: rich, chewy, and chocolatey, with a bittersweet, toothsinking caramel and an abundance of pecans. The first step in our testing was to create a rich and nutty brownie base. Since we already had a good brownie recipe, we simply took it to new heights by adding chocolate chips (in addition to bittersweet and unsweetened chocolate) along with chopped pecans. Then we grappled with the caramel. We knew that a traditional caramel sauce would be too thin and runny for this purpose, so we created a foolproof and simple caramel with just the right consistency. By adding corn syrup with the sugar and cooking the mixture covered for the first few minutes, we prevented the sugar from seizing, and as a safeguard against burning the caramel, we reduced the heat to medium-low once the caramel reached a very pale golden color, which allowed us to monitor it as it cooked to a beautiful light amber. With the addition of just 6 tablespoons heavy cream, this caramel had enough textural contrast when layered with the brownie batter, and was thick enough to spread over the top of the cooled baked brownies.

CARAMEL
| | |
|---|---|
| ¼ | cup plus 2 tablespoons heavy cream |
| ¼ | teaspoon salt |
| ¼ | cup water |
| 2 | tablespoons light corn syrup |
| 1¼ | cups (8¾ ounces) sugar |
| 2 | tablespoons unsalted butter |
| 1 | teaspoon vanilla extract |

BROWNIES
| | |
|---|---|
| ¾ | cup (3¾ ounces) unbleached all-purpose flour |
| ½ | teaspoon baking powder |
| 8 | tablespoons (1 stick) unsalted butter, cut into 1-inch pieces |
| 4 | ounces bittersweet chocolate, chopped |
| 2 | ounces unsweetened chocolate, chopped |
| 2 | large eggs, at room temperature |
| 1 | cup (7 ounces) sugar |

¼ teaspoon salt

2 teaspoons vanilla extract

⅔ cup chopped pecans

⅓ cup semisweet chocolate chips

GARNISH

25 pecan halves, toasted

**1. TO MAKE THE CARAMEL:** Mix the cream and salt in a small bowl. Combine the water and corn syrup in a medium saucepan. Pour the sugar into the center of the saucepan, taking care not to let sugar crystals adhere to the sides of the pan. Gently stir with a clean spatula to thoroughly moisten the sugar. Cover and bring to a boil over medium-high heat. Cook, covered and without stirring, until the sugar is completely dissolved and the liquid is clear, 3 to 5 minutes. Uncover and continue to cook, without stirring but gently swirling the pan occasionally, until a pale golden color, 3 to 5 minutes more. Reduce the heat to medium-low and continue to cook (swirling occasionally) until the caramel is light amber-colored and registers about 360 degrees on a candy or instant-read thermometer, about 1 to 3 minutes longer. Remove the saucepan from the heat, add the cream to the center of the pot, and stir with a whisk or spatula until the bubbling subsides, being sure that your hand isn't directly over the pot (the mixture will bubble and steam vigorously). Stir in the butter and vanilla and transfer the caramel to a microwaveable measuring cup or bowl and set aside.

**2. TO MAKE THE BROWNIES:** Adjust an oven rack to the lower-middle position and heat the oven to 325 degrees. Line a 9-inch-square baking pan with aluminum foil, allowing the extra foil to hang over the edges of the pan. Spray the foil-lined pan with nonstick cooking spray. Combine the flour and baking powder in a small bowl and set aside.

**3.** Melt the butter and bittersweet and unsweetened chocolates in a heatproof bowl set over a saucepan of barely simmering water, stirring occasionally until smooth; set aside to cool. When the chocolate has cooled slightly, whisk the eggs in a large bowl, add the sugar, salt, and vanilla, and whisk until incorporated. Whisk the melted chocolate mixture into the egg mixture. Add the flour mixture and stir until almost combined. Stir in the chopped pecans and chocolate chips.

**4.** Distribute half of the brownie batter in the prepared baking pan. Drizzle ¼ cup of the caramel over the brownie batter. Drop the remaining brownie batter over the caramel layer; spread evenly and into corners of the pan. Drizzle an additional ¼ cup caramel over the top. Using the tip of a butter knife, swirl the caramel and batter. Bake the brownies until a

toothpick inserted into the center comes out with only a few moist crumbs attached, 35 to 40 minutes. Cool to room temperature on a wire rack, 1 to 2 hours.

**5.** Heat the remaining caramel (you should have about ¾ cup) in the microwave until hot and pourable but still thick, 45 to 60 seconds, stirring once or twice; pour the caramel over the brownies. Using a rubber spatula, spread the caramel to cover the surface. Refrigerate the brownies uncovered until fully chilled, at least 2 hours or overnight.

**6.** Remove from the baking pan by lifting the foil extensions. Cut into 25 evenly sized squares. Press a pecan half onto the surface of each brownie. Serve chilled or at room temperature.

**WHERE THINGS CAN GO WRONG:** The caramel is very thick and sticky. To drizzle it over the brownies, it must be quite warm. If necessary, reheat it in the microwave.

**WHAT YOU CAN DO AHEAD OF TIME:** The brownies can be refrigerated in an airtight container for up to 5 days. Let stand at room temperature at least 15 minutes before serving.

## NOTES FROM THE TEST KITCHEN
### FOOLPROOF CARAMEL 101: A VISUAL GUIDE

**1. DAMPEN WITH A SPATULA.** After pouring the sugar into the center of the pan, gently stir with a clean spatula until the sugar is damp. Cover until the mixture boils and the sugar dissolves completely; remove the lid.

**2. PALE GOLDEN.** Cook until the bubbles show a faint golden color, then lower the heat. Full gold bubbles mean you've gone too far.

**3. LIGHT AMBER.** Cook for 1 to 3 minutes more, until the mixture is light amber (honey colored). Remove the pan from the heat.

**4. MEDIUM AMBER.** Add the cream, butter, and vanilla which will cause the caramel to turn a darker shade of amber.

To create neat edges, trim ¼ inch off the borders around the baked block before cutting it into bars.

# RASPBERRY STREUSEL BARS

MAKES TWENTY-FOUR 2-INCH SQUARES

**WHAT MAKES THIS A BEST RECIPE:** In our quest to develop the best recipe for raspberry bars, we tested dozens of recipes, most of which suffered from dry toppings and skimpy jam fillings. We love these bars, not only because they have just the right balance of rich, buttery shortbread, bright, tangy fruit filling, and crisp streusel topping, but also because they are easy. We created a simple shortbread bottom crust that also forms the basis of a simple streusel topping. And since we think the whole point of these bars is the raspberry flavor, we use both preserves and fresh raspberries (which we mashed lightly for easy spreading). These bars are packed with serious raspberry flavor.

| | |
|---|---|
| 2 ½ | cups (12½ ounces) unbleached all-purpose flour |
| ⅔ | cup (4¾ ounces) granulated sugar |
| ½ | teaspoon salt |
| 16 | tablespoons (2 sticks) plus 2 tablespoons unsalted butter, at room temperature and cut into ½-inch pieces |
| ¼ | cup (1¾ ounces) packed light or dark brown sugar |
| ½ | cup (1½ ounces) old-fashioned rolled oats |
| ½ | cup pecans, chopped fine |
| ¾ | cup raspberry preserves |
| ¾ | cup (3½ ounces) fresh raspberries |
| 1 | tablespoon fresh lemon juice |

**1.** Adjust an oven rack to the middle position and heat the oven to 375 degrees. Line a 13 by 9-inch baking pan with aluminum foil, allowing the extra foil to hang over the edges of the pan. Spray the foil-lined pan with nonstick cooking spray.

**2.** With an electric mixer, mix the flour, granulated sugar, and salt on low speed in a large bowl until combined, about 5 seconds. With the mixer on low, add 16 tablespoons of the butter, one piece at a time, and continue mixing until the mixture resembles damp sand, 1 to 1½ minutes. (If using a food processor, process the flour, granulated sugar, and salt until combined, about 5 seconds. Scatter 16 tablespoons of the butter pieces over the flour mixture and pulse until the mixture resembles damp sand, about twenty 1-second pulses.)

**3.** Measure 1¼ cups of the flour mixture into a medium bowl and set aside; distribute the remaining flour mixture evenly in the bottom of the prepared baking pan. Using your hands or a flat-bottomed measuring cup, firmly press the mixture into an even layer to form a bottom crust. Bake until the edges are beginning to brown, 14 to 18 minutes.

**4.** While the crust is baking, add the brown sugar, oats, and nuts to the reserved flour mixture; toss to combine. Work in the remaining 2 tablespoons butter by rubbing the mixture between your fingers until the butter is fully incorporated. Pinch the mixture with your fingers to create hazelnut-sized clumps; set the streusel aside.

**5.** Combine the preserves, raspberries, and lemon juice in a small bowl; mash with a fork until combined but some berry pieces remain.

**6.** Spread the filling evenly over the hot crust; sprinkle the streusel topping evenly over the filling (do not press streusel into filling). Return the pan to the oven and bake until the topping is deep golden brown and the filling is bubbling, 22 to 25 minutes. Cool to room temperature on a wire rack, 1 to 2 hours; remove from the baking pan by lifting the foil extensions. Using a chef's knife, cut into squares and serve.

**WHERE THINGS CAN GO WRONG:** To avoid frail bars that fall apart in your hands, be sure to press the bottom crust down firmly and evenly into the pan. As for the filling, if your raspberries are very tart, only add 1 or 2 teaspoons of lemon juice or the filling will be too sharp.

**WHAT YOU CAN DO AHEAD OF TIME:** The bars are best eaten the day they are made, but they can be stored in an airtight container at room temperature for up to 3 days (the crust and streusel will soften slightly with storage).

## NOTES FROM THE TEST KITCHEN

### FRUIT MAKES THE DIFFERENCE
We added fresh raspberries to preserves to get a cohesive filling that remained bright and full of raspberry flavor, even after baking, but, frozen raspberries can be substituted for the fresh; be sure to thaw them before combining them with the raspberry preserves.

### OUR FAVORITE RASPBERRY PRESERVES
On the hunt for the best possible preserves to use in these bars, we tested a variety of jams and preserves, looking for the one with a flavor that speaks loudly of raspberry, without tartness or cloying sweetness. **Smucker's Red Raspberry Preserves** was the best of the bunch. Tasters praised its "classic, clean flavor" and noted that it had just the right amount of seeds.

### THE PROBLEM WITH RASPBERRY BARS
We tested dozens of raspberry bar recipes and uncovered several recurring problems.

**SANDY, DRY STREUSEL.** Using the same dough (without modification) for both the top and bottom layers resulted in a crumbly topping.

**SKIMPY JAM.** Tasters felt cheated by a skimpy, overcooked layer of jam, which got lost between thick, cookie-like layers.

**TOO OATY.** Too many oats and not enough flour created a streusel topping that melted right into the filling.

# CHOCOLATE-MINT BUTTER COOKIES
MAKES ABOUT 4 DOZEN 2½-INCH COOKIES

**WHAT MAKES THIS A BEST RECIPE:** Chocolate butter cookies usually taste bland or surrender their crisp, delicate appeal to a chewy, brownie-like texture. We love these cookies because they have it all: a strong chocolate flavor and a perfectly crisp texture. The chocolate flavor comes from a large quantity of cocoa powder, which we "bloomed" with espresso powder in melted butter to release volatile flavor compounds and boost the underlying chocolate flavor of the cookies (see page 284). With hopes of replicating the best after-dinner mint you have ever tasted, we added mint extract, which complemented the deep chocolate flavor with its fresh, cool essence. This dough is easy to work with, and the cookies can be cut into any desired shape, or simply rolled into a log and sliced. Though refined enough to serve plain, chocolate glaze and a drizzle of white chocolate add a nice finishing touch.

COOKIES

20  tablespoons (2½ sticks) unsalted butter, at room temperature
½   cup (2 ounces) Dutch-processed cocoa powder
1   teaspoon instant espresso powder
1   cup (7 ounces) sugar
¼   teaspoon salt
2   large egg yolks
2   teaspoons mint extract
2¼  cups (11¼ ounces) unbleached all-purpose flour

GLAZE

4   ounces bittersweet chocolate, chopped
4   tablespoons (½ stick) unsalted butter
2   tablespoons light corn syrup
1   teaspoon vanilla extract
1   cup (6 ounces) white chocolate chips, melted

**1. FOR THE COOKIES:** Adjust an oven rack to the middle position and heat the oven to 375 degrees. Melt 4 tablespoons of the butter in a medium saucepan over medium heat (or in a medium microwave-save bowl, on medium power for about 30 seconds). Add the cocoa powder and espresso powder; stir until the mixture forms a smooth paste. Set aside to cool, 15 to 20 minutes.

**2.** With an electric mixer, mix the remaining 16 tablespoons butter, sugar, salt, and cooled cocoa mixture on high speed in a large bowl until well combined and fluffy, about 1 minute, scraping down the sides of the bowl once or twice. Add the yolks and mint extract and mix on medium speed until thoroughly combined, about 30 seconds. Scrape down the sides of the bowl. With the mixer on low speed, add the flour in three additions, waiting until each addition is incorporated before adding the next and scraping down the sides of the bowl after each addition. Continue to mix until the dough forms a cohesive ball, about 5 seconds. Turn the dough onto the counter; divide into three 4-inch disks. Wrap each disk in plastic wrap and refrigerate until the dough is firm yet malleable, 45 to 60 minutes. (Alternatively, shape the dough into a log, 2 inches in diameter and about 12 inches long; use parchment paper or plastic wrap to roll into a neat cylinder. Chill until very firm and cold, at least 1 hour.)

**3.** Roll out 1 of the dough disks between 2 large sheets of parchment paper to an even thickness of ³⁄₁₆ inch. (If the dough becomes soft and sticky, slide the rolled dough on the parchment onto a baking sheet and rechill until firm, about 10 minutes.) Peel the parchment from one side of the dough, and cut into desired shapes using a cookie cutter(s); using a thin metal spatula, place the shapes on a parchment-lined baking sheet, spacing them about 1 inch apart. Gather the dough scraps and chill. (For cylinder-shaped dough, simply slice the cookies ¼ inch thick and place on parchment-lined baking sheets.)

**4.** Bake until the cookies show slight resistance to the touch, 10 to 12 minutes, rotating the baking sheet halfway through the baking time. Cool for 5 minutes, then, using a spatula, transfer the cookies to a wire rack; cool completely. Repeat steps 3 and 4 with the remaining dough disks and scraps, rerolling the scraps just once.

**5.** FOR THE GLAZE: Melt the chocolate and butter in the microwave (see page 267), and mix until smooth. Stir in the corn syrup and vanilla, and mix until shiny. Use the back of a spoon to spread a scant 1 teaspoon of the glaze almost to the edge of each cookie. (If necessary, reheat to increase the fluidity of the glaze.) Let dry until the glaze is set, at least 20 minutes. Drizzle the white chocolate over the glazed cookies. Let dry for at least 20 minutes before serving.

**WHERE THINGS CAN GO WRONG:** Bake these cookies just until they show slight resistance to the touch. If they are baked until they darken around the edges, the cookies will turn slightly bitter and lose much of their complex chocolate flavor.

**WHAT YOU CAN DO AHEAD OF TIME:** The cookies can be stored (unglazed) in an airtight container at room temperature for up to 3 days. Proceed with the recipe from step 5. The disks of dough can be wrapped tightly in plastic wrap and refrigerated for up to 2 days, or frozen for up to 1 month. Thaw frozen dough in the refrigerator. Before rolling, let the dough stand at room temperature for 15 minutes to soften.

## NOTES FROM THE TEST KITCHEN

### HOW TO TELL IF THEY'RE DONE
We found that for the perfect texture, take the cookies out of the oven at just the right moment. The secret is to use a fork or finger to gently press the center of a cookie; slight resistance tells you that the cookies are done. If they yield easily, they are underdone and need more time to crisp.

### KEY STEPS TO MAXIMUM CHOCOLATE FLAVOR

**1. ADD COCOA SOLIDS.** Start with cocoa powder. It has more cocoa solids than other forms of chocolate and the most intense flavor.

**2. UP THE COMPLEXITY.** The bitter, roasted notes of espresso powder accentuate similar qualities in the cocoa powder.

**3. "BLOOM" IN HOT BUTTER.** Mixing both powders with hot, melted butter makes more flavor available to the taste buds.

# PEANUT BLOSSOM COOKIES

MAKES ABOUT 8 DOZEN COOKIES

**WHAT MAKES THIS A BEST RECIPE:** When Freda Smith of Gibsonburg, Ohio, entered her peanut blossoms in the 1957 Pillsbury Bake-Off, she created a cookie sensation that would endure for nearly five decades. Since Freda's recipe is where it all began, we used it as a starting point to create our own version. Although her recipe produced a good and chewy peanut butter cookie, we wanted more peanut flavor. Like Freda, we favored creamy peanut butter (cookies made with chunky peanut butter had a craggy texture and appearance), but we supplemented it with some finely ground roasted and salted peanuts, which added a deep peanut flavor to the cookies without compromising their smooth texture. While most recipes, including Freda's, call for the Kisses to be pressed into the cookies immediately after baking, we found that placing the chocolates on the cookies during the last two minutes of baking stabilized and set the exterior of the chocolate, and kept the interior smooth and creamy.

2¾ cups (13¾ ounces) unbleached all-purpose flour
½ teaspoon salt
½ teaspoon baking soda
½ teaspoon baking powder
1 cup roasted, salted peanuts
16 tablespoons (2 sticks) unsalted butter, softened but still cool
¾ cup (5¼ ounces) packed dark brown sugar
¾ cup (5¼ ounces) granulated sugar
1 cup creamy peanut butter
2 large eggs, at room temperature
2 teaspoons vanilla extract
96 Hershey's Chocolate Kisses (from two 1-pound bags), wrappers removed

**1.** Adjust an oven rack to the middle position and heat the oven to 350 degrees. Line 2 baking sheets with parchment paper.

**2.** Whisk 1¾ cups of the flour, salt, baking soda, and baking powder together in a medium bowl. Process the remaining 1 cup flour and peanuts in a food processor until ground, about fifteen 1-second pulses, then stir into the flour mixture.

**3.** With an electric mixer, beat the butter and sugars on medium-high speed in a large bowl until fluffy, about 3 minutes. Add the peanut butter and continue to beat until combined. Add the eggs, one at a time, beating after each addition, until incorporated, about 30 seconds, then beat in the vanilla, scraping down the sides of the bowl as needed. Reduce the speed to low, add the flour mixture in two batches, and mix until incorporated. Cover the bowl and refrigerate the dough until stiff, about 30 minutes.

**4.** Roll twenty 1-inch balls of dough and space them 2 inches apart on one of the baking sheets. Bake until just set and beginning to crack, 9 to 11 minutes, rotating the baking sheet from front to back halfway through baking (while the cookies are baking, roll another 20 balls of dough and place on the second baking sheet). Working quickly, remove the sheet from the oven and firmly press one Kiss in the center of each cookie. Bake until lightly golden, about 2 minutes. Transfer the baking sheet to a wire rack to cool for 5 minutes, then transfer the cookies directly to the wire rack to finish cooling. Repeat rolling and baking the remaining cookies. Cool completely. (The cookies will be cool enough to eat after about 30 minutes, but the Kisses will take 2 hours to set completely.)

**WHERE THINGS CAN GO WRONG:** Knowing when to add the chocolate Kiss is key to the success of this recipe. If you add the Kiss too soon, the chocolate will take too long to firm up; if you add it too late, the cookie, firming as it cools, may break under the pressure.

**WHAT YOU CAN DO AHEAD OF TIME:** The cookies are best eaten the day they are made, but they can be stored in an airtight container at room temperature for up to 3 days. The dough can be rolled into 1-inch balls and frozen in an even layer on a parchment-lined plate or baking sheet (don't let them touch or they will fuse together) until completely firm, 2 to 3 hours. When the dough balls are firm, transfer them to a zipper-lock bag and freeze for up to 1 month. Bake frozen cookies for 2 to 4 minutes longer than normal.

# CHOCOLATE TOFFEE BUTTER COOKIES

MAKES ABOUT 5 DOZEN COOKIES

**WHAT MAKES THIS A BEST RECIPE:** The grand-prize winner of our Christmas cookie recipe contest, these cookies can't be beat. Submitted by Mary Hay Glass of Arlington, Virginia, this recipe delivers rich and buttery cookies punctuated by bits of sweet toffee, and adorned with melted semisweet chocolate and a sprinkling of toasted pecans. Besides being tasty, this recipe is straightforward and easy to make, and follows the basic creaming method for making cookies. The dough is rolled into logs, then flattened into rectangles and refrigerated until firm. All that is left to do is slice (which is easy because of the chilled dough) and bake the cookies until perfectly browned around the edges. And depending upon how you apply the chocolate and pecan garnishes, these cookies can look quite different.

- 2⅓ cups (11⅔ ounces) unbleached all-purpose flour
- ½ teaspoon baking powder
- ½ teaspoon salt
- 16 tablespoons (2 sticks) unsalted butter, softened but still cool
- 1 cup (7 ounces) packed light brown sugar
- 1 large egg
- 1 teaspoon vanilla extract
- 1 cup Heath Toffee Bits (without chocolate)
- 1½ cups (9 ounces) semisweet chocolate chips
- 1 tablespoon vegetable oil
- ⅔ cup pecans, toasted and chopped fine

**1.** Whisk the flour, baking powder, and salt together. With an electric mixer, beat the butter and brown sugar on medium speed until fluffy, about 3 minutes. Add the egg and vanilla and beat until combined, about 30 seconds. Reduce the speed to low, add the flour mixture in two batches, and mix until incorporated. Stir in the toffee bits. Divide the dough in half and roll each piece into a log about 9 inches long and 1½ inches in diameter. Flatten the logs until 2½ inches wide. Wrap each log in plastic wrap and refrigerate until firm, about 1½ hours.

**2.** Adjust the oven racks to the upper-middle and lower-middle positions and heat the oven to 350 degrees. Line 2 baking sheets with parchment paper.

**3.** Using a chef's knife, cut the dough into ¼-inch slices; transfer to baking sheets, spacing 1 inch apart. Bake until just browned around the edges, 10 to 12 minutes, rotating the rack position and direction of the baking sheets halfway through the baking time. Cool cookies completely on the baking sheets. Use the remaining dough to make a second batch of cookies.

**4.** Transfer the baked cookies to a wire rack set in a baking sheet. Melt the chocolate chips in the microwave (see below), add the oil, and mix until smooth. Dip part of each cookie into the melted chocolate or drizzle the chocolate over the cookies with a spoon. Sprinkle the pecans over the chocolate. Let sit until the chocolate sets, about 1 hour.

**WHERE THINGS CAN GO WRONG:** Make sure that you thoroughly chill the dough before slicing, or it will be too soft and the cookies will be misshapen. At the store, buy the Heath Toffee Bits without chocolate, or the recipe will not come out right.

**WHAT YOU CAN DO AHEAD OF TIME:** The cookies are best eaten the day they are made, but they can be stored in an airtight container at room temperature for up to 3 days.

## NOTES FROM THE TEST KITCHEN

**HOW TO MELT CHOCOLATE**

**IN A MICROWAVE.** Place the chocolate in a microwave-safe bowl and microwave for 45 seconds. Stir and keep microwaving until the mixture is smooth, checking and stirring at 15 second intervals.

**ON THE STOVETOP.** Bring a pan of water to a gentle simmer and set a metal bowl over the pan (but not touching the water). Add the chocolate and stir gently until melted.

# DARK CHOCOLATE MOUSSE
## MAKES 3½ CUPS (6 TO 8 SERVINGS)

**WHAT MAKES THIS A BEST RECIPE:** Chocolate mousse usually falls into one of two categories: rich, creamy, and dense, or light and airy (but with all the flavor impact of chocolate milk). This recipe falls in between those two extremes: rich but not dense, chocolatey but not cloying, light and silky but not unsubstantial. The toughest challenge was ramping up the chocolate without destroying the texture. Most recipes call it quits at just 4 or 5 ounces. The trick to adding more, as it turned out, was the liquid-to-solid ratio; as we increased the chocolate, we had to increase the liquid, or we ended up with a gritty paste that wouldn't combine with the beaten egg whites. The secret: just add water. We were able to accommodate 8 ounces of bittersweet chocolate plus 2 ounces of cocoa—and the texture was silkier than ever. Just 2 egg yolks made our mousse rich and smooth, while the egg whites, whipped to soft peaks, created a silky texture, and whipped cream added volume.

- 8 ounces bittersweet chocolate, chopped fine
- 2 tablespoons Dutch-processed cocoa powder
- 1 teaspoon instant espresso powder
- 5 tablespoons water
- 1 tablespoon brandy
- 2 large eggs, separated
- 1 tablespoon sugar
- ⅛ teaspoon salt
- 1 cup plus 2 tablespoons chilled heavy cream

**1.** Melt the chocolate, cocoa powder, espresso powder, water, and brandy in a medium heatproof bowl set over a saucepan filled with 1 inch of barely simmering water, stirring frequently until smooth. Remove from the heat.

**2.** Whisk the egg yolks, 1½ teaspoons sugar, and salt in a medium bowl until the mixture lightens in color and thickens slightly, about 30 seconds. Pour the melted chocolate mixture into the egg mixture and whisk until thoroughly combined. Let cool until slightly warmer than room temperature, 3 to 5 minutes.

**3.** With an electric mixer, beat the egg whites on medium-low speed in a large bowl until frothy, 1 to 2 minutes. Add the remaining 1½ teaspoons sugar, increase the mixer speed to medium-high, and beat until soft peaks form when the beaters are lifted, about 1 minute. Whisk the last few strokes by hand, making sure to scrape any unbeaten whites from the bottom of the bowl. Using a whisk, stir about one-quarter of the beaten egg whites into the chocolate mixture to lighten it; gently fold in the remaining egg whites with a rubber spatula until a few white streaks remain.

**4.** In a large bowl, whip the cream with an electric mixer on medium speed until it begins to thicken, about 30 seconds. Increase the speed to high and whip until soft peaks form, about 15 seconds longer. Using a rubber spatula, gently fold the whipped cream into the mousse until no white streaks remain. Spoon the mousse into 6 to 8 individual serving dishes or goblets. Cover with plastic wrap and refrigerate until set and firm, at least 2 hours.

**WHAT YOU CAN DO AHEAD OF TIME:** The mousse can be wrapped tightly in plastic wrap and refrigerated for up to 1 day. Let stand at room temperature for 10 minutes before serving.

## GREAT DISCOVERIES
### WHY YOU CAN'T JUST SUBSTITUTE PREMIUM CHOCOLATE

When developing this recipe, I stuck to our winning brand of supermarket chocolate, Ghirardelli. Thinking that perhaps premium, high-end chocolates might make an even better mousse, I gave them a try. But no dice. The resulting mousse was stiff and grainy and more bitter than it was sweet. It turns out that these more expensive brands have between 62 and 70 percent chocolate liquor—higher than Ghirardelli, which has 60 percent. Substituting them doesn't work because they are inherently starchier and less sweet. The solution? If you're a fan of truly dark chocolate and want to use one of these brands, increase the water to 7 tablespoons, add another egg, and up the sugar to 3 tablespoons.

SANDRA WU | ASSOCIATE EDITOR, COOK'S ILLUSTRATED

## NOTES FROM THE TEST KITCHEN

**THE PERFECT MOUSSE TEXTURE**
Going easy on the egg whites, omitting the butter, and adding a small amount of water yielded just the right texture. This is how it should look.

DARK CHOCOLATE MOUSSE

# LIGHT ALMOND SUGAR COOKIES

MAKES 24 COOKIES

**WHAT MAKES THIS A BEST RECIPE:** Anyone who has ever eaten a good sugar cookie can attest that they are addictively rich and delicate, especially when discretely flavored with almond. For *The Best Light Recipe*, we wondered whether it would even be possible to develop an acceptable lower-fat version since this cookie relies on only a few basic ingredients (butter, sugar, eggs, flour, and vanilla). Right off the bat we were able to reduce the butter in our original recipe from 10 to just 5 tablespoons, which saved us 3.5 grams of fat per cookie. The lesser amount of butter caused a decrease in flavor, but a combination of vanilla and almond extracts picked up the slack. To pack even more almond flavor, we ground sliced almonds with the sugar and coated the cookies in the sweet, nutty mix before baking them. At last we had a light sugar cookie that we could be proud of, with just 3 grams of fat and 90 calories.

- ¾    cup (3¾ ounces) unbleached all-purpose flour
- ½    cup (2 ounces) cake flour
- ½    teaspoon baking powder
- ¼    teaspoon salt
- 5    tablespoons unsalted butter, at room temperature
- 1⅓  cups (9⅓ ounces) sugar
- 1    large egg, lightly beaten
- 1    teaspoon vanilla extract
- ½    teaspoon almond extract
- ¼    cup sliced almonds

**1.** Adjust an oven rack to the middle position and heat the oven to 375 degrees. Line 2 baking sheets with parchment paper.

**2.** Whisk the flours, baking powder, and salt together in a medium bowl; set aside. With an electric mixer, beat the butter and 1 cup of the sugar on medium speed until light and fluffy, 3 to 5 minutes, scraping down the sides of the bowl as needed. Add the egg, vanilla, and almond extract and continue to beat at medium speed until combined, 30 to 60 seconds. Add the flour mixture and continue to beat at low speed until just combined, 30 to 60 seconds, scraping down the sides of the bowl as needed.

**3.** Process the remaining ⅓ cup sugar with the almonds in a food processor until finely ground, 10 to 15 seconds; transfer to a shallow bowl. Working with a level tablespoon of dough each time, roll the dough into 1-inch balls. (If the dough is too soft to roll, refrigerate it until firm.) Carefully roll the balls in the almond sugar and place them on the prepared baking sheets, spacing them about 2½ inches apart (you will fit 12 cookies on each baking sheet).

**4.** Bake the cookies, one sheet at a time, until the edges are light golden and the centers are just set, 9 to 11 minutes, rotating the sheet halfway through baking (do not overbake). Cool the cookies on the baking sheets for 5 minutes, then serve warm, or transfer to a wire rack and cool completely. Bake the second batch of cookies while the first batch cools.

**WHERE THINGS CAN GO WRONG:** We find that if the dough is too soft it is difficult to roll into balls; 10 or 15 minutes in the refrigerator will remedy this problem.

**WHAT YOU CAN DO AHEAD OF TIME:** The cookies are best eaten the day they are made, but they can be stored in an airtight container at room temperature for up to 3 days.

## GREAT DISCOVERIES

### YOU CAN CUT THE BUTTER BY HALF

When we developed this cookie recipe (and others) for our light cookbook, we were shocked to discover how much butter we could take out before the taste and texture began to suffer. Here we cut the amount of butter in half eliminating 5 tablespoons, and while we had to use both cake flour and all-purpose flour to adjust the texture, there was little else we had to do to the recipe as a result.

JULIA COLLIN DAVISON | SENIOR FOOD EDITOR, BOOKS

## NOTES FROM THE TEST KITCHEN

### THE BEST OVEN TEMPERATURE

In developing this recipe, we quickly discovered that proper baking times and temperatures can really make or break these cookies. Normally, we bake cookies at 350 degrees; however, these sugar cookies didn't spread enough at this temperature. We found that a 375-degree oven was just right. The cookies spread to a perfect 2½-inch diameter and became just lightly browned at the very edges.

# LIGHT NEW YORK CHEESECAKE
## WITH STRAWBERRY TOPPING
### SERVES 12

**WHAT MAKES THIS A BEST RECIPE:** Since one modest slice of cheesecake has close to 600 calories and more fat than most people should consume in a day (43 grams), and just about every cookbook recipe for reduced-fat cheesecake is a rubbery, gummy mess, chock full of artificial and off flavors, this recipe makeover proved to be one of our greatest challenges for *The Best Light Recipe*. We tried a whole slew of substitutions for the 2½ pounds of cream cheese in our full-fat cheesecake, from fat-free cream cheese and ricotta, to tofu and lowfat mayonnaise. Light cream cheese, drained cottage cheese, and yogurt cheese (see the easy recipe at right), which we mixed in a food processor until ultra creamy, turned out to be the perfect combination. The cream cheese and cottage cheese created a rich and creamy cake with just the right density, and the yogurt provided the trademark tang that is essential to any great New York cheesecake. After the cheesecake had chilled, we knew we had achieved perfection. Each slice kept its shape, and each bite felt satiny on the tongue. At just 400 calories and 13 grams of fat (topping included), we were in cheesecake heaven.

### CRUST

- 9 whole graham crackers (5 ounces), broken into rough pieces and processed in a food processor to fine, even crumbs (about 1¼ cups)
- 4 tablespoons (½ stick) unsalted butter, melted
- 1 tablespoon sugar

### FILLING

- 1 pound 1 percent cottage cheese
- 1 pound light cream cheese, at room temperature (see page 258)
- 8 ounces (1 cup) lowfat yogurt cheese
- 1½ cups (10½ ounces) sugar
- ¼ teaspoon salt
- ½–1 teaspoon grated lemon zest
- 1 tablespoon vanilla extract
- 3 large eggs, at room temperature

### STRAWBERRY TOPPING

- 1 pound strawberries (about 1 quart), washed, dried, hulled, and cut lengthwise into ¼- to ⅜-inch wedges
- ¼ cup sugar
  Pinch salt
- ½ cup strawberry jam
- 1 tablespoon fresh lemon juice

## NOTES FROM THE TEST KITCHEN

### TO MAKE YOGURT CHEESE
Line a fine-mesh strainer, set over a deep container, with 3 paper coffee filters or a double layer of cheesecloth. Spoon 16 ounces (2 cups) plain lowfat yogurt into the lined strainer, cover, and refrigerate for 10 to 12 hours (about 1 cup of liquid will drain out of the yogurt). Transfer to a covered container and refrigerate—it will keep for about 1 week.

### A TRULY RELIABLE SPRINGFORM PAN
A springform pan is an essential piece of equipment for making New York Cheesecake. In addition to a smooth working buckle, we find the most crucial feature on a reliable springform pan to be its ability to resist leakage. **Frieling's Handle-It Glass Bottom Springform** ($31.95) is our favorite pan, both for its solid construction and tempered-glass bottom, which makes it ideal not just for baking but also for serving. While we usually find transferring a cake off of the bottom of a springform pan daunting, given that this one is both invisible and has no rim to catch the knife's edge, we were able to place the cake pan bottom directly on a platter. We also like the fact that the Frieling has handles, which are helpful when removing the pan from the oven.

### TAKE ITS TEMPERATURE
To ensure a properly baked cheesecake, we found it best to bake the cake to an internal temperature of 150 degrees. Although it may seem unnecessary, an instant-read thermometer inserted into the cake is the most reliable means of judging the doneness of the cheesecake.

**1. FOR THE CRUST:** Adjust an oven rack to the middle position and heat the oven to 325 degrees. In a medium bowl, stir together the graham cracker crumbs, melted butter, and sugar until combined. Transfer the mixture to a 9-inch springform pan and press evenly into the pan bottom. Bake the crust until fragrant and beginning to brown, 10 to 15 minutes. Cool on a wire rack. Increase the temperature to 500 degrees.

**2. FOR THE FILLING:** Meanwhile, line a medium bowl with a clean dish towel or several layers of paper towels. Spoon the cottage cheese into the bowl and let drain for 30 minutes.

**3.** Process the drained cottage cheese in a food processor until smooth and no visible lumps remain, about 1 minute, scraping down the sides of the bowl as needed. Add the cream cheese and yogurt cheese and continue to process until smooth, 1 to 2 minutes, scraping down the sides of the bowl as needed. Add the sugar, salt, lemon zest, and vanilla and continue to process until smooth, about 1 minute, scraping down the sides of the bowl as needed. With the machine running, add the eggs, one at a time, and continue to process until smooth.

**4.** Being careful not to disturb the baked crust, spray the insides of the springform pan with vegetable oil spray. Set the springform pan on a rimmed baking sheet. Pour the cheese filling into the cooled crust.

**5.** Bake for 10 minutes. Without opening the oven door, reduce the oven temperature to 200 degrees and continue to bake until an instant-read thermometer inserted into the center of the cheesecake reads 150 degrees, about 1½ hours.

**6.** Transfer the cake to a wire rack and run a paring knife around the edge of the cake to loosen. Cool the cake at room temperature until barely warm, 2½ to 3 hours, running a paring knife around the edge of the cake every hour or so. Wrap the pan tightly in plastic wrap and refrigerate until cold, at least 3 hours.

**7. FOR THE TOPPING:** Toss the berries, sugar, and salt in a medium bowl and let stand until the berries have released some juice and the sugar has dissolved, about 30 minutes, tossing occasionally to combine.

**8.** Process the jam in a food processor until smooth, about 8 seconds. Transfer the jam to a small saucepan and bring to a simmer over medium-high heat. Simmer, stirring frequently, until dark and no longer frothy, about 3 minutes. Stir in the lemon juice, then gently stir the warm jam into the strawberries. Cover with plastic wrap and refrigerate until cold, at least 2 hours or up to 12.

**9. TO UNMOLD THE CHEESECAKE:** Wrap a hot kitchen towel around the springform pan and let stand for 10 minutes. Remove the sides of the pan and blot any excess moisture from the top of the cheesecake with paper towels. Let the cheesecake stand at room temperature about 30 minutes before slicing. To serve, spoon a portion of the topping over each slice.

**WHERE THINGS CAN GO WRONG:** If you are making your own yogurt cheese, allow at least 12 hours for the yogurt to drain, otherwise the texture of the cake will be loose. Be sure to use light cream cheese in this recipe—it is most commonly sold in tubs, not blocks (see page 258). Fat-free cream cheese will yield a rubbery cake, and Neufchâtel cheese (marketed as reduced-fat cream cheese) will boost the fat and calories.

**WHAT YOU CAN DO AHEAD OF TIME:** The cottage cheese can be drained and the yogurt cheese can be made up to 2 days ahead. The cheesecake can be wrapped tightly in plastic wrap and refrigerated for up to 1 day.

## GREAT DISCOVERIES
### YOGURT CHEESE SAVES THE DAY

Light cheesecake proved to be one of the most challenging test kitchen makeovers the book team tackled this year. I spent weeks making cheesecakes before we even came close to success since lowfat dairy alone does not equal a good lowfat cheesecake. Many of the recipes I researched used yogurt to cut out some of the cream cheese but these cakes were much too soft. Not willing to give up on yogurt, especially since I liked the tangy flavor it lent the cheesecake, I decided to make yogurt cheese (though you can buy it in natural food stores and Middle Eastern markets, where it is labeled laban or labana). It worked like a charm as a stand-in for some of the cream cheese, and had enough structure to deliver a perfectly formed wedge of cheesecake. But don't limit your use of yogurt cheese to cheesecake alone since it's also great used in lots of other ways—as a stand-in for full-fat cream cheese in dips and spreads, on bagels, or dolloped on baked potatoes or atop creamy soup. If you're making your own, just be sure to avoid buying yogurt containing modified food starch, gelatin, or gums since they prevent it from draining.

DIANE UNGER | TEST COOK, BOOKS

# A GUIDE TO ESSENTIAL BAKEWARE

Though its manufacturers are loath to admit it, choosing quality bakeware is pretty simple. All the usual jargon about clad aluminum cores and anodized coatings remains in full force, but a dozen years of testing have left us even more skeptical than usual about bells and whistles when it comes to shopping for cake pans and cookie sheets. In fact, in all our testing we certainly found that price doesn't always equal performance. The design details that matter may be the ones you least expected. Here's what to look for—and what to avoid.

## CAKE PAN

**TESTING NOTES:** We're still searching for the ultimate cake pan: one with high, straight sides; a dark, nonstick finish; and handles, which most manufacturers consider unnecessary. Until then, both our test kitchen winner and "best buy" option (below) score two out of three. Nine-inch cake pans are the standard size, and you'll need two for most recipes. (If you want to bake in a square pan instead, drop down to the 8-inch size—the surface area is comparable to a 9-inch round pan.)

**WHAT TO AVOID:**
- Light-colored tinned or stainless steel pans, which brown and release poorly
- Sloped sides, which produce flared cakes that are impossible to split evenly

**TEST KITCHEN FAVORITE**
★ CHICAGO Metallic Professional Nonstick, $14.95
**BEST BUY:** The supermarket standard BAKER'S SECRET cake pan ($3.99) is a bit short and has sloped sides, but it browns and releases easily, has helpful handles, and boasts a winning price tag.

## COOKIE SHEET

**TESTING NOTES:** When it comes to light-versus dark-colored metal bakeware, the cookie sheet is the exception. All of the dark-colored, nonstick cookie sheets we tested consistently overbrowned the bottoms of cookies. Light-colored sheets, on the other hand, were prone to sticking, but because we always bake cookies on parchment paper, we chose the (much) lesser of two evils.

**WHAT TO AVOID:**
- Dark finishes
- Lightweight sheets, which are prone to warping
- Sheets with only one handle (difficult to rotate during baking) or four sides (difficult to transfer cookie-loaded parchment paper from sheet to cooling rack)

**TEST KITCHEN FAVORITE**
★ VOLLRATH Cookie Sheet, $19.95

## MUFFIN TIN

**TESTING NOTES:** Thanks to excellent heat absorption, dark-colored metal pans produce muffins and cupcakes that not only brown better but also rise higher and sport more nicely domed tops when compared with those baked in shiny, reflective tins. Choose a moderately priced muffin tin with reasonable heft (no more than 2 pounds).

**WHAT TO AVOID:**
- Flimsy pans that buckle when filled with heavy batter
- Heavy pans (some of our contenders weighed in at well over 2 pounds), which provide an unwelcome one-arm workout

**TEST KITCHEN FAVORITE**
★ WILTON Ultra-Bake, $9.99

## LOAF PAN

**TESTING NOTES:** The refusal of much of the bakeware industry to embrace the good common sense of handles has always left us puzzled. Loaf pans are a good example. All of the dark, nonstick pans we tested browned nicely and released cleanly, so we gave the nod to those that are easy to carry as well. Though often referred to as "9 by 5-inch loaf pans," few meet those exact dimensions. We prefer pans with a width of just under 5 inches, which produce loaves with taller, rounder tops. Many recipes yield two loaves, so you might as well buy two pans.

**WHAT TO AVOID:**
- Pans without handles
- Light-colored pans, which deter browning

**TEST KITCHEN FAVORITE**
★ BAKER'S SECRET Non-Stick Loaf Pan (8½ by 4½ inches), $3.99

## SPRINGFORM PAN

**TESTING NOTES:** The disappointing truth: All springform pans leak. This means that using them in a water bath can be problematic (we recommend double-wrapping the pan with aluminum foil to make it leakproof). We picked out the least leaky contenders, then chose the only model with helpful handles and a clear glass bottom to boot. Nine-inch pans are the standard size.

**WHAT TO AVOID:**
- Rimmed bottoms, which make it difficult to slide a spatula under the cake to remove it

**TEST KITCHEN FAVORITE**
★ FRIELING Handle-It (9-Inch) Glass Bottom, $31.95

## FLUTED TART PAN

**TESTING NOTES:** We love these clever pans—the fluted edges and false bottom allow even a novice baker to turn out elegant-looking desserts with not much effort. But we can't condone splurging on pricey nonstick models when the generic tinned steel pans, sold in most stores for around $8, work just as well. (There's so much fat in buttery tart dough that it wouldn't stick to flypaper, much less a pan.) Our tart recipes are generally developed to fit a 9-inch pan, but 11-inch pans are also common.

**WHAT TO AVOID:**
- Nonremovable bottoms
- Expensive nonstick pans

**TEST KITCHEN FAVORITE**
★ Tinned Steel Fluted Tart Pan with Removable Bottom, about $8

## BAKING PAN

**TESTING NOTES:** We stock plenty of these pans in the test kitchen, where they handle everything from lasagna to sticky buns. Sturdy Pyrex is our first choice here: dishwasher-safe, handy handles, and scratch-resistant. The 13 by 9-inch pan is the best all-around option, but the 17 by 11-inch model turns out super-sized casseroles, while the 8-inch- and 9-inch-square pans are good for smaller batches of cornbread or brownies.

**WHAT TO AVOID:**
- Aluminum pans, which can react with the acids in tomato-based recipes

**TEST KITCHEN FAVORITE**
★ PYREX Bakeware 13 by 9-Inch Baking Dish, $8.95

## WHEN PYREX EXPLODES

Pyrex pie plates and baking dishes are standard issue in the test kitchen, but over the years we've learned that they are prone to shattering when exposed to sudden and extreme temperature changes. Naturally, this prohibits their use under a broiler or over direct stovetop heat, but the tempered glass bakeware is also vulnerable to sudden drops in temperature, known in the industry as downshock. Downshock would result from adding cold liquid to a hot Pyrex dish or from placing a hot dish directly on a cold or wet surface. It is considered safe, however, to transfer a Pyrex dish directly from the refrigerator or freezer to a hot oven, provided it has been properly pre-heated—some ovens use the broiler element to heat up to the desired temperature.

## PIE PLATE

**TESTING NOTES:** Pie making is hard work—we understand why lots of cooks want to show off the finished product in a handsome, heavy piece of French ceramic pottery. (We're less certain why so many others trust their creations to flimsy EZ Foil disposable aluminum pans.) But neither option turns out evenly browned crusts as reliably as the trusty, inexpensive Pyrex. The Pyrex pie plate is scratch-resistant, its wide lip makes it easy to shape decorative fluted crusts, and its see-through glass is the best choice for monitoring a crust's browning progress.

**WHAT TO AVOID:**
- Ceramic pie plates
- Flimsy, disposable aluminum pie plates
- Opaque plates

**TEST KITCHEN FAVORITE**
★ PYREX (9-Inch) Pie Plate, $5

## KITCHEN WORKHORSE: JELLYROLL PAN

In the test kitchen, we keep stacks of rimmed aluminum baking sheets (known as jellyroll pans—half-sheet pans, in restaurant lingo) and use them for a wide assortment of everyday tasks: roasting vegetables, catching drips in the oven, and, yes, baking the occasional jellyroll or sheet cake. Fitted with the right-sized wire cooling rack, this versatile pan can stand in for a roasting pan; it also makes an acceptable cookie sheet, though the rimmed design prevents a quick sliding of cookies to the cooling rack. Though similar pans are available in cookware shops in a variety of materials, sizes, and finishes, we purchase ours at a restaurant supply store in the industry standard size of 16 by 12 inches and recommend that you do the same. If you do buy retail, however, a good alternative is the **WearEver Commercial Jellyroll Pan** ($10.99).

# CONVERSIONS

SOME SAY COOKING IS A SCIENCE AND AN ART. We would say that geography has a hand in it, too. Flour milled in the United Kingdom and elsewhere will feel and taste different from flour milled in the United States. So we cannot promise that the loaf of bread you bake in Canada or England will taste the same as a loaf baked in the States, but we can offer guidelines for converting weights and measures. We also recommend that you rely on your instincts when making our recipes. Refer to the visual cues provided. If the bread dough hasn't "come together in a ball," as described, you may need to add more flour—even if the recipe doesn't tell you so. You be the judge. For more

information on conversions and ingredient equivalents, visit our Web site at www.cooksillustrated.com and type "conversion chart" in the search box.

The recipes in this book were developed using standard U.S. measures following U.S. government guidelines. The charts below offer equivalents for U.S., metric, and Imperial (U.K.) measures. All conversions are approximate and have been rounded up or down to the nearest whole number. For example:

| | | |
|---|---|---|
| 1 teaspoon | = | 4.9292 milliliters, rounded up to 5 milliliters |
| 1 ounce | = | 28.3495 grams, rounded down to 28 grams |

## VOLUME CONVERSIONS

| U.S. | METRIC |
|---|---|
| 1 teaspoon | 5 milliliters |
| 2 teaspoons | 10 milliliters |
| 1 tablespoon | 15 milliliters |
| 2 tablespoons | 30 milliliters |
| ¼ cup | 59 milliliters |
| ⅓ cup | 79 milliliters |
| ½ cup | 118 milliliters |
| ¾ cup | 177 milliliters |
| 1 cup | 237 milliliters |
| 1¼ cups | 296 milliliters |
| 1½ cups | 355 milliliters |
| 2 cups | 473 milliliters |
| 2½ cups | 592 milliliters |
| 3 cups | 710 milliliters |
| 4 cups (1 quart) | 0.946 liter |
| 1.06 quarts | 1 liter |
| 4 quarts (1 gallon) | 3.8 liters |

## WEIGHT CONVERSIONS

| OUNCES | GRAMS |
|---|---|
| ½ | 14 |
| ¾ | 21 |
| 1 | 28 |
| 1½ | 43 |
| 2 | 57 |
| ½ | 71 |
| 3 | 85 |
| 3½ | 99 |
| 4 | 113 |
| 4½ | 128 |
| 5 | 142 |
| 6 | 170 |
| 7 | 198 |
| 8 | 227 |
| 9 | 255 |
| 10 | 283 |
| 12 | 340 |
| 16 (1 pound) | 454 |

## CONVERSIONS FOR INGREDIENTS COMMONLY USED IN BAKING

Baking is an exacting science. Because measuring by weight is far more accurate than measuring by volume, and thus more likely to achieve reliable results, in our recipes we provide ounce measures in addition to cup measures for many ingredients. Refer to the chart below to convert these measures into grams.

| INGREDIENT | OUNCES | GRAMS |
|---|---|---|
| 1 cup all-purpose flour* | 5 | 142 |
| 1 cup whole wheat flour | 5½ | 156 |
| | | |
| 1 cup granulated (white) sugar | 7 | 198 |
| 1 cup packed brown sugar (light or dark) | 7 | 198 |
| 1 cup confectioners' sugar | 4 | 113 |
| | | |
| 1 cup cocoa powder | 3 | 85 |
| | | |
| **Butter†** | | |
| 4 tablespoons (½ stick, or ¼ cup) | 2 | 57 |
| 8 tablespoons (1 stick, or ½ cup) | 4 | 113 |
| 16 tablespoons (2 sticks, or 1 cup) | 8 | 227 |

*U.S. all-purpose flour, the most frequently used flour in this book, does not contain leaveners, as some European flours do. These leavened flours are called self-rising or self-raising. If you are using self-rising flour, take this into consideration before adding leavening to a recipe.
† In the United States, butter is sold both salted and unsalted. We generally recommend unsalted butter. If you are using salted butter, take this into consideration before adding salt to a recipe.

## OVEN TEMPERATURES

| FAHRENHEIT | CELSIUS | GAS MARK (IMPERIAL) |
|---|---|---|
| 225 | 105 | ¼ |
| 250 | 120 | ½ |
| 275 | 130 | 1 |
| 300 | 150 | 2 |
| 325 | 165 | 3 |
| 350 | 180 | 4 |
| 375 | 190 | 5 |
| 400 | 200 | 6 |
| 425 | 220 | 7 |
| 450 | 230 | 8 |
| 475 | 245 | 9 |

## CONVERTING TEMPERATURES FROM AN INSTANT-READ THERMOMETER

We include doneness temperatures in many of our recipes, such as those for poultry, meat, and bread. We recommend an instant-read thermometer for the job. Refer to the table above to convert Fahrenheit degrees to Celsius. Or, for temperatures not represented in the chart, use this simple formula:

Subtract 32 degrees from the Fahrenheit reading, then divide the result by 1.8 to find the Celsius reading.

### EXAMPLE:

"Roast until the juice runs clear when the chicken is cut with a paring knife or the thickest part of the breast registers 160 degrees on an instant-read thermometer." To convert:

160° F − 32 = 128°
128° ÷ 1.8 = 71° C (rounded down from 71.11)

# COLOR PHOTO CREDITS

## By Daniel J. van Ackere:

Cheese Straws, p. 2 • Baked Brie en Croûte, p. 9 • Parker House Rolls, p. 87
Coffeecake Muffins, p. 91 • Chicken Breasts with Bacon, Rosemary, and Lemon, p. 179
Light Chicken Parmesan, p. 185 • Seared Salmon with Balsamic Glaze, p. 218
Sesame-Ginger Shrimp, p. 235 • Spicy Baked Shrimp, p. 236
Light New York Cheesecake, p. 292

## By Keller + Keller:

Stuffed French Toast, p. vi • Green Salad with Roasted Pears and Blue Cheese, p. 12
Cool and Creamy Macaroni Salad, p. 15 • Chicken Noodle Soup, p. 18
Beef and Vegetable Soup, p. 22 • Hearty Slow-Cooker Beef Stew, p. 27
Hearty Vegetable Soup, p. 31 • Oven-Fried Onion Rings, p. 40
Sugar-Glazed Roasted Carrots, p. 51 • Short-Order Home Fries, p. 61
Down 'n' Dirty Rice, p. 65 • Orange Drop Doughnuts, p. 99
Pepperoni Pan Pizza, p. 102 • Creamy Carbonara, p. 109 • Pasta Primavera, p. 117
Slow-Cooker Bolognese Sauce, p. 127 • Stuffed Flank Steak, p. 135
Sunday-Best Garlic Roast Beef, p. 141 • French Dip Sandwiches, p. 143
Slow-Cooker Beer-Braised Short Ribs, p. 144 • Oven-Barbecued Beef Brisket, p. 147
Sloppy Joes, p. 155 • Old-Fashioned Roast Pork, p. 166 • Cubanos, p. 169
Easy Jerk Chicken, p. 174 • Cheesy Basil-Stuffed Chicken Breasts, p. 183
Freezer Chicken Enchiladas, p. 191 • Crispy Roast Chicken and Potatoes, p. 200
Alabama BBQ Chicken, p. 212 • Creole Crab Cakes, p. 222
Shrimp Jambalaya, p. 239 • Southern Pecan Praline Pie, p. 250
Pecan–Sour Cream Coffee Cake, p. 262 • Tipsy Squire, p. 269
Boston Cream Cupcakes, p. 277 • Chocolate Toffee Butter Cookies, p. 287

## By Carl Tremblay:

Poached Shrimp Salad with Avocado and Grapefruit, p. 11
Daube Provençal, p. 35 • The Ultimate Vegetable Torta, p. 43
Pan-Roasted Broccoli with Spicy Southeast Asian Flavors, p. 47
Sweet Potato Casserole, p. 66 • Huevos Rancheros, p. 72
Skillet Strata with Spinach and Smoked Gouda, p. 79
Flaky Buttermilk Biscuits, p. 83 • Marinara Sauce, p. 106
Light Meat and Cheese Lasagna, p. 121 • Pepper-Crusted Filet Mignon, p. 128
Glazed All-Beef Meat Loaf, p. 152 • Veal Scaloppini with Lemon-Parsley Sauce, p. 160
Chicken Kiev, p. 180 • Moroccan Chicken with Olives and Lemon, p. 195
Chicken Fajitas, p. 204 • Old-Fashioned Chocolate Layer Cake, p. 240
Deep-Dish Apple Pie, p. 243 • Free-Form Summer Fruit Tart, p. 255
Strawberry Cream Cake, p. 272 • Ultimate Turtle Brownies, p. 280
Dark Chocolate Mousse, p. 289

# INDEX